Mastering Microsoft OneNote

Team Collaboration Made Easy

Charles Waghmare

Apress®

Mastering Microsoft OneNote: Team Collaboration Made Easy

Charles Waghmare
Matunga
Mumbai, Maharashtra, India

ISBN-13 (pbk): 979-8-8688-2865-2 ISBN-13 (electronic): 979-8-8688-2866-9
https://doi.org/10.1007/979-8-8688-2866-9

Managing Director, Apress Media LLC: Welmoed Spahr
Acquisitions Editor: Smriti Srivastava
Editorial Assistant: Marina Engler

Cover designed by eStudioCalamar

Cover image designed by pikisuperstar on Freepik

Distributed to the book trade worldwide by Springer Science+Business Media New York, 1 New York Plaza, New York, NY 10004. Phone 1-800-SPRINGER, fax (201) 348-4505, e-mail orders-ny@springer-sbm.com, or visit www.springeronline.com. Apress Media, LLC is a Delaware LLC and the sole member (owner) is Springer Science + Business Media Finance Inc (SSBM Finance Inc). SSBM Finance Inc is a **Delaware** corporation.

For information on translations, please e-mail booktranslations@springernature.com; for reprint, paperback, or audio rights, please e-mail bookpermissions@springernature.com.

Apress titles may be purchased in bulk for academic, corporate, or promotional use. eBook versions and licenses are also available for most titles. For more information, reference our Print and eBook Bulk Sales web page at http://www.apress.com/bulk-sales.

Any source code or other supplementary material referenced by the author in this book is available to readers on GitHub. For more detailed information, please visit https://www.apress.com/gp/services/source-code.

If disposing of this product, please recycle the paper

"Blessed are those who find wisdom, those who gain understanding." —Proverbs 3:13

To begin, I want to express my gratitude to Lord Jesus Christ for giving me another chance to author this book. I attribute all my achievements to Him and use this moment to offer praise and thanks for everything He has done in my life. God bless.

My Dedication

This book will always hold a special place in my heart, as I penned this book during the time my dear father, late Mr. David Genuji Waghmare, passed away. I dedicate this work to both my beloved father and my beloved late mother, Mrs. Kamala David Waghmare, who departed for their heavenly abode within three years of each other.

I thank my parents for their lasting impact on my life and career and for their continued support. I also dedicate this book to my wife, Mrs. Priya Waghmare, for her unwavering love and encouragement.

Table of Contents

About the Author

Charles David Waghmare —presently a DBA (Doctor of Business Administration) scholar from the prestigious SP Jain School of Global Management and an MBA from the same prestigious B-School—has over 18 years of industry experience in IT, engineering, and energy sectors.

Charles is presently working with a global energy leader since 2019 as an information management consultant in the Microsoft 365 space. Before that, he worked for Capgemini for eight years in various roles including Viva Engage community manager and manager of the Drupal-based enterprise knowledge management system. He also developed a knowledge management platform for Capgemini's Digital Customer Experience (DCX) organization using SharePoint Online to manage client references and knowledge assets related to artificial intelligence (AI) and customer experience (CX). Further, he adopted Microsoft Azure chatbots to automate communication channels with the customers.

Charles also worked for ATOS (erstwhile SIEMENS Information Systems Limited) for five years. During his tenure there, he was a community manager of SAP-based communities, where he utilized TechnoWeb 2.0—a Viva Engage-like platform and on-premises SharePoint to manage SAP user-based communities. Also, Charles was a global rollout manager for a structured document management system built in on-premises SharePoint.

Charles has penned several books on Microsoft 365 technologies, such as Viva Engage, SharePoint Online, Azure chatbots, Microsoft Purview, Microsoft Loop, and Microsoft Project, and on ChatGPT. Further, he loves reading motivational books in his spare time, his favorite being *The Monk Who Sold His Ferrari*, *The 5 AM Club*, and *The Everyday Hero Manifesto*.

About the Technical Reviewer

Kasam Shaikh is a four-time recipient of the prestigious Microsoft Most Valuable Professional (MVP) award in AI making him the first and only Indian professional under the age of 40 to earn this honor three times consecutively. A recognized global AI speaker, published author, and tech influencer, Kasam is widely known for his contributions to the AI ecosystem through his YouTube channel, mentoring initiatives, and thought leadership. He currently serves as an apps and AI architect, driving digital transformation and AI adoption across business units. As the founder of Dear Azure – Az-INDIA, the largest Azure AI community in the region, he plays a key role in nurturing AI talent and fostering innovation. Additionally, he is acknowledged as a career expert in AI by rediffGurus and leads the Gen AI Expert Community at the practice level within his organization.

Acknowledgments

I wish to express my heartfelt gratitude to the following individuals who have profoundly impacted my life:

Late **Mr. Anil Malvankar**, former Deputy General Manager at SIEMENS, who graciously offered me my first professional opportunity at SIEMENS. His mentorship and guidance were invaluable, and I remain deeply appreciative of his support until his passing in April 2024.

Late **Mr. Alwin Fernandis**, my cherished friend. Though he is no longer with us, his memory endures in my heart, and his influence continues to inspire me.

Introduction

Microsoft OneNote is a digital notebook designed to help general audiences such as educators, IT professionals, and executives manage content and collaborate across teams and disciplines. OneNote provides a flexible structure consisting of notebooks, sections, and pages, reflecting traditional note-taking methods augmented by digital capabilities. Users can input text, draw, record audio, embed files, and clip web content within their notes. Its functionality supports lesson planning, technical documentation, meeting notes, and brainstorming.

What Is in the Book

This book on Microsoft OneNote equips readers with essential skills to organize digital notebooks using sections, pages, and tags. It covers capturing diverse content such as text, images, and audio, while enabling effective collaboration through shared notebooks. Readers learn role-specific applications, integration with Microsoft 365 tools, and best practices for secure note management. Advanced features like optical character recognition (OCR), handwriting recognition, and audio search further enhance productivity and information retrieval.

Audience

This book aims to equip readers with practical knowledge to use OneNote effectively as a digital notebook for enhanced productivity. It offers actionable templates and workflow examples tailored for various professions:

- **Educators**: Lesson planning, student assessment, curriculum development
- **IT Professionals**: Incident logs, technical documentation, internal wikis
- **Executives**: Meeting records, strategic outlines, KPI monitoring

Readers will learn integration with Microsoft 365 tools, apply professional templates, ensure secure note management, and explore advanced features like OCR and audio capture, empowering them to achieve efficient collaboration and innovative digital note-taking practices.

CHAPTER 1

Introduction to Microsoft OneNote: Understanding the Platform

Microsoft OneNote is a comprehensive, cloud-based digital note-taking platform that has developed into a foundational knowledge management solution within the Microsoft 365 suite. Initially intended for unstructured note capture, OneNote now offers structured notebooks, sections, pages, support for rich media, and seamless cross-device synchronization. This enables users to organize ideas, documents, meetings, research, and projects within a unified workspace. The application is accessible on Windows, macOS, the web, iOS, and Android, with notebooks securely stored and synchronized via OneDrive and SharePoint, ensuring real-time access and collaboration across devices and teams.

OneNote's recent advancements include substantial enhancements powered by Microsoft 365 Copilot, evolving the platform from a passive information repository to an intelligent, AI-assisted environment. Copilot in OneNote provides capabilities such as summarizing content, generating meeting notes, extracting action items, rewriting text, and responding to natural-language queries based on users' own notes and Microsoft 365 files, thereby facilitating easier comprehension and reuse of information. A noteworthy addition is Copilot Notebooks—persistent, AI-enabled workspaces allowing integration of OneNote pages, Word documents, PowerPoint presentations, PDFs, and Copilot interactions, supported by features like notebook-level summaries, audio overviews, and insight generation.

In tandem with AI developments, Microsoft continues to refine OneNote's core functionality and security, introducing improvements such as integrated image cropping, advanced multilingual proofing, enhanced touch and pen input, updated

C. Waghmare, *Mastering Microsoft OneNote*, https://doi.org/10.1007/979-8-8688-2866-9_1

task tags, and Microsoft Purview sensitivity labels to address enterprise compliance needs. OneNote maintains deep integration with the broader Microsoft 365 roadmap, leveraging ongoing investments in Copilot intelligence, collaborative features, and governance and aligning with other tools including Teams, Outlook, Planner, Loop, and SharePoint to enable comprehensive information workflows.

Consequently, modern OneNote serves not merely as a digital notebook, but as a flexible platform supporting personal knowledge management, academic endeavors, instruction, business documentation, and project coordination. It successfully combines unstructured creativity with organized structure, AI-powered insights, and enterprise-grade security to address the requirements of contemporary digital workplaces.

Introduction

This chapter will provide a comprehensive overview of utilizing Microsoft OneNote as a structured and collaborative digital note-taking platform, emphasizing the creation, management, and organization of notebooks through seamless OneDrive integration. It will commence by detailing the process for users to create notebooks, securely store them in OneDrive, and thus enable accessibility across various devices and platforms. The discussion will address the establishment of multiple notebooks to differentiate academic, professional, and personal content and will outline the option to create notebooks directly from the OneDrive interface. By illustrating both methods, the chapter will demonstrate workflow flexibility while reinforcing OneDrive as the primary repository for OneNote notebooks.

Subsequently, the chapter will explore the procedures for opening and accessing notebooks stored either in the cloud or locally on a computer. Guidance will be provided on viewing recently accessed notebooks, browsing the complete list of available notebooks, and selecting whether to open them via the desktop application or a web browser. This section will highlight continuity for users transitioning from previous OneNote versions and underscore seamless access irrespective of storage location. Emphasis will also be placed on navigation efficiency to ensure users can promptly locate and resume work within their notebooks.

A significant portion of the chapter will be devoted to notebook sharing and permission management. It will clarify that notebooks are private by default and explain how sharing can be facilitated through OneNote or OneDrive. The chapter will delineate sharing options, including sending links, specifying view or edit permissions, inviting collaborators both internal and external, and administering access centrally from OneDrive. The process of deleting unique permissions to restore inherited access will also be explained, supporting consistent and simplified security management. Various permission levels will be reviewed, alongside methods for managing, editing, and revoking user access.

In conclusion, the chapter will address the creation, renaming, coloring, movement, deletion, and linking of sections to enhance notebook organization. The use of internal links to sections and pages will be demonstrated as a means of constructing indexes or reference structures, thereby streamlining navigation within extensive notebooks. Collectively, this chapter aims to equip readers with the knowledge required to employ OneNote as a well-organized, shareable, and scalable knowledge management solution.

Create a Notebook and Store in OneDrive

To create a notebook stored in OneDrive, start by launching the OneNote application as shown in Figure 1-1. Upon initial use, a default notebook will be provided, and its name appears in the upper-left corner of the interface. The name we have given is *"French Language Learning Links."*

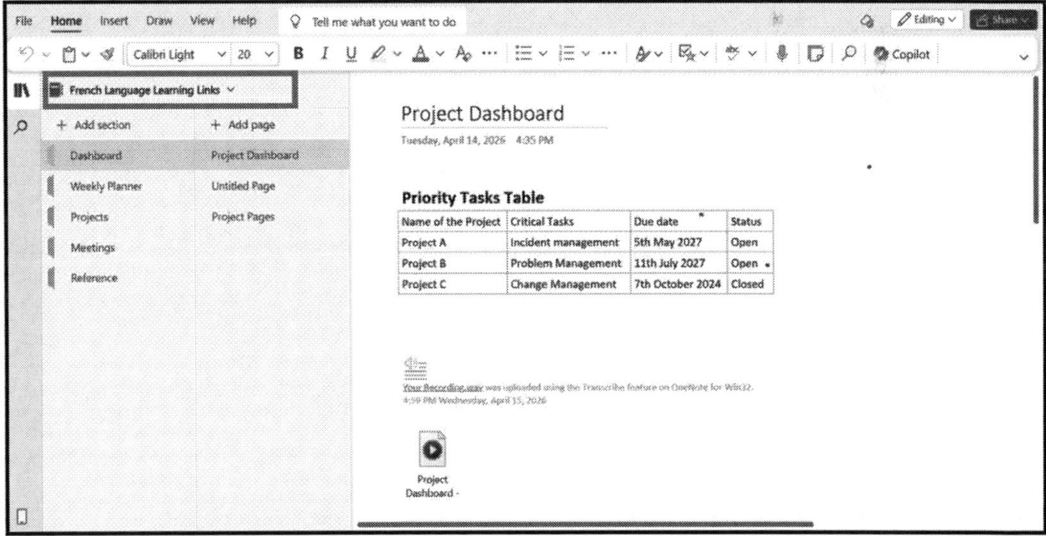

Figure 1-1. *Homepage of a OneNote notebook*

As you accumulate different sections within your notes, you may find it beneficial to establish separate notebooks for various categories, such as annual project timelines, academic subjects, or personal routines like family activities. To create a new notebook, proceed to the bottom of the panel, and click "Add notebook" as shown in Figure 1-2. Enter your desired notebook name, such as "French Language Learning Links," then press Enter or click "Create" as shown in Figure 1-3. The newly created notebook will appear and is ready for note-taking, with its title displayed at the top as shown in Figure 1-1.

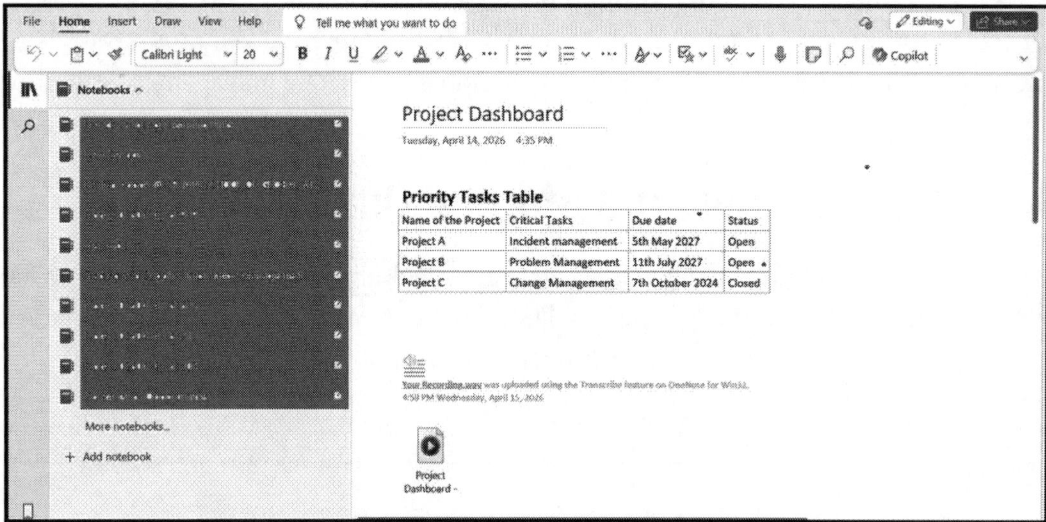

__Figure 1-2.__ Option to "Add notebook"

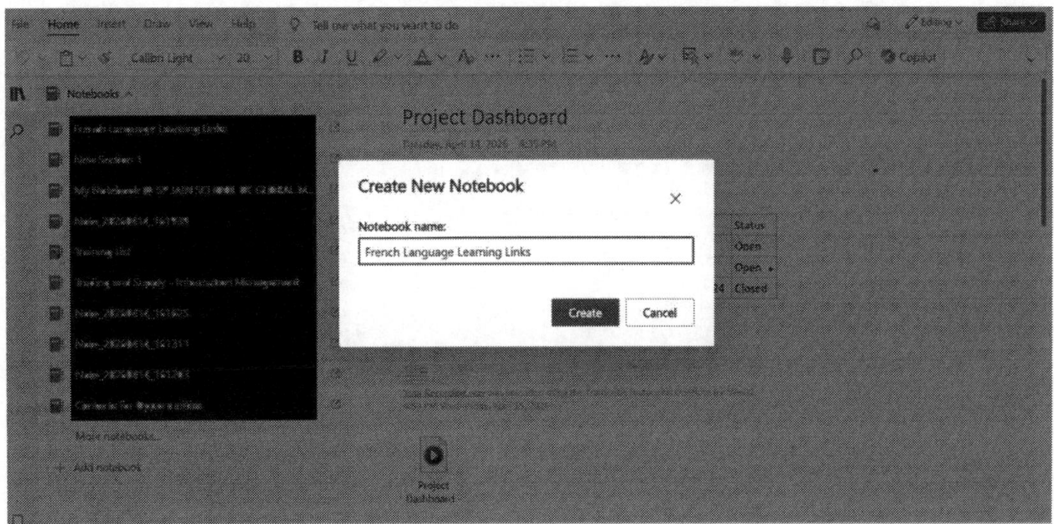

Figure 1-3. *Name for a new notebook*

This notebook is saved in the OneDrive document library associated with your Microsoft account. Access OneDrive as shown in Figure 1-4. In OneDrive, you can categorize files by Word, Excel, PowerPoint, PDF, and more. Under More options, you will see different additional categories as shown in Figure 1-5. One of the categories is OneNote and once selected you will see all OneNote files as shown in Figure 1-6.

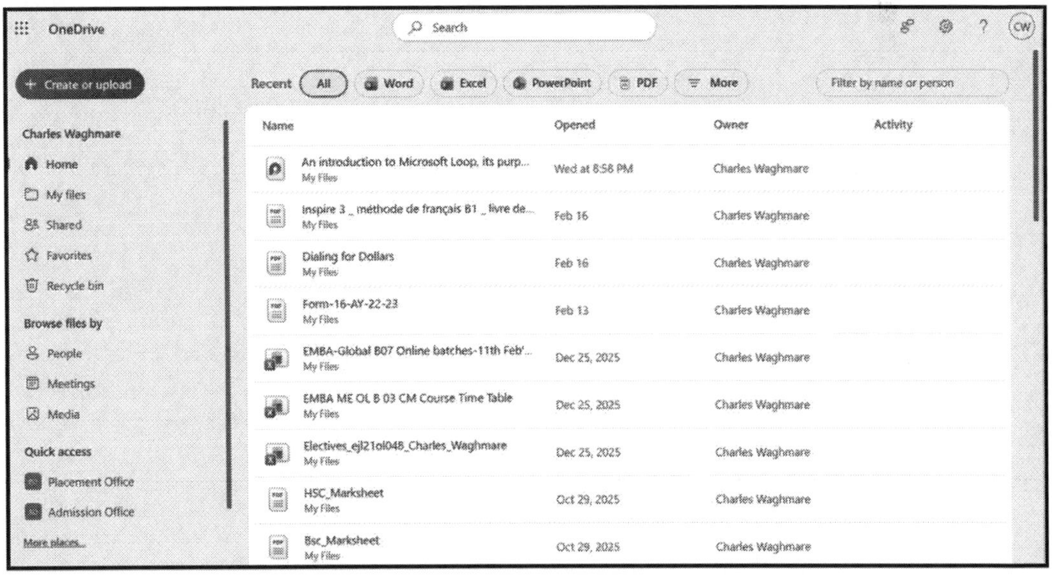

Figure 1-4. *OneDrive homepage*

Figure 1-5. *More option containing additional categories*

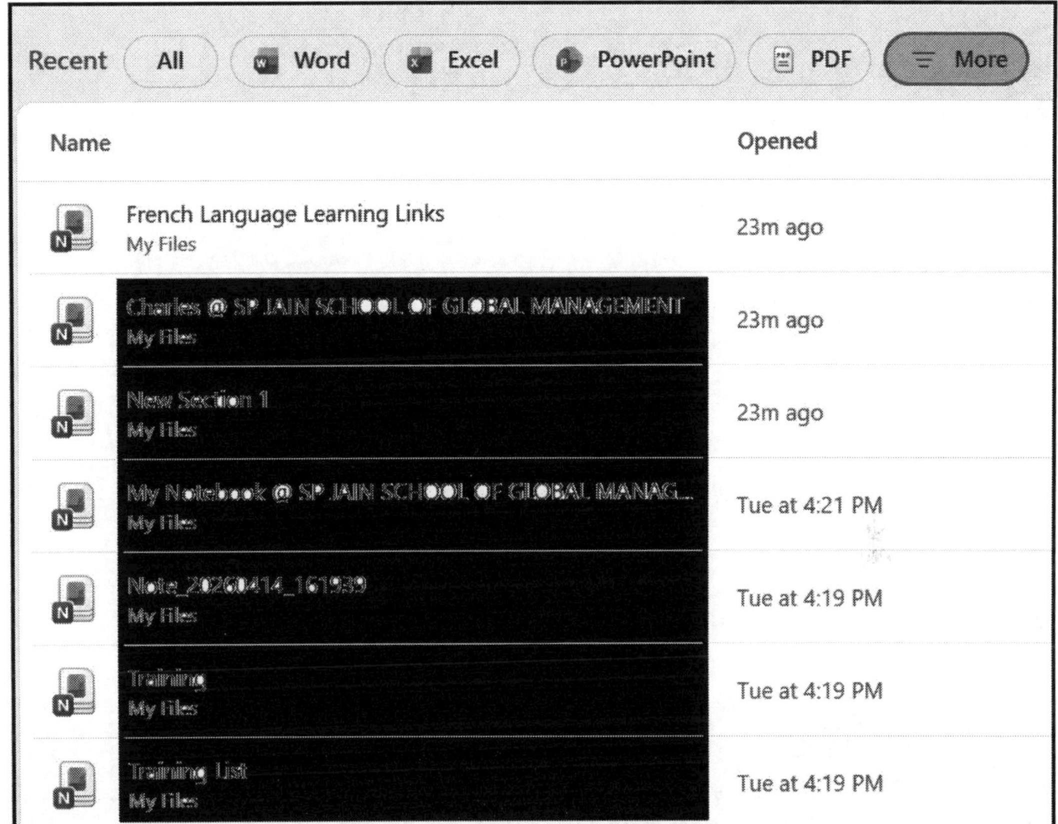

Figure 1-6. *Access to a list of OneNote files in OneDrive*

Notebooks can also be created directly from OneDrive by clicking the “New” button on the toolbar and choosing “OneNote notebook” as shown in Figure 1-7. The process is similar: assign a name as shown in Figure 1-8 such as “Learning Spanish Language,” and the notebook will be created as shown in Figure 1-9 and gets saved in the OneDrive document library as shown in Figure 1-10. Whether you are working in OneDrive, OneNote, or OneNote for the web, notebooks can be created according to your workflow preferences.

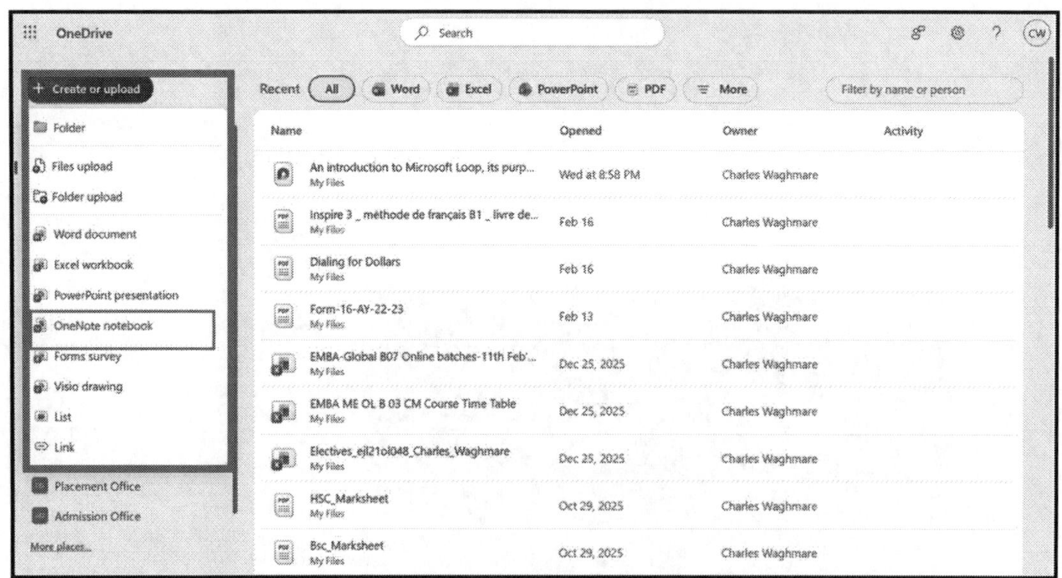

***Figure 1-7.** Creating OneNote notebook from OneDrive*

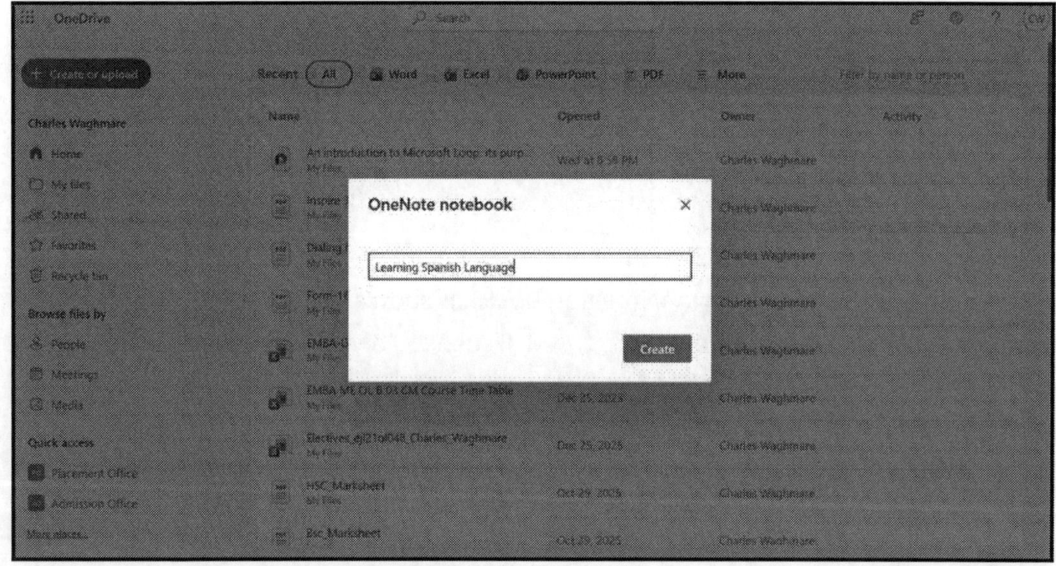

***Figure 1-8.** Assign Name to new OneNote notebook*

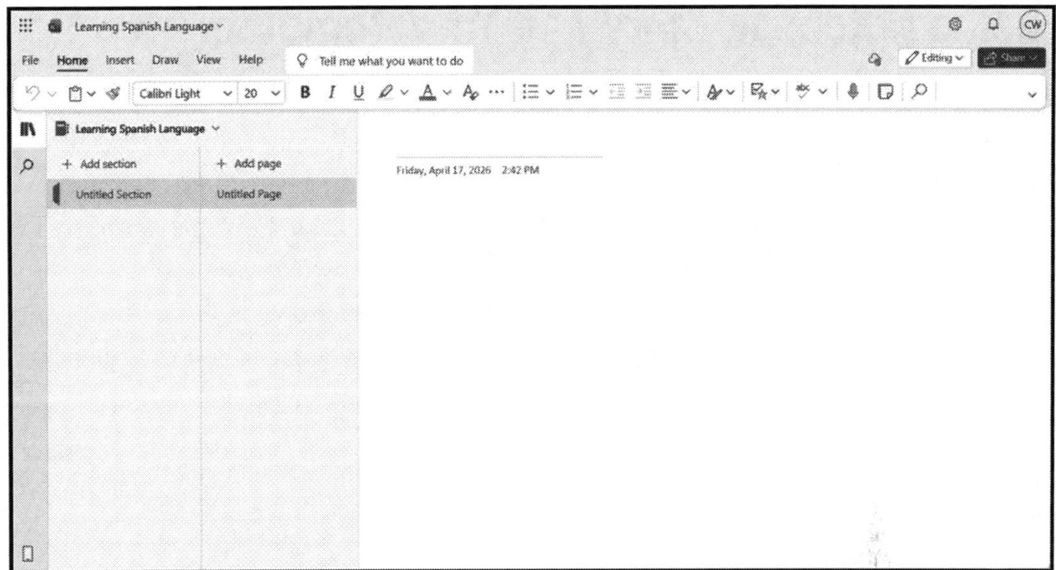

Figure 1-9. *Notebook gets created*

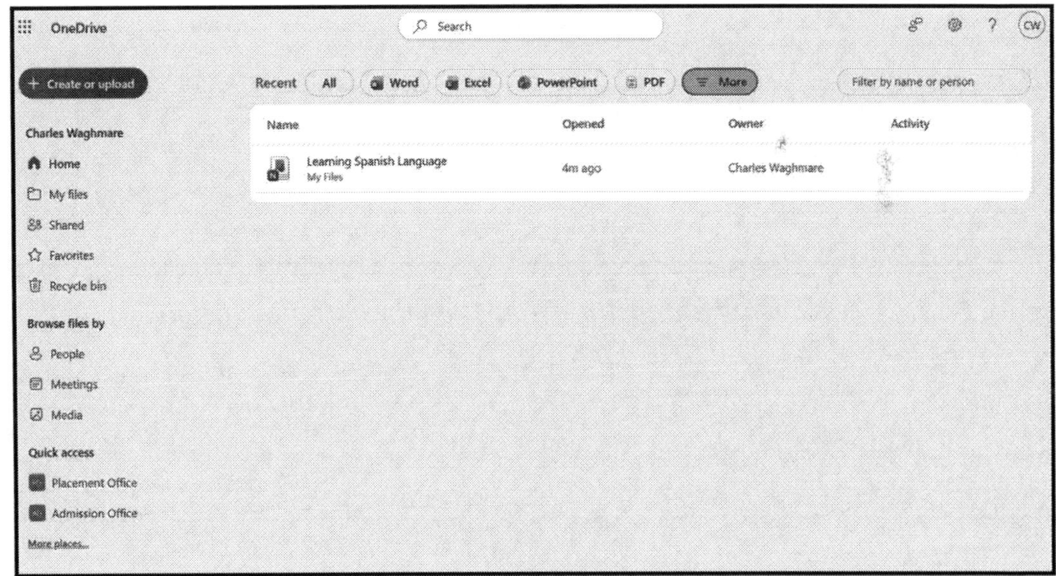

Figure 1-10. *OneNote becomes accessible from OneDrive*

Open a Notebook Stored on Your Computer

To open a notebook stored on your computer, follow these steps. If you have notebooks saved locally that you previously used with another OneNote application, such as the OneNote app or OneNote 2016, you can also open them in OneNote. First, click the downward-facing arrow next to your currently open notebook as shown in Figure 1-11; then you will see a list of the latest accessed notebooks as shown in Figure 1-12. Next, click "More notebooks" to view a list of all your notebooks as shown in Figure 1-13, whether they're stored in the cloud (like on OneDrive) or saved locally on your device.

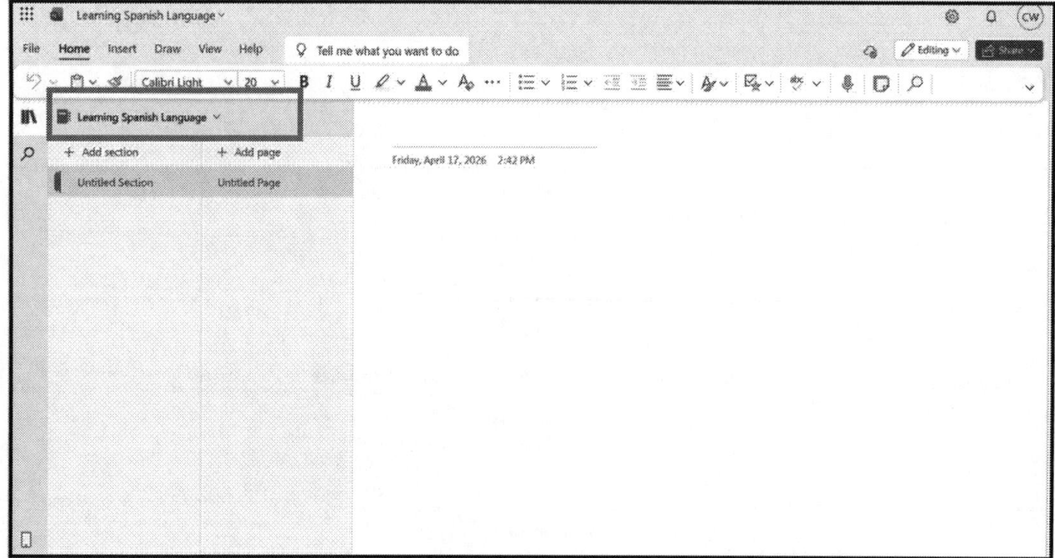

Figure 1-11. *Access downward-facing arrow from the current notebook*

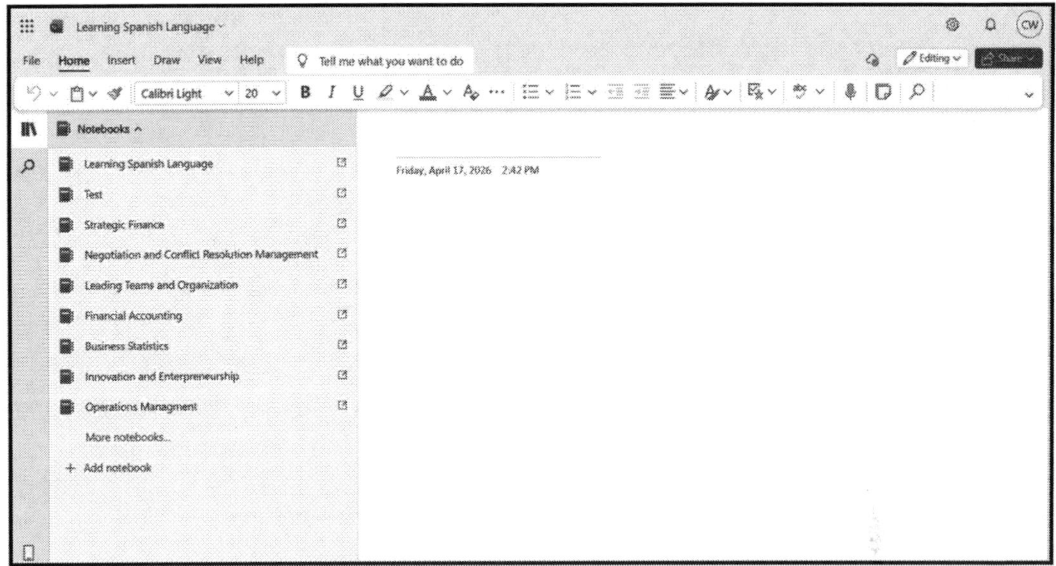

Figure 1-12. *List of the latest accessed notebooks*

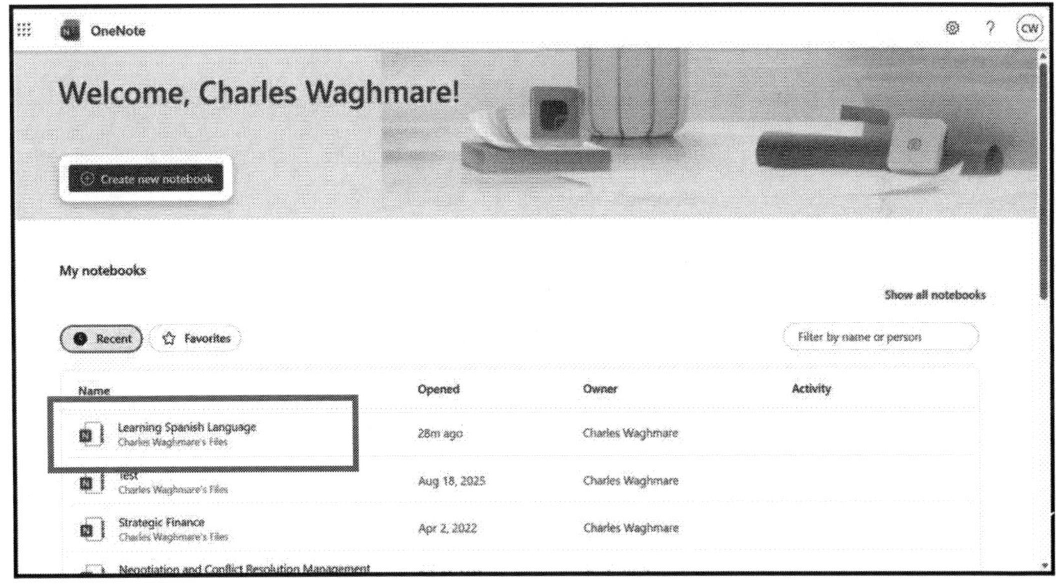

Figure 1-13. *List of all notebooks*

As shown in Figure 1-13, this list displays each notebook's name, such as "Learning Spanish Language," and when you last accessed it and organizes the most recent ones at the top. Locate the notebook you want—such as "Strategic Finance"—and check the box next to it as shown in Figure 1-14. You can open either in the browser or OneNote app.

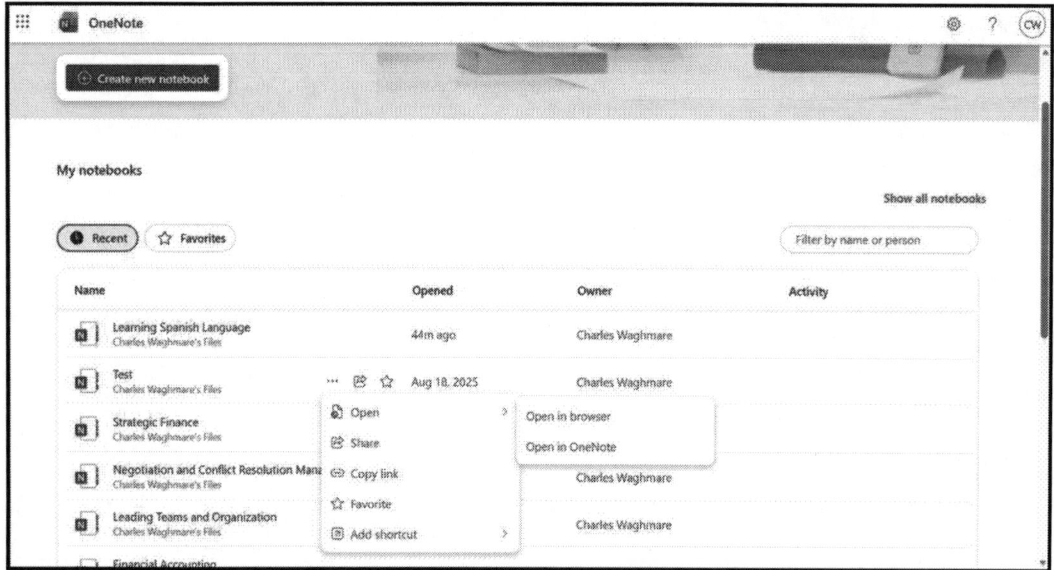

***Figure 1-14.** Open a specific notebook*

Click "Open in browser" to begin opening the selected notebook in the browser, and you will see this notebook as shown in Figure 1-15.

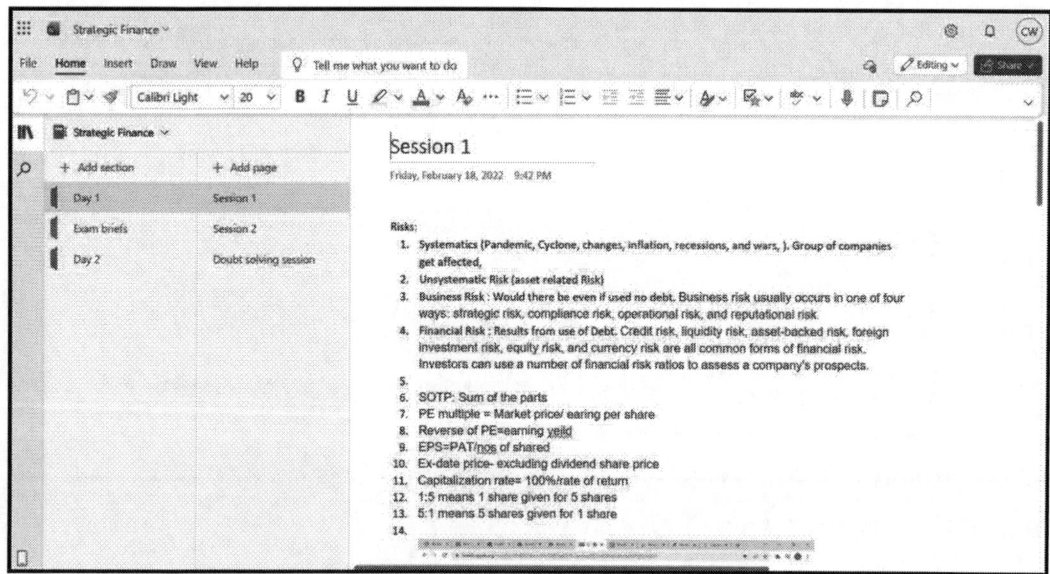

***Figure 1-15.** Strategic Finance OneNote notebook*

Share a Notebook

Notebooks accessed through OneNote are private by default until the owner decides to share them. If you own a notebook stored in your OneDrive document library, it remains private until you grant access to others, similar to files created or uploaded to OneDrive. Sharing can be managed directly from the OneNote application by clicking the "Share" button located in the upper-right corner or by pressing the keyboard shortcut Ctrl+Shift+E to open the Share Send Link menu. Once you click the "Share" button, you will see three options, Share Entire Notebook, Copy Link to Notebook, and Manage Access, as shown in Figure 1-16.

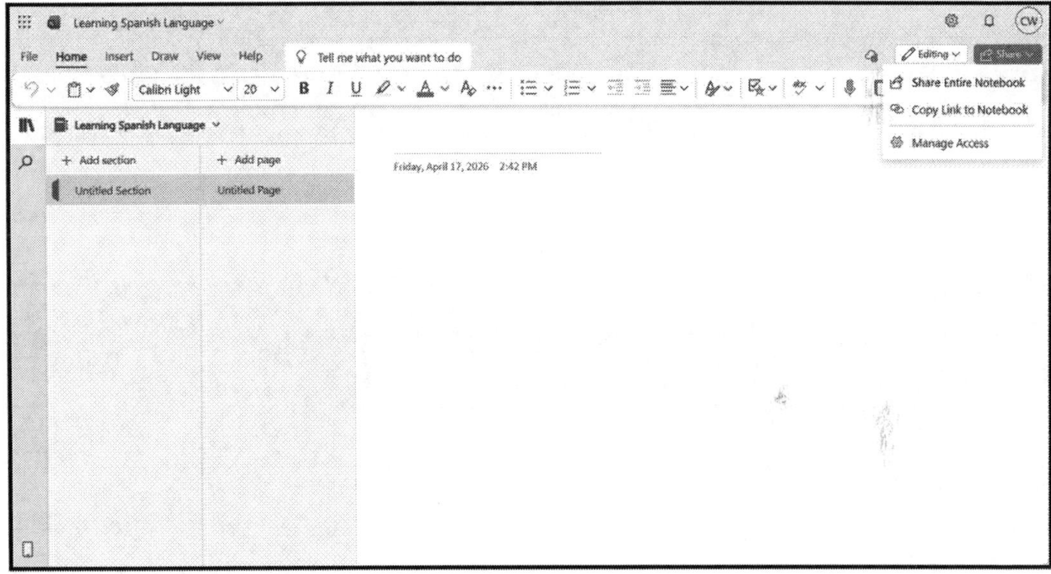

***Figure 1-16.** Options available under the Share feature*

Before entering the intended recipient's name or email address, review the current sharing permissions as shown in Figure 1-17. By default, the setting called as "Can View" which is a view only permission may be enabled as shown in Figure 1-18. This option can be adjusted to restrict access to individuals within your organization, users who already have access, or specific people. As shown in Figure 1-18, the default access of "Can view" can be changed to "Can edit."

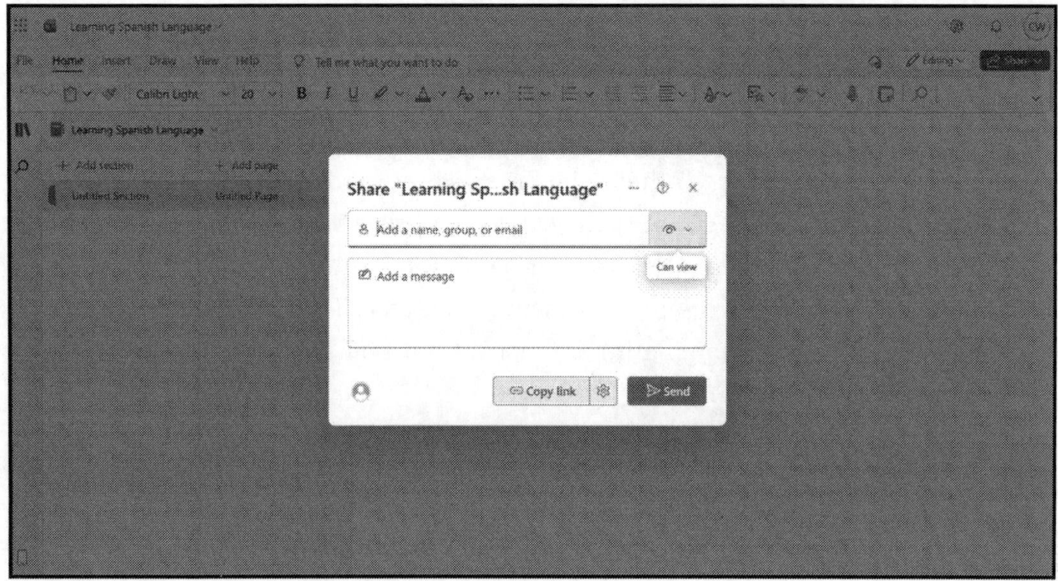

Figure 1-17. *Default view-only permission*

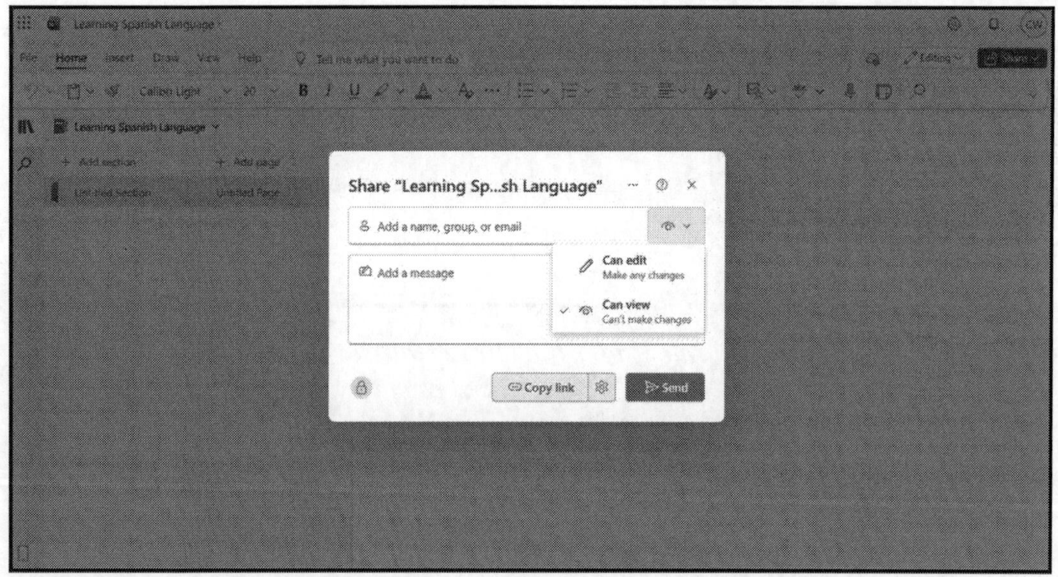

Figure 1-18. *Permissions changed to edit only permission*

To invite a collaborator, enter their name or email address—external participants can also be added via their email as shown in Figures 1-17 and 1-18. You can send a OneNote link via Outlook as shown in Figure 1-19. Multiple users or groups can be included if necessary. Using the "Copy link" button as shown in Figure 1-20, the notebook link can be copied and shared via MS Teams or copied into an Office document.

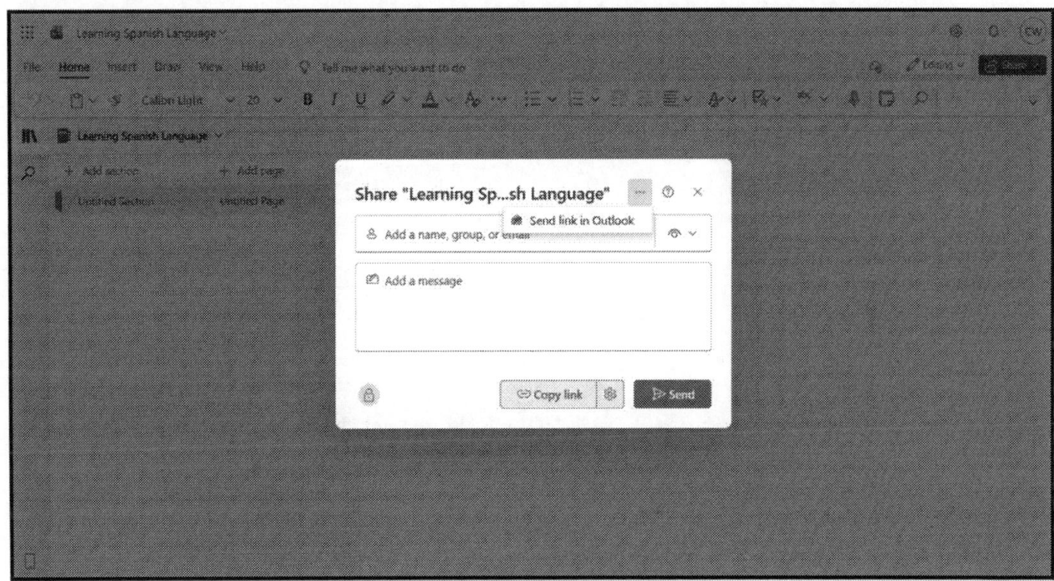

Figure 1-19. *Notebook link sent via Outlook option*

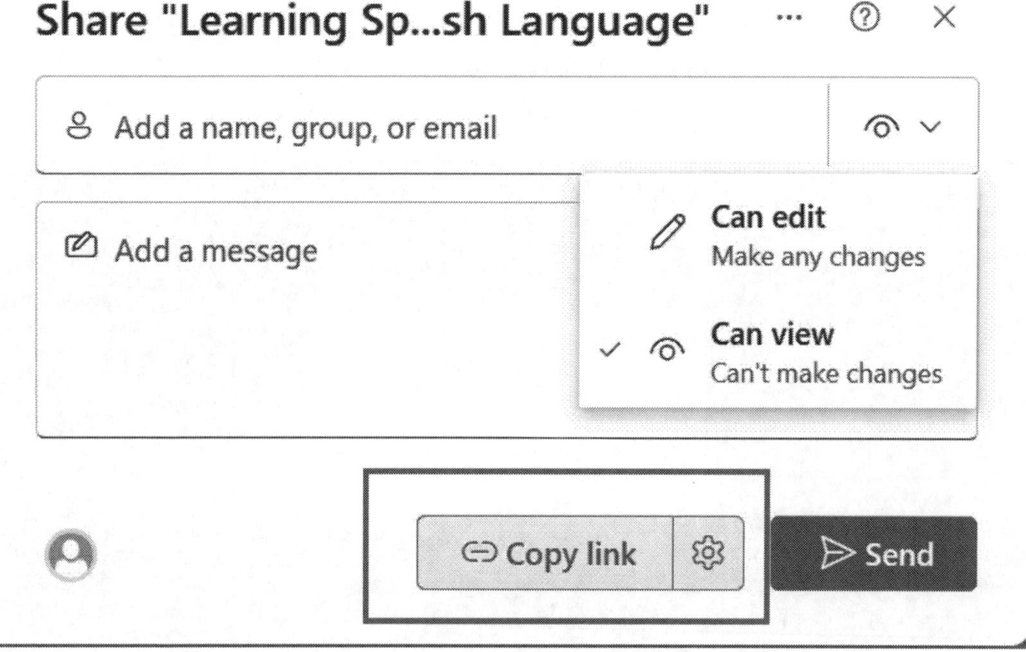

Figure 1-20. *Copy link button*

Optionally, an accompanying message can be added. Once ready, click "Send" to notify recipients, who will receive an email with a link to the shared notebook. Upon clicking the link, invited users will have access based on the permissions set.

Other two options under the Share feature are Copy Link to Notebook and Manage Access as shown in Figure 1-21.

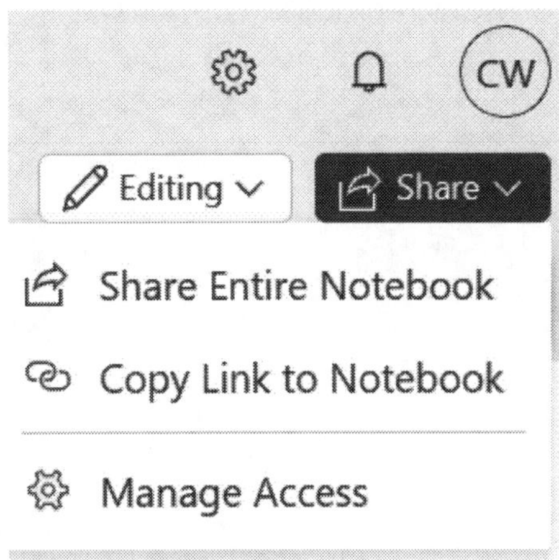

Figure 1-21. *Options under the Share button*

Once Copy Link to Notebook is clicked, the notebook link gets copied as shown in Figure 1-22.

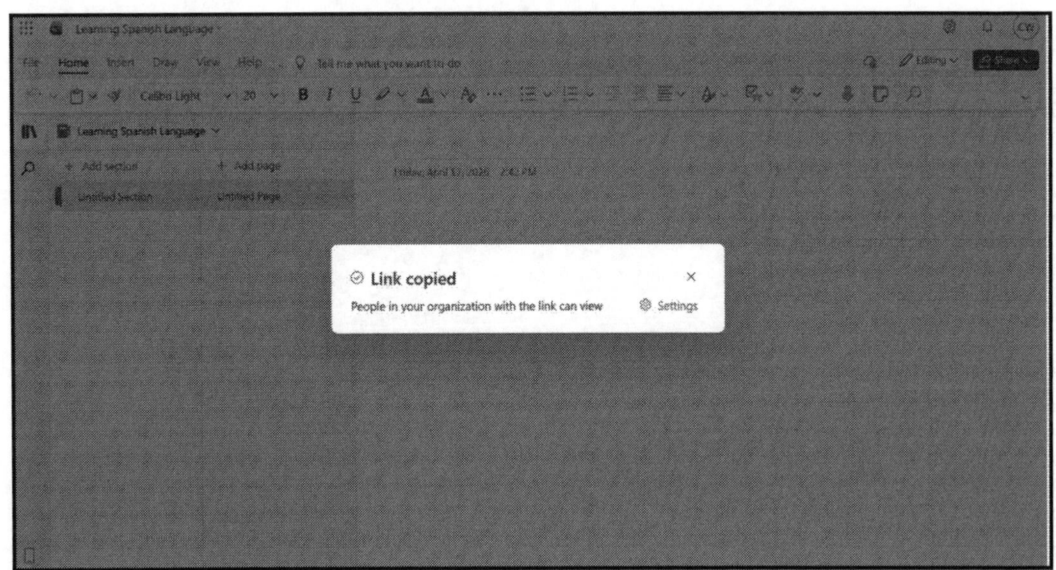

Figure 1-22. *Copied link of OneNote notebook*

Upon clicking Manage Access, one can see a screen as shown in Figure 1-23, using which we can grant access to people or groups by the Grant Access feature as shown in Figure 1-24.

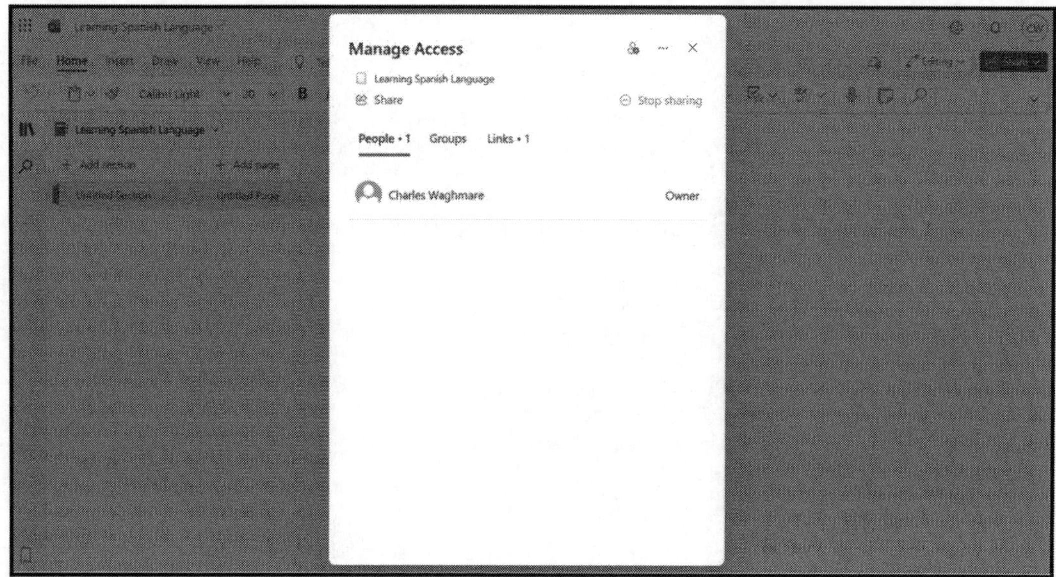

***Figure 1-23.** Manage Access page of notebook*

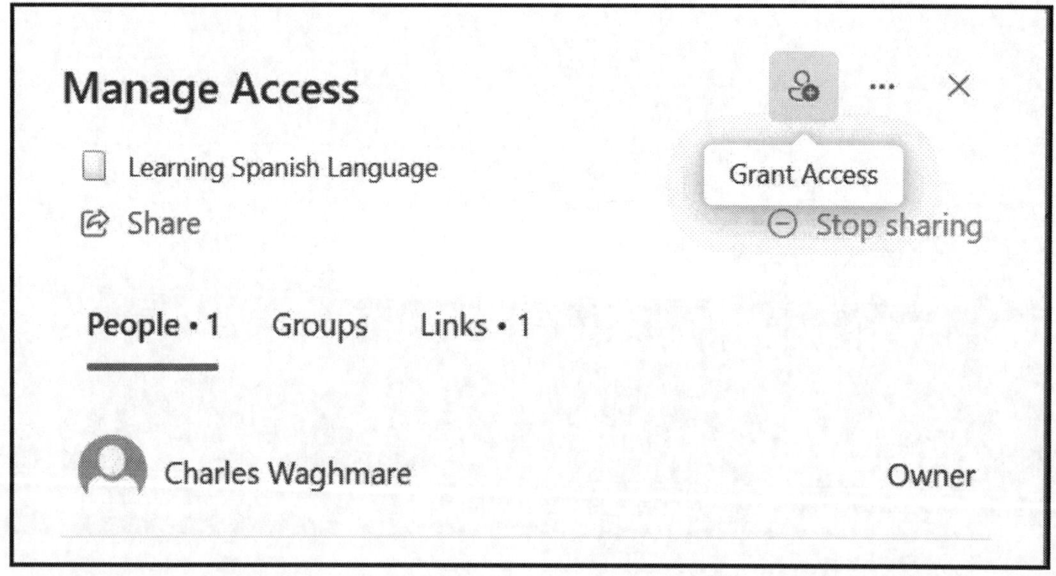

***Figure 1-24.** Click Grant Access option*

"Can View" and "Can Edit" type of access can be granted as shown in Figure 1-25. Further, a custom message can be send to users while granting access.

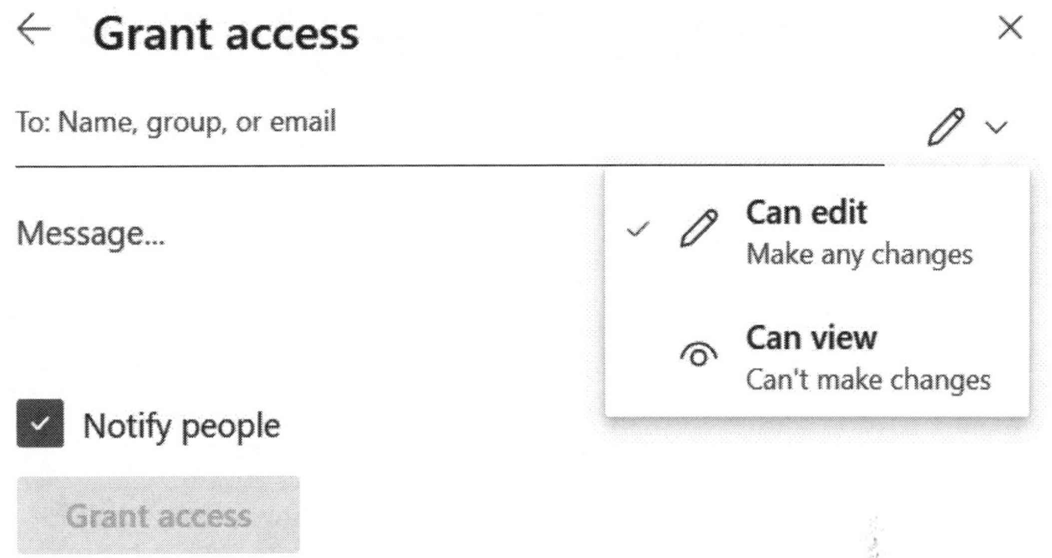

***Figure 1-25.** Grant access to a user or group*

Notebook sharing can also be managed through the OneDrive document library. This can be achieved by clicking the Advanced settings tab as shown in Figure 1-26; you will land on the permission settings of this notebook in OneDrive as shown in Figure 1-27.

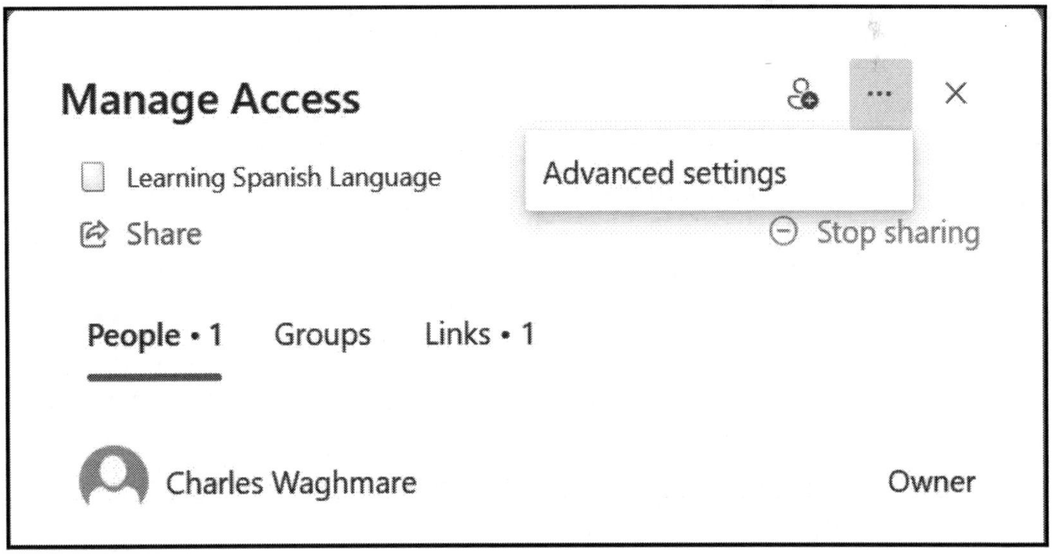

***Figure 1-26.** Advanced settings*

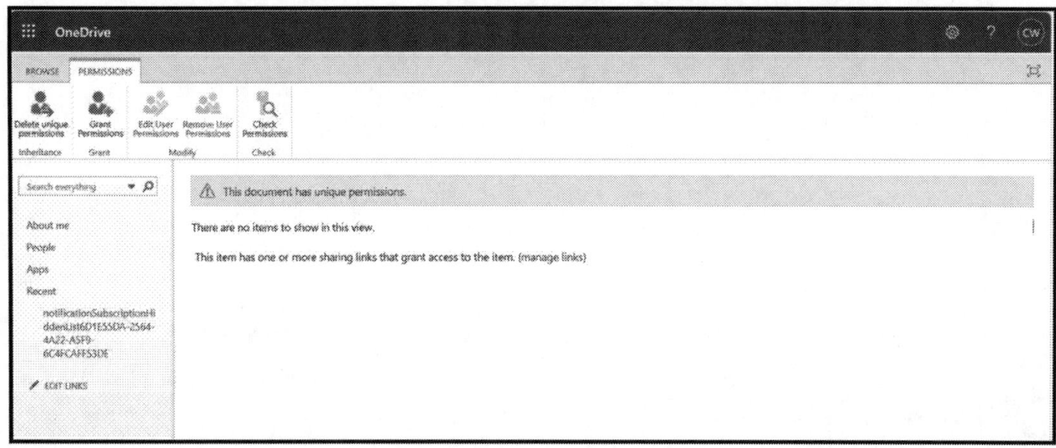

Figure 1-27. *Manage notebook permissions on OneDrive*

You can grant, edit or view access, remove existing permissions and check existing user permissions; these options are available in OneDrive as shown in Figure 1-28.

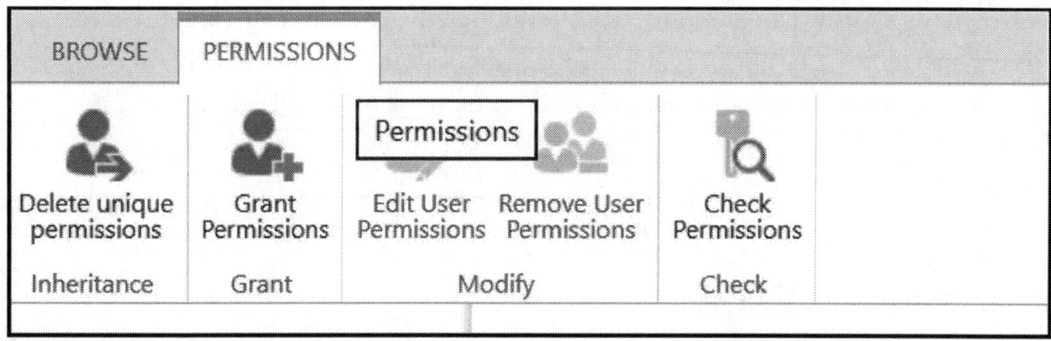

Figure 1-28. *Manage permissions of notebook in OneDrive*

If you want to delete unique permissions, then look for the option "Delete unique permissions," and click OK as shown in Figure 1-29. Deleting unique permissions in OneNote removes custom access settings and restores inherited permissions from the parent notebook, section, or SharePoint library, ensuring consistent security across all related content items globally. Deleting unique permissions means removing special sharing settings so the OneNote page or notebook uses the same access permissions as its parent, making sharing simpler and consistent.

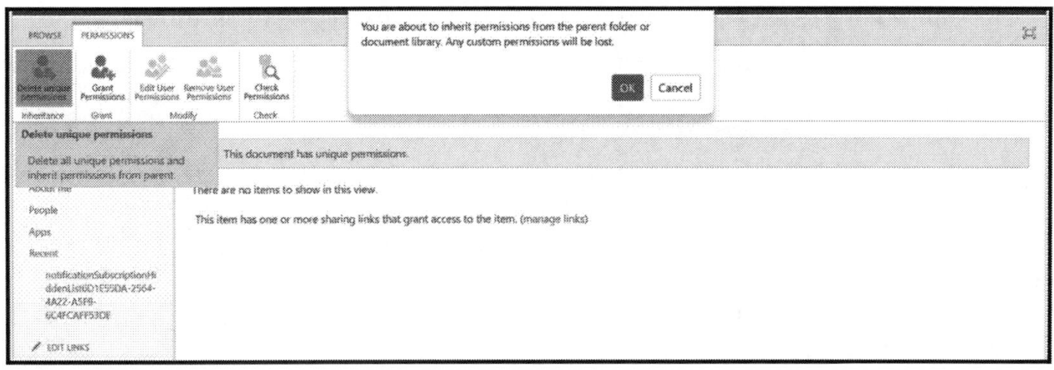

***Figure 1-29.** Delete unique permissions*

While granting permissions, OneNote offers different types of permissions such as full control, design, edit, contribute, read, and restricted view. Permission confirmation can be sent via email as shown in Figure 1-30.

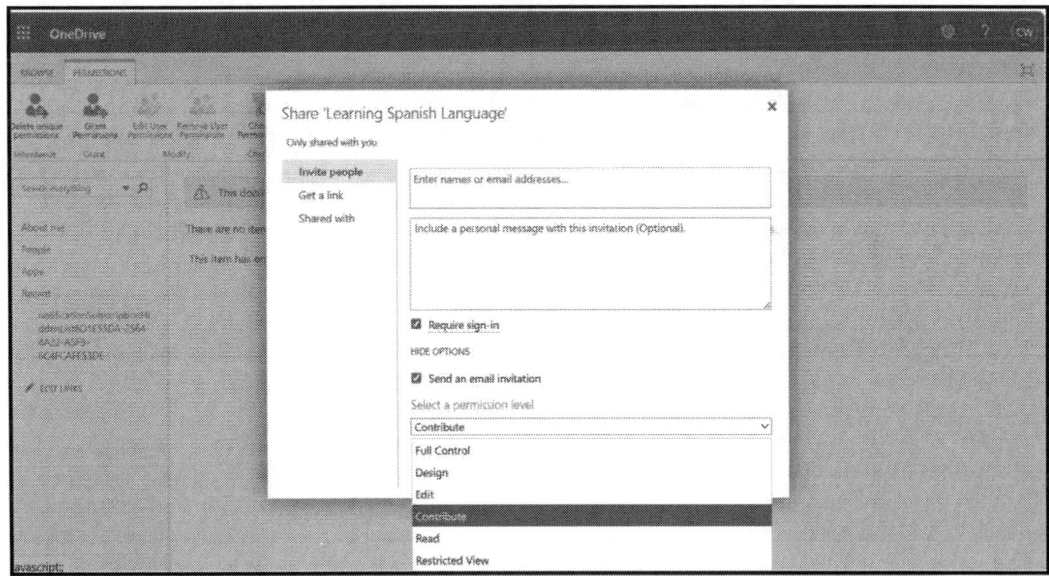

***Figure 1-30.** Grant permissions*

The Check Permissions feature offers to check the permission of existing users as shown in Figure 1-31, and a summary of existing permissions can be seen in Figure 1-32.

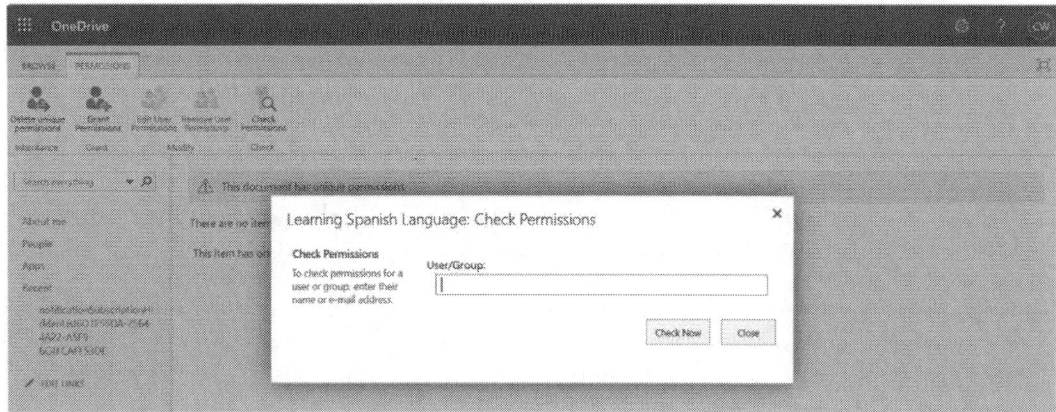

Figure 1-31. *Check existing user permissions*

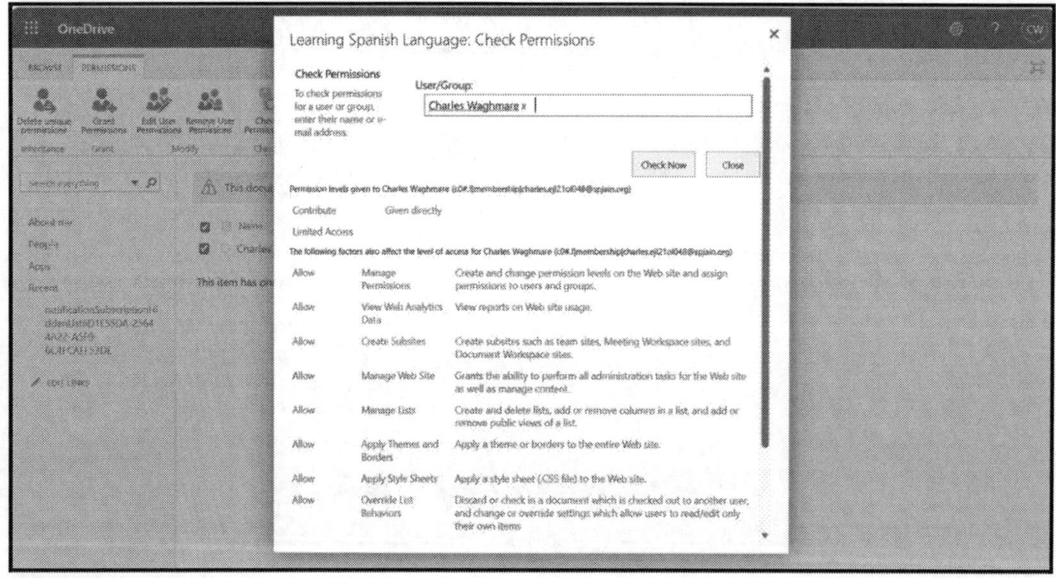

Figure 1-32. *Permission summary*

To edit user permissions, select a user as shown in Figure 1-33, and then edit user permissions.

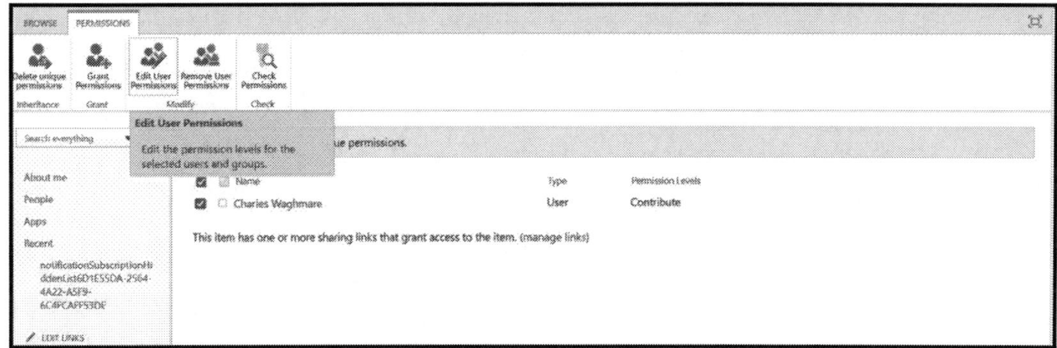

Figure 1-33. *Select a user for editing permissions*

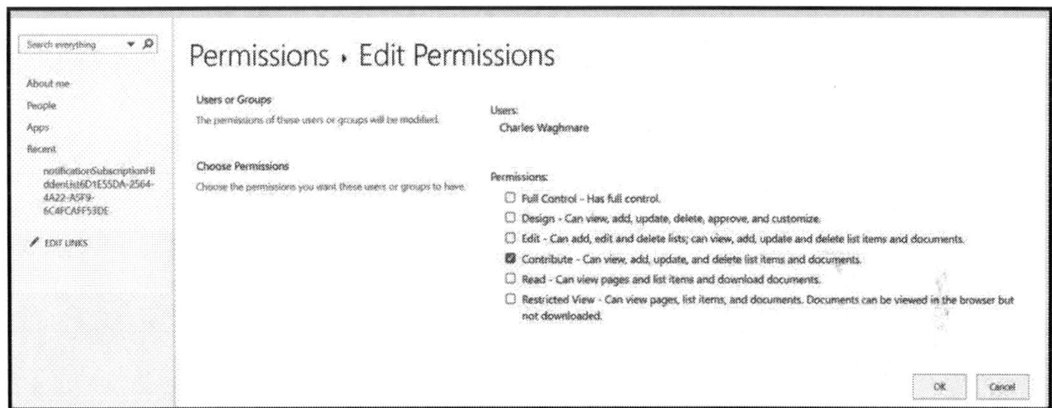

Figure 1-34. *Edit user permissions with different permission types*

Finally, to remove user permissions, select a user and remove permissions as shown in Figure 1-35.

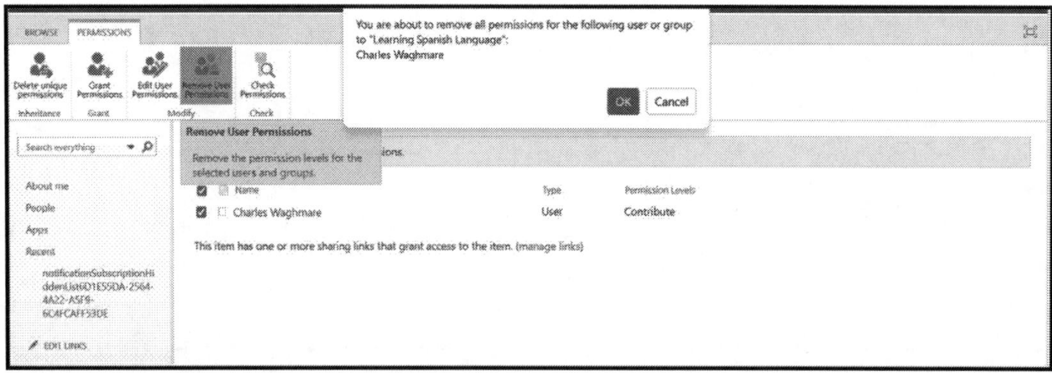

***Figure 1-35.** Remove user permissions*

It is essential to note that Microsoft OneNote does not possess its own independent permission model. All aspects of access control, sharing, and permission management for OneNote notebooks are dictated by the storage platform utilized—OneDrive or SharePoint. When a notebook is shared, permissions such as view, edit, or full control are inherited directly from the associated OneDrive folder or SharePoint document library where the notebook resides. Consequently, the permissions discussed in this chapter—including granting access, modifying user rights, revoking access, or reinstating inherited permissions—are based on SharePoint and OneDrive mechanisms, rather than controls specific to OneNote.

Within the OneNote application, users interact with a streamlined sharing interface; however, these operations correspond to SharePoint-level permission settings at their core. OneNote does not provide granular, page-level permissions, custom role definitions, or unique access policies distinct from its storage platform. Any advanced management of permissions, audit trails, or inheritance must therefore be conducted within OneDrive or SharePoint.

This differentiation is crucial for establishing appropriate expectations. OneNote's primary focus is on content creation and organization, while security, governance, and access control are managed through SharePoint and OneDrive, ensuring uniformity throughout Microsoft 365. Recognizing this structural relationship enables users to facilitate collaboration securely and aligns OneNote usage with enterprise governance standards.

Create a OneNote Section

Organizing sections within a notebook is an effective method for categorizing similar pages of content. If the section and page panes are not visible, it is possible that navigation has been hidden as shown in Figure 1-36; this can be toggled by selecting the corresponding notebook icons, which switch between "Show Navigation" and "Hide Navigation" as shown in Figures 1-36 and 1-37, respectively.

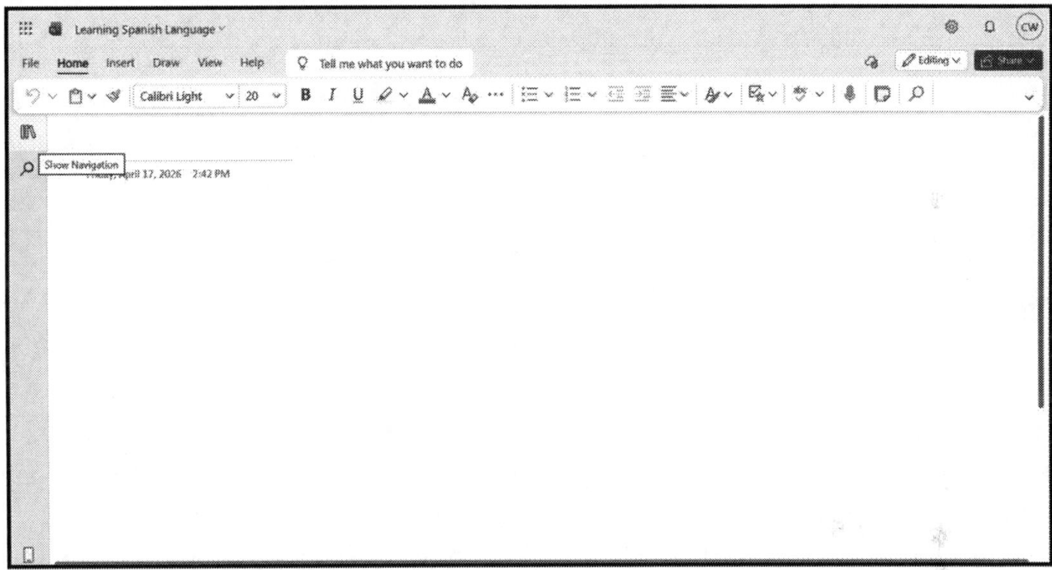

Figure 1-36. *Show Navigation"*

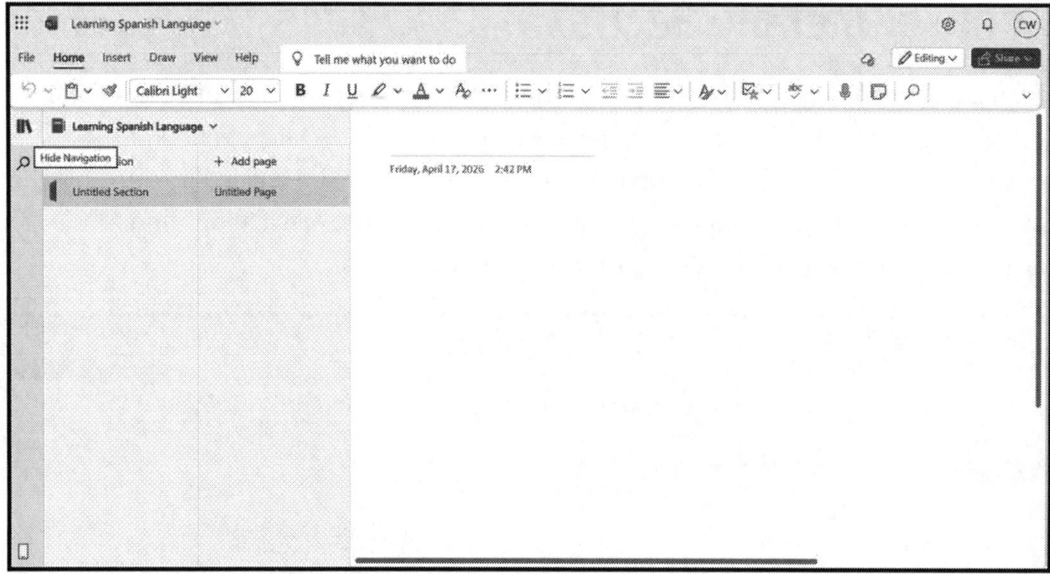

Figure 1-37. *Hide Navigation"*

Proceed with section pane and select "+Add section" as shown in the Figure 1-38. Once we click on "+Add section" a windows pops up as shown in Figure 1-39 to add title as "Comprehension Oral" of the new section to be created. Once we click OK as shown in Figure 1-39, section gets created as shown in Figure 1-40.

A default section with the title "Untitled Section" will always appear as shown in Figure 1-41 which is included by default when a notebook is created.

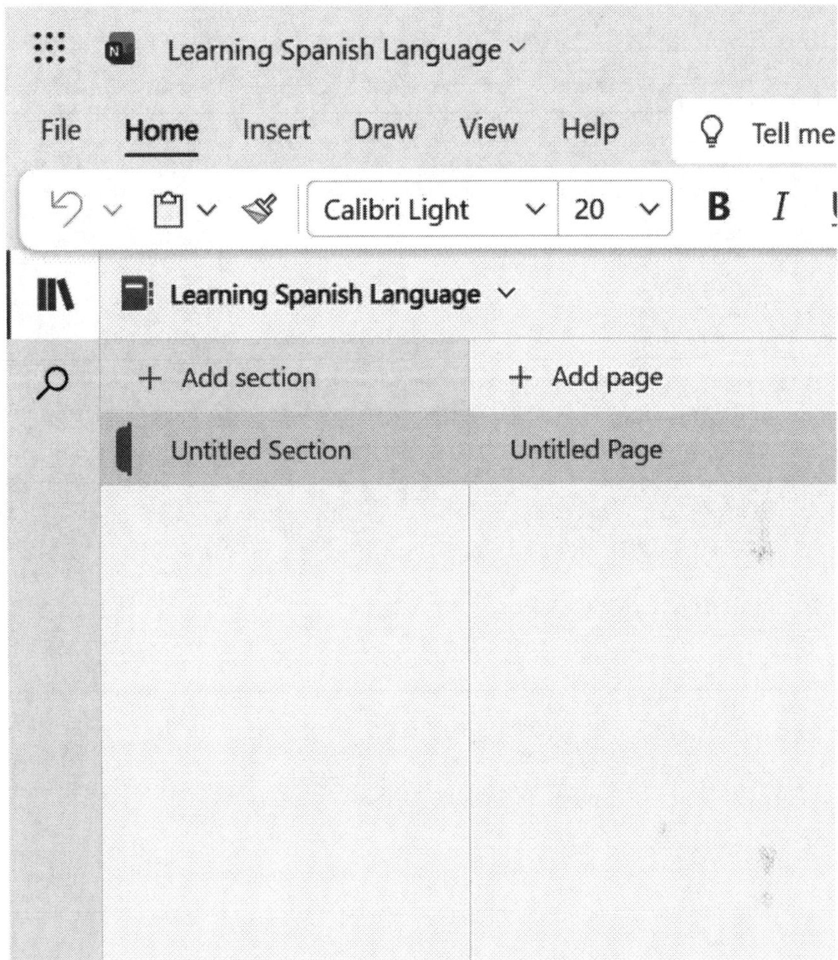

Figure 1-38. *"+ Add section" to create a new section*

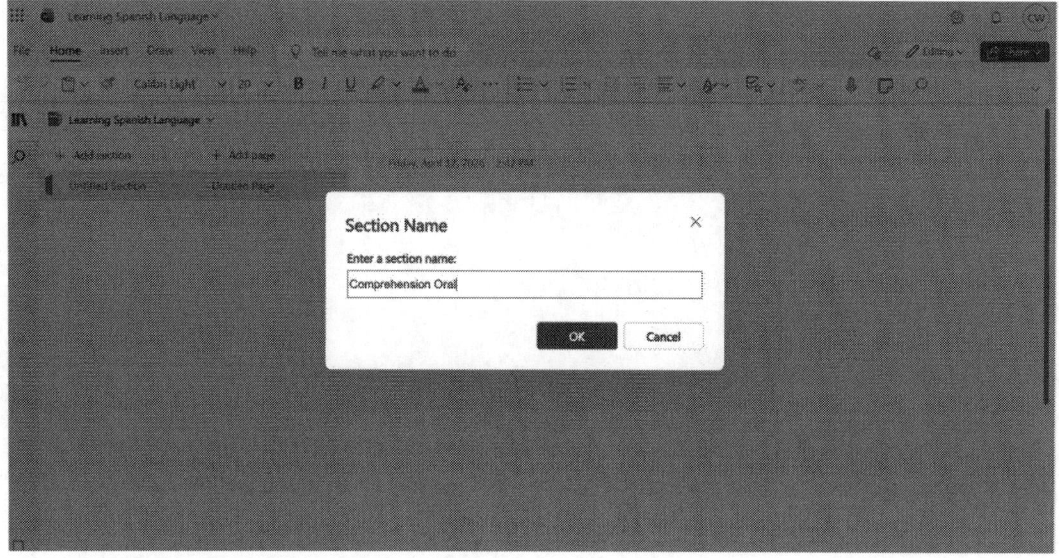

Figure 1-39. *Title of the new section*

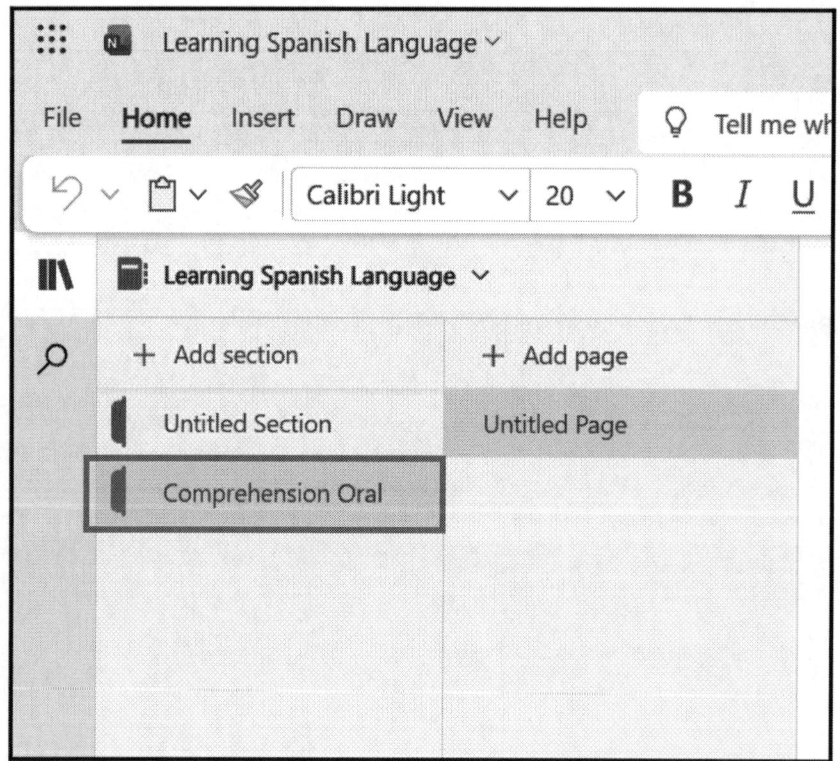

Figure 1-40. *New section gets created*

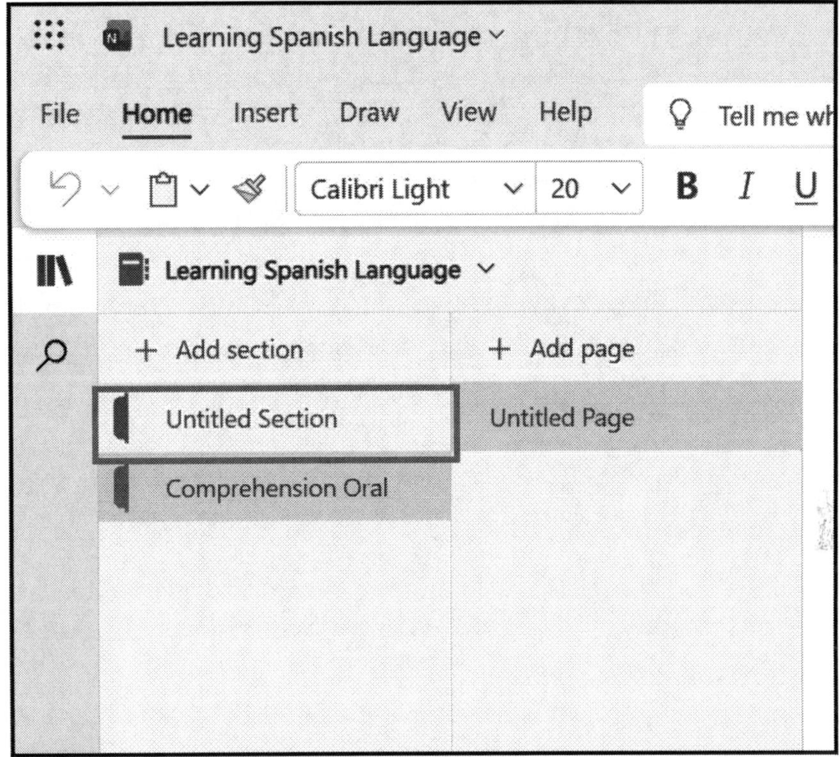

Figure 1-41. *Default section—Untitled Section*

Renaming either section is straightforward; simply select the section as shown in Figure 1-42, and enter the desired name, such as "Comprehension Written," then press Enter button to confirm as shown in Figure 1-43.

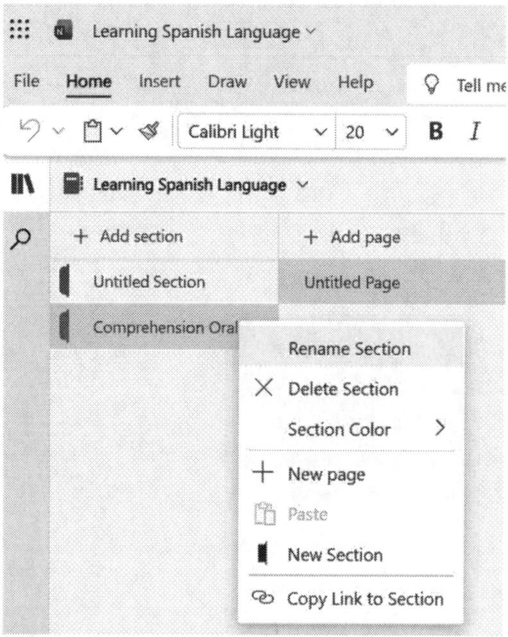

Figure 1-42. *Access rename option*

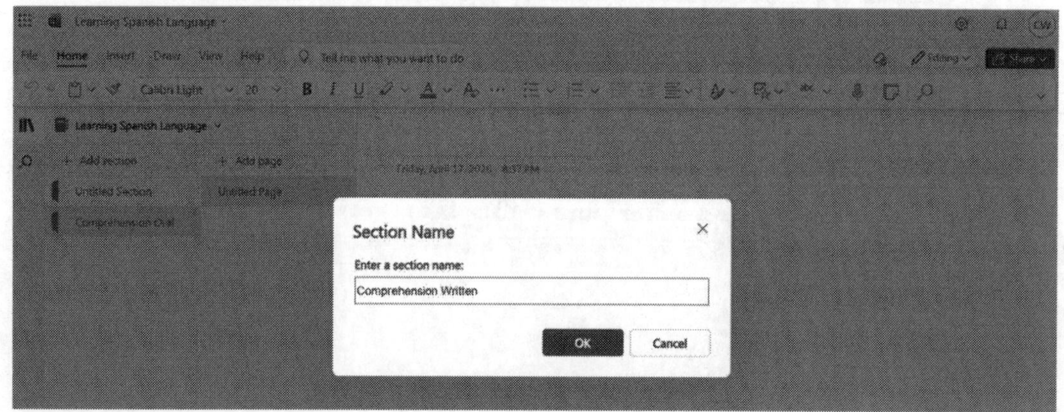

Figure 1-43. *Update name*

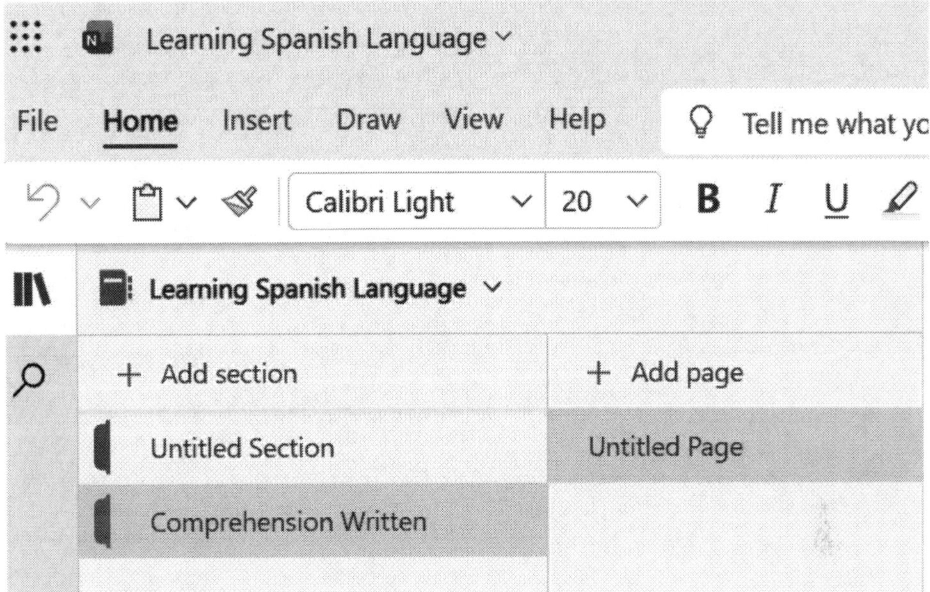

Figure 1-44. *Updated name is visible*

Each section is represented as a tab on the left, with a distinct color assigned for differentiation. For example, "Untitled Section" may display charcoal blue while others could have colors like green as seen in Figure 1-44. To adjust the color of a section, right-click the section; choose "Section Color," as shown in Figure 1-45; and select from the available palette, let's say red. Upon selection, the tab color updates accordingly as shown in Figure 1-46.

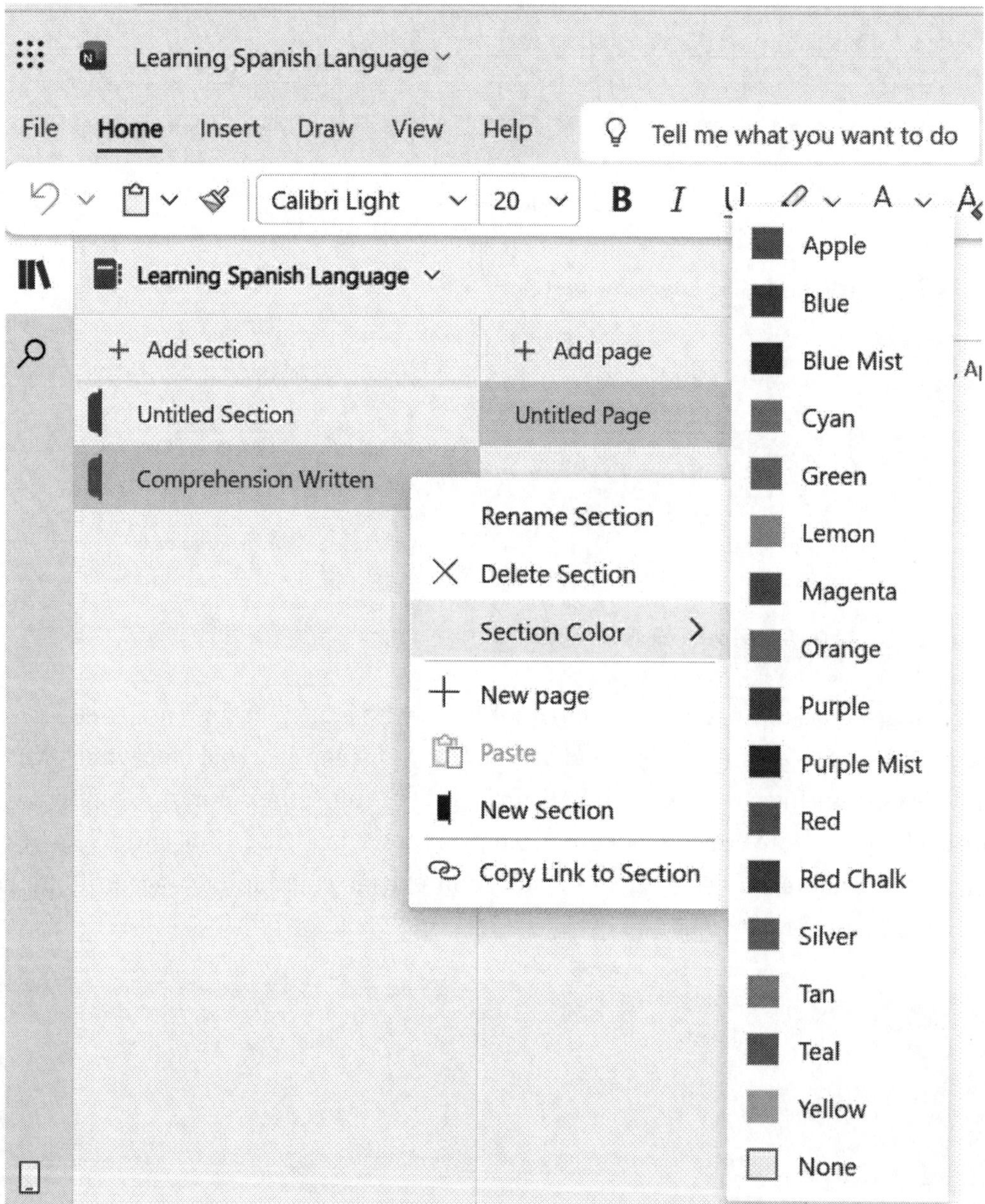

***Figure 1-45.** Access Section Color option*

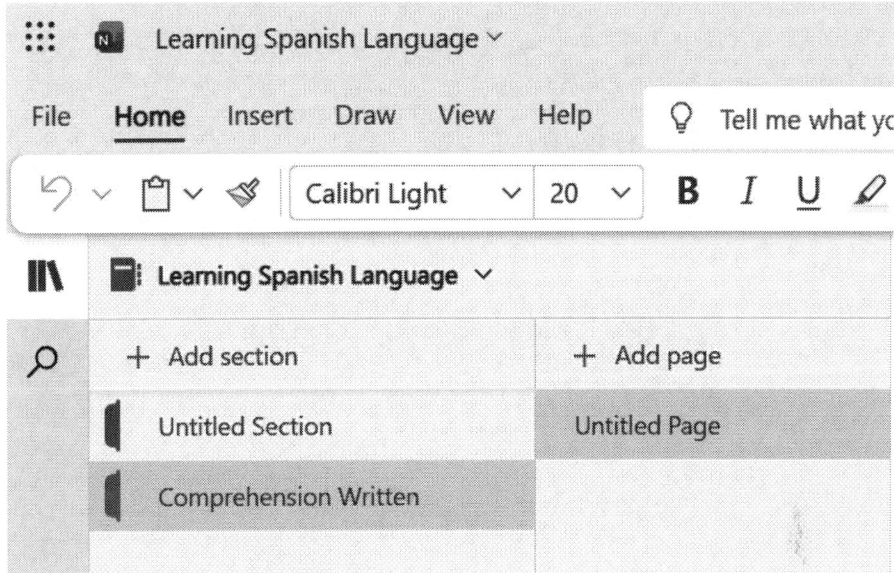

Figure 1-46. *Section color updated*

Navigating between multiple sections is facilitated through both mouse selection and keyboard shortcuts. These tools enhance notebook structure and promote greater organization. Further, sequence of the sections can be changed easily by dragging section names with the help of a mouse. Figure 1-47 shows the section sequence as "Untitled Section", "Comprehension Written" before change and Figure 1-48 shows section sequence as "Comprehension Written, "Untitled Section" after change.

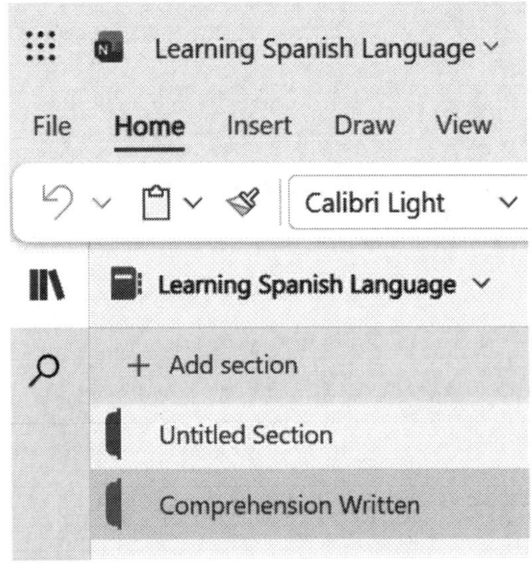

Figure 1-47. *Section before moving*

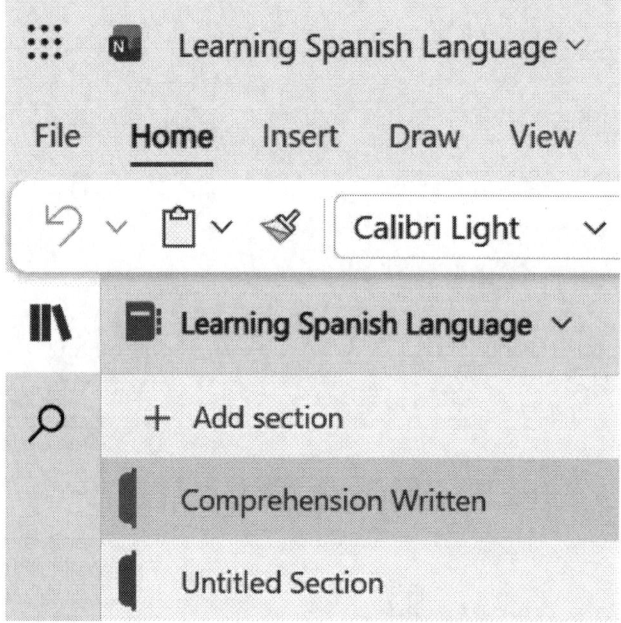

Figure 1-48. *Section after moving*

To delete a section, right-click its name and select "Delete Section" as shown in Figure 1-49. Confirm your choice as shown in Figure 1-50, and it will disappear from the notebook as shown in Figure 1-51.

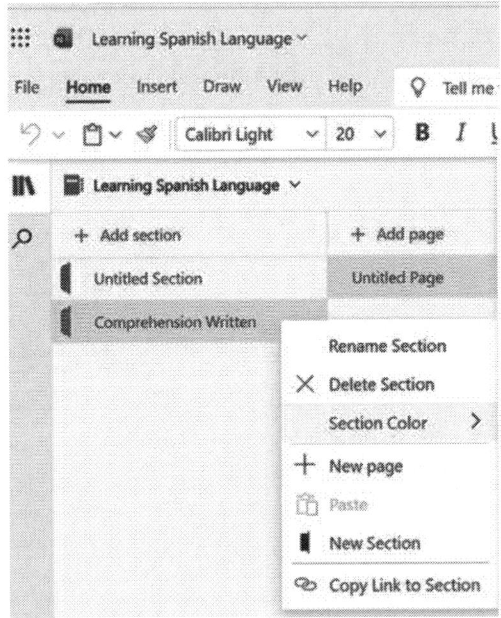

***Figure 1-49.** Access option to delete a section*

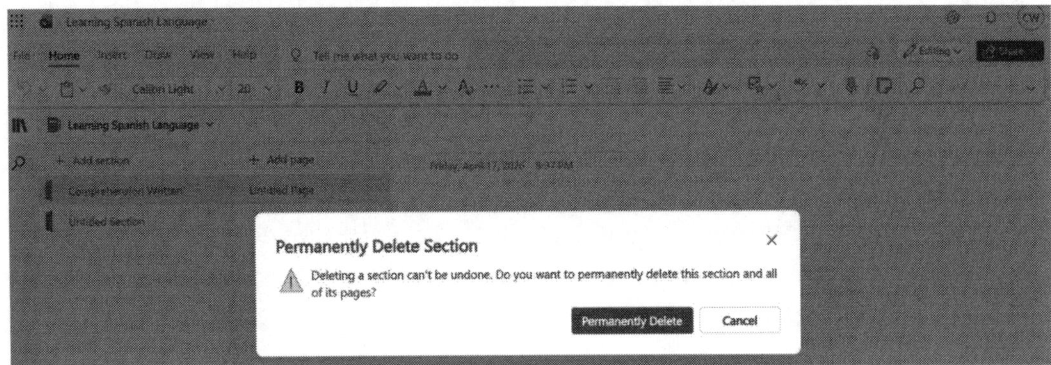

***Figure 1-50.** Confirm deletion*

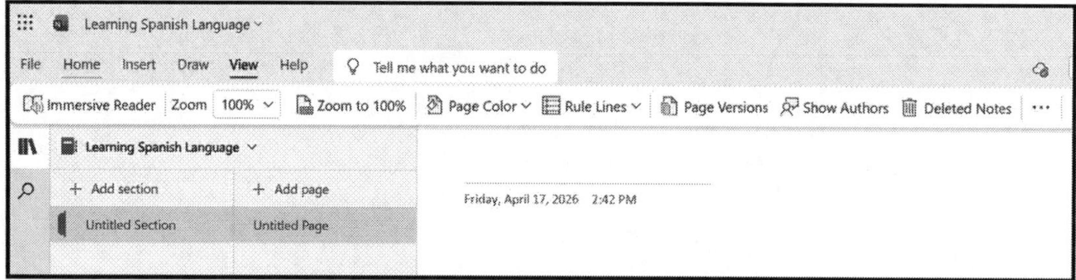

Figure 1-51. *Deletion successfully completed*

Create a Linked Section

Over time, you may accumulate various types of notes for multiple projects. To organize your material efficiently, you can create an index, table of contents, or other reference points by linking to specific sections or pages. Begin by right-clicking "Comprehension Oral" and selecting "Copy Link to Section" as shown in Figure 1-52. Navigate to your desired destination—for instance, "Comprehension Written"—right-click in the appropriate location and choose "Paste." The resulting link, when selected, will direct you immediately to the "Comprehension Oral" section as shown in Figure 1-53.

In Figure 1-53, you will observe that the link is embedded within a container. To manage this link, right-click on it. Under the link menu, accessible via the arrow, you may open, edit, copy, or remove the link as necessary as shown in Figure 1-54. If required, click outside the area to deselect. This process applies equally to individual pages within a section: simply right-click the relevant page and follow the aforementioned steps to copy its link.

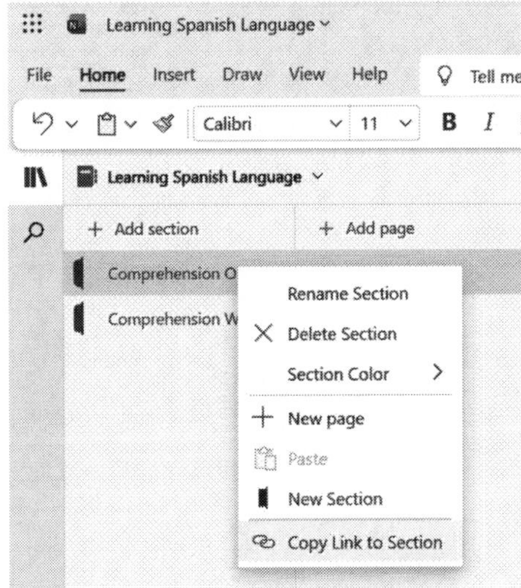

Figure 1-52. *Select "Copy Link to Section"*

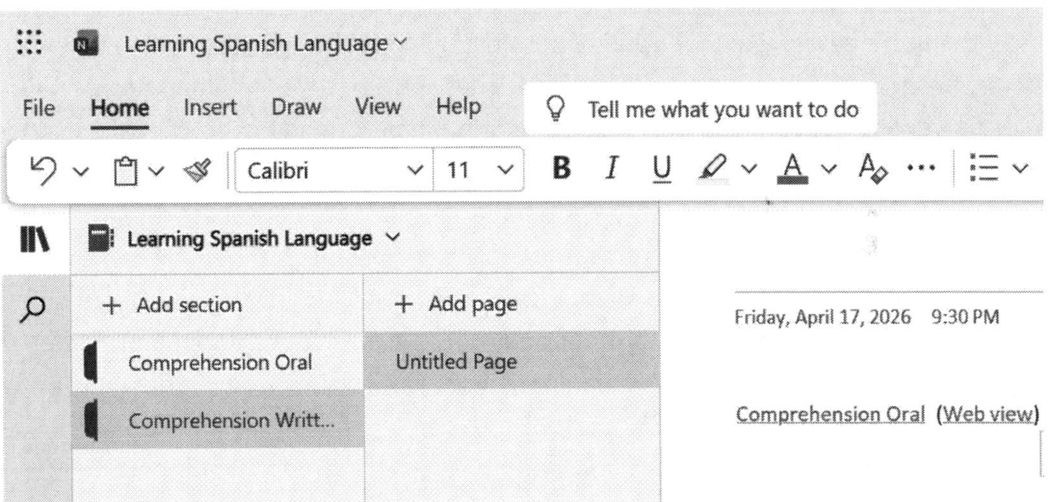

Figure 1-53. *Link is copied in the Comprehension Written section*

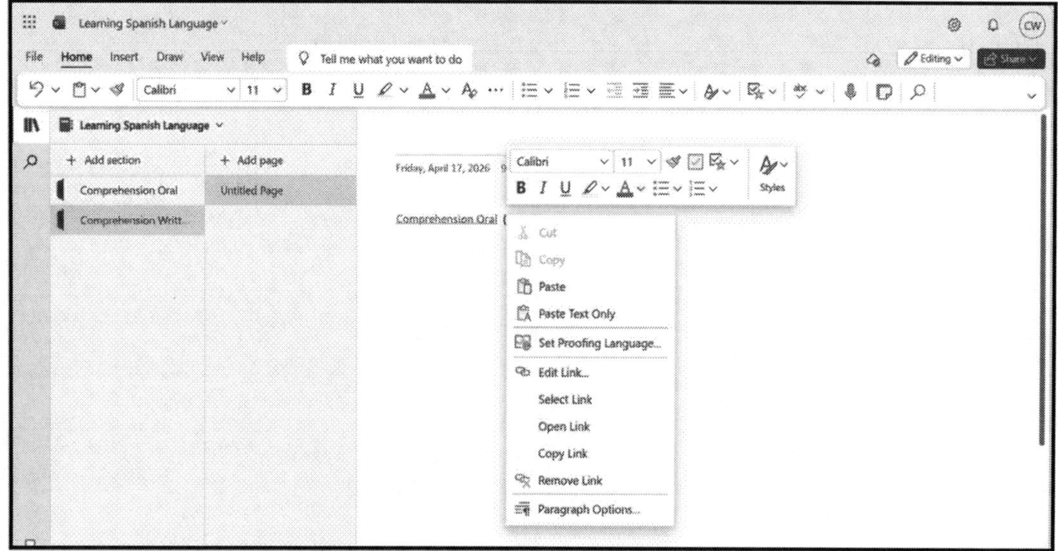

Figure 1-54. *Managing links in OneNote*

With this we have come to the end of this chapter. This chapter explained how Microsoft OneNote was used as a structured digital workspace for creating, storing, and managing notebooks through OneDrive integration. It described the process of creating notebooks using OneNote as well as directly from OneDrive, ensuring secure cloud storage and cross-device accessibility. The chapter also covered how users organized multiple notebooks for academic, professional, or personal purposes and accessed them either through the OneNote application or a web browser. Guidance was provided on opening recently used notebooks, browsing all available notebooks, and maintaining continuity for users working across different devices or migrating from earlier OneNote versions.

In addition, the chapter detailed how notebooks were shared and how permissions were managed to support collaboration. It explained default privacy settings, sharing entire notebooks or links, assigning view or edit access, and inviting internal or external collaborators. Permission management through both OneNote and OneDrive was discussed, including editing, removing, and restoring inherited permissions for consistent security. The chapter further demonstrated how sections were created, renamed, color-coded, moved, deleted, and linked to improve organization and navigation. By the end of the chapter, readers gained a clear understanding of how OneNote supported efficient note organization, controlled collaboration, and effective knowledge management within a unified Microsoft 365 environment.

This chapter provides a practical overview of Microsoft OneNote, covering note creation, organization, and management for academic and professional use. In the next chapter, readers will learn how to create and navigate pages, apply formatting for clarity, and use OneNote Class Notebook for collaboration and assignment management. The chapter also covers research organization, training program development, annotation techniques, and designing digital lesson plans

CHAPTER 2

Getting Started with Microsoft OneNote

In the previous chapter, we have seen how Microsoft OneNote functions as a structured digital workspace for creating, storing, and managing notebooks through OneDrive integration. It explained notebook creation using OneNote and OneDrive, ensuring secure cloud storage and cross-device access. The chapter described organizing and accessing multiple notebooks for academic, professional, and personal use, including working across devices and older versions. It also covered notebook sharing, permission settings, and collaboration management. Additionally, the chapter demonstrated managing sections through renaming, color-coding, moving, deleting, and linking, helping readers understand effective organization, controlled collaboration, and knowledge management within Microsoft 365.

In this chapter, we will address a variety of topics including creating, moving, and deleting pages; making subpages; rearranging content using the Cut, Copy, and Paste tools; working in full screen mode; utilizing page templates for efficiency; building a page index; leveraging OneNote for academic research management; developing training programs; annotating and reviewing work; and designing digital lesson plans.

Create, Move, and Delete a Page

When a new section is added to a notebook, such as a project management section, a corresponding page is automatically generated within that section (e.g., an initially untitled page) as shown in Figure 2-1. Each newly created page features a date and timestamp indicating when it was created as highlighted in Figure 2-1. The area above this information serves as a placeholder for naming the page; for instance, meetings can be organized by month or year according to the specific needs of the notebook. For

C. Waghmare, *Mastering Microsoft OneNote*, https://doi.org/10.1007/979-8-8688-2866-9_2

example, one might name a page "Jan meetings" to categorize content accordingly as shown in Figure 2-2. This title is displayed both on the page itself and within the page pane as highlighted in Figure 2-2.

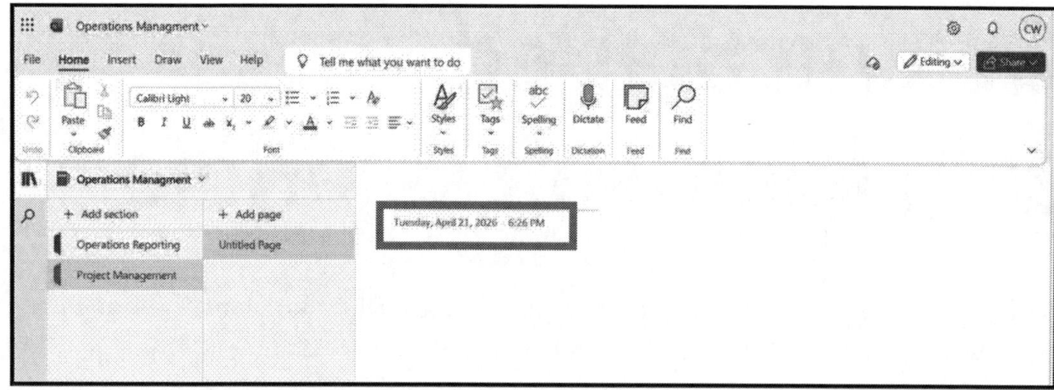

Figure 2-1. *Default page exists for a new section*

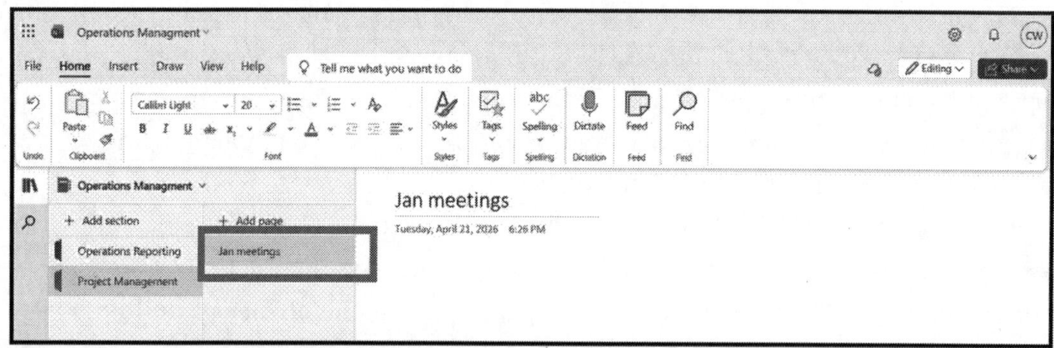

Figure 2-2. *Title for the page updated*

To create additional pages within a section, there are several available methods. With the page pane open, clicking "Add page" at the top as shown in Figure 2-3 will generate a new untitled page as shown in Figure 2-4. Alternatively, the keyboard shortcut Ctrl+N quickly creates a new page. Right-clicking an existing page also provides an option to add a new page below the selected one as shown in Figure 2-5.

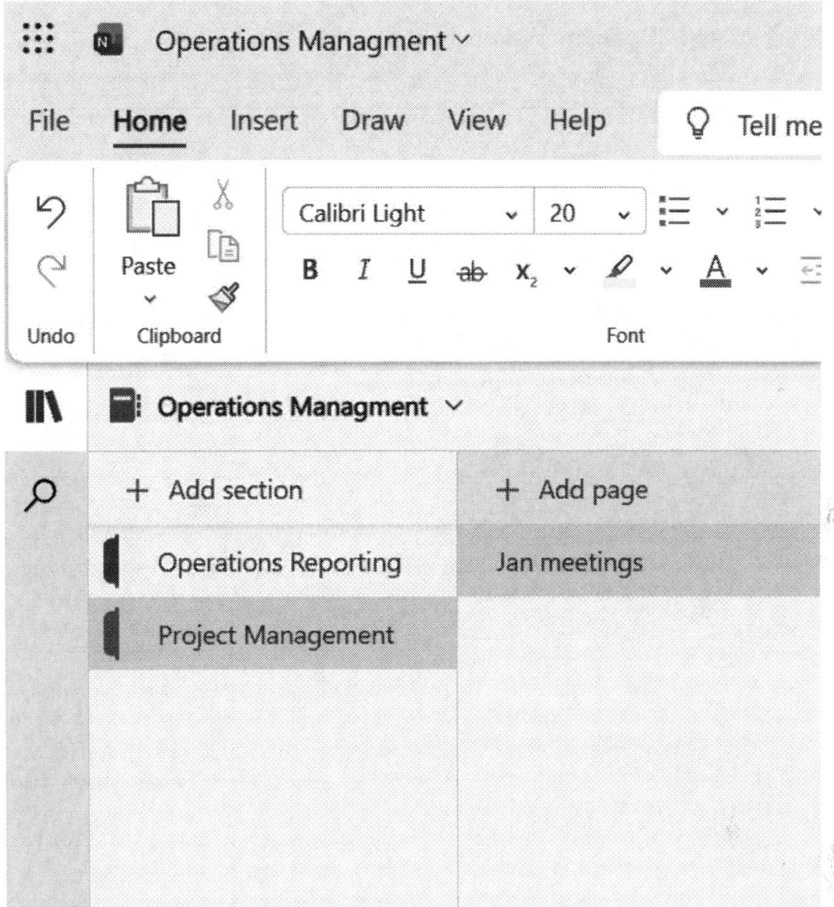

Figure 2-3. *Add page to create a new page*

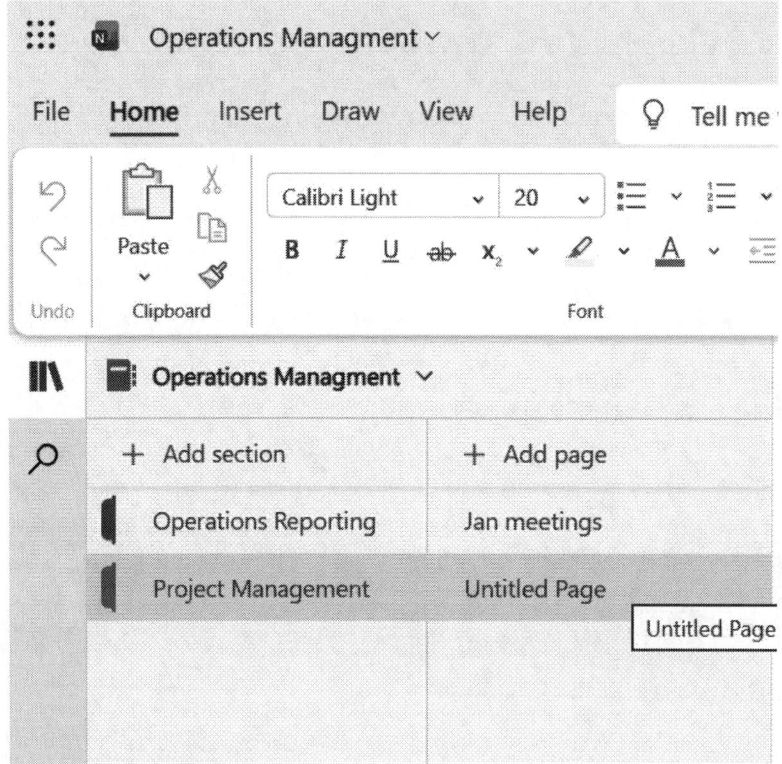

Figure 2-4. *Untitled page created*

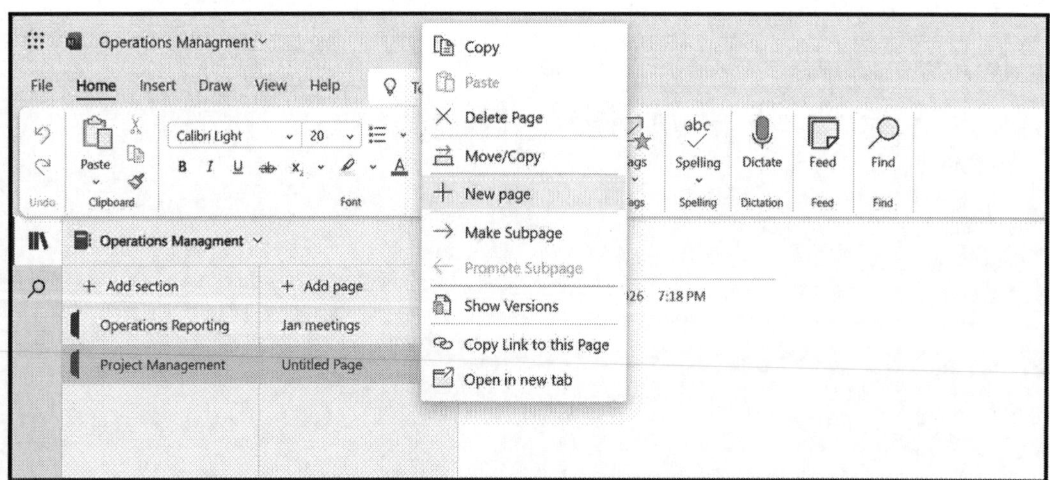

Figure 2-5. *Create a new page from an existing page*

If it becomes necessary to delete a page—whether due to redundancy or unnecessary content—right-clicking the page and selecting “Delete Page” as shown in Figure 2-6 will remove it from the page pane. The deleted page, for example, “Jan Meetings,” is moved to the Deleted Notes area, accessible via the View ribbon, where it remains temporarily (similar to the Recycle Bin) before permanent deletion after 60 days as shown in Figure 2-7. In Microsoft 365, retention periods are not fixed by default—they depend on how retention policies or labels are configured. Microsoft 365 supports flexible retention from 1 day to indefinite (forever), with most organizations using 1 year, 3 years, 5 years, or 7 years based on compliance needs.

Within this view, users may right-click to restore a deleted page or choose to delete it permanently as shown in Figure 2-8. To restore a deleted page, it will ask for the notebook where it needs to be restored as shown in Figure 2-9.

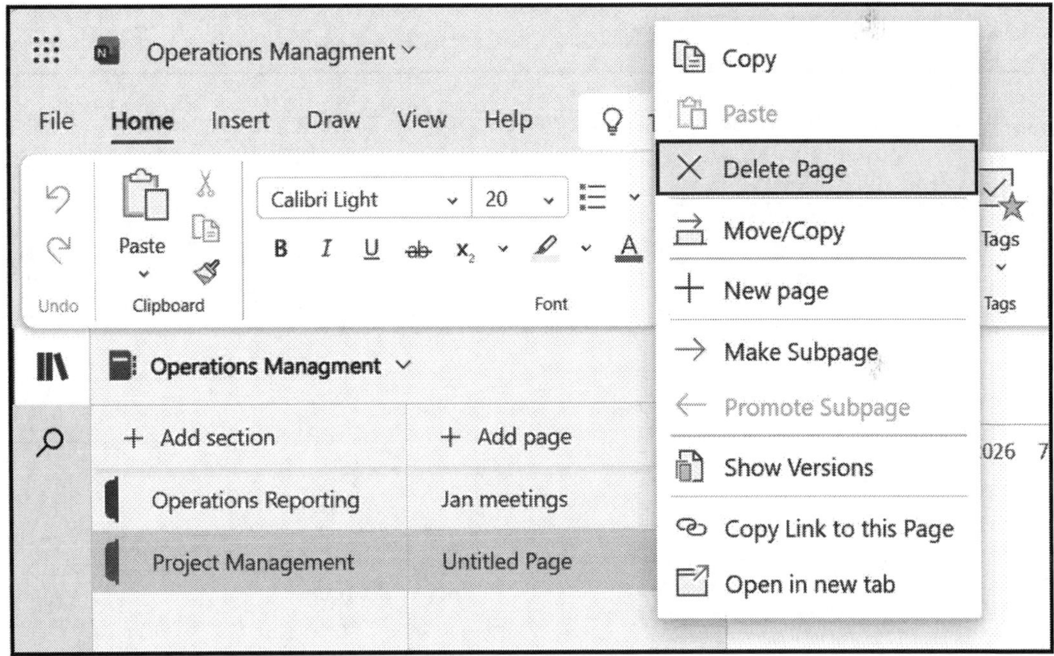

Figure 2-6. *Option to delete a page*

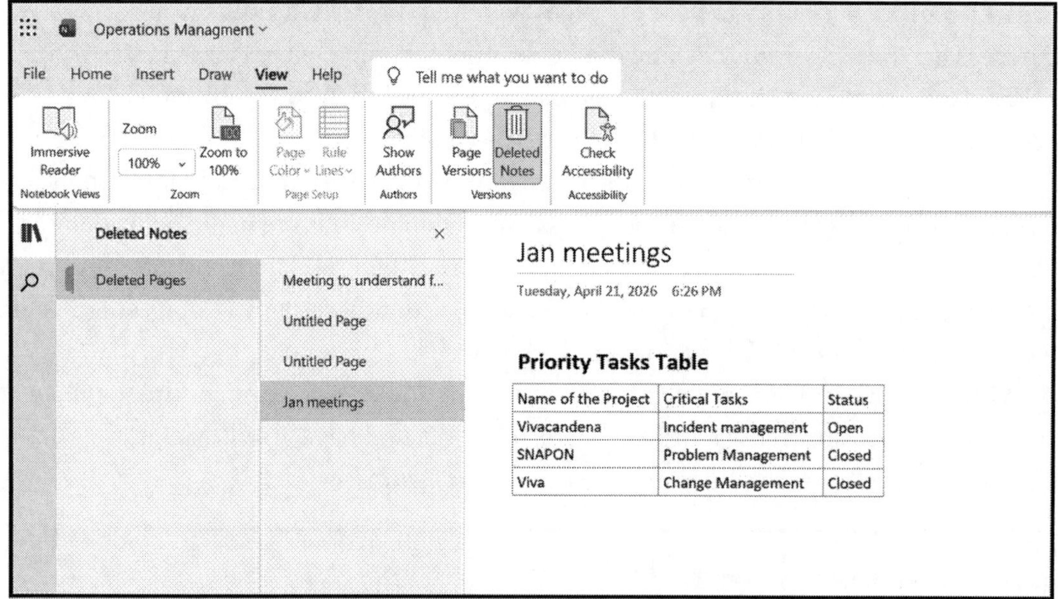

***Figure 2-7.** Deleted page in OneNote Recycle Bin*

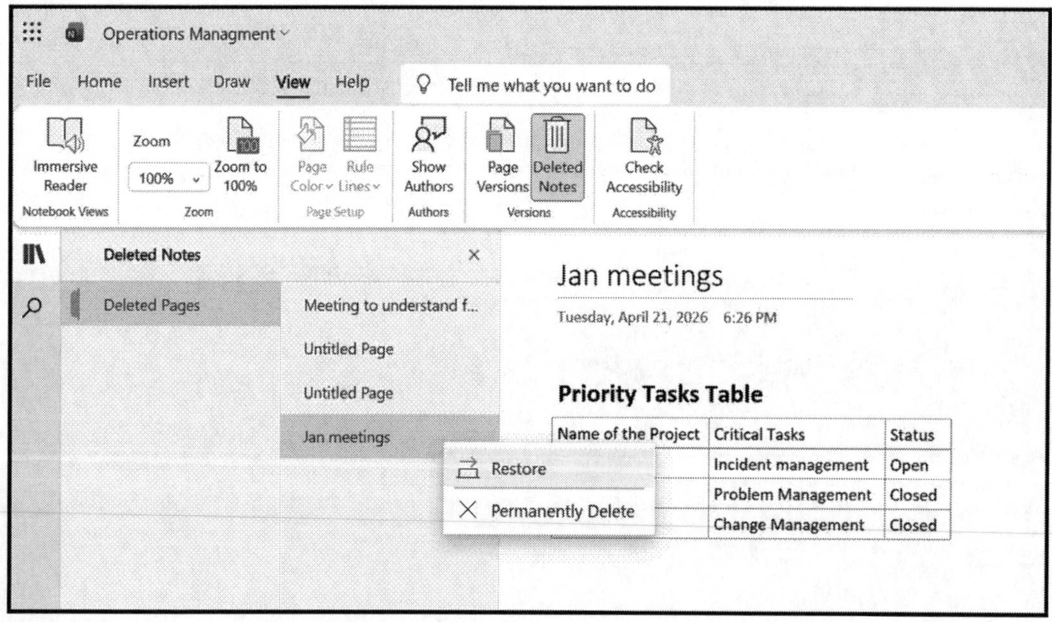

***Figure 2-8.** Deleted page to restore from Recycle Bin*

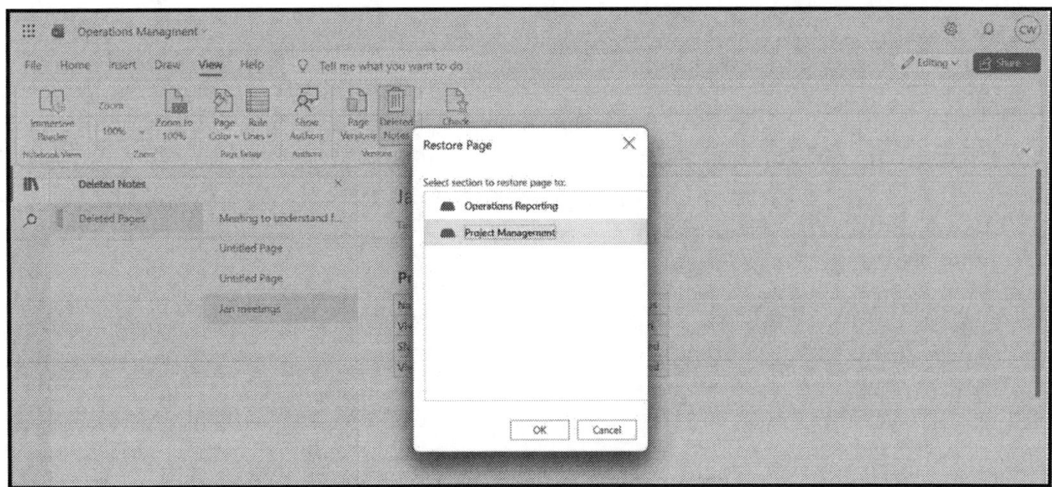

***Figure 2-9.** Choose source notebook for restoration*

Pages can be reorganized within the notebook by right-clicking a page to access the "Move/Copy" function as shown in Figure 2-10, facilitating relocation or duplication either within the same notebook or to another notebook. Alternatively, pages can be repositioned by dragging and dropping them within the notebook. To copy a page to a different notebook, use the right-click menu, select "Move/Copy," navigate to the desired notebook and section, and choose whether to move or copy the page as shown in Figure 2-11. Once completed, the original page remains, and a duplicate is placed in the specified location. In summary, these procedures enable efficient creation, movement, and deletion of pages within the notebook environment.

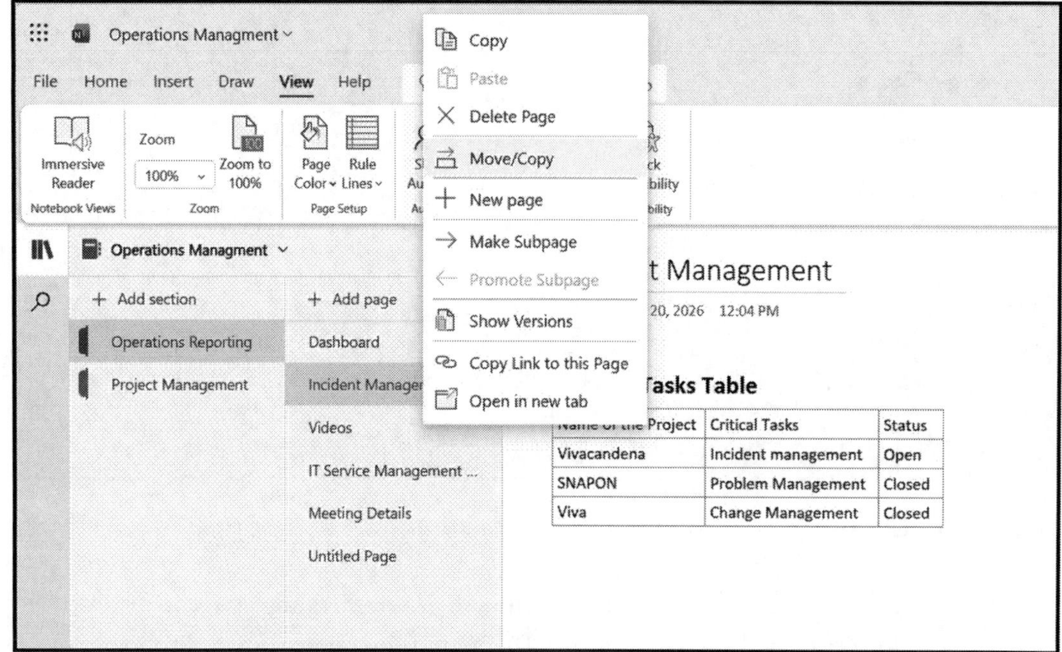

Figure 2-10. *Move pages option*

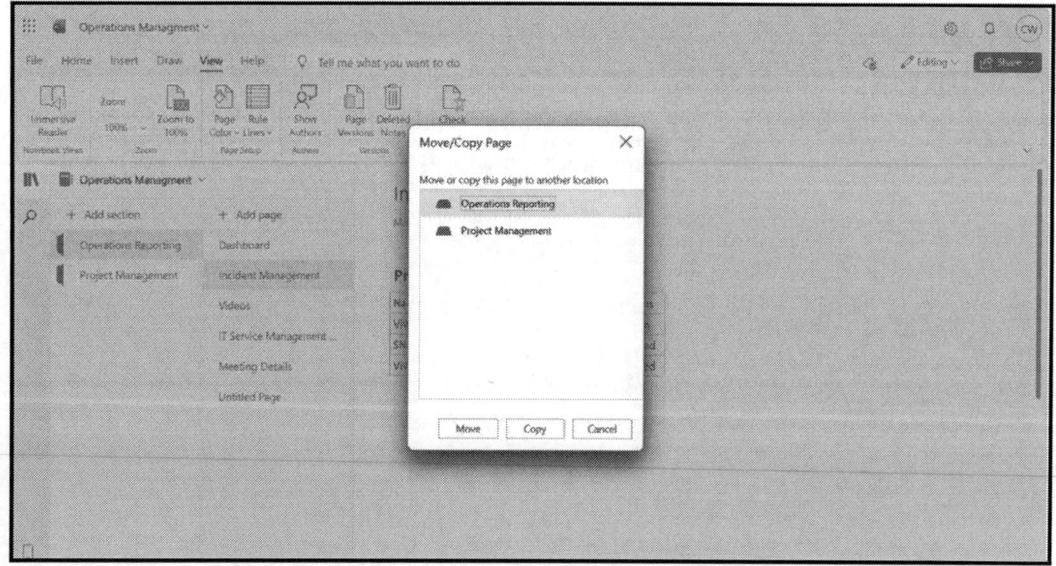

Figure 2-11. *Choose move or copy options to move/copy page*

Make a Subpage

Pages may be organized at multiple hierarchical levels within a section, serving as an effective strategy for structuring course content. For example, the primary chapter title functions as a level one page, while each associated page is designated as a subordinate level two page. Within the Cooking Classes section, there are seasonal pages—Winter, Spring, Summer, and Fall as shown in Figure 2-12. The Soup page should be nested as a subpage under the Fall page by right-clicking and selecting "Make Subpage" from the menu. To create a subpage, we have to create a page and by using the "Make Subpage" function, we can make it a subpage. Create a "Soup" page as shown in Figure 2-13 and apply the "Make Subpage" function as shown in Figure 2-14. The "Soup" page now is a subpage for the "Fall" page as shown in Figure 2-15.

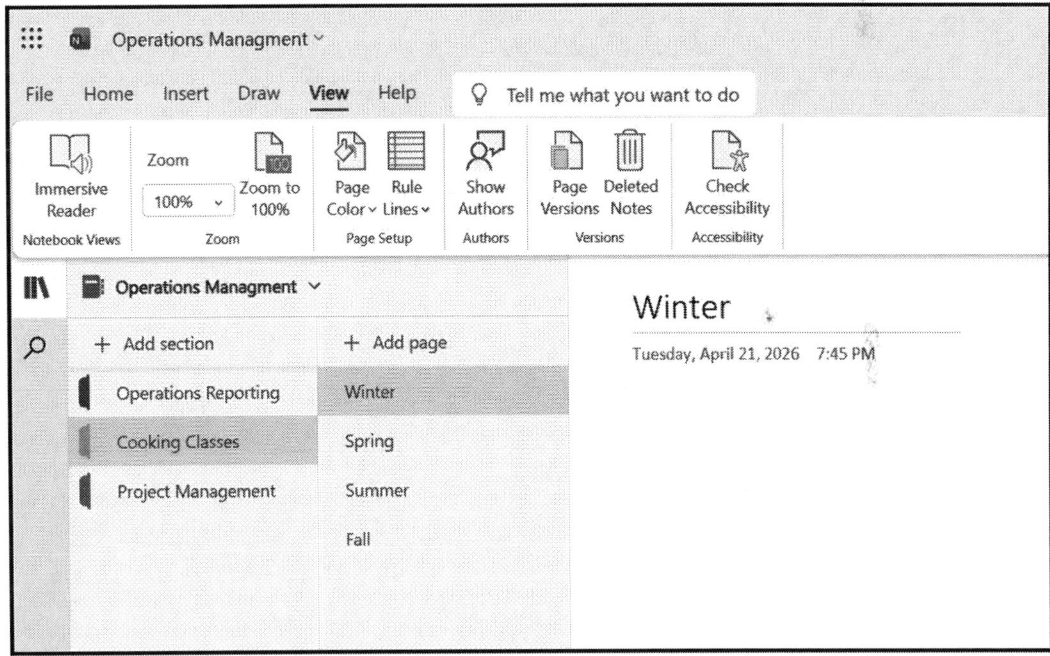

Figure 2-12. *Section and its pages heirarchy*

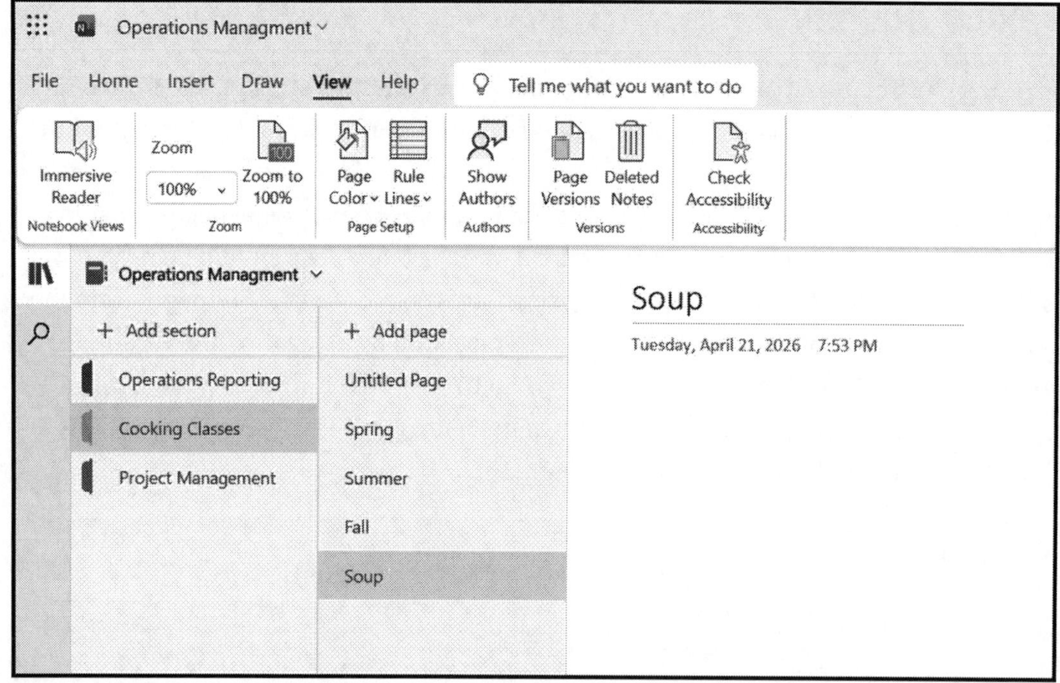

Figure 2-13. *Creation of "Soup" page*

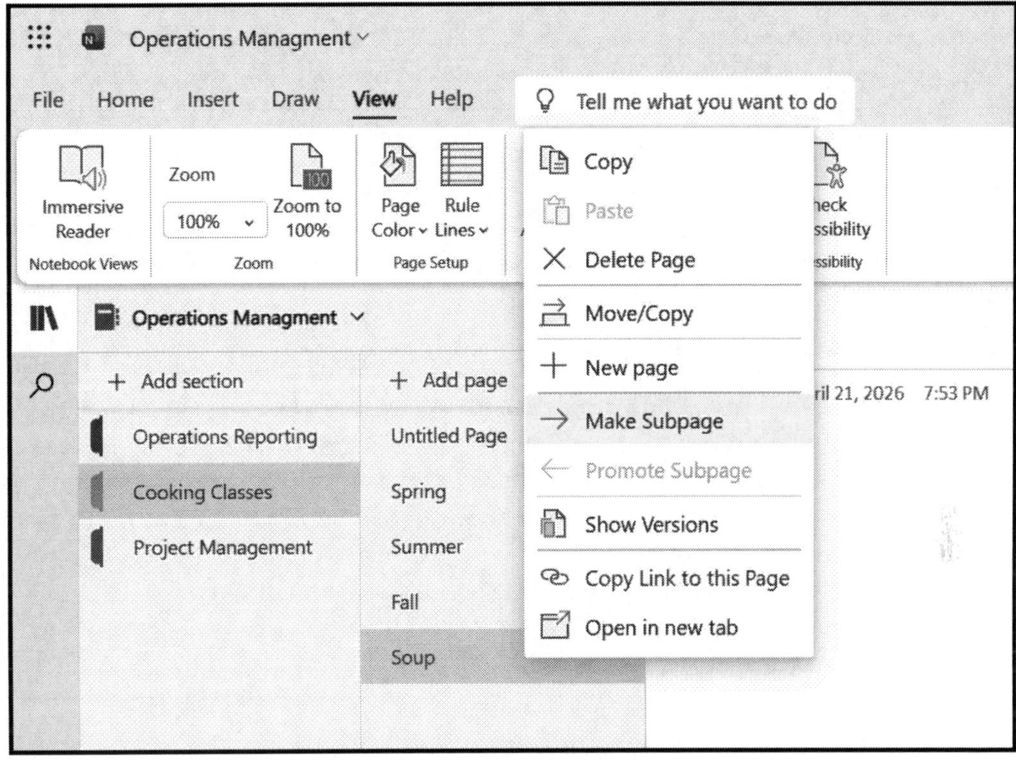

__Figure 2-14.__ Apply the "Make Subpage" function

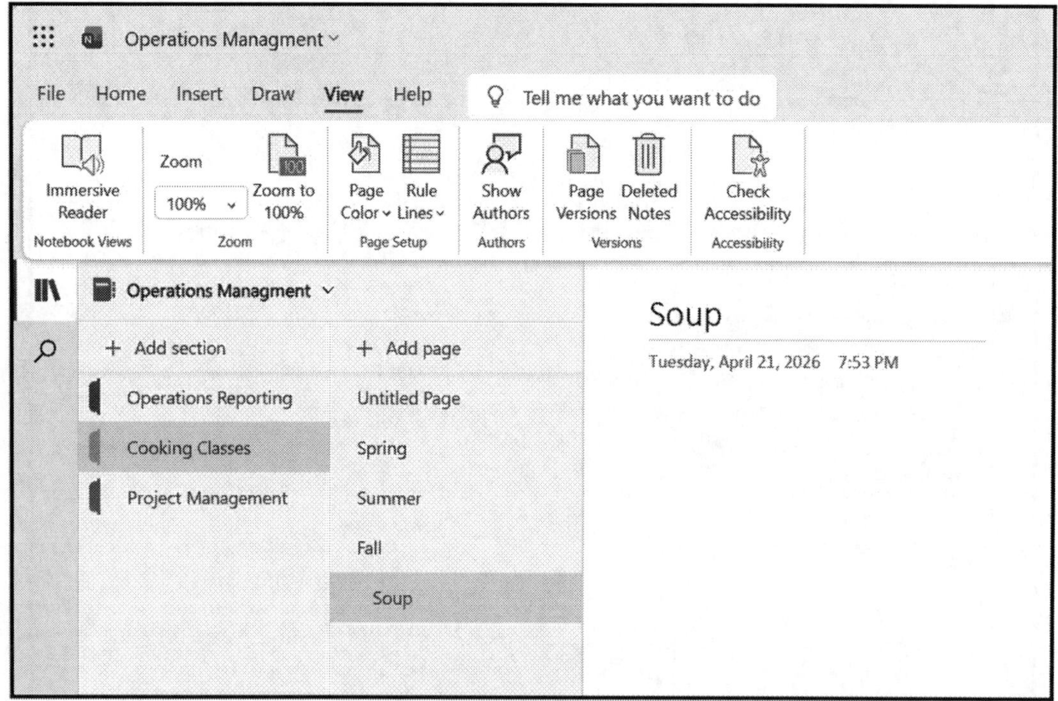

Figure 2-15. *Creation of a "Soup" subpage*

Additional hierarchical levels can be introduced; for instance, level two subpages subordinate to the Soup page are "Salt" and "Pepper" as shown in Figure 2-16. While OneNote technically allows multiple subpage levels, maintaining a hierarchy beyond 2–3 levels is generally not recommended due to reduced usability and navigation challenges. In addition of you can use, "Promote Subpage" as shown in Figure 2-17 to retract one step behind at a time as being a page. That means a subpage two levels down can be a page as shown in Figure 2-18. Furthermore, a keyboard shortcut—Ctrl+Alt+Shift+N—can quickly generate a new subpage beneath the currently selected page. When moving a parent page with subpages, the entire group is transferred together, preserving the organizational structure regardless of expansion status. This method supports cohesive grouping and efficient management of notes using subpages.

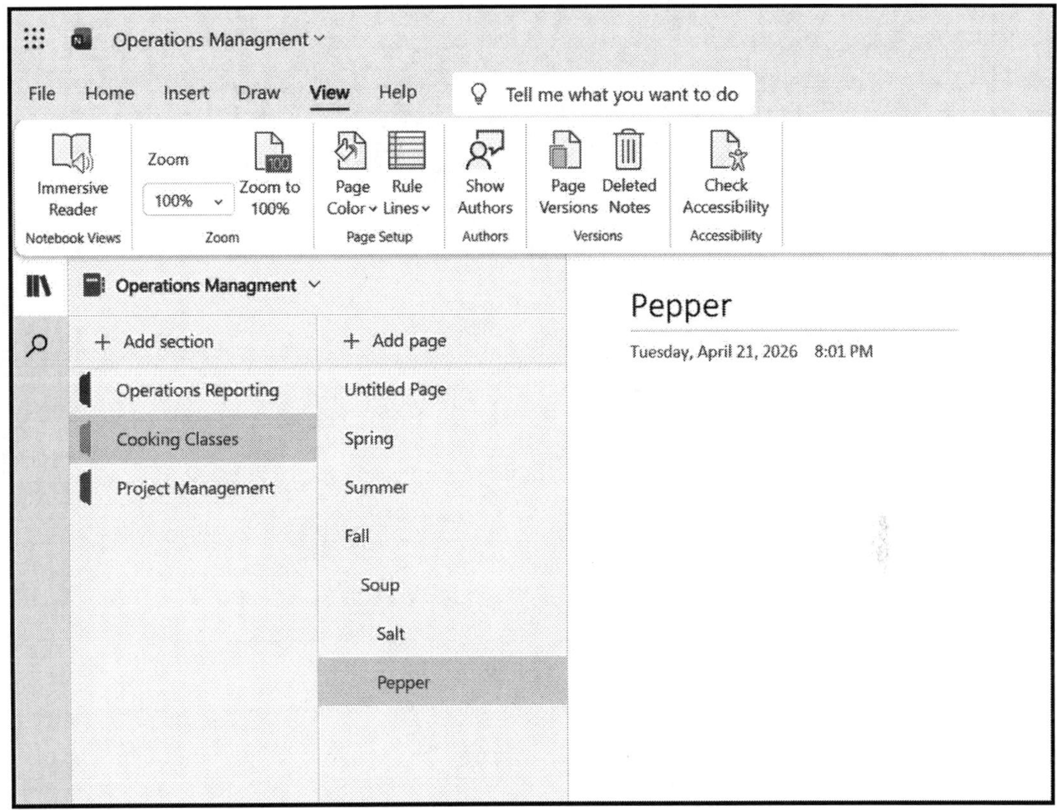

Figure 2-16. *Creating multiple subpages*

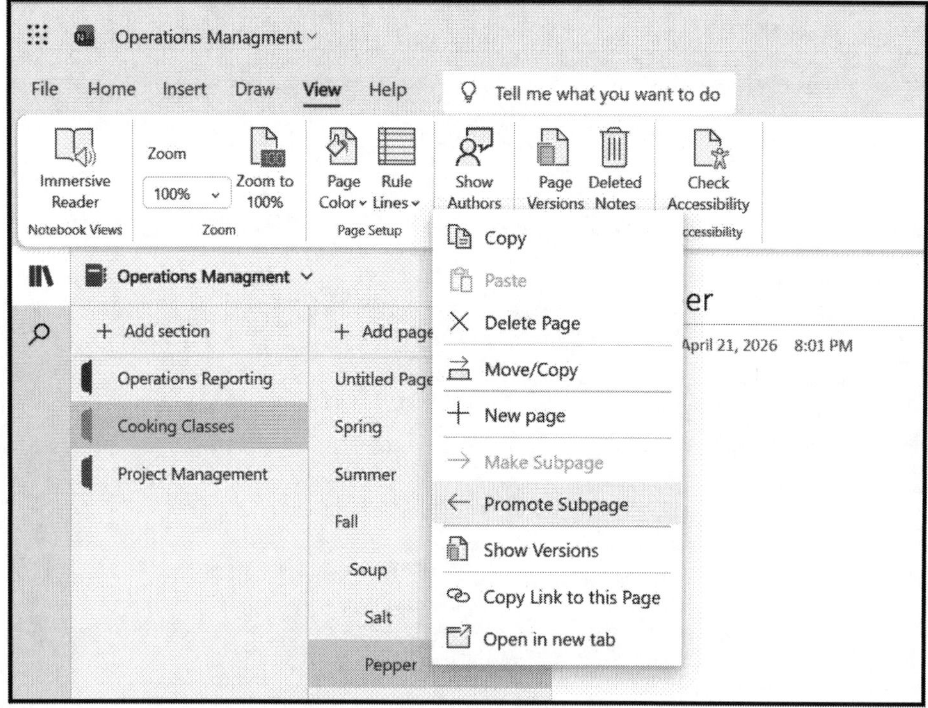

Figure 2-17. *Use the Promote Subpage function*

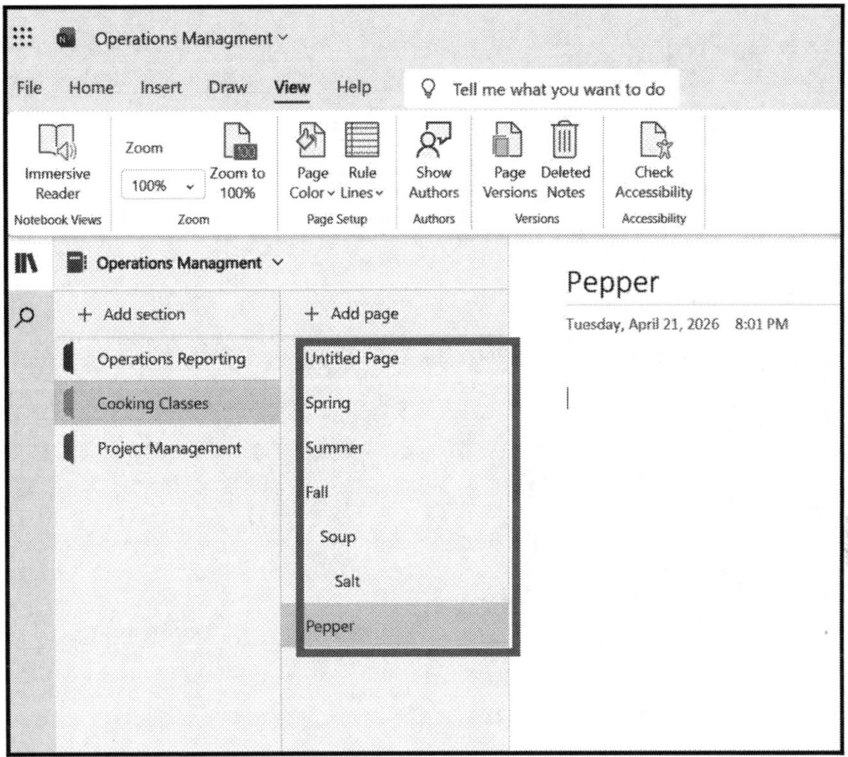

Figure 2-18. *Pepper is now a page*

Rearranging with the Cut, Copy, and Paste Tools

When content is added to a notebook page, it is placed within a note container, as illustrated by the image (gray background) displayed in Figure 2-19. Selecting this frame with a click will activate the four-way arrow, and the contents of the container will appear grayed out, indicating that all items within have been selected. Hovering the mouse over this area reveals a frame that delineates the boundaries of the note container as shown in Figures 2-19 and 2-20.

Figure 2-19. *Image and text inside a container*

Figure 2-20. *Text delineates image*

To utilize Clipboard tools such as Cut, Copy, and Paste, you must first select the desired content. If you choose Cut or Copy at this point, all elements within the note container will be copied to the clipboard. To select specific items as shown in Figure 2-21, simply click outside of the container and then select an individual image or piece of text; a frame will appear around the selected item, allowing you to cut or copy only that particular element.

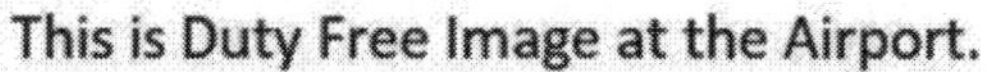

Figure 2-21. Image delineates Text

To utilize clipboard tools such as Cut, Copy, and Paste, you must first select the desired content. If you choose Cut or Copy at this point, all elements within the note container will be copied to the clipboard. To select specific items as shown in Figure 2-22, simply click outside of the container and then select an individual image or piece of text; a frame will appear around the selected item, allowing you to cut or copy only that particular element.

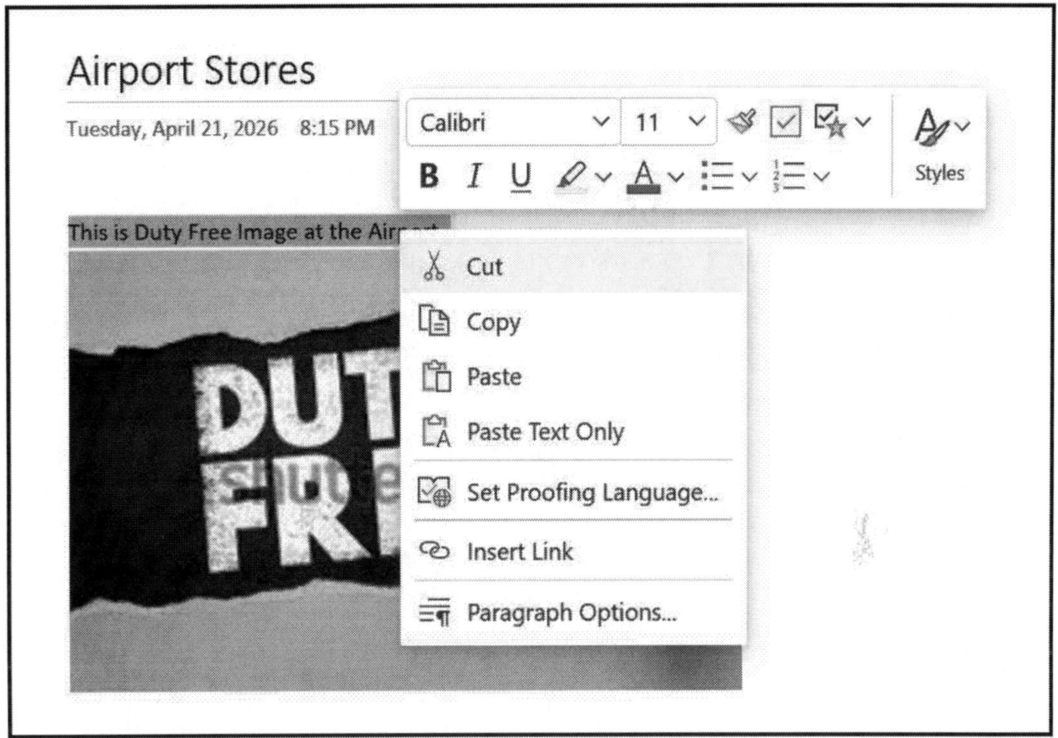

Figure 2-22. *Selecting a specific content from the container*

If you wish to select all contents within the note container, select the frame and use the options from the pop-up window as shown in Figure 2-23.

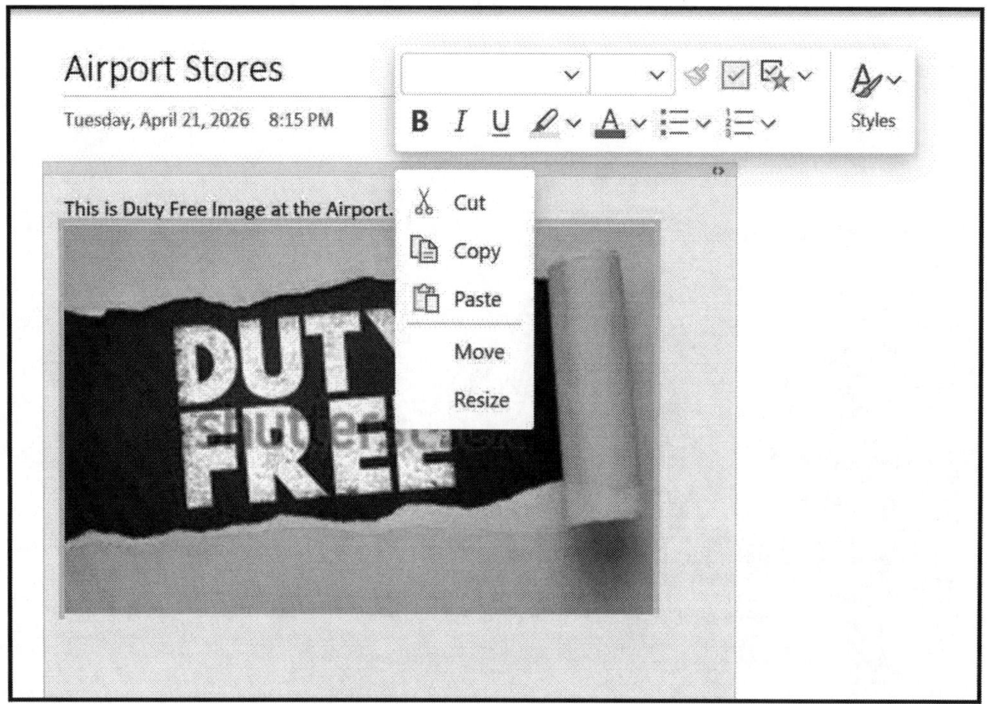

Figure 2-23. *Selecting the entire container*

To paste the content, navigate to the target page, position your cursor, and use either the right-click menu or the clipboard's Paste function. The pasted content in the Videos page will appear at the cursor's location, including all images within the original note container as shown in Figure 2-24.

***Figure 2-24.** Content from the container pasted into a new page*

Additionally, content can be copied from a notebook page and pasted into external applications such as Teams chats, Outlook email messages, Word documents, or PowerPoint presentations.

Working in Full Screen Mode

If you have numerous notes on a page and require maximum workspace—particularly when working on a smaller screen—it is advisable to utilize full screen mode. This can be accessed by clicking the double-headed arrow as shown in Figure 2-25 located in the upper-right corner to enter full screen mode as shown in Figure 2-26. Activating this view conceals the ribbon and navigation panes on the left, while providing a streamlined toolbar containing essential selection and markup tools such as Object Selection, Typed Text Mode, and the Lasso tool for selecting objects. One can revert to the original view as shown in Figure 2-29.

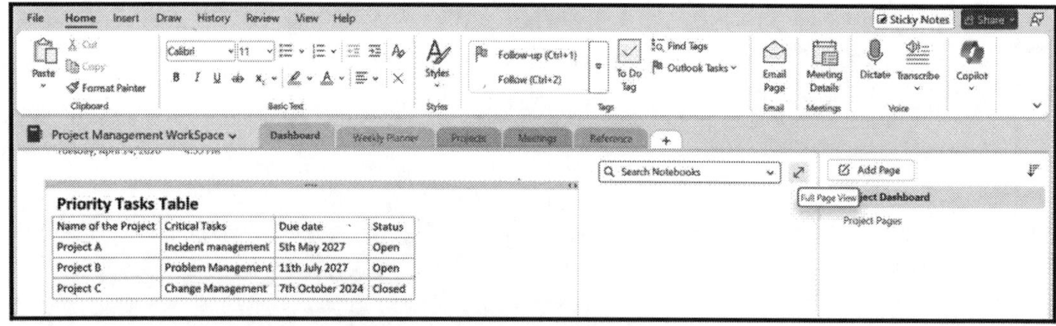

Figure 2-25. *Option to view the full page*

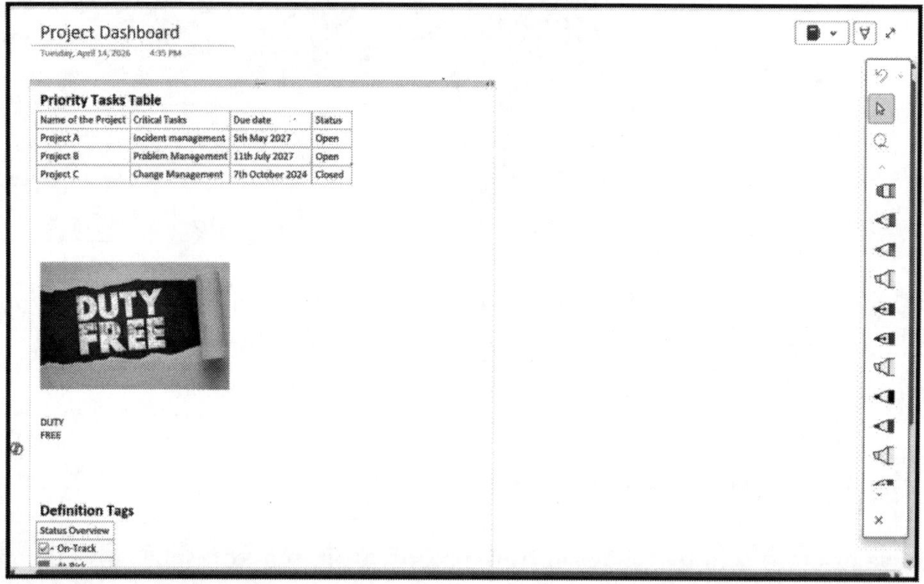

Figure 2-26. *Full page view*

To adjust the spacing between note containers, click "Insert Space" as shown in Figure 2-27. By positioning your cursor you can then click and drag to control the amount of space inserted between images or within note containers as shown in Figure 2-28, enabling you to add typed or handwritten notes as needed. The interface also offers pens, an eraser for annotating your notes, shape tools, a ruler, and options for inserting mathematical equations.

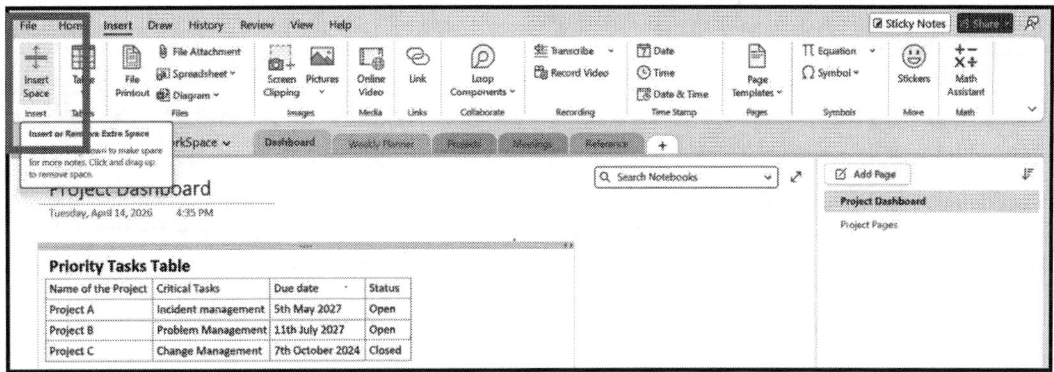

Figure 2-27. Option to access "Insert Space"

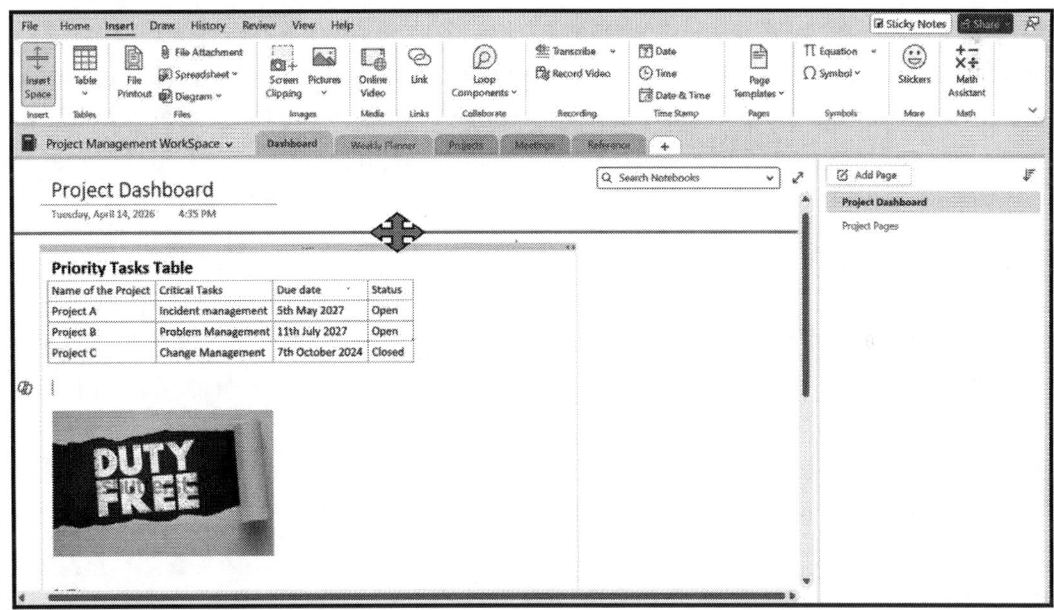

Figure 2-28. Control space

When you are ready to return to the standard view, the two-headed arrow will be replaced by a four-way arrow; click this to exit full screen mode as shown in Figure 2-29. If you were previously in Drawing mode, the indicator may display "Drawing," though this action will still close full screen mode. By following these steps, you can efficiently maximize your workspace and seamlessly toggle between full screen and normal modes as required.

Figure 2-29. *Revert to normal view*

Save Time with Page Templates

Whenever you take notes—whether it's during a meeting, on a call, or at a conference—you probably already have a preferred way to organize them, such as separating out tasks, listing attendees, and highlighting action items. You can streamline this process by using pre-built templates to bring more order to your notes. You'll find Page Templates on the Insert ribbon as shown in Figure 2-30. Click there, then head over to the Pages group. When you click Page Templates, you'll see a list of the templates you've used recently as shown in Figure 2-31. If yours is empty, don't worry, just click Page Templates at the bottom to browse all available options.

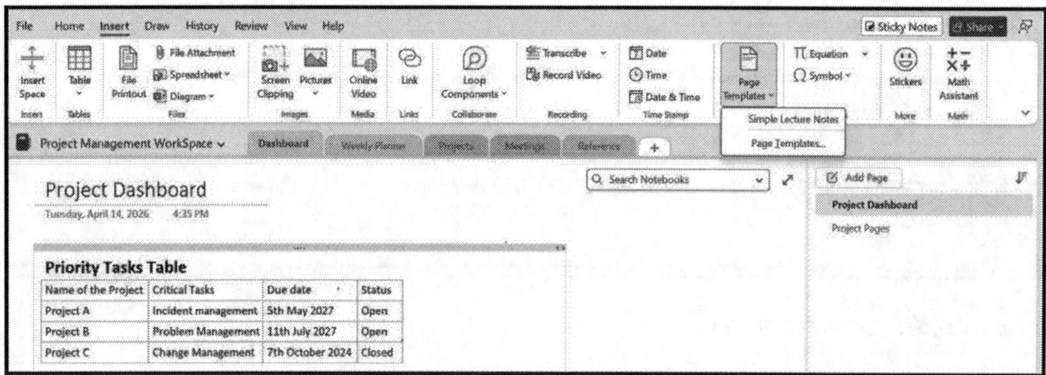

Figure 2-30. *Insert Ribbon option*

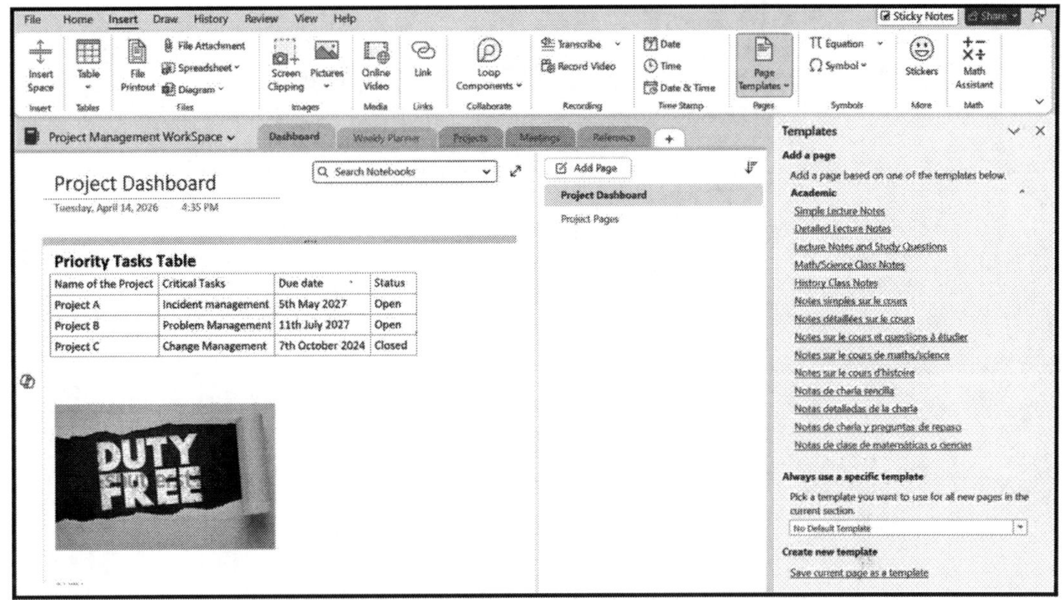

***Figure 2-31.** List of available templates*

Once you click Simple Lecture Notes, a page with a template gets created as shown in Figure 2-32, and this is the latest accessed template as shown in Figure 2-32. [Once you click Simple Lecture Notes a page with template gets created as shown in Figure 2-32 and however this is latest accessed templated as shown in same Figure 2-32 in the menu bar.] The Templates pane will open on the right side, where you can explore various categories. For example, those in academia might expand the Academic category to discover relevant templates. Choosing "Simple Lecture Notes" from that section, for instance, creates a new page titled "Title" for you to update, as shown in Figure 2-32, complete with built-in sections for Today's Topics, Lecture Topic, Important Dates, and Important People.

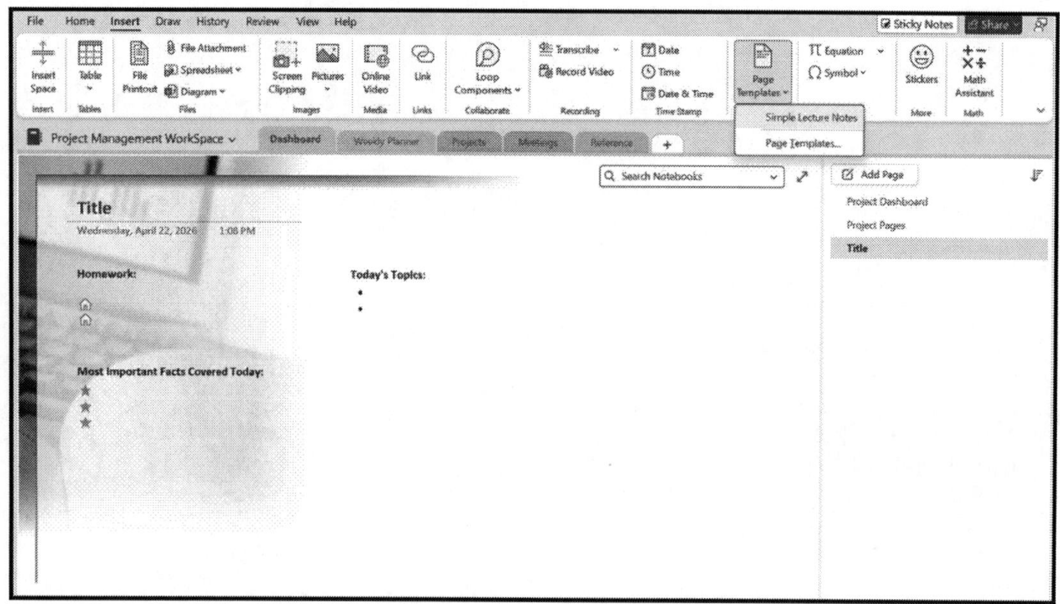

Figure 2-32. *Display of Latest accessed template*

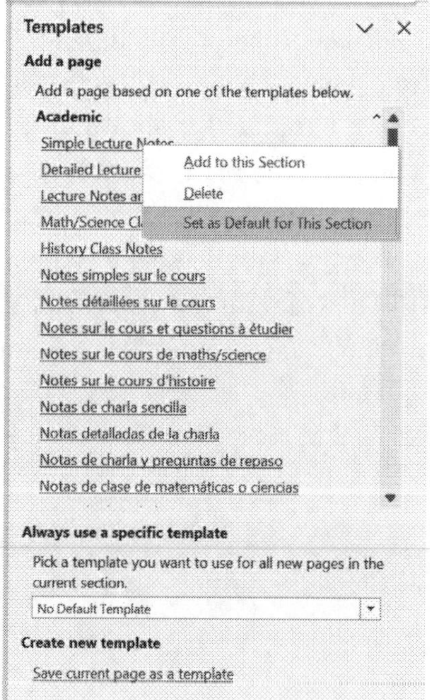

Figure 2-33. *Configuring the default Page template*

To see more, you can collapse Academic and expand Planners as shown in Figure 2-34. Here, there are a few templates to choose from. If one suits your needs, switch to your Event Planning section and select, say, the Prioritized To Do List template. This gives you containers labeled Simple To Do List, Prioritized To Do List, and Project To Do List, each with a ready-made To Do label for your tasks.

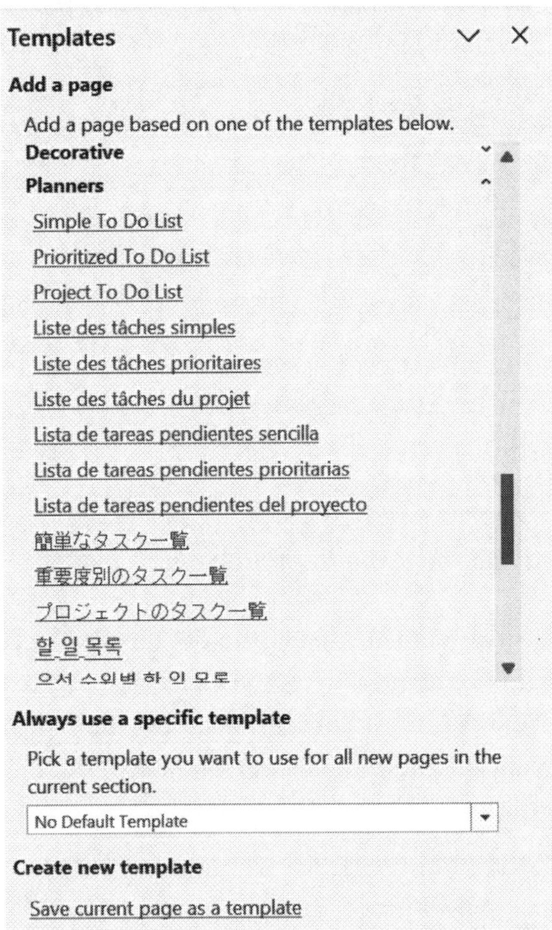

***Figure 2-34.** Setting up the Planners template*

Next, set up a meeting detail template in your Event Planning section by expanding Business. You'll find several formats for project overviews and meeting notes. Adding a template inserts a new page just like before. For example, choosing Detailed Meeting Notes as shown in Figure 2-35 provides a structure with sections you can customize. Rename Meeting Details to Planning/Logistics Details, change Summary to Action

Items, or modify any part to suit your workflow. When you're happy with your edits, save your current page as a reusable template from the Templates pane, give it a name, and set it as the default for new pages in this section if you like.

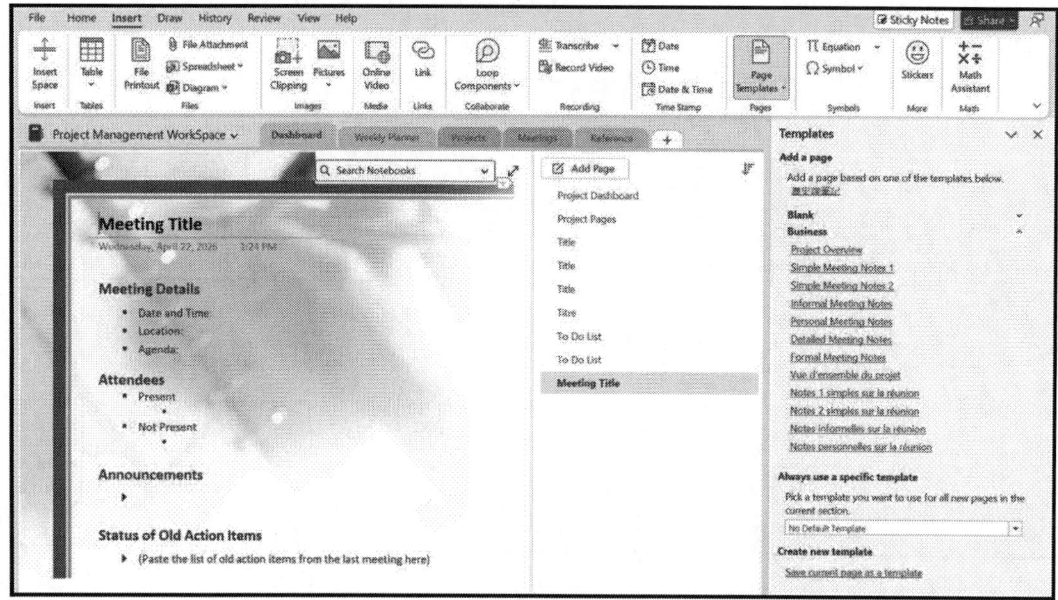

***Figure 2-35.** Detailed Meeting Notes template page*

Once saved, your custom template appears under the My Templates category as shown in Figure 2-36 in the Templates pane. You can access and use these templates anytime or apply them in different sections. After closing the Templates pane, try adding a new page—it'll automatically use your custom template instead of starting blank. With these pre-built templates, your notes will be much more organized and structured.

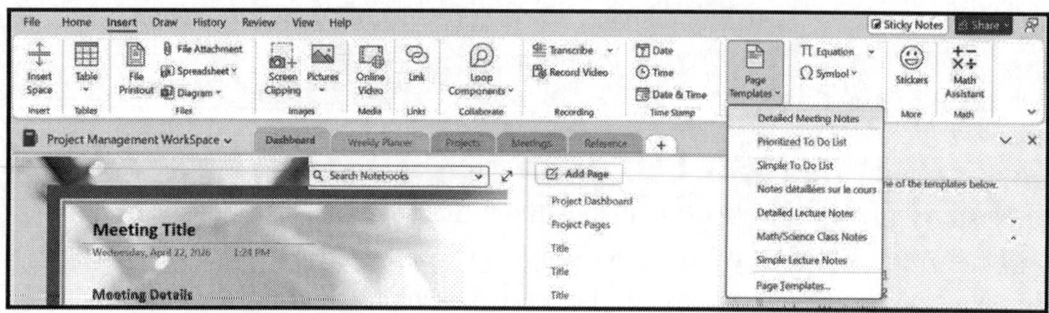

***Figure 2-36.** List of templates accessed*

Create a Page Index

OneNote offers a valuable feature that allows users to efficiently create hyperlinks to new pages, while automatically naming those pages. For example, in a section titled "Goals," you might have a page named "Goal Index" serving as a master index or a table of contents for your collection of related content as shown in Figure 2-37.

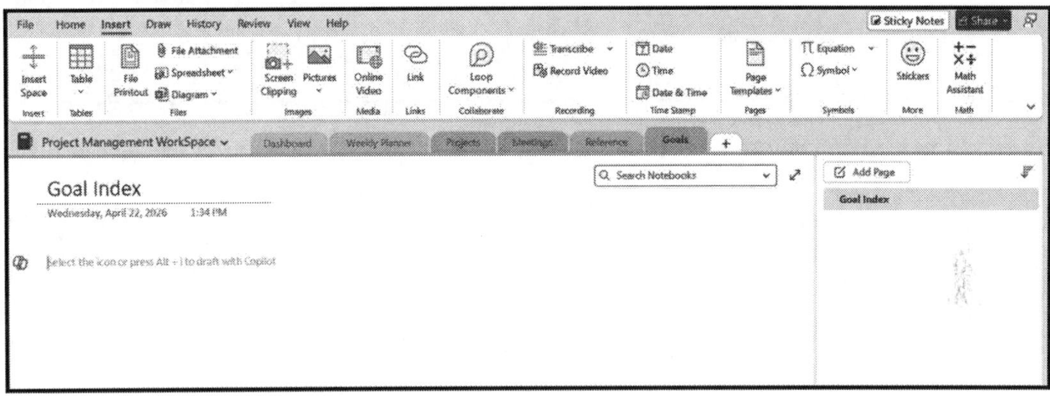

Figure 2-37. *Creating a master index–"Goal Index"*

To utilize this shortcut, begin by typing two open square brackets followed by the desired name for your new page, then type two closing square brackets as shown in Figure 2-38. As soon as you complete the brackets, OneNote instantly generates the new page with the specified title and inserts a hyperlink with a dashed underline, signifying its interactive nature as shown in Figure 2-39. The newly created page appears within your section, allowing you to navigate directly from your index. This streamlined approach enables rapid setup of an organized index as shown in Figure 2-40 while simultaneously establishing named, linked pages within your notebook.

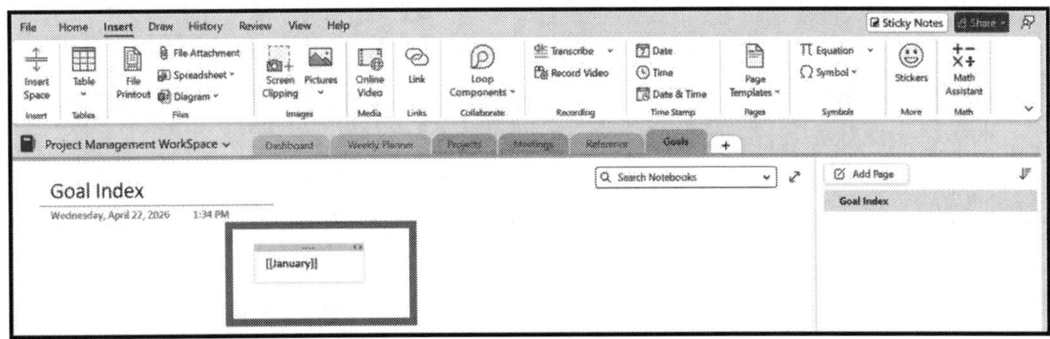

Figure 2-38. *Creation of an index—January*

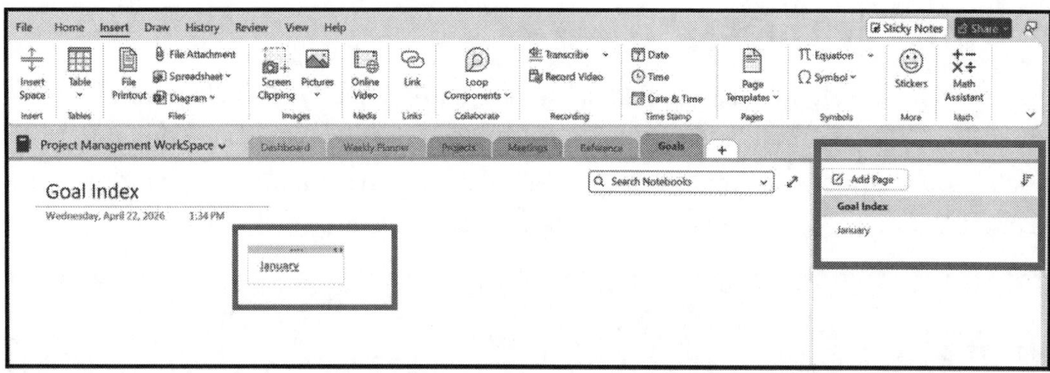

Figure 2-39. *January page gets created*

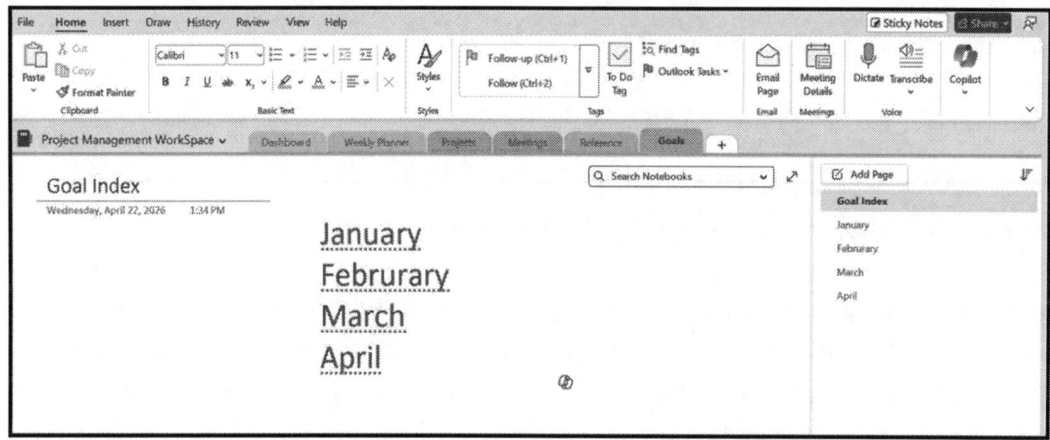

Figure 2-40. *Creation of indexes*

Using OneNote for Academic Research Management

Microsoft OneNote serves as an effective academic research management platform when its notebook hierarchy and content-capture tools are applied systematically. A dedicated research notebook can be created for each research project, thesis, or subject area. Within this notebook, sections may be organized according to research stages such as literature review, research questions, methodology, data collection, analysis, and draft writing. Each section can then contain individual pages representing specific articles, book chapters, datasets, interviews, or conceptual notes. This structure mirrors the academic research lifecycle, ensuring logical segregation and quick retrieval of information. Pages allow free-form content placement, enabling researchers to mix typed text, handwritten annotations, figures, and references without rigid formatting constraints. The Insert ribbon plays a central role in academic research workflows by enabling the direct inclusion of scholarly material. PDF articles, Word documents, Excel datasets, and PowerPoint slides can be inserted as printouts or embedded files for inline annotation. Screen clipping and online video insertion support visual research material, while hyperlinks connect notes to journal repositories, citation managers, and institutional databases. Researchers can insert tables to summarize literature comparisons, equations for quantitative studies, and date/timestamps to track intellectual progress. As shown in Figure 2-41, together, sections and pages supported by the Insert ribbon allow researchers to centralize fragmented research assets into a coherent, navigable academic workspace, reducing dependence on scattered folders, emails, or physical notes.

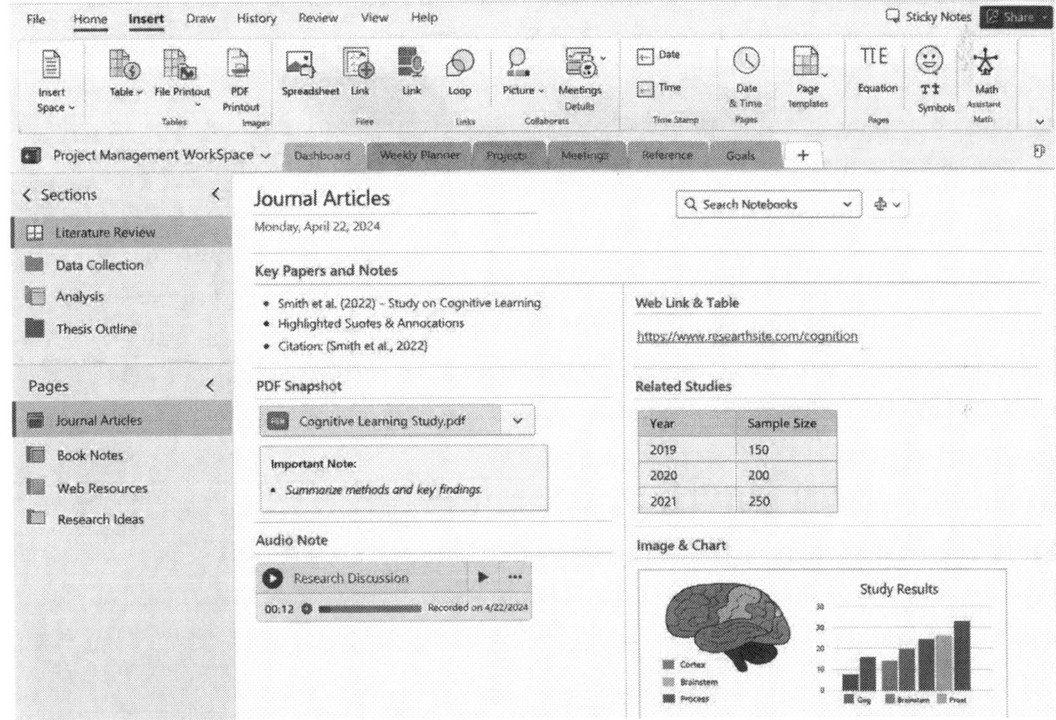

Figure 2-41. *An example of a research project using Microsoft OneNote*

In addition to facilitating basic organization, OneNote significantly enhances academic productivity by supporting annotation, synthesis, and iterative knowledge development. The ability to insert PDF printouts enables researchers to highlight, underline, and comment directly on scholarly documents, thereby replicating and surpassing traditional marginal note-taking methods. Audio recordings from lectures, conferences, or interviews can be incorporated and revisited alongside written notes, promoting multimodal reference and comprehension. Visual materials such as diagrams, conceptual frameworks, and experimental setups can also be embedded and annotated, which fosters visual understanding.

Furthermore, internal page linking allows users to connect theories, citations, and empirical evidence across various sections, transforming OneNote into a dynamic personal knowledge base (PKB) rather than a static repository. The tagging system enhances research management by marking essential findings, citations requiring verification, methodological considerations, or future research directions. The search functionality, bolstered by advanced optical character recognition (OCR), enables efficient retrieval of text within both scanned articles and images, thereby improving information recall.

As research progresses, pages can be duplicated and revised, preserving earlier iterations through version history for reflective analysis. Integration with OneDrive cloud sync ensures seamless cross-device accessibility, permitting researchers to engage with literature on tablets, annotate content on laptops, and summarize findings on mobile devices. Collaborative features support shared notebooks, allowing supervisors, co-authors, or research teams to review notes, provide feedback, and contribute analyses in real time. By utilizing structured sections, flexible pages, and the comprehensive content-integration capabilities of the Insert ribbon, Microsoft OneNote serves as a robust academic research management platform, effectively supporting all stages of the research process—from literature review to synthesis and scholarly dissemination.

Use Microsoft OneNote for Annotating and Reviewing Academic Research Work

Microsoft OneNote can be strategically configured as a dedicated academic annotation and review space by thoughtfully applying its notebook hierarchy and content-insertion capabilities. Researchers may begin by creating a specialized notebook exclusively for evaluation and review activities, distinct from general research collection. Sections within this notebook can represent review themes such as initial reading, critical evaluation, revision notes, peer review feedback, or supervisor comments. Each reviewed article or manuscript can be allocated its own page, enabling focused and interruption-free analysis. This page-based approach supports deep reading while preserving contextual separation between multiple works. The Insert ribbon becomes central to academic review practices by enabling direct engagement with scholarly materials. By inserting research papers as PDF printouts, reviewers can annotate directly over the original text, marking conceptual gaps, methodological concerns, or theoretical strengths using highlights, ink, and margin comments. Charts, tables, and figures extracted from papers can be inserted independently, allowing targeted critique without visual clutter. Inserted tables support structured evaluation matrices—such as originality, rigor, and contribution—while links connect commentary to authoritative sources or citation databases. Screenshots and clipped figures may be embedded to capture visual evidence during comparative analysis. Timestamps inserted at review milestones help document assessment timelines, which is particularly valuable for thesis supervision, grant evaluation, or journal reviewing. Through disciplined use of sections, pages, and Insert ribbon tools, OneNote becomes a self-contained review environment that aligns closely with formal academic evaluation standards. An example of how Microsoft OneNote can be used for annotating and reviewing academic research work is shown in Figure 2-42.

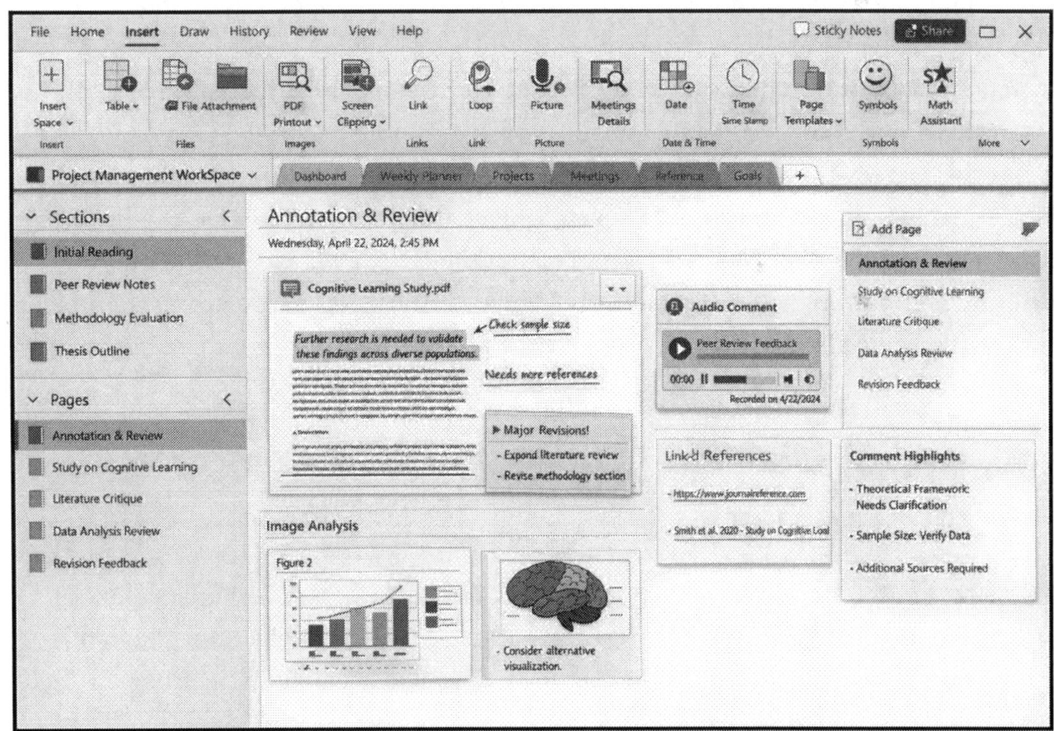

Figure 2-42. *Annotating and reviewing using OneNote*

OneNote significantly advances the academic review process by enabling iterative analysis, reflective annotation, and collaborative scholarly feedback. Users can augment pages with layered insights through a combination of typed critiques and handwritten annotations, delivering the depth characteristic of traditional peer review while enhancing readability and organization. The ability to insert audio notes facilitates immediate verbal reflections during reading sessions, manuscript evaluations, or research meetings, ensuring that nuanced assessments are captured efficiently. Direct insertion of equations and symbols allows for precise commentary on quantitative analyses or theoretical frameworks. Comment containers may be systematically organized—such as by conceptual issues, literature alignment, or clarity and structure—thereby fostering structured revision guidance. Internal linking between pages enables reviewers to connect recurring observations across multiple manuscripts or compare methodological approaches across studies. With optical character recognition, annotated keywords within scanned documents remain searchable, expediting retrieval of prior feedback. As manuscripts progress through revisions, OneNote's page duplication and version history features preserve historical feedback while facilitating new commentary, thereby supporting transparent editorial cycles. When notebooks are shared, co-reviewers, supervisors, or editorial board members may contribute asynchronously, promoting continuity without overwriting individual perspectives. Cloud synchronization ensures that reviewers can annotate materials seamlessly across devices, whether on tablets during readings or desktops during formal reporting. Through its integration of structured layouts, diverse annotation tools, and collaborative workflows, Microsoft OneNote serves as a comprehensive platform for academic reviewing, supporting rigorous critique, reflective synthesis, and scholarly accountability across the research lifecycle.

How to Use Microsoft OneNote for Training Program Creation

Microsoft OneNote serves as an integrated platform for the creation, management, and maintenance of training programs by capitalizing on its organized yet adaptable notebook structure. A dedicated *training program notebook* can be established for each course, certification path, onboarding process, or professional development initiative. Within each notebook, sections may delineate essential phases such as *program overview, learning objectives, module content, practical exercises, assessments,* and *trainer notes.* These sections may contain multiple pages that correspond to specific lessons, workshops, or learning units, enabling trainers to organize content sequentially and preserve instructional coherence. The page format provides flexibility, supporting comprehensive lesson planning, detailed instructional materials, and clear performance criteria without restrictive layouts. Additionally, metadata like dates and author notes can be appended to track program revisions and scheduling. This systematic framework ensures consistency across training deliveries while accommodating customization for varied learner groups. Section grouping allows clustering of advanced modules or elective topics, enhancing the scalability of training initiatives. Through well-defined sections and pages, OneNote facilitates both structured and reference-based learning, making it an effective tool for academic, corporate, and professional education.

Microsoft OneNote empowers trainers to convert static instructional outlines into dynamic and interactive training materials. Integrated features such as File Attachment and PDF Printout enable the embedding of manuals, policy documents, research papers, and other reference materials directly within lesson pages, ensuring immediate access for learners during training sessions. The ability to insert images and screen clippings facilitates the illustration of workflows, processes, and system navigation steps, which is especially beneficial for technical or software-focused instruction. Videos sourced from local files or online platforms reinforce conceptual understanding by accommodating visual and auditory learning preferences. Tables created via the Insert ribbon provide a structured format for presenting training agendas, module breakdowns, competency matrices, and comparison frameworks. Audio recording capabilities allow trainers to incorporate voice explanations, walkthroughs, and revision summaries within lesson pages, supporting asynchronous learning and self-paced review. Equations and symbols deliver precise content relevant to mathematics, finance, engineering, and data analysis. Date and timestamps track training updates, modifications, and session timelines. Page templates available through the Insert ribbon standardize lesson layouts, promoting uniformity across modules and streamlining preparation efforts. By integrating diverse content formats on a single lesson page, OneNote enables trainers to develop learner-centered programs that foster comprehension, engagement, and retention.

Beyond content creation, Microsoft OneNote supports the full training lifecycle through assessment management, collaboration, and continuous improvement mechanisms. Dedicated sections can be created for evaluations, feedback collection, and learner progress tracking. Pages may contain quizzes, reflective questions, checklists, or case studies that assess knowledge acquisition and skill application. Trainers can insert forms, spreadsheets, or links to assessment tools, consolidating evaluation artifacts within the training notebook. Annotation tools enable trainers to review assignments, provide contextual feedback, and highlight areas for improvement directly on submitted materials. Internal page links allow trainers to connect assessment results with corresponding training modules, creating transparent learning pathways. OneNote's collaborative features support co-authoring of training content by subject matter experts, instructional designers, and peer reviewers, ensuring accuracy and relevance. Shared notebooks enable distributed teams to contribute updates, while version history preserves content evolution over successive training cycles. Tagging features can highlight action items such as curriculum updates, learner difficulties, or post-training follow-ups. Cloud synchronization through OneDrive ensures training materials remain accessible across devices, supporting in-person, hybrid, and remote training environments. As training needs evolve, existing pages and sections can be duplicated and adapted, significantly reducing redevelopment effort. Through structured organization, rich content integration, and collaborative refinement, Microsoft OneNote functions as a scalable training program creation platform that supports instructional design, delivery, evaluation, and long-term knowledge preservation. An example of how OneNote can be used for training program creation is shown in Figure 2-43.

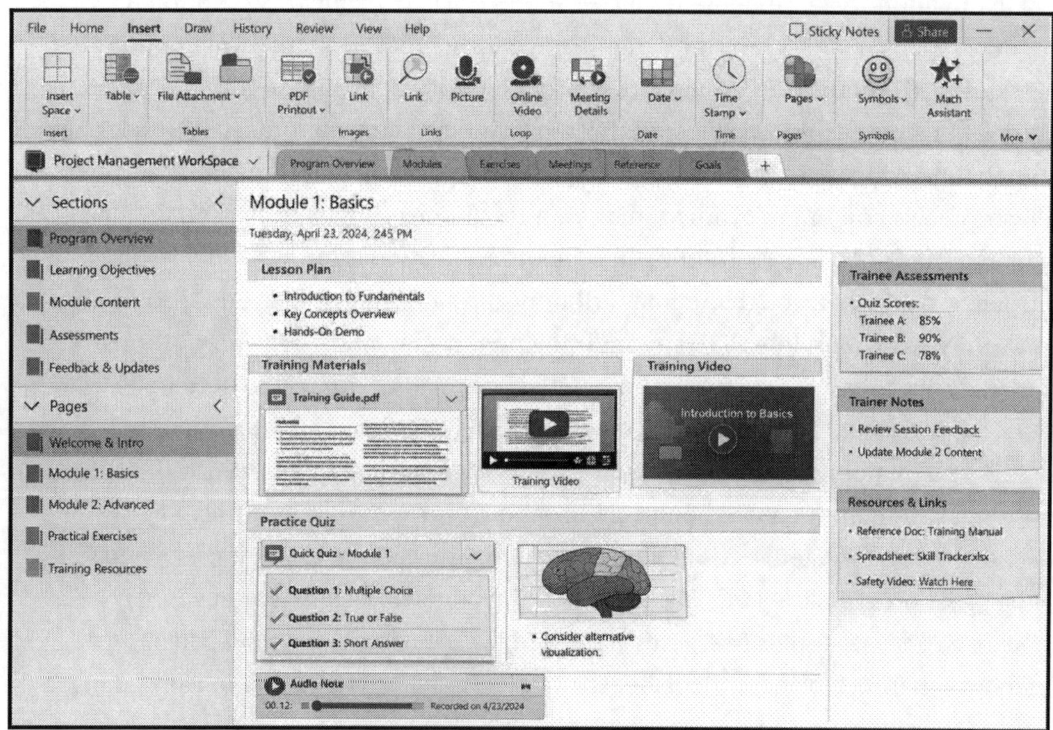

***Figure 2-43.** Training program creation using OneNote*

Building Digital Lesson Plans

Microsoft OneNote provides an efficient and adaptable platform for developing comprehensive digital lesson plans aligned with contemporary, student-centered pedagogical approaches. Educators are able to establish dedicated notebooks for specific courses, subjects, or academic terms, utilizing sections to correlate instructional materials with curriculum units, weekly timelines, or thematic modules. Individual pages within each section can be designated for particular lessons, enabling instructors to articulate learning objectives, instructional methods, necessary resources, and assessment criteria within a unified structure. The flexible format of OneNote pages allows educators to organize content strategically—such as commencing with lesson outcomes, then progressing through instructional material, guided exercises, independent work, and reflective activities—without limitations imposed by static document templates.

Educators are able to incorporate PDF printouts of worksheets, syllabi, or reading materials directly into lesson pages, facilitating inline annotation and contextual reference throughout instruction. Images, diagrams, and screen captures can be embedded to visually clarify concepts, processes, or experiments, while online videos and recorded audio clips accommodate diverse learning styles and support blended or flipped classroom methods. Tables inserted via the ribbon provide a structured format for presenting lesson schedules, activity timelines, or evaluation rubrics, enhancing clarity and consistency. Audio recordings may be included to offer explanatory commentary or revision summaries, enabling learners to review material independently. The use of date and timestamps assists in tracking lesson delivery and updates, fostering reflective practice and iterative improvement. For disciplines requiring symbolic representation, equations and mathematical symbols can be precisely inserted, upholding academic standards. Furthermore, reusable page templates contribute to a standardized lesson design across sessions, streamlining preparation and maintaining instructional quality. Through the integration of organized structure and multimedia resources, OneNote equips educators with the tools to develop digital lesson plans that are flexible, engaging, and reusable, thereby elevating lesson planning from static documentation to an advanced instructional design process supporting teaching, learning, and ongoing curriculum refinement. An example of how OneNote can be used for building digital lesson plans is shown in Figure 2-44.

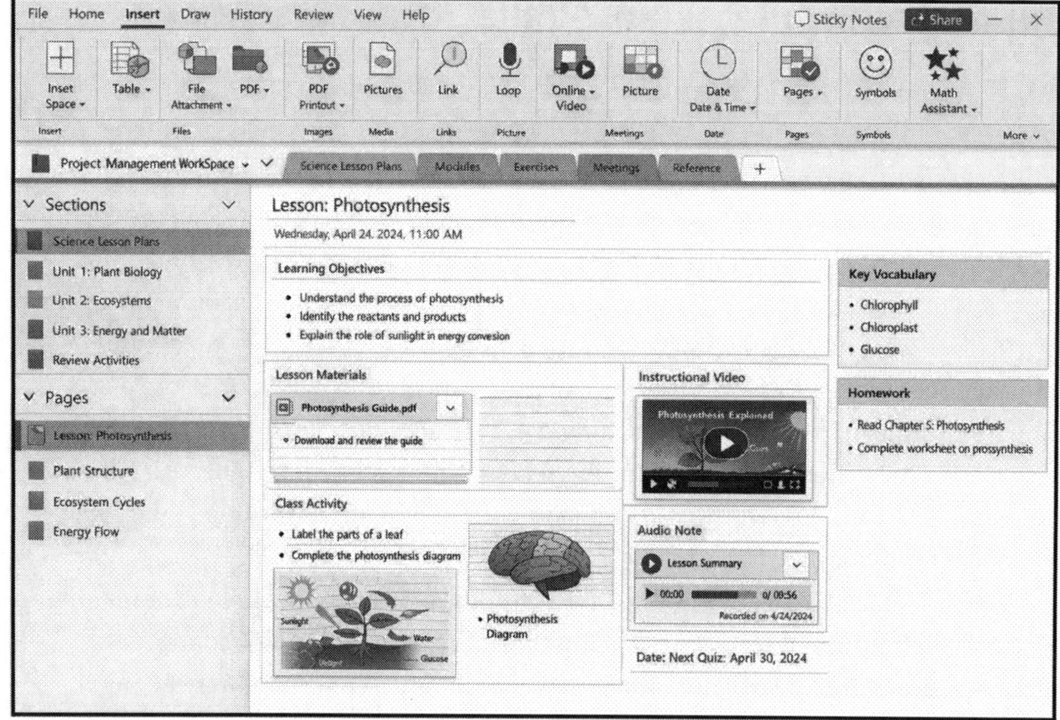

Figure 2-44. *Building digital lesson plans using OneNote*

Knowledge Management Patterns: Personal Knowledge Base vs. Team Knowledge Base vs. Knowledge Base

Microsoft OneNote supports effective knowledge management through evolving patterns from personal to organizational use. Its features enable users to capture ideas, collaborate, and formalize information for long-term access. With notebooks, sections, and pages, OneNote streamlines transitions from individual notes to team and enterprise-wide knowledge systems, keeping information organized and accessible. Microsoft OneNote facilitates layered knowledge management strategies that progress from individual use to organization-wide systems, enabling a smooth transition from personal learning initiatives to institutional intelligence. As shown in Figure 2-45, knowledge management patterns are divided into personal, team, and organizational knowledge.

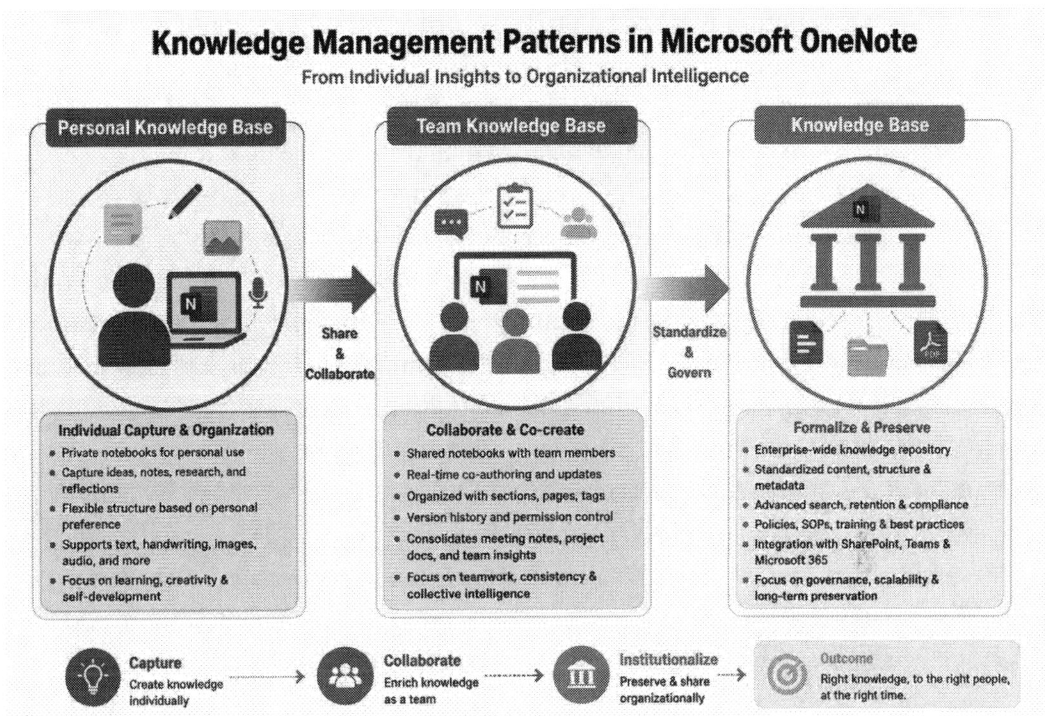

Figure 2-45. *Knowledge patterns*

At its core, the personal knowledge base (PKB) within OneNote empowers individual users to systematically capture, organize, and reflect on information. Users can create customized notebooks for diverse purposes, such as study notes, meeting documentation, brainstorming, and research synthesis. The platform's flexible structure—incorporating pages, sections, and adaptable note containers—supports unstructured data entry, including text, handwritten annotations, images, and audio content. This design fosters innovation and expedites knowledge capture in an environment without rigid oversight, making it well-suited to self-directed learning and individual productivity.

On a collaborative scale, the team knowledge base (TKB) leverages OneNote's capabilities for collective input, knowledge sharing, and iterative refinement within shared notebooks. Through integration with Microsoft Teams and SharePoint, team notebooks enable real-time co-authoring, comprehensive version control, and granular permission settings. In contrast to personal systems, TKBs benefit from structured organization utilizing consistent sectioning, standardized naming conventions, and tagging protocols to promote clarity and uniformity. Within project contexts, these shared resources facilitate centralized meeting records, task management, and the accumulation of team knowledge, thereby minimizing information silos and supporting enhanced collaboration. The TKB framework transforms individual contributions into collective organizational insights that evolve through ongoing participation.

At the enterprise level, the organizational knowledge base (KB) extends beyond individual and team boundaries to deliver a robust, scalable solution for knowledge governance. While OneNote may function as a supplementary tool, seamless integration with platforms like SharePoint enables centralized knowledge retention. Enterprise-level notebooks commonly contain policies, procedures, training materials, and institutional memory. Effective governance is essential, incorporating defined structures, metadata, retention schedules, and controlled access rights to ensure compliance and long-term viability. The focus at this stage shifts toward standardization, discoverability, and maximizing knowledge reuse across the entire organization.

These three tiers operate cohesively within the OneNote ecosystem. Knowledge typically originates in personal notebooks, evolves through team collaboration, and is ultimately formalized within organizational repositories. This progression ensures valuable insights are preserved and systematically converted into reusable assets. Through this continuum, Microsoft OneNote acts as a comprehensive platform, bridging informal knowledge collection with structured knowledge management—thereby advancing productivity, cooperation, and organizational learning.

With this, we have come to the end of this chapter. In this chapter, we have learned various topics such as creating, moving, and deleting a page; making a subpage; rearranging with the Cut, Copy, and Paste tools; working in full screen mode; saving time with page templates; creating a page index; using OneNote for academic research management; training program creation; annotating and reviewing academic research work; building digital lesson plans; and knowledge management patterns.

In the next chapter, we will see an overview of Microsoft OneNote's advanced input and capture features, highlighting the use of handwritten, audio, and video notes. We will learn how Draw tools such as pen styles, highlighters, and the laser pointer support clear and expressive note-taking. Precision and navigation tools including the Panning Hand, Ruler, Ink to Text, and Ink Replay will be discussed to improve accuracy and usability. Also, we will learn about the Transcribe feature, showing how spoken content can be converted into searchable notes.

CHAPTER 3

Exploring Handwritten and Audio Notes in Microsoft OneNote

In the previous chapter, we discussed the core concepts and practical capabilities of Microsoft OneNote, focusing on effective everyday usage. It explains how to work with pages and apply formatting tools to create well-structured, visually clear notes. The chapter highlights OneNote's value in education and training through features such as Class Notebook, digital lesson planning, training program creation, and academic research management. It also covers annotation and reviewing techniques that support feedback, collaboration, and content refinement. Overall, the chapter builds a strong foundation for using OneNote as a versatile tool for learning, teaching, research, and professional documentation. In the current chapter, we will explore the capabilities of handwritten notes and audio and video notes in Microsoft OneNote. In the handwritten notes section, we will cover the Draw menu and the different pens for formatting text such as pen, fountain pen, brush pen, highlighter, and laser pointer. Further, we cover features such as Panning Hand, Ruler, Ink to Text, and Ink Replay. In the last section, we will learn how to use the Transcribe feature to create audio and video notes.

Enhance your note-taking capabilities with Microsoft Office applications. Microsoft 365 offers comprehensive solutions for organizing and managing notes, leveraging the integration of its various apps and services. This connectivity allows users to capture, share, and access notes from multiple platforms. In this chapter, you will learn how to expand your personal note collection through screen capture and speech-to-text features, automate meeting notes, collaborate effectively in Microsoft Teams meetings, organize notes alongside tasks and to-dos, and engage in collaborative note-taking on a digital whiteboard.

C. Waghmare, *Mastering Microsoft OneNote*, https://doi.org/10.1007/979-8-8688-2866-9_3

Handwrite Digital Notes

If you enjoy taking handwritten notes, OneNote lets you use digital ink on digital paper. You can draw or write by hand in all OneNote apps, whether it's OneNote for Microsoft 365, Windows 10, the web, or mobile devices. Here, I'll demonstrate using the "Draw" menu in the OneNote desktop app as shown in Figure 3-1.

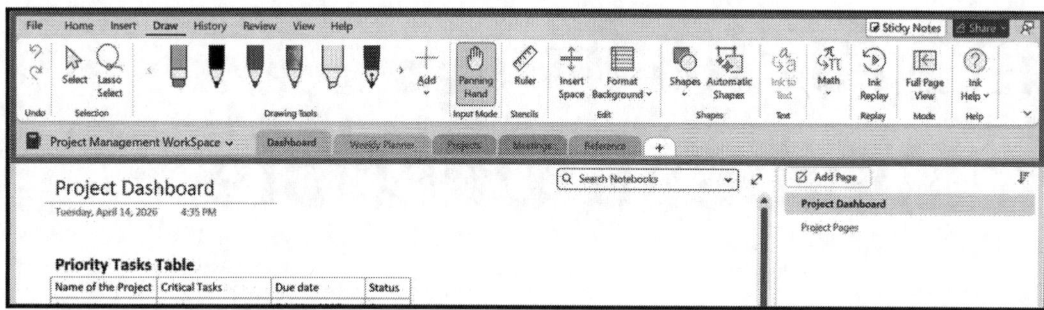

Figure 3-1. *"Draw" menu in the Microsoft desktop app*

To begin, click the Draw menu at the top. In the middle of the ribbon, you'll see an eraser, pens, and a highlighter for drawing called Drawing Tools as shown in Figure 3-2. Next, choose a pen—click one to the right of the eraser, for example, the red-colored pen. When selected, it appears slightly above the others as shown in Figure 3-3, indicating you're in handwriting mode. You're now ready to write, not type, on the page. Clicking the pen again lets you change the ink thickness and color as shown in Figure 3-4.

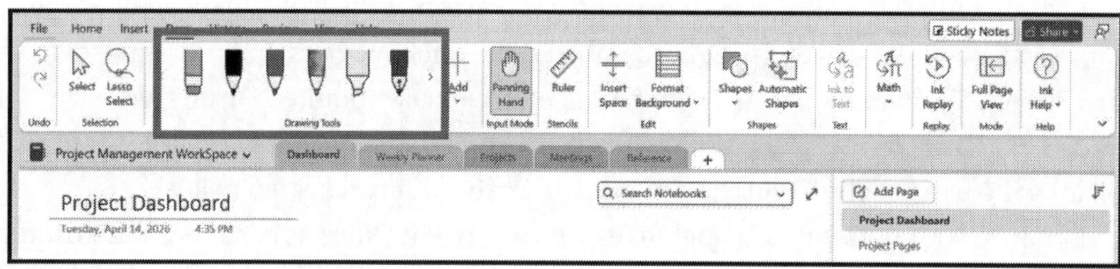

Figure 3-2. *Drawing tools*

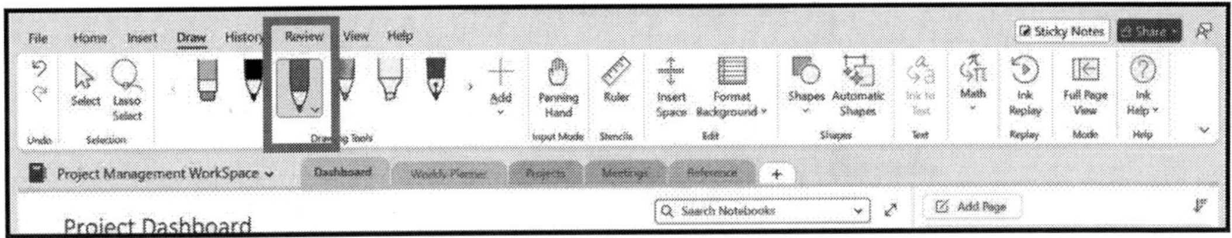

***Figure 3-3.** Selected pen appears above others*

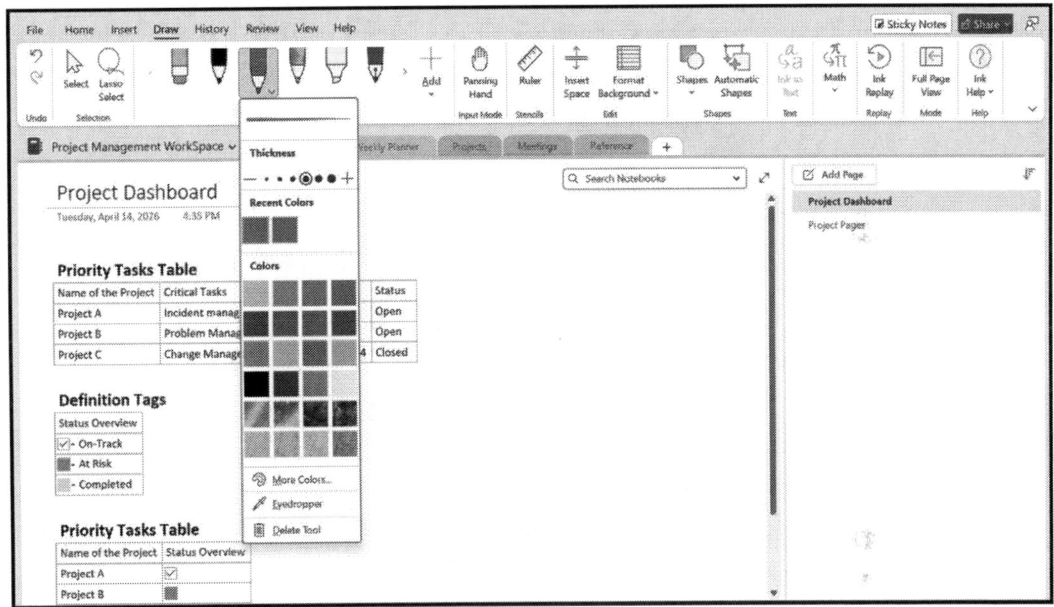

***Figure 3-4.** Option to choose ink thickness and color through clicking*

At the top, adjust the thickness with the circle or the plus/minus signs as shown in Figure 3-4-1. Below, select your ink color; several solid colors and textured options like rainbow, galaxy, volcano, and ocean are available, as well as glitter inks, as shown in Figure 3-4-1. I'll stick with purple for now.

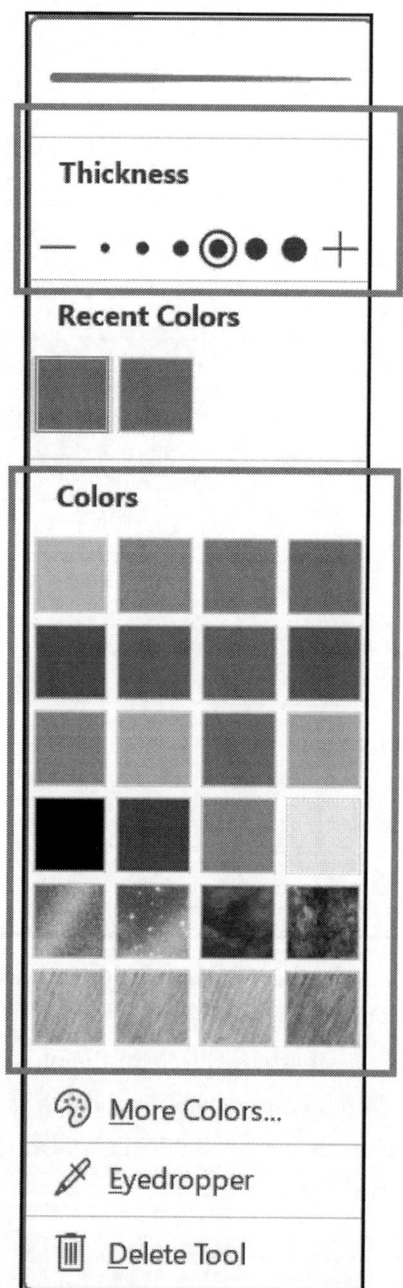

Figure 3-4-1. *Option to change ink thickness and ink colors*

Click outside this panel to return to your note. If you notice any stray marks, pick up the eraser tool to remove them as shown in Figures 3-5 and 3-5-1. Then erase the stray or unwanted text as shown in Figure 3-6. Re-select your preferred pen, then start writing anywhere on the notebook page as shown in Figure 3-7.

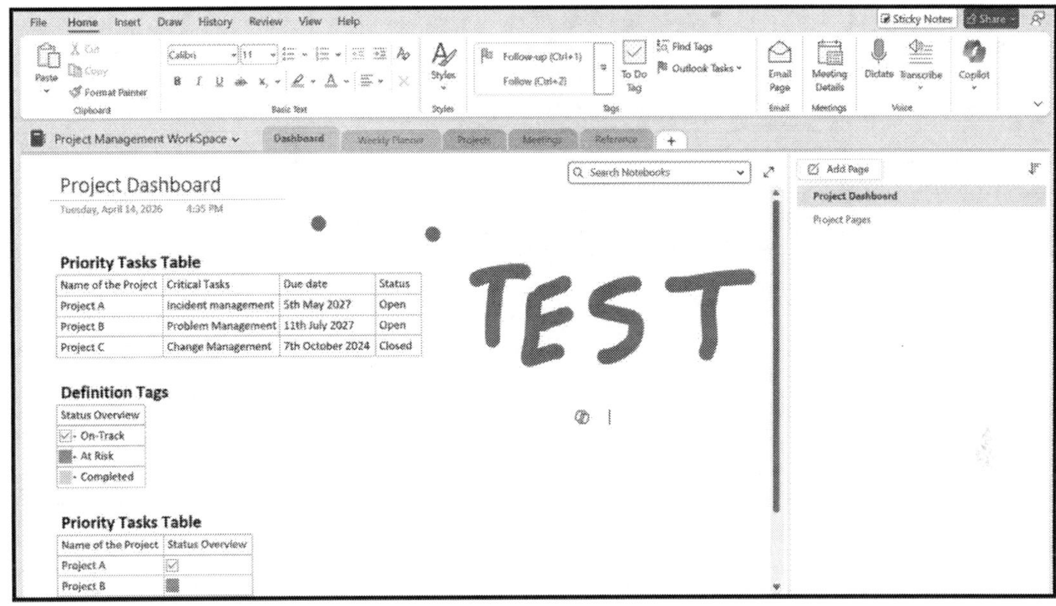

Figure 3-5. *Stray marks using red ink*

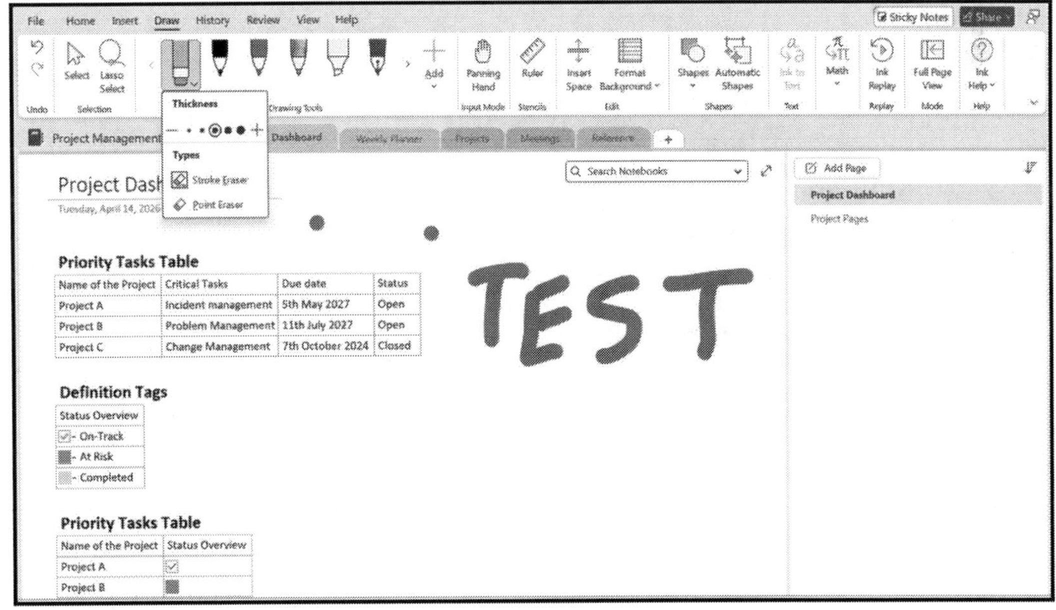

Figure 3-5-1. *Eraser tool*

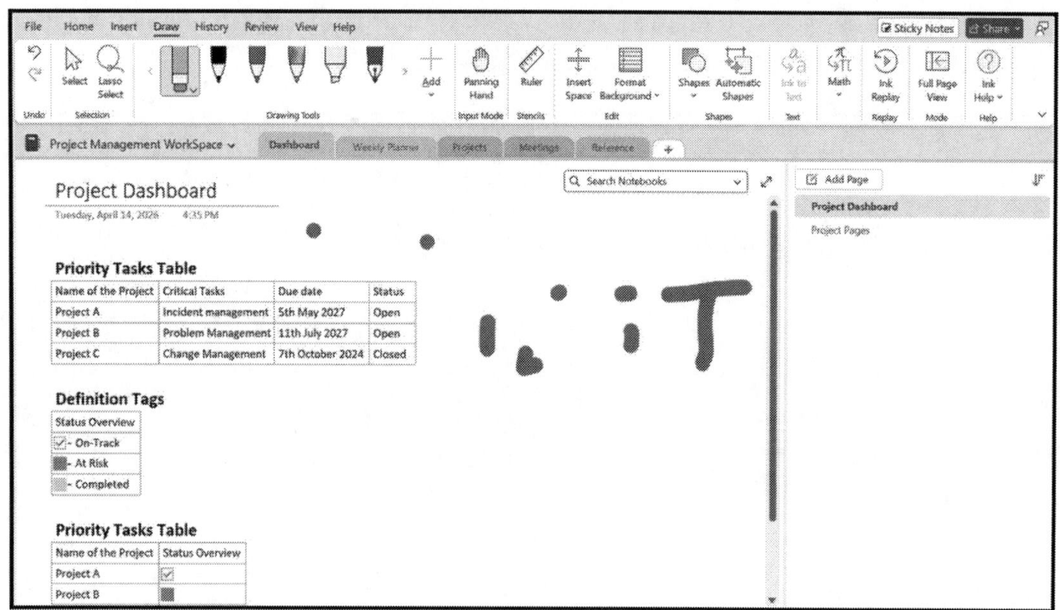

***Figure 3-6.** Erase is in progress*

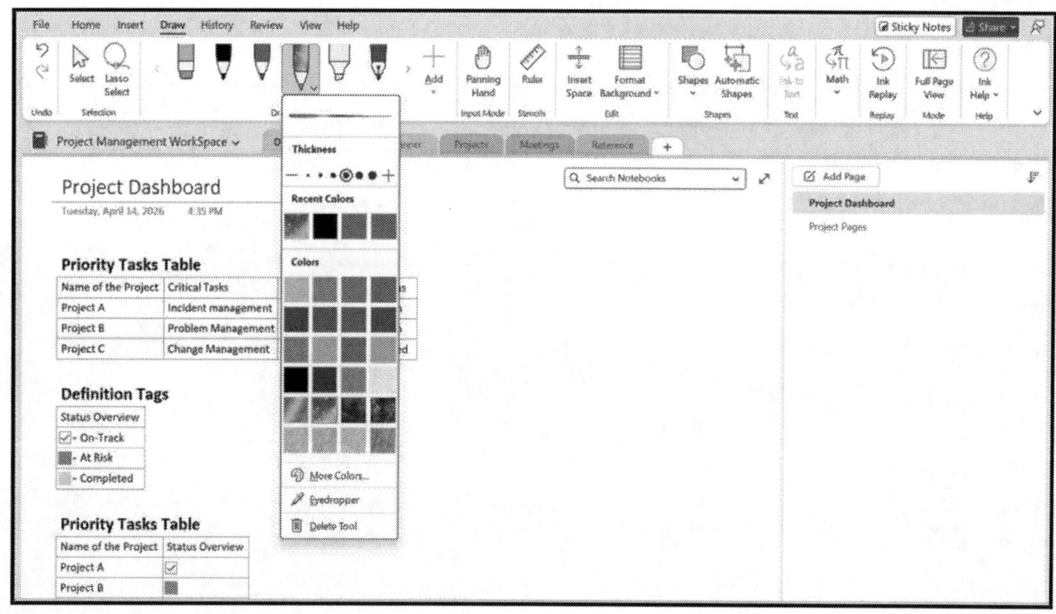

***Figure 3-7.** Clicking a new pen*

If you've used other OneNote versions, you might know about "Ink to Text," which converts handwriting into typed text as shown in Figures 3-8 and 3-9. Its accuracy depends on your handwriting neatness as shown in Figure 3-10.

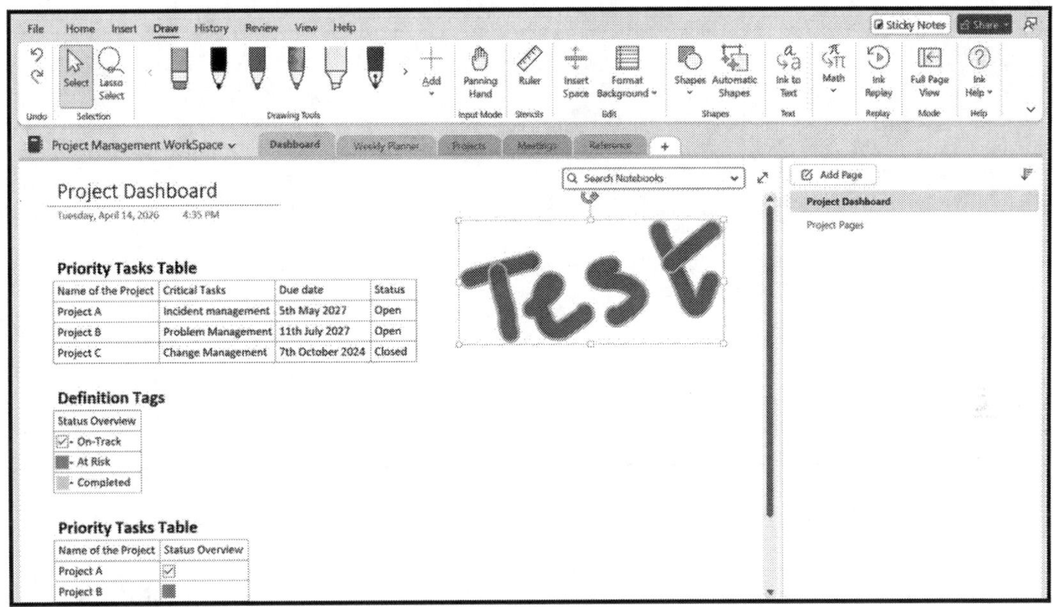

Figure 3-8. *Text before using "Ink to Text"*

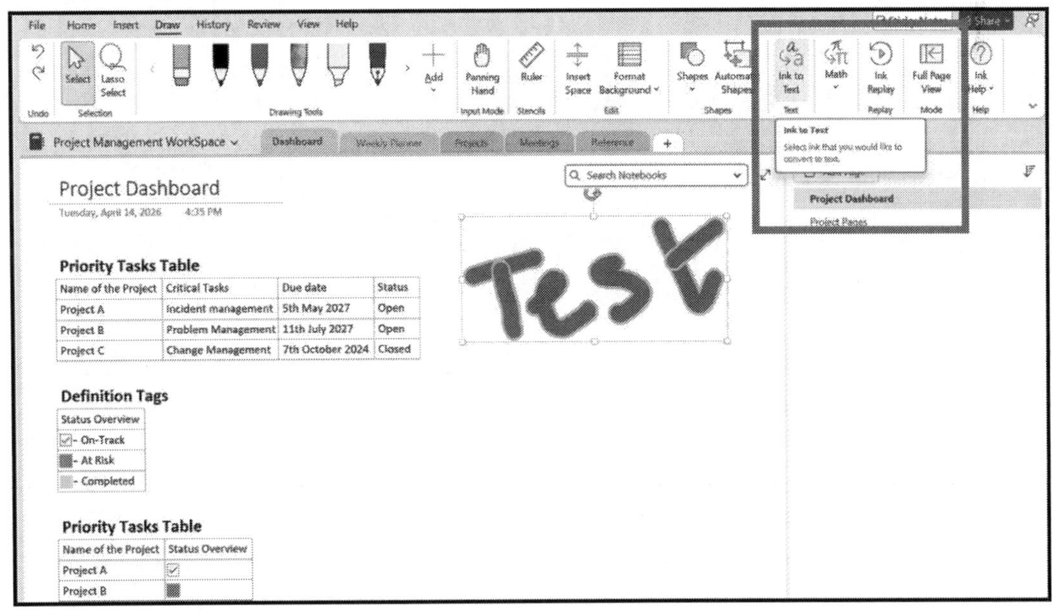

Figure 3-9. *"Ink to Text" feature*

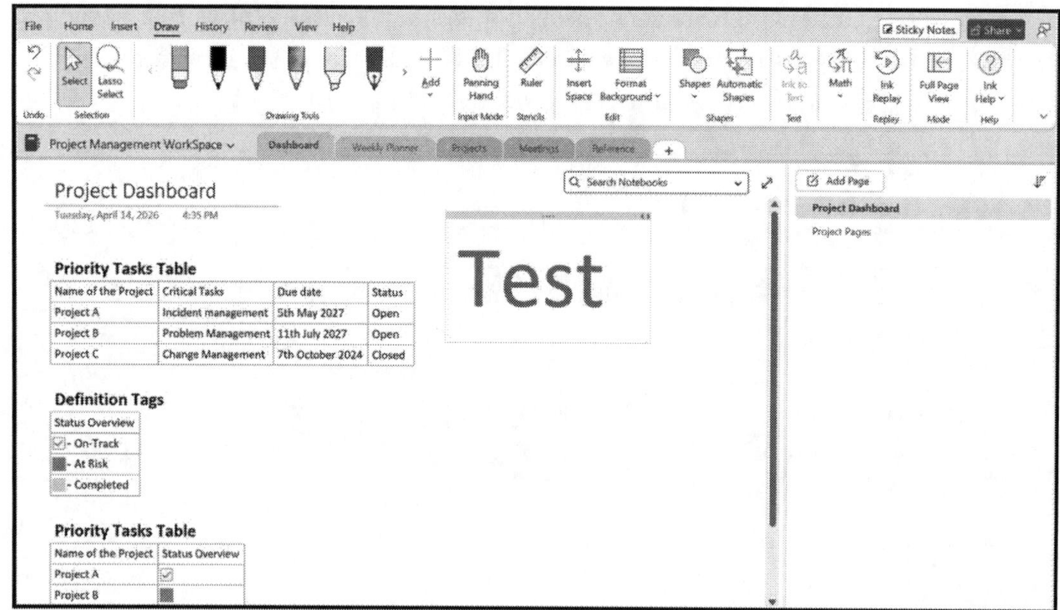

***Figure 3-10.** Text after using "Ink to Text" feature*

Further, you can use the Ink Replay feature to understand in detail how the ink got converted into text as shown in Figures 3-11, 3-11-1, 3-11-2, 3-11-3, and 3-11-4.

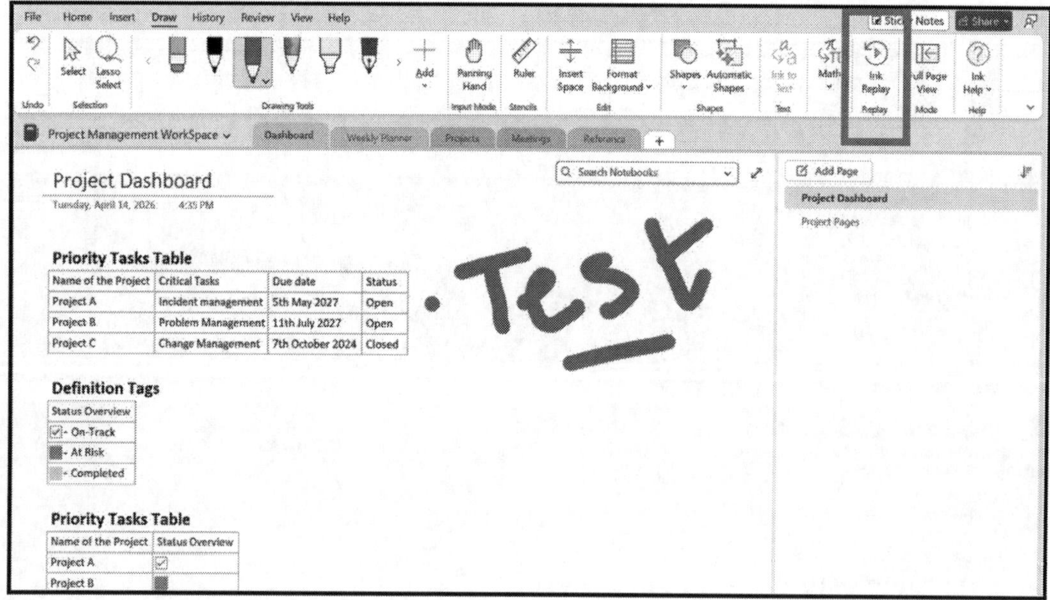

***Figure 3-11.** Text before using "Ink Replay"*

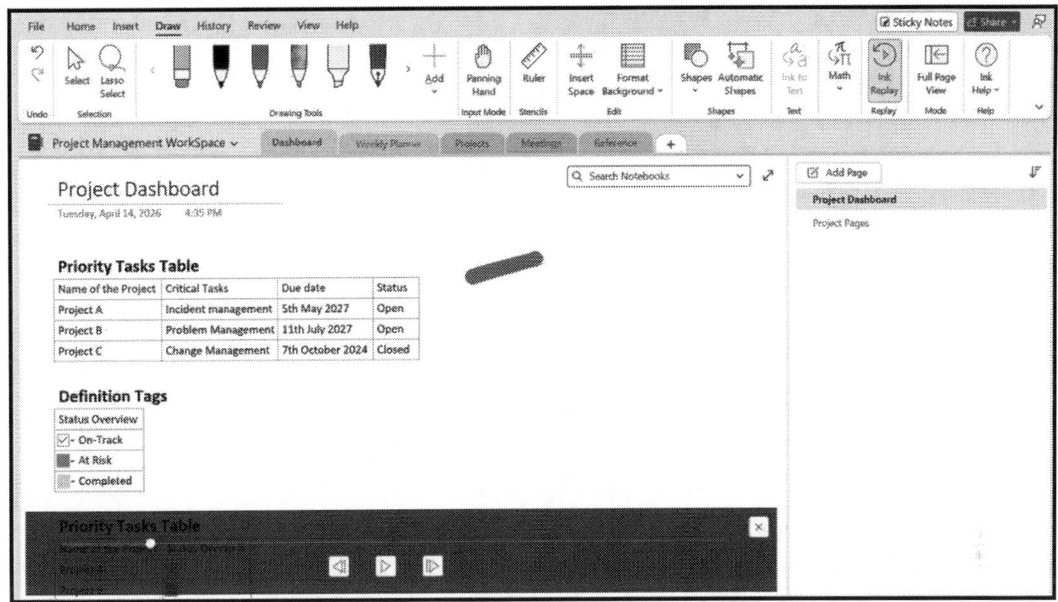

Figure 3-11-1. *"Ink Reply" feature displaying sequence of Drawing starting with "-"*

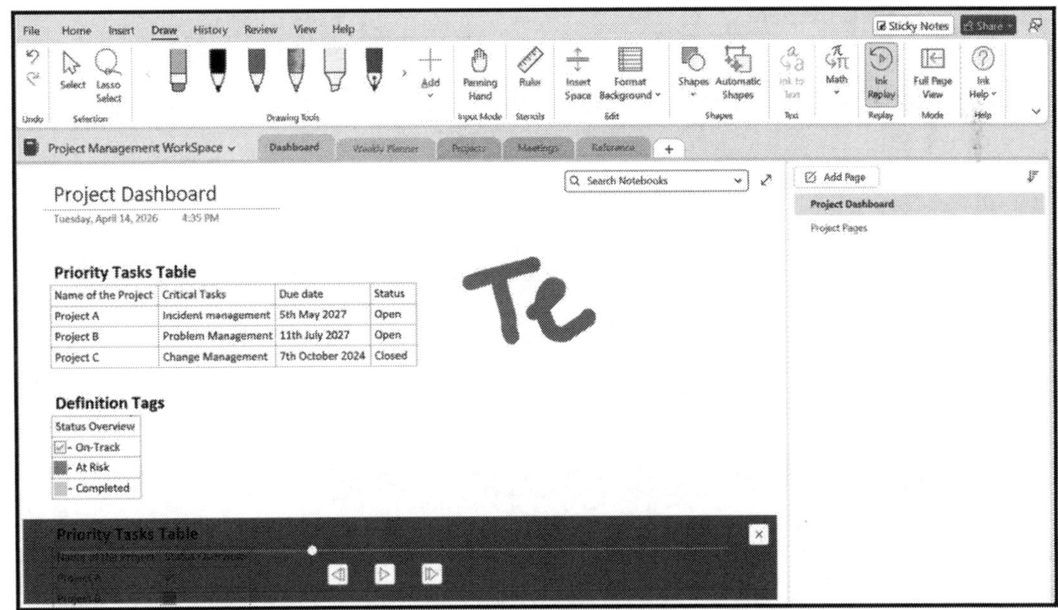

Figure 3-11-2. *"Ink Reply" feature: "Ink Reply" feature displaying sequence of Drawing with -"Te"*

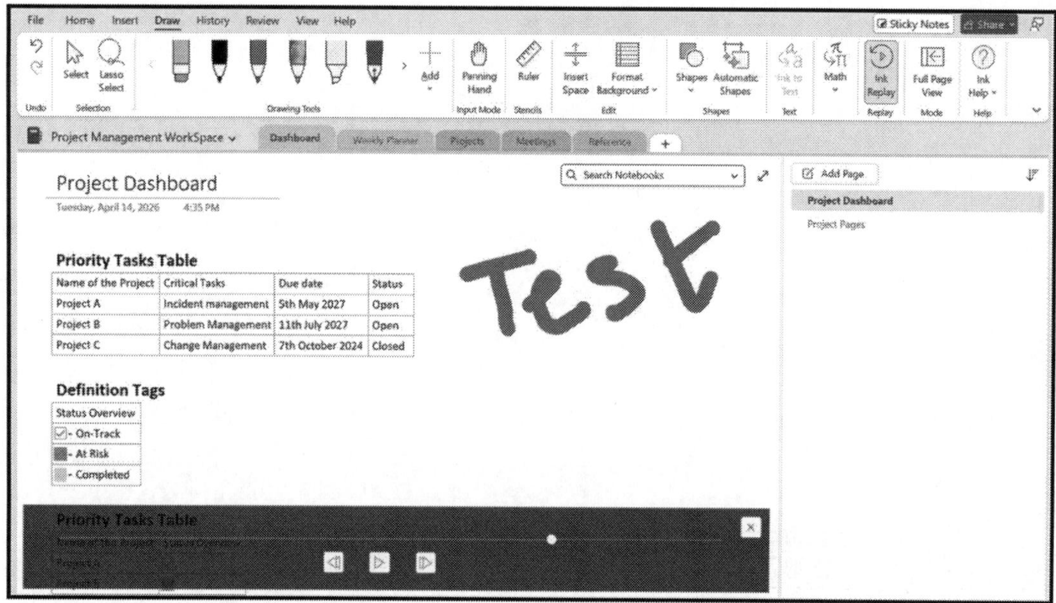

***Figure 3-11-3.** "Ink Reply" feature displaying sequence of Drawing with - "Test"*

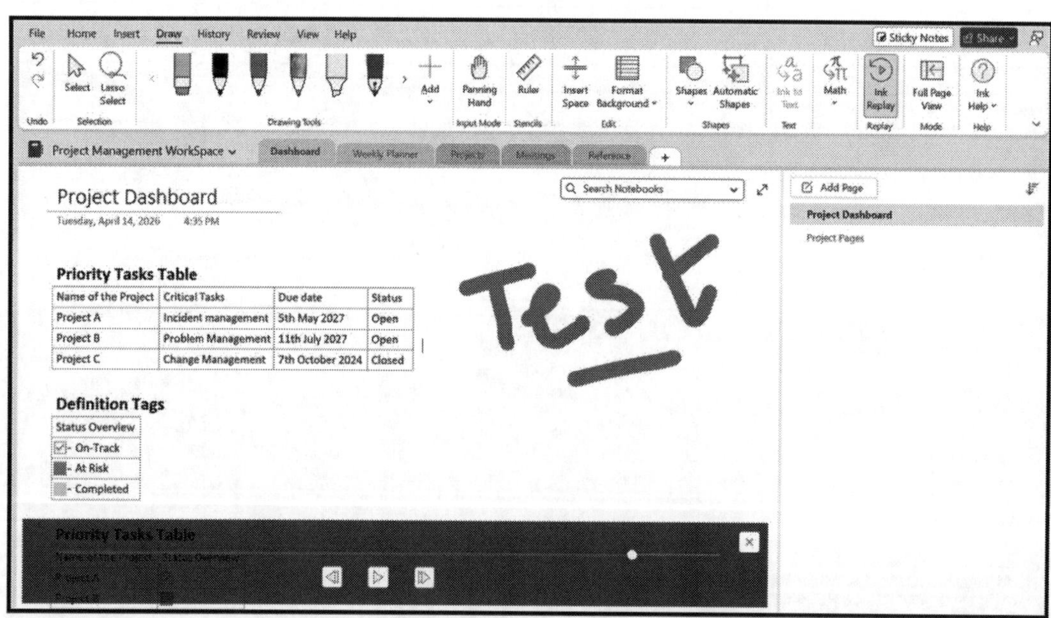

***Figure 3-11-4.** "Ink Reply" feature returning original drawing with word "Test" and with an underline "_"*

Under the Draw menu, you can change the drawing tools in terms of pen, highlighter, fountain pen, and brush pen as shown in Figure 3-12.

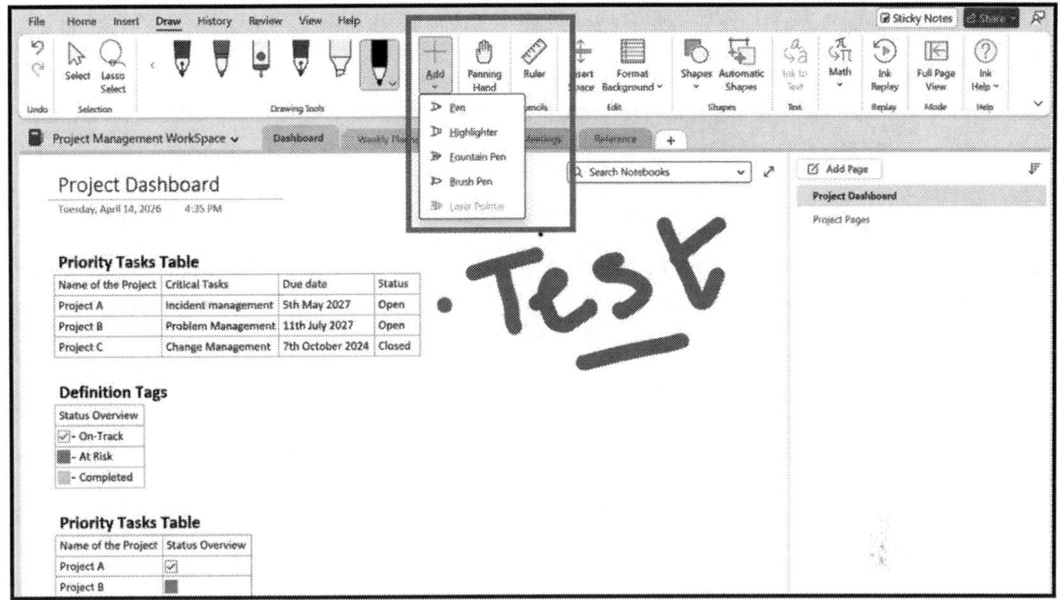

***Figure 3-12.** Add more drawing tools*

Once you choose Pen, the text changes to a pen written format as shown in Figure 3-13.

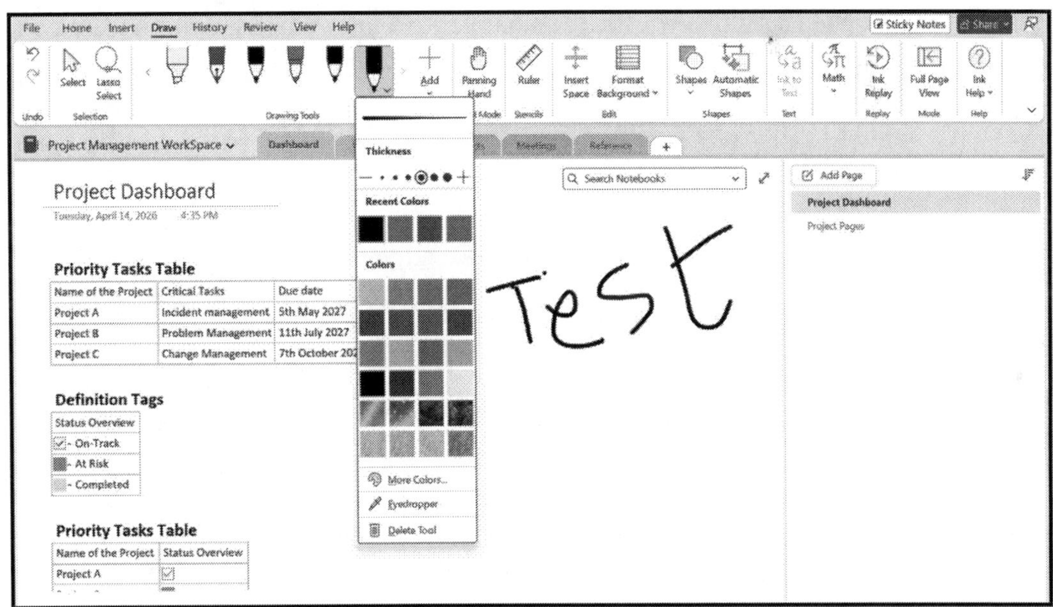

***Figure 3-13.** Pen type written format*

Once you choose Highlighter, the text changes to a highlighted written format as shown in Figure 3-14.

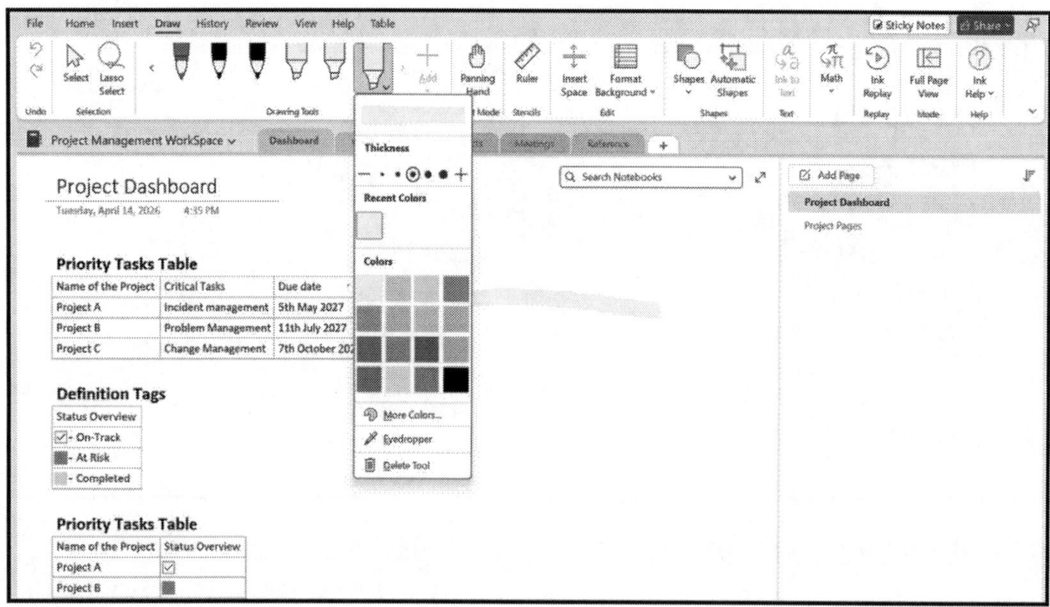

***Figure 3-14.** Highlighter type written format*

Once you choose Fountain Pen, the text changes to a fountain pen written format as shown in Figure 3-15.

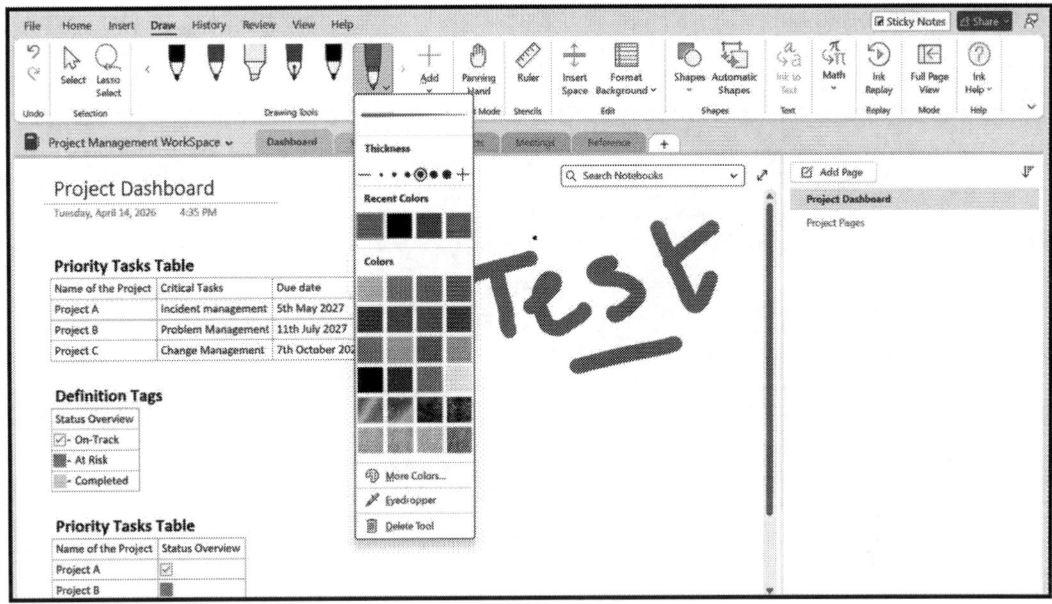

Figure 3-15. Fountain pen type written format

Once you choose Brush Pen, the text changes to a brush pen written format as shown in Figure 3-16.

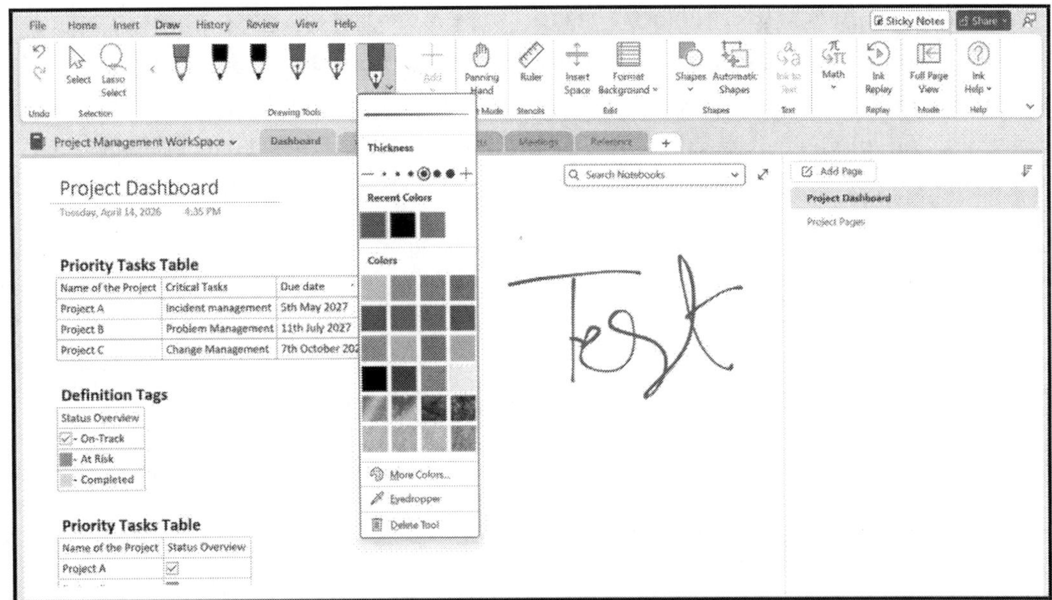

Figure 3-16. Brush pen type written format

Once you choose Laser Pointer, a laser can be pointed toward the text as shown in Figure 3-17.

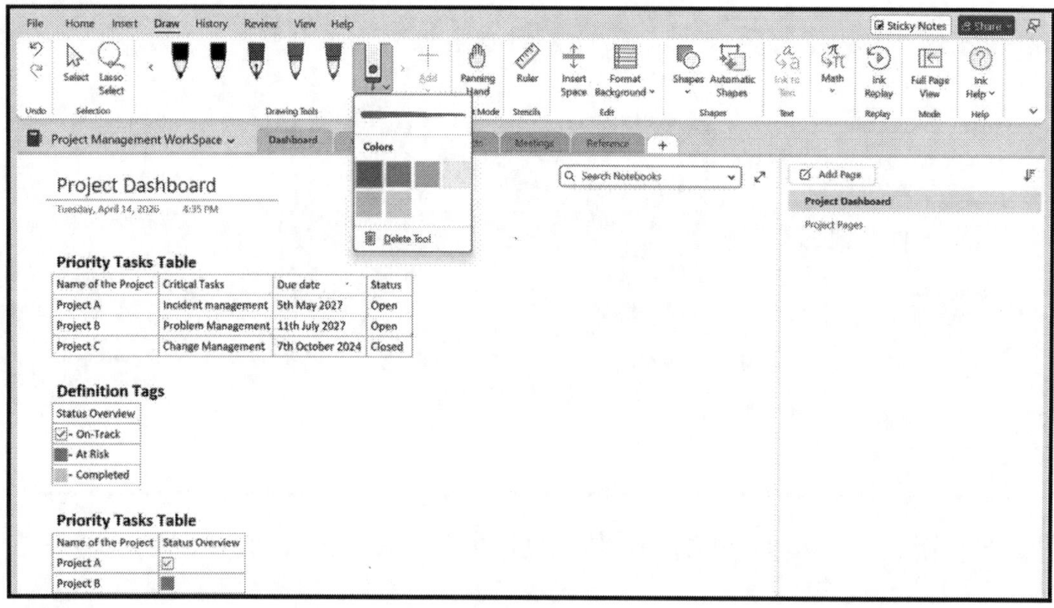

Figure 3-17. *Laser pointer to highlight text*

The Ruler tool helps users align, measure, and draw straight lines accurately on a OneNote page, especially when working with ink or diagrams as shown in Figure 3-18. It can be rotated to any angle, making it useful for creating neat handwritten notes, shapes, or layouts. The ruler is particularly effective on touch-enabled devices when used with a stylus.

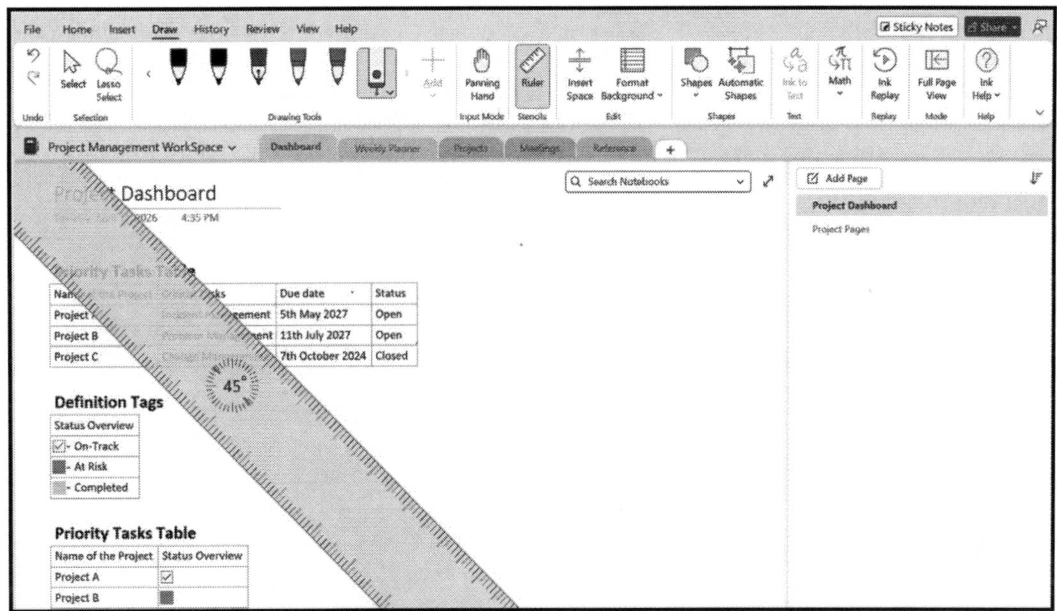

Figure 3-18. *Ruler in OneNote*

Note A stylus is a pen-like tool for interacting with touchscreens, enabling precise writing, drawing, and navigation. It's especially handy in apps like Microsoft OneNote for handwriting notes, sketching, annotating, and using features like the Ruler.

The Panning Hand tool as shown in Figure 3-19 allows users to move around the OneNote page freely without accidentally writing or selecting content. It is especially useful when navigating large or zoomed-in pages containing extensive notes or diagrams. By temporarily disabling ink or selection, Panning Hand ensures smooth and controlled page movement.

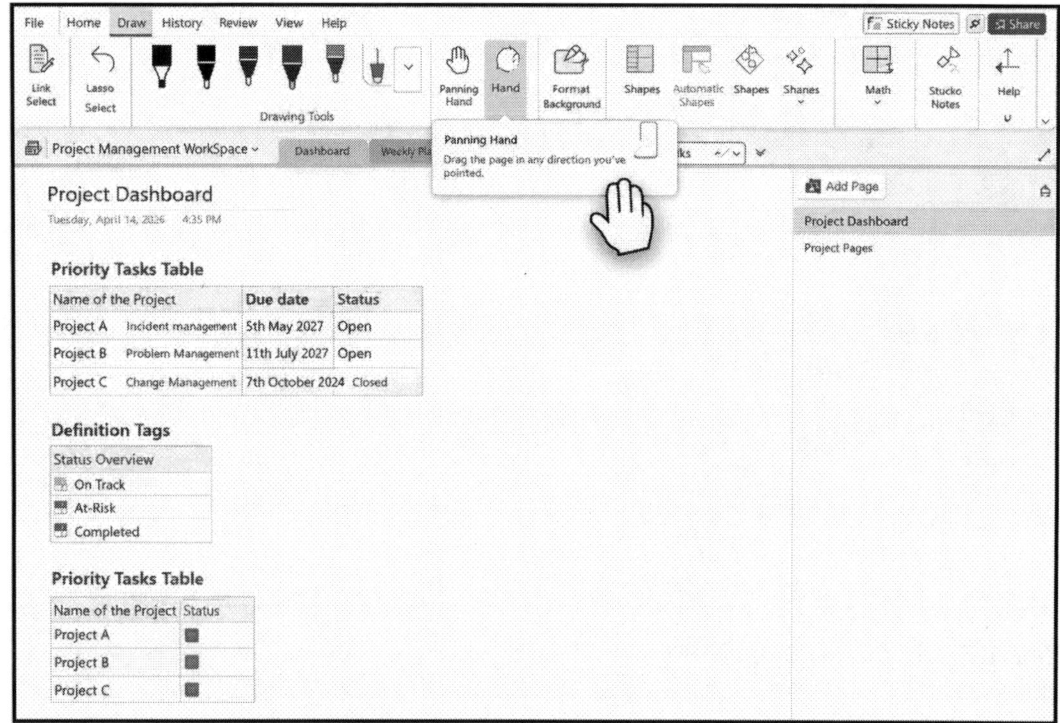

Figure 3-19. *Panning image*

Record Audio and Video in Microsoft OneNote

When attending a class or meeting, users have the ability to record audio and transcribe spoken content into written text. The audio recording functionality is available across several OneNote applications; however, access to the Transcribe feature specifically requires OneNote for Microsoft 365. This section will outline how to utilize the Transcribe tool.

It's important to understand where and how the **Transcribe** feature works in Microsoft OneNote. While transcription can be very useful, it's **not available in all versions of OneNote**. Right now, you'll only find this feature in **OneNote for Microsoft 365**, and its availability depends on Microsoft's cloud services. If you're using OneNote for Windows 10, on the web, or on mobile devices, you might be able to record audio but won't necessarily have access to all of the transcription features described here.

The Transcribe feature is also **dependent on your region and language**. The range of supported languages differs, and how well transcription works can vary based on the language or dialect you choose. Whether transcription is available may depend on factors like Microsoft's service rollout, your organization's settings, or data privacy requirements—which means it could be turned off by administrators or restricted by policy in certain places.

Additionally, transcription in OneNote requires **OneDrive cloud storage** because your audio files must be uploaded and processed online before transcripts are created. This means you need to be connected to the internet. Because of these requirements, consider transcription as a **conditional feature** in OneNote—not something that's guaranteed in every situation. Understanding these limitations allows users to set realistic expectations and make sure they use the Transcribe feature only where it's truly supported.

In OneNote for Microsoft 365, the Transcribe option can be accessed from the Home ribbon—within the Voice group as shown in Figure 3-20—or the Insert ribbon under the Recording group as shown in Figure 3-21. Both locations offer identical functionality. Clicking the Transcribe button initiates transcription, while clicking the downward arrow provides options either to start transcription or simply to record audio for later insertion on the page.

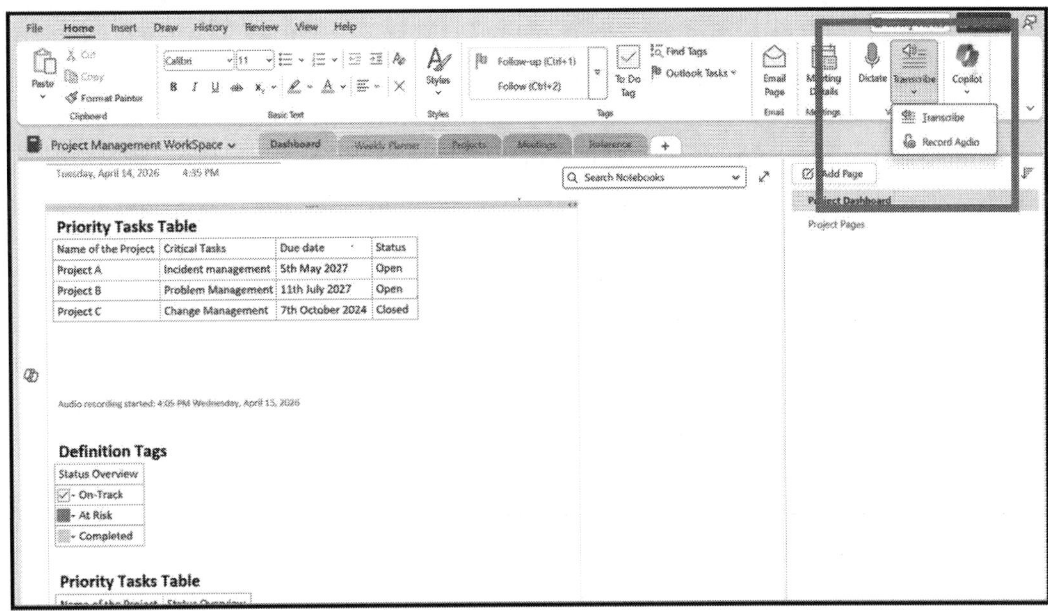

***Figure 3-20.** Transcribe from the Home menu*

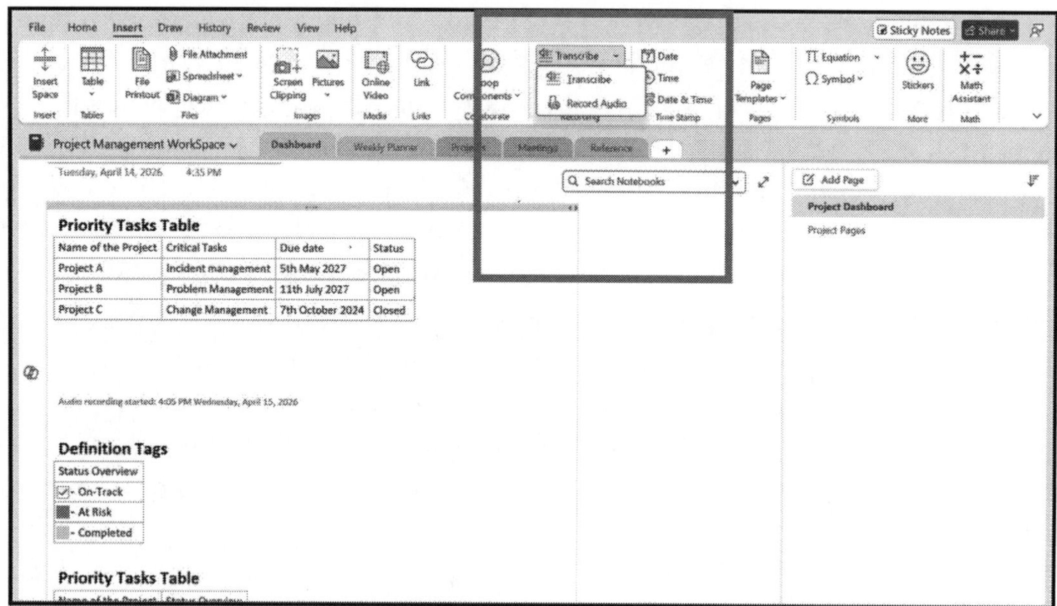

Figure 3-21. Transcribe from the Insert menu

Upon launching Transcribe, a dedicated panel appears on the right as shown in Figure 3-22. The user should select the appropriate language for the recording. Available languages include multiple dialects, particularly for English as shown in Figure 3-23. If you possess an audio file supported by OneNote (e.g., .wav or .mp4), it can be uploaded for transcription into written form as shown in Figure 3-24. To create a new recording, initiate the process, after which the panel will display a microphone icon and a timer indicating the duration of the current session as shown in Figure 3-25. Users may then save and transcribe the audio file, selecting the relevant notification to proceed as shown in Figure 3-26. It is important to note that files are uploaded to OneDrive, specifically to the document library associated with the logged-in user account.

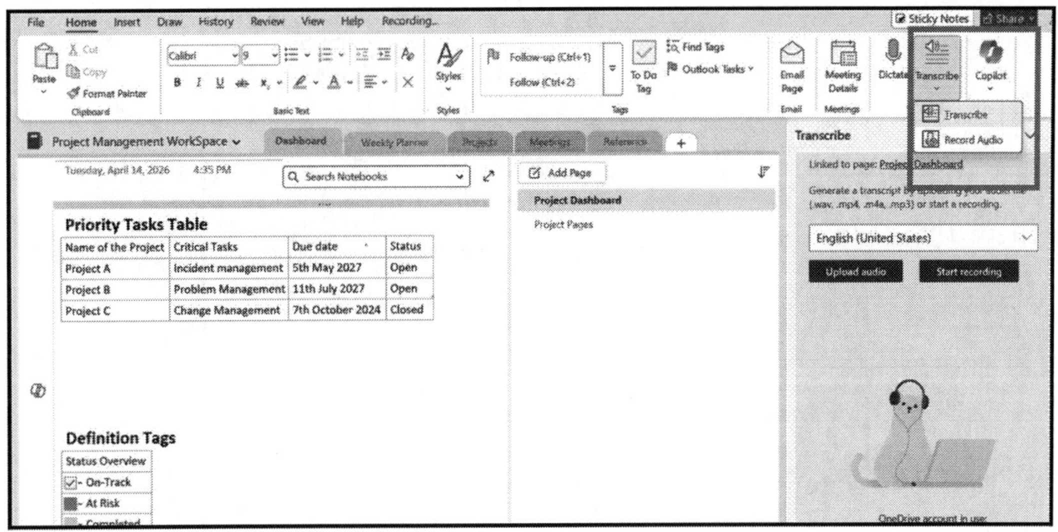

Figure 3-22. *Transcribe panel*

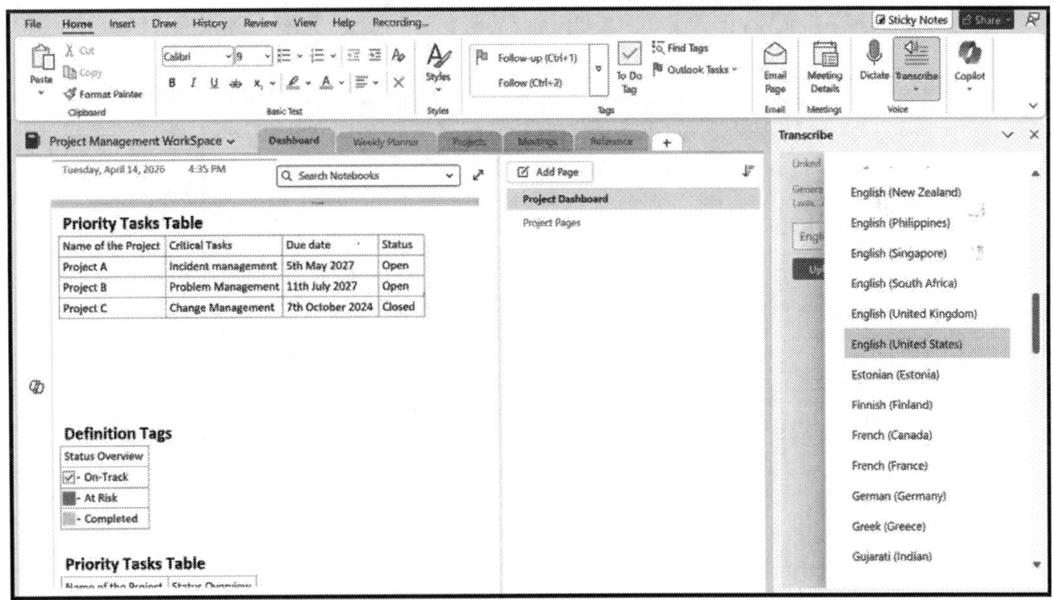

Figure 3-23. *Select languages*

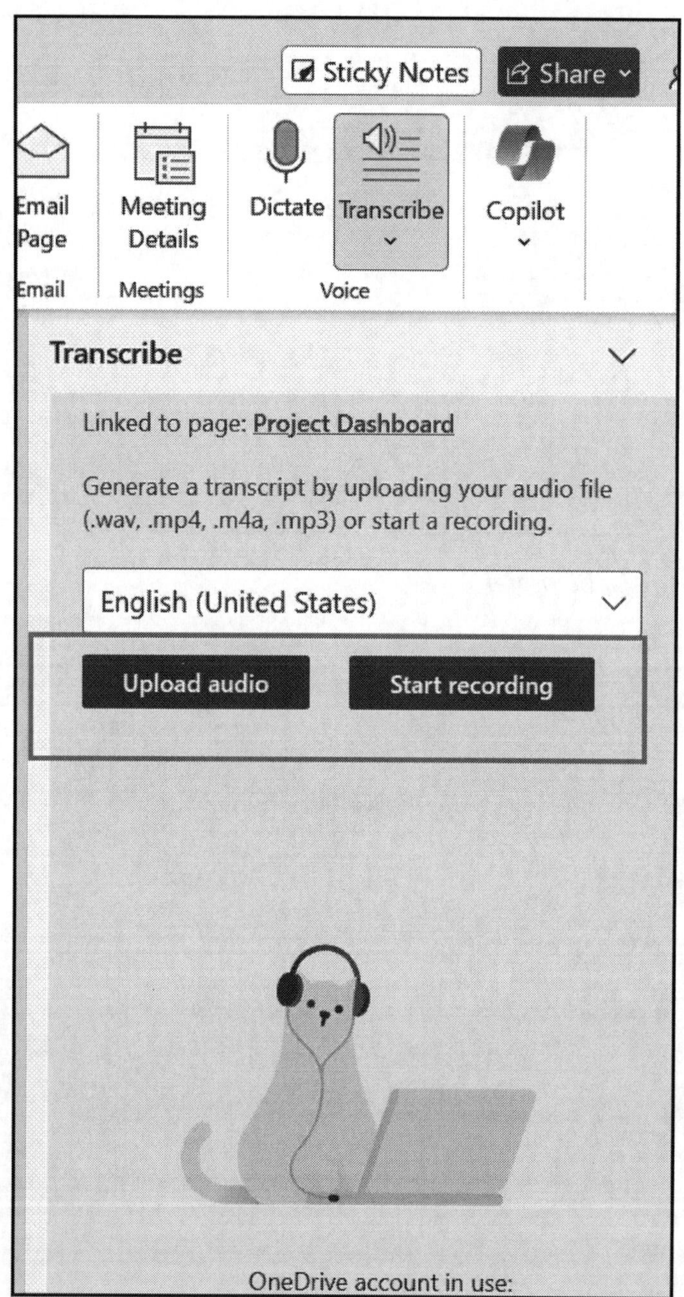

Figure 3-24. *Functionality to upload or start recording*

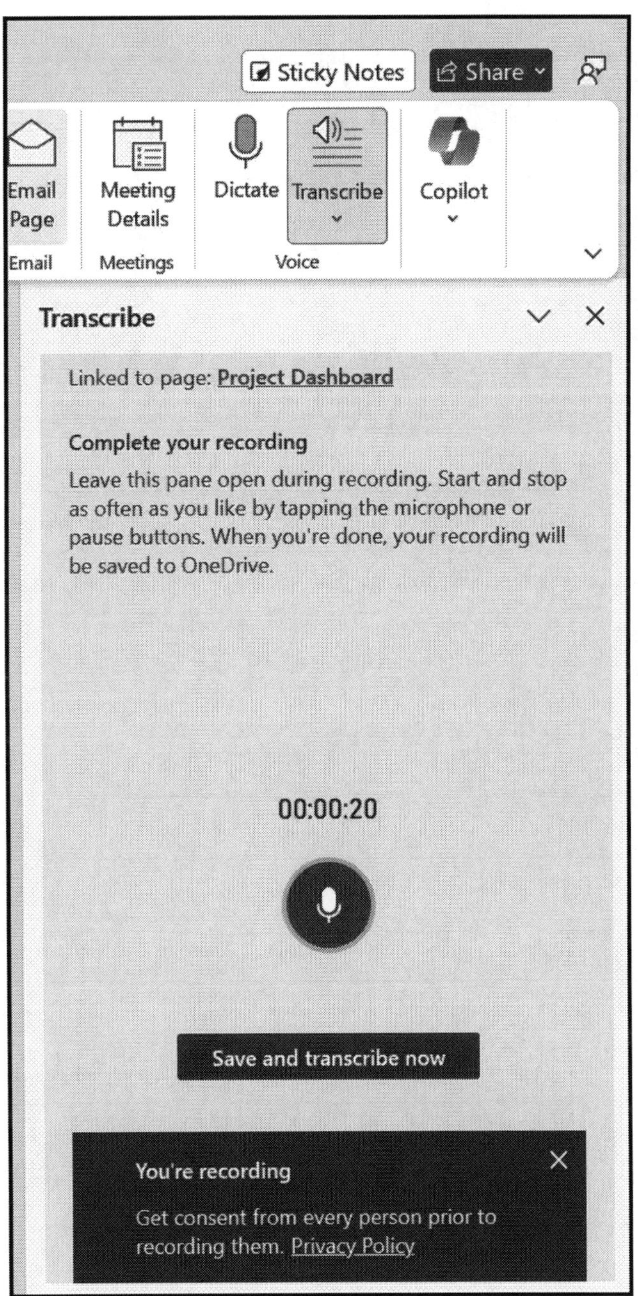

Figure 3-25. *New record creation*

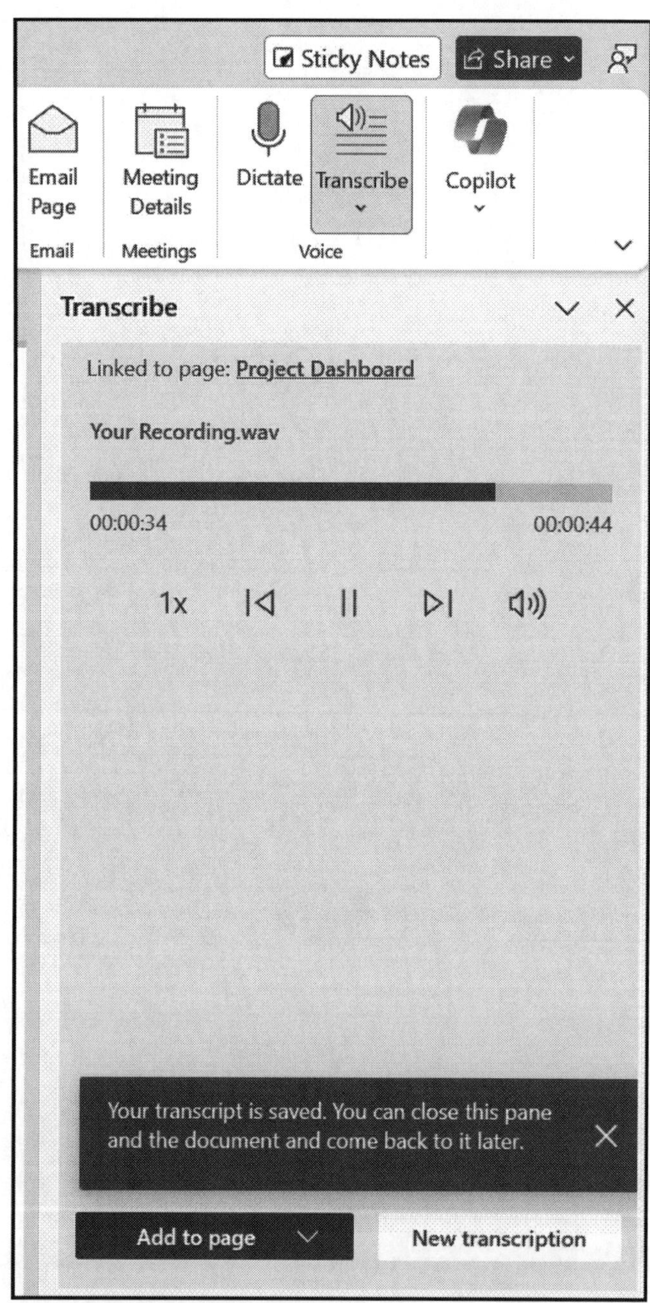

Figure 3-26. *Save and transcribe*

Also, as shown in Figure 3-26, once transcription begins, OneNote confirms the process and offers progress notifications. Saving time depends on the length and size of the recording. Post-upload, the note container on the left includes the audio file, playback controls, and metadata such as upload method and timestamp. On the right, users can change playback speed, navigate through the recording, and adjust volume.

As shown in Figure 3-27, to add the transcript to the page, click "Add to page," choosing from options that include plain text and inclusion of speaker names, timestamps, or both. After selection, the transcript appears alongside the original audio recording, allowing for further review and editing if necessary. Note that only one transcription per page is permitted. To start a new transcription without losing previous data, copy existing content elsewhere or create a new page.

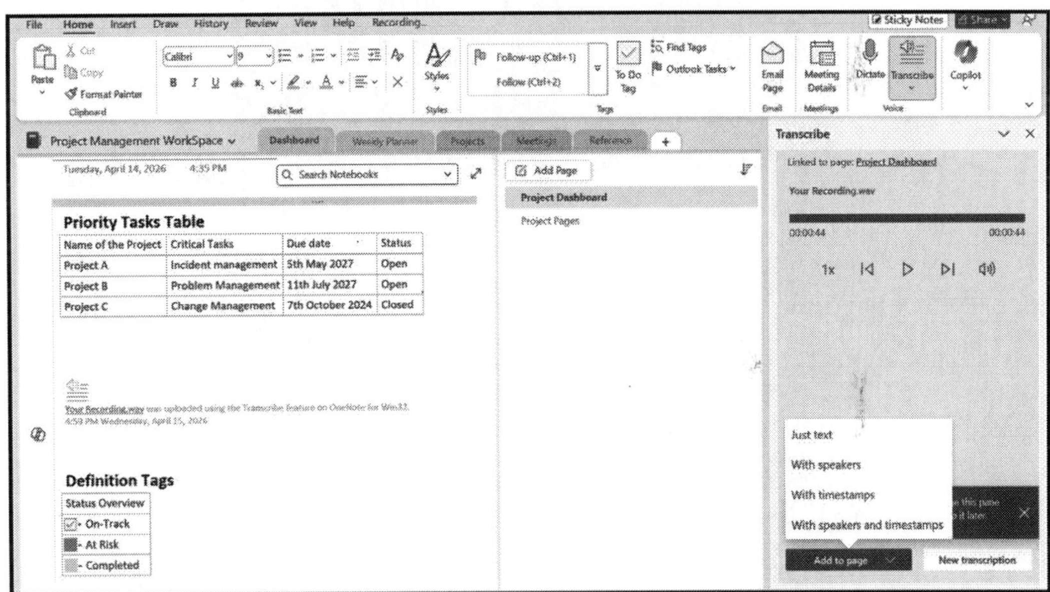

Figure 3-27. Add transcript to page

If initiating another transcription, OneNote will prompt a warning indicating that the current transcript must be moved or will be overwritten as shown in Figure 3-28. Canceling this action preserves the transcript.

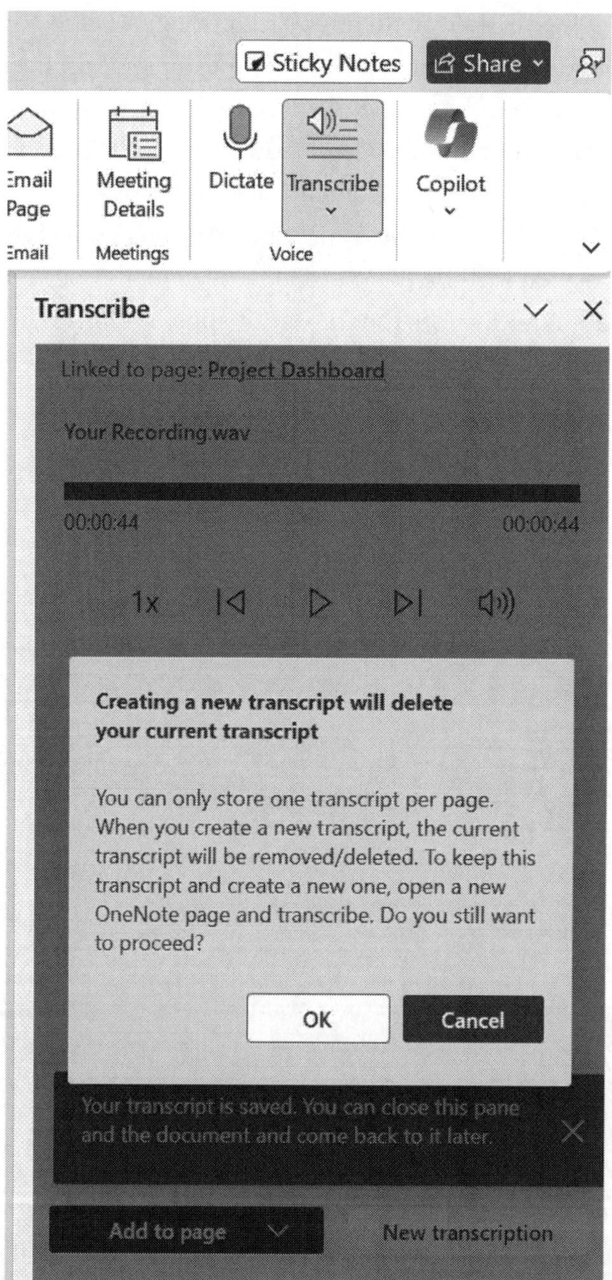

Figure 3-28. *Initiate another transcription*

Additionally, for those interested solely in audio recording without transcription, the Record Audio feature is accessible via the same dropdown menu on either the Insert or Home ribbon. Recorded audio is saved as a WMA file and displayed in a note container, with contextual ribbons providing playback controls and timestamps as shown in Figure 3-29. Unlike the Transcribe feature, audio recording alone does not generate a written transcript. This outlines the process for recording and transcribing audio notes within OneNote for Microsoft 365.

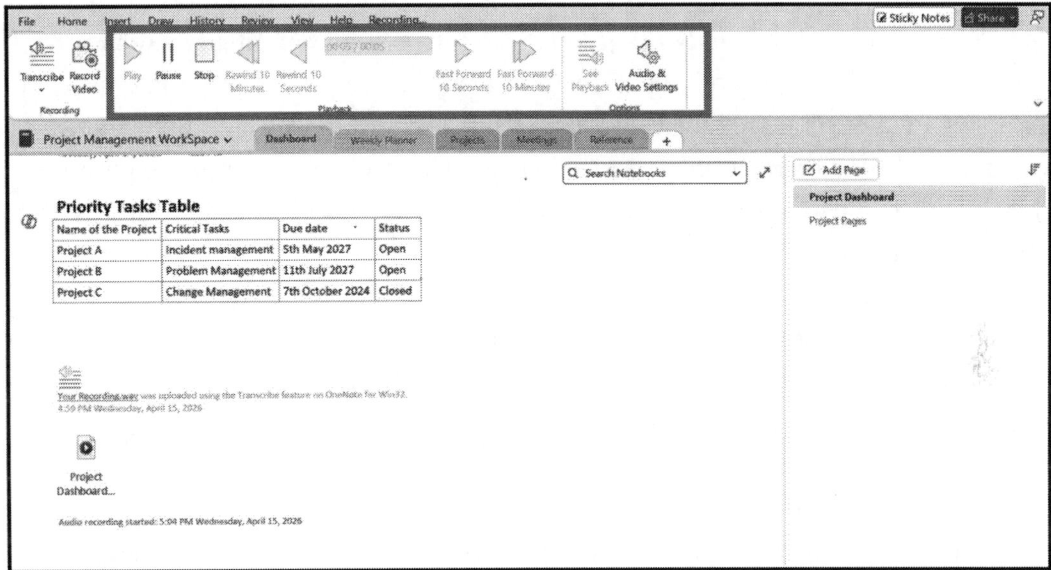

Figure 3-29. Audio recording with transcription

Pros and Cons

It is essential to delineate the scope and intended use of the Ink Replay capability as referenced in the above section. Microsoft OneNote provides comprehensive support for digital ink—including handwriting input, drawing tools, ink-to-text conversion, and visual annotation—but Ink Replay should not be regarded as an integral or standalone feature within typical note-taking workflows in OneNote.

Within OneNote, ink-related functionalities are predominantly designed to facilitate free-form handwriting, sketching, highlighting, and annotation, rather than supporting conversational or threaded reply features. Core ink tools—such as Ink to Text, Ink to Shape, pen customization, and highlighters—are inherently available in OneNote to enhance the capture and refinement of handwritten notes.

Unlike Outlook or document review platforms, OneNote does not offer structured, threaded ink replies or comment-based ink conversations. Ink markings added in

OneNote serve as static annotations that visually augment the content, enabling users to emphasize concepts, clarify details, or provide handwritten feedback within a note. These marks are not tracked as replies and do not constitute part of a communication workflow.

This distinction is important for establishing accurate expectations about OneNote's capabilities with regard to handwriting. OneNote serves as a robust digital notebook for capturing and organizing handwritten materials, whereas ink-based reply and response workflows are more comprehensively supported in other Microsoft 365 applications. Recognizing this differentiation allows users to apply ink features appropriately and mitigates any confusion between annotation-oriented and communication-driven functionalities.

Microsoft continues to advance OneNote by integrating AI-driven features through **Microsoft Copilot**, thereby enhancing the utility of handwritten notes and meeting content beyond standard digital capture. When handwritten materials are stored electronically, AI supports the **interpretation, summarization, and organization of ink-based content**, particularly as handwriting is transcribed into text. With Copilot, users can produce accurate summaries, identify key information, and restructure handwritten content into organized formats, which streamlines the review and repurposing of notes. These enhancements are particularly beneficial for students, educators, and professionals who utilize free-form writing during learning or brainstorming sessions.

For meetings, AI functionalities are primarily delivered via **Microsoft Teams and Copilot**, rather than being embedded directly within OneNote itself. Once meeting recordings and transcriptions are available, Copilot analyzes this data to extract themes, decisions, and action items. These insights can then be referenced or manually added to OneNote pages to supplement meeting documentation. While OneNote does not provide real-time meeting analysis, it acts as a central repository for storing AI-generated summaries, tasks, and highlights sourced from Teams or Copilot. It should be noted that access to these AI capabilities depends on specific licenses and services, and their availability varies according to tenant configuration. Collectively, OneNote and Copilot enable workflows in which natural inputs—such as handwriting and speech—are elevated by AI, contributing to enhanced understanding, clarity, and productivity.

Finally, we have come to the end of this chapter. This chapter provides a comprehensive overview of Microsoft OneNote's advanced input and capture capabilities, focusing on handwritten, audio, and video notes. It explains how users can leverage the Draw menu tools—including various pen styles, highlighters, and the laser pointer—to create expressive and organized handwritten content. Navigation and precision tools such as the Panning Hand, Ruler, Ink to Text, and Ink Replay enhance usability and accuracy. The chapter concludes with the Transcribe feature, demonstrating how spoken content can be converted into searchable notes. Together, these features empower users to capture ideas naturally and efficiently within OneNote. In the next chapter, we will learn about collaboration using Microsoft OneNote, by learning integration with Teams and embedding videos.

CHAPTER 4

Collaboration and Sharing Using OneNote

The previous chapter provided a comprehensive overview of Microsoft OneNote's advanced input and capture capabilities, focusing on handwritten, audio, and video notes. It explained how users can leverage the Draw menu tools—including various pen styles, highlighters, and the laser pointer—to create expressive and organized handwritten content. Navigation and precision tools such as the Panning Hand, Ruler, Ink to Text, and Ink Replay enhance usability and accuracy. The chapter concluded with the Transcribe feature, demonstrating how spoken content can be converted into searchable notes. Together, these features empower users to capture ideas naturally and efficiently within OneNote. In this chapter, we will learn about collaboration using Microsoft OneNote, by learning integration with Teams and embedding videos.

This chapter presents two sub-sections: one focuses on leveraging multimedia content and the other focuses on Microsoft Copilot with AI capabilities within Microsoft OneNote to improve collaboration, organization, and productivity. It outlines methods for embedding online videos from platforms such as YouTube or Vimeo into OneNote pages, either by inserting direct links or utilizing the Insert ➤ Online Video feature. The chapter details how embedded videos can be accessed seamlessly within the notebook interface, thereby facilitating easy retrieval of educational materials and references. Furthermore, it covers the procedure for recording videos directly within OneNote using the Record Video function, describing how these recordings are stored at the cursor location along with playback controls and timestamps.

In addition to video integration, the chapter discusses how users can insert files, images, hyperlinks, Excel spreadsheets, and Visio diagrams via the Insert menu, thus enabling the centralization of diverse resources within a single notebook. This approach supports well-structured documentation and ensures prompt access to supplementary materials.

C. Waghmare, *Mastering Microsoft OneNote*, https://doi.org/10.1007/979-8-8688-2866-9_4

A significant portion of the chapter is dedicated to the application of Copilot in OneNote. It explains how Copilot assists users by summarizing extensive notes, generating concise meeting summaries suitable for management, creating organized to-do lists, and developing actionable project plans from unstructured content. The chapter also demonstrates Copilot's ability to facilitate conversational research within notes, enabling users to efficiently identify key insights, responsibilities, and decisions across extensive notebooks. In summary, the chapter illustrates how OneNote, empowered by Copilot, functions as a robust platform for intelligent content management, analysis, and collaboration.

Embed an Online Video in OneNote

Online videos from platforms such as YouTube or Vimeo may be embedded directly into a notebook page and viewed within the page interface. The process is as follows: first, locate the desired video on a supported site. For example, after searching for a copyright-free video on YouTube, copy the hyperlink from the address bar or use the Share option beneath the video player to obtain the link. Select "Copy" in the Share menu, confirming the link has been copied to your clipboard. Paste the link in your OneNote and it will appear as shown in Figure 4-1.

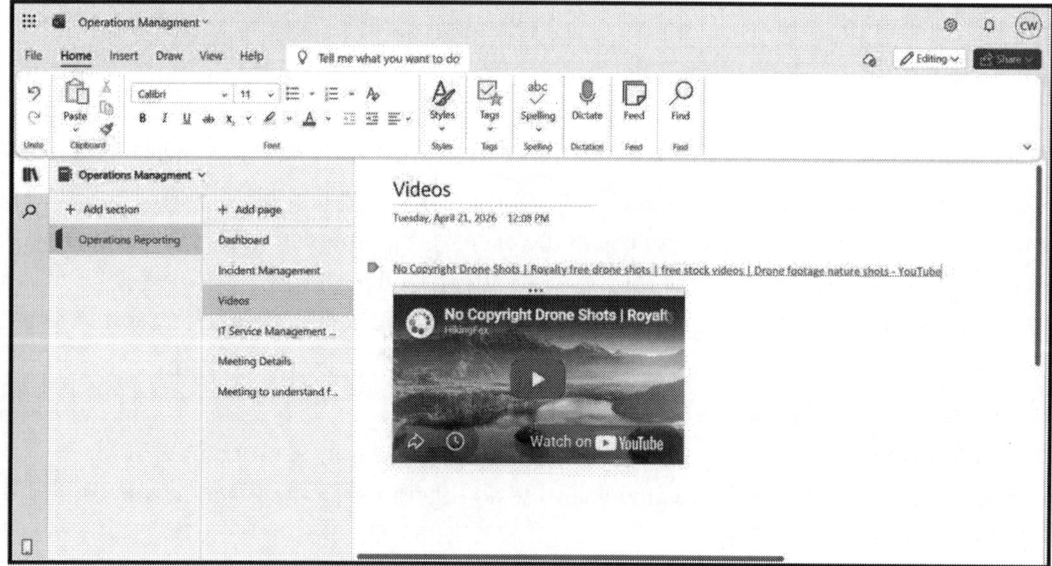

Figure 4-1. *Video embedded in a OneNote page*

There is another way to embed a video into a OneNote page through the Insert menu. Position the cursor at the intended location, navigate to the Insert ribbon as shown in Figure 4-2, and select Online Video from the media group as shown in Figure 4-3. Paste the video address into the provided field using the Ctrl+V keyboard shortcut, then click OK. To review which video formats are supported, click "View supported video," which will redirect you to the Microsoft Help and Training site containing detailed instructions and a link to a list of compatible embedded video types.

Upon clicking OK, the video will appear on the notebook page as shown in Figure 4-4, featuring a link to the source and playback controls that allow you to view the video directly within the frame. This procedure enables seamless integration of online videos into your notebook notes.

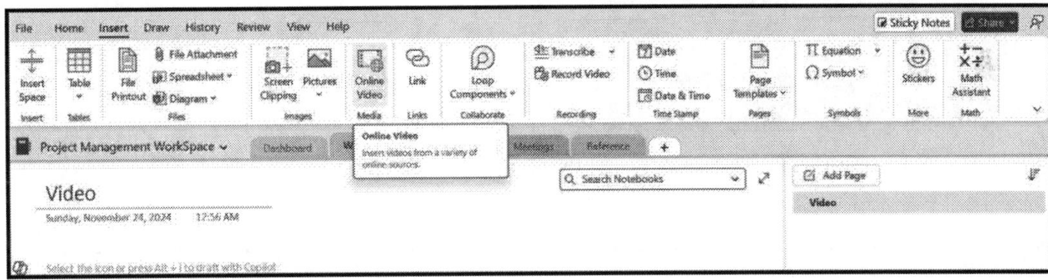

Figure 4-2. Navigate to Online Video option

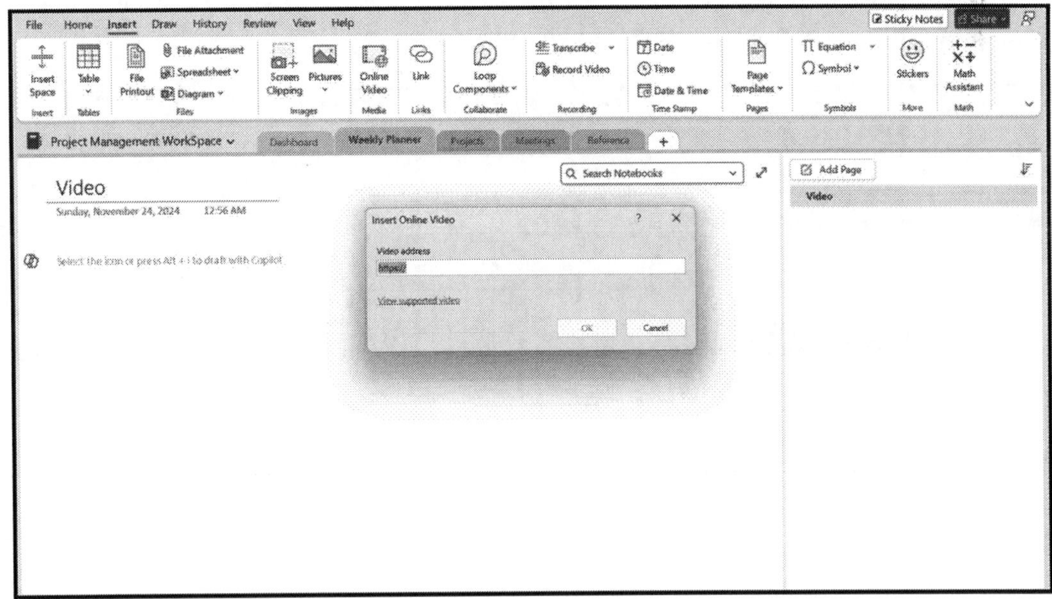

Figure 4-3. Insert online video link

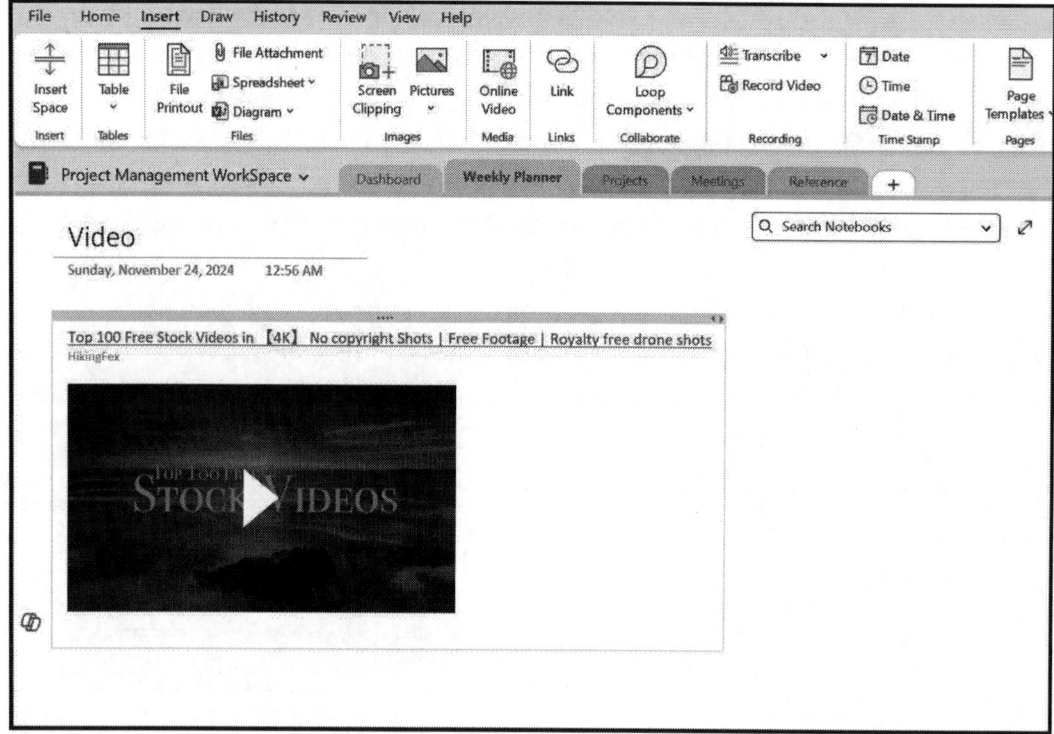

Figure 4-4. *Video is published via OneNote*

One can also record a video and embed in OneNote. Access the "Record Video" option from the Insert menu as shown in Figure 4-5.

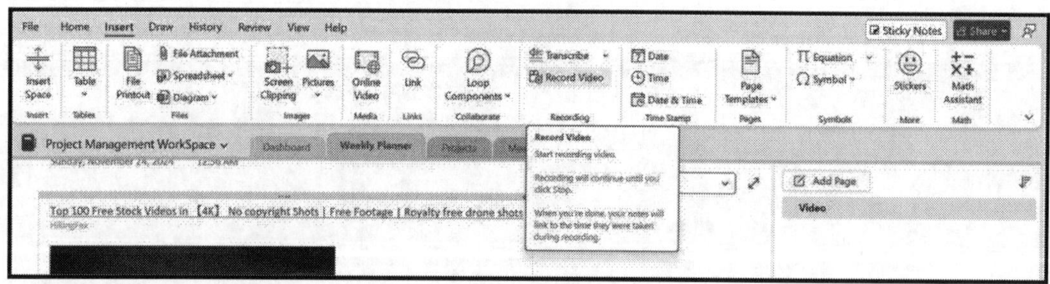

Figure 4-5. *Access Record Video option*

Place the cursor in the notebook where you would like to save this recorded video. After that, click Record Video and a video will open using your default camera, and recording will start as shown in Figure 4-6.

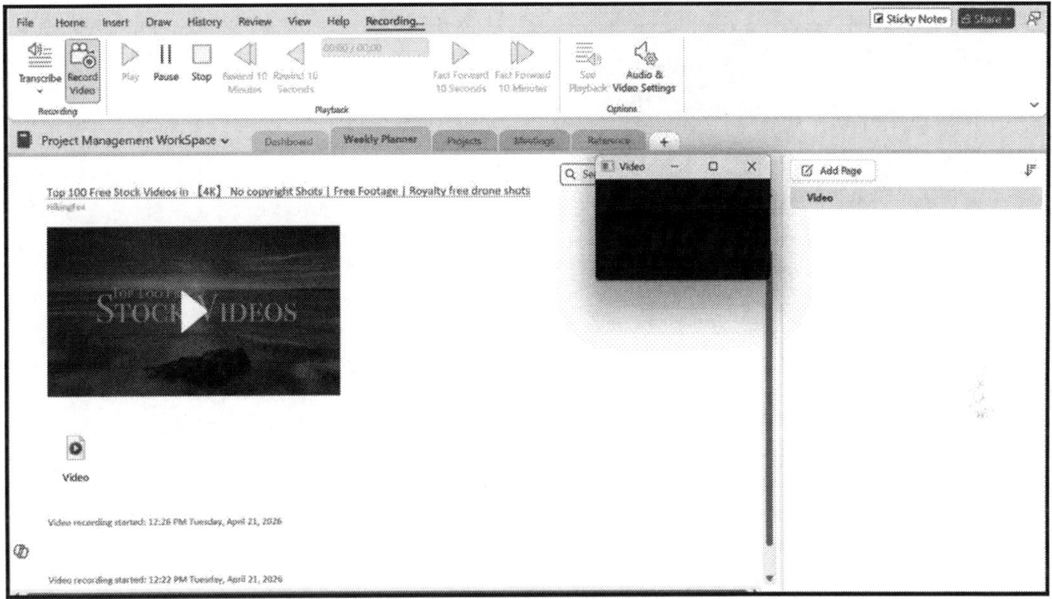

Figure 4-6. *Recording started*

Once recording is started, a Playback menu appears at the ribbon which contains options such as stop, play, forward, and others, and after you close this video, it will get saved at the location where we had placed the cursor before the start of the recording as shown in Figure 4-7. This Playback menu disappears the moment the video is deleted from OneNote.

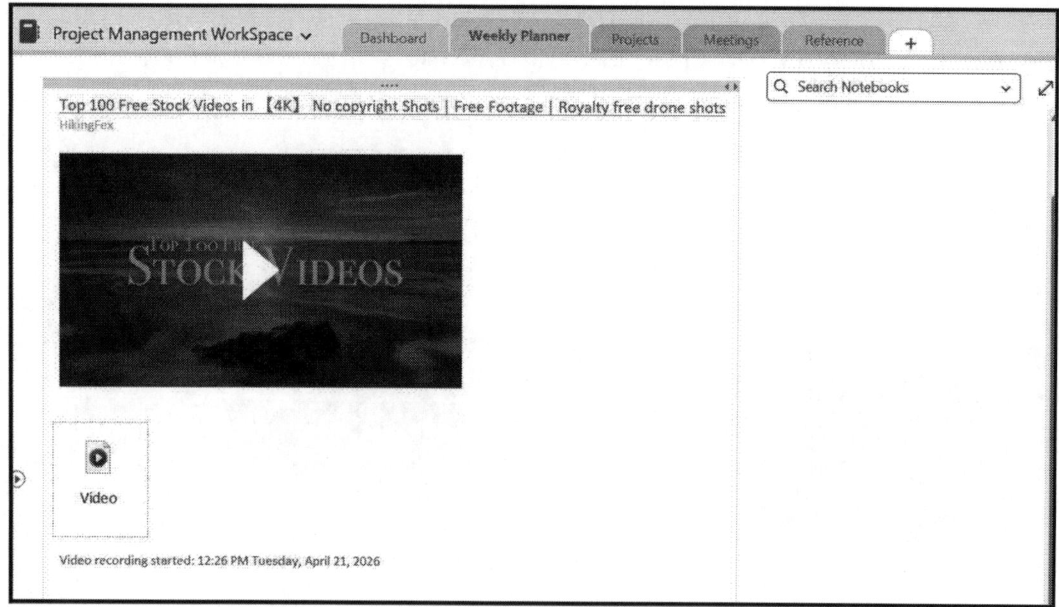

***Figure 4-7.** Recording saved with timestamp*

Besides inserting and recording a video, one can insert pictures such as from a "From File" as shown in Figure 4-8, "From Camera" as shown in Figure 4-9 and "From Online" - as shown in Figure 4-10 into OneNote very similar to the way we have just seen for inserting videos. The Files option is accessible under the Insert menu, and files can be embedded into OneNote from the local machine, camera, and online resources as shown in Figure 4-8.

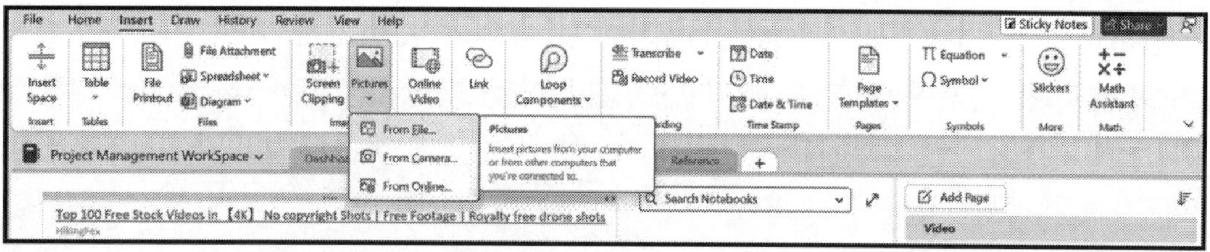

***Figure 4-8.** Access insert picture option*

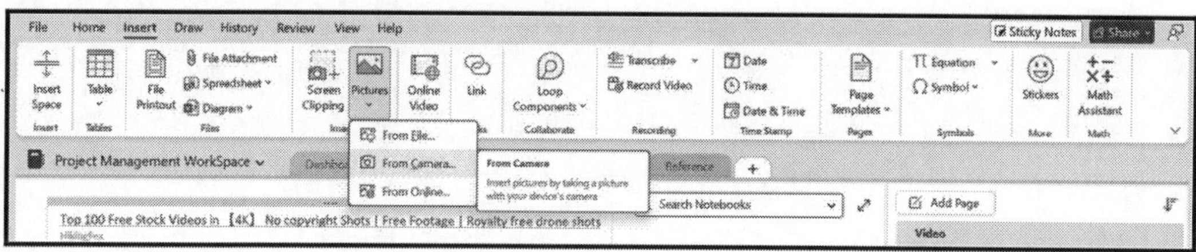

***Figure 4-9.** Insert picture from camera*

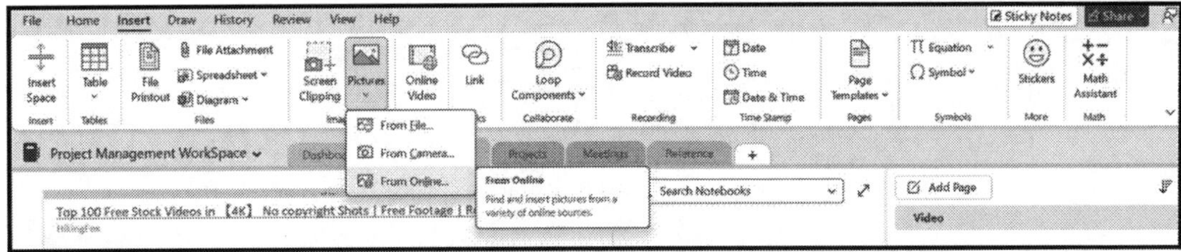

Figure 4-10. *Insert picture from online resources*

Besides video files and pictures, one can insert links into OneNote very similar to the way we did while following the steps for videos and images. The option to insert links is also available under the Insert menu as shown in Figure 4-11. This feature is very helpful to group useful links in a single place.

Finally, one can insert files as attachment from the local machine as shown in Figure 4-12, as well as existing Excel files and new Excel files as shown in Figure 4-13. One can also insert existing Visio and new Visio files as shown in Figure 4-14.

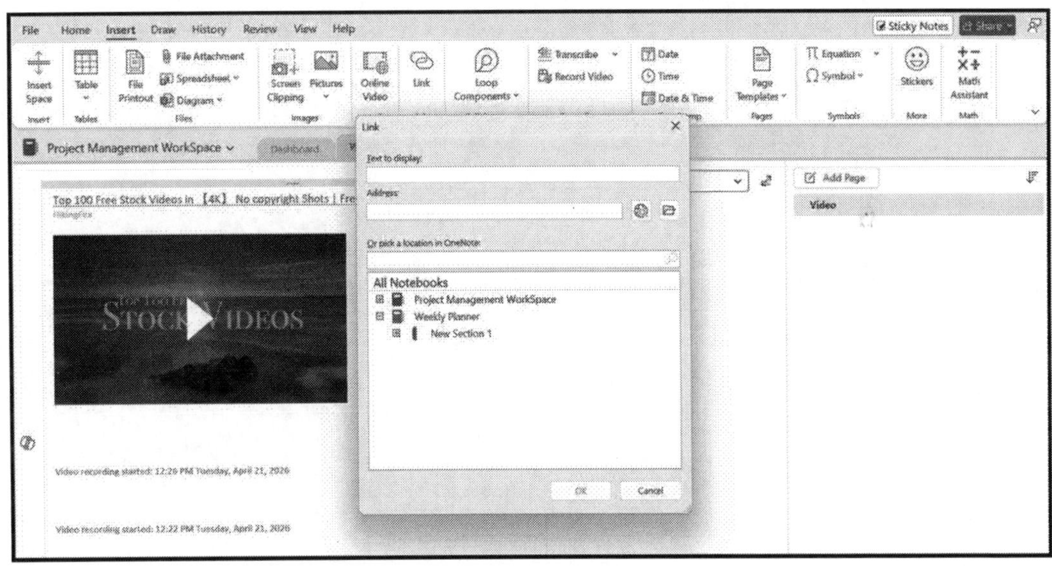

Figure 4-11. *Insert links into OneNote*

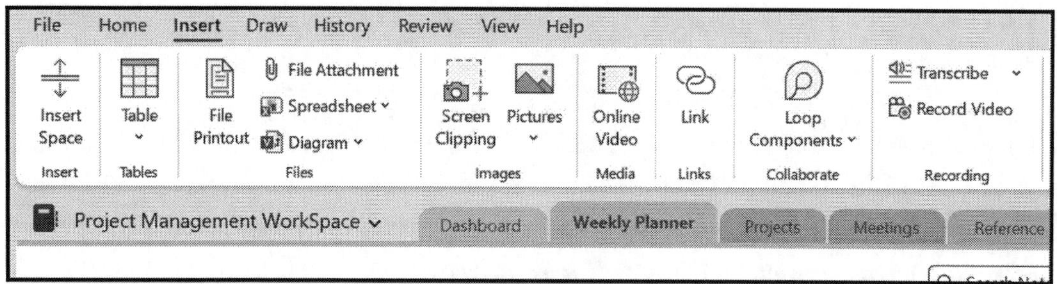

Figure 4-12. *Insert files as attachment into OneNote*

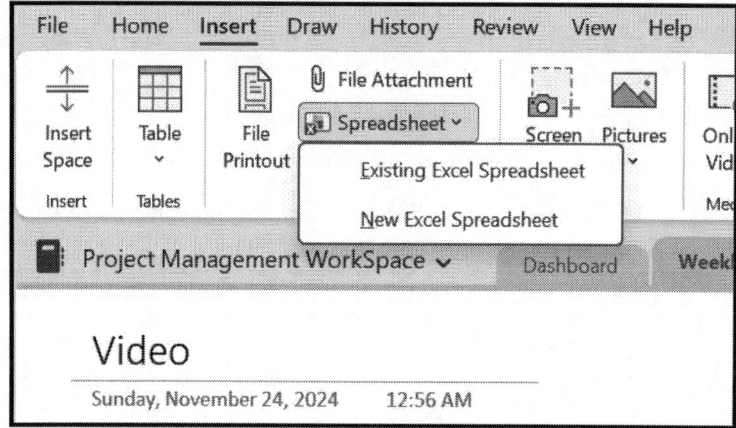

Figure 4-13. *Insert Excel as attachment into OneNote*

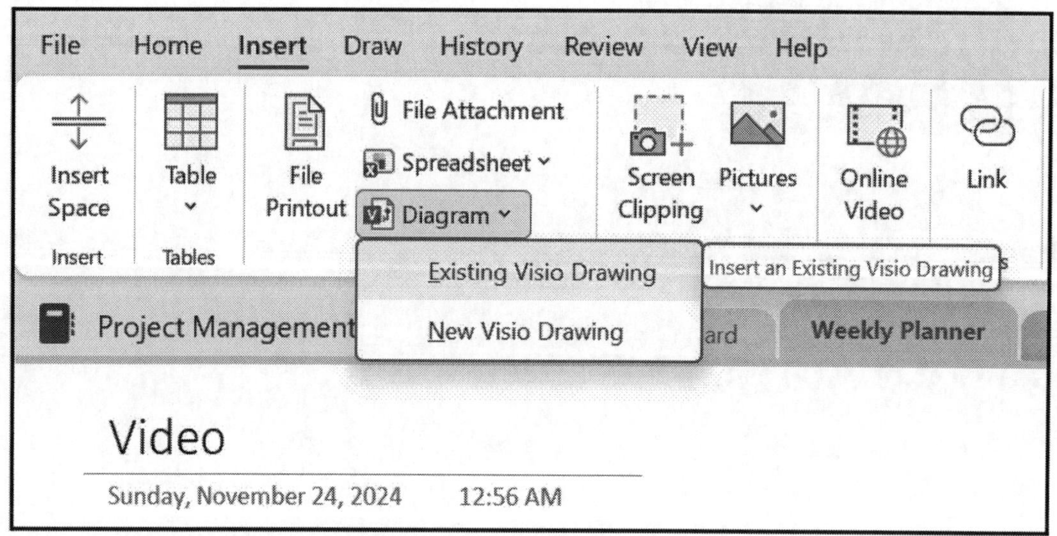

Figure 4-14. *Insert Visio as attachment into OneNote*

So far we have seen where to find OneNote commands and how to use collaboration features like embedding media, inserting files or links, and sharing content. The next section will demonstrate how Copilot guidance covers working with your notes—summarizing, creating action lists, and drafting plans—based on notebook content and your prompt. Outputs vary depending on your license, settings, and platform and should be reviewed before use.

Collaboration pages guide you through user interface (UI) steps for sharing and embedding content, while Copilot pages offer AI-driven examples for transforming notes into summaries or lists. Always verify names, dates, and decisions in Copilot outputs before sharing.

The interface provides consistent tools for configuring collaboration, whereas Copilot offers context-based suggestions but doesn't replace manual controls. Use the UI for accurate sharing and Copilot for refining your work—review all AI-generated drafts to ensure reliability and avoid over-promising.

Use Copilot in OneNote

Microsoft Copilot is an AI-driven assistant designed to boost productivity and efficiency across Microsoft 365 apps like Word, Excel, PowerPoint, Outlook, and Teams. By leveraging large language models and Microsoft Graph data, Copilot understands user context and generates relevant outputs such as drafting documents, analyzing data, creating presentations, and summarizing communications. It also streamlines collaboration and allows organizations to build custom AI assistants with Copilot Studio. Copilot simplifies complex tasks, automates routine processes, and operates within Microsoft's secure and compliant framework, marking a significant advance in digital assistance. In this chapter, we will see how Copilot serves as an AI assistant within Microsoft OneNote, providing support for tasks such as summarizing notes into actionable items, creating to-do lists, and generating project plans. Copilot facilitates the identification of essential information within your notes, enabling effective decision-making and improving comprehension of context and key insights.

Microsoft uses the name "Copilot" for several different products. Before starting this course, let me clarify how the Copilot name applies to using it in OneNote. If you visit Microsoft's official website at microsoft.com/microsoft-copilot and scroll down, you'll see that to enable Copilot in OneNote or other Microsoft 365 applications (like Word or PowerPoint), you need a paid Copilot subscription through either a personal account or a work or school (business) account. For individuals, the subscription is called Copilot Pro, which allows access to Copilot features in Microsoft 365 apps such as Word, Excel, PowerPoint, OneNote, and Outlook. If your Microsoft account is associated with work or school, that's a business account, requiring a Copilot for Microsoft 365 subscription. Usually, if you're using a work or school account, your IT department will handle your Copilot setup, so Copilot will be available in your Microsoft 365 apps automatically.

Summarize Your Notes

Copilot efficiently summarizes meeting notes, extracting essential points and highlighting critical information. For instance, consider the notes from the Minutes of Meeting (MoM) of an IT service stakeholders meeting as shown in Figure 4-15.

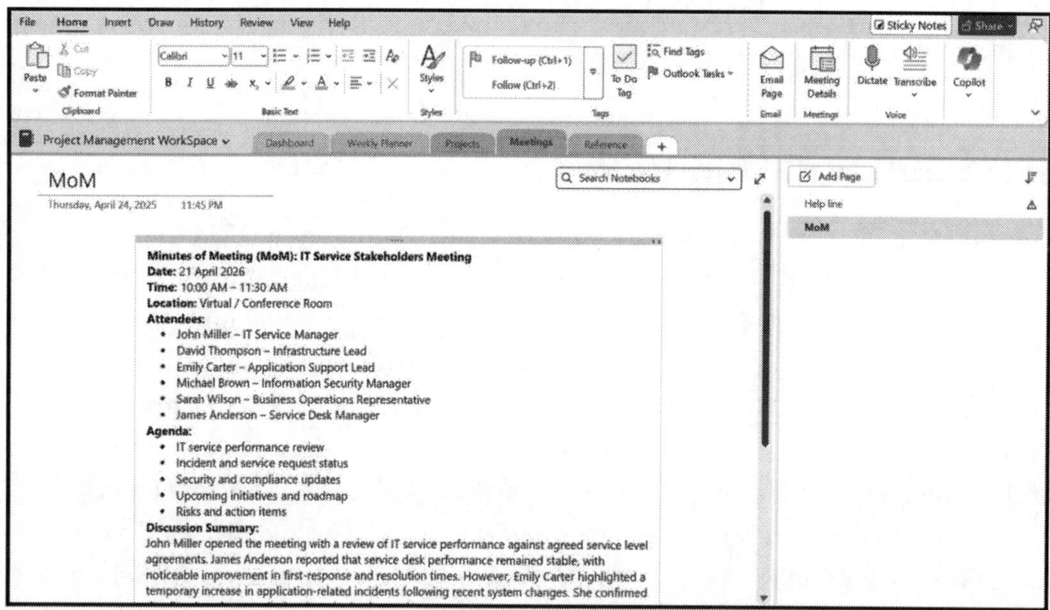

Figure 4-15. *MoM of an IT service stakeholders meeting*

Given the substantial amount of content, users may need to prepare for subsequent meetings while also providing an overview to management. As shown in Figure 4-16, by selecting Copilot from the home ribbon, the Copilot pane opens, offering options such as summarizing notes, drafting to-do lists, listing pros and cons, and several others as shown in Figure 4-17 and additional default prompts as shown in Figure 4-18.

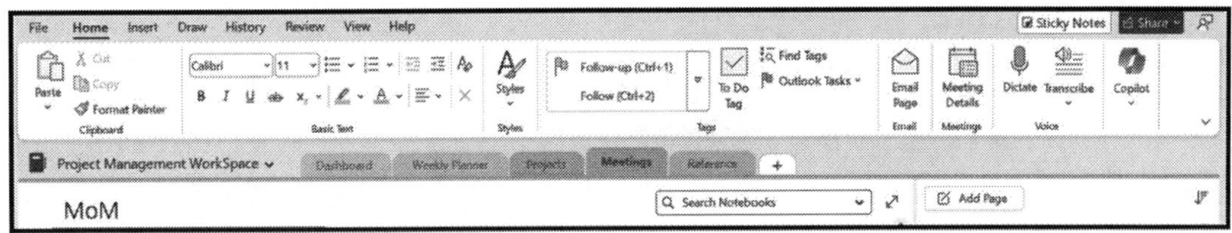

Figure 4-16. *Copilot in the ribbon*

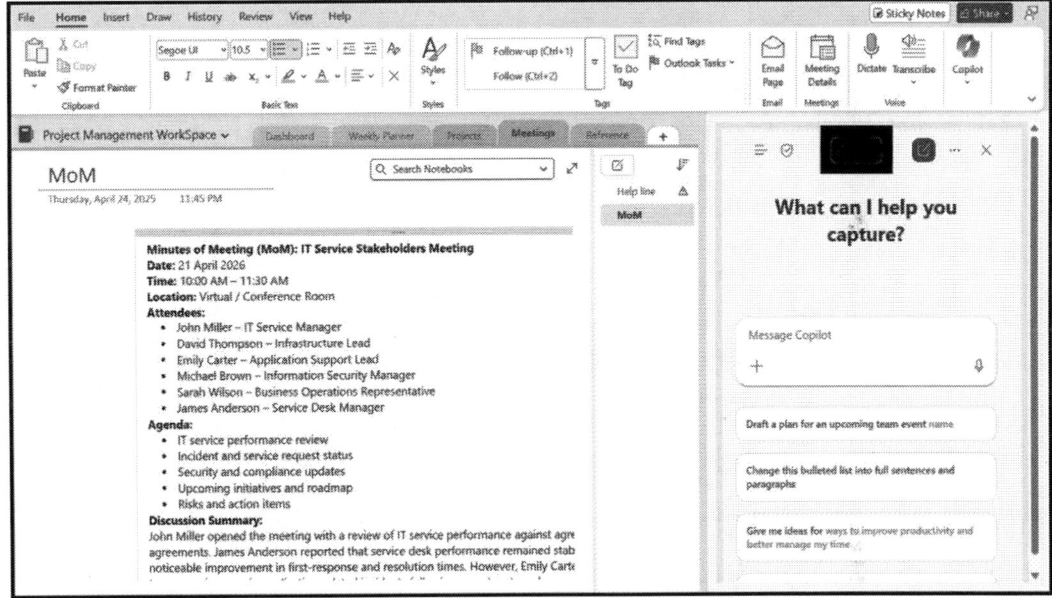

Figure 4-17. *Copilot in OneNote with default prompts*

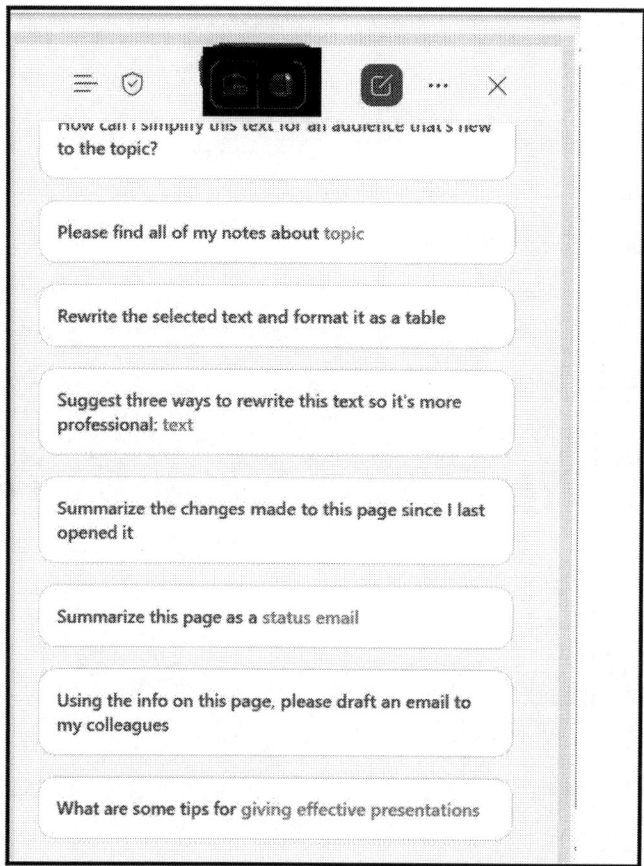

Figure 4-18. *Additional default prompts*

To generate a tailored summary, users can enter instructions in the compose box—for example, "Create a summary of these meeting notes. At the end, provide a bullet list of action items, and create a separate section highlighting Emily's contributions to the meeting" as shown in Figure 4-19. This ensures that specific requirements are addressed, such as detailing individual input for management review. To maintain a professional perspective, users might add "Compose this summary in the third person," which prevents direct address and enhances suitability for managerial communication.

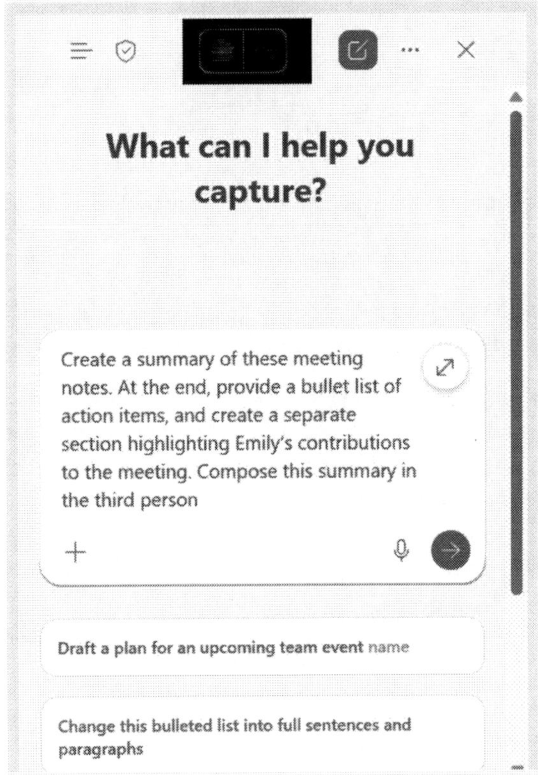

Figure 4-19. *Create a summary of MoM—prompt*

The prompt applies to all notes unless a particular text is selected. Upon sending the instructions, Copilot produces a comprehensive summary that meets the specified criteria, including action items and a dedicated section for Emily's contributions as shown in Figures 4-20 and 4-21. The summary can then be copied into emails or documents after review and necessary edits as shown in Figure 4-21.

Copilot also facilitates further analysis by enabling follow-up questions or custom prompts. Suggested queries—such as identifying main topics discussed or listing Sarah's or John's assigned action items—allow for focused examination of meeting outcomes. Additionally, users can request insights, such as unique selling points derived from the notes. Even when a complete summary is not required, Copilot offers valuable perspectives and helps distill critical information from meeting documentation.

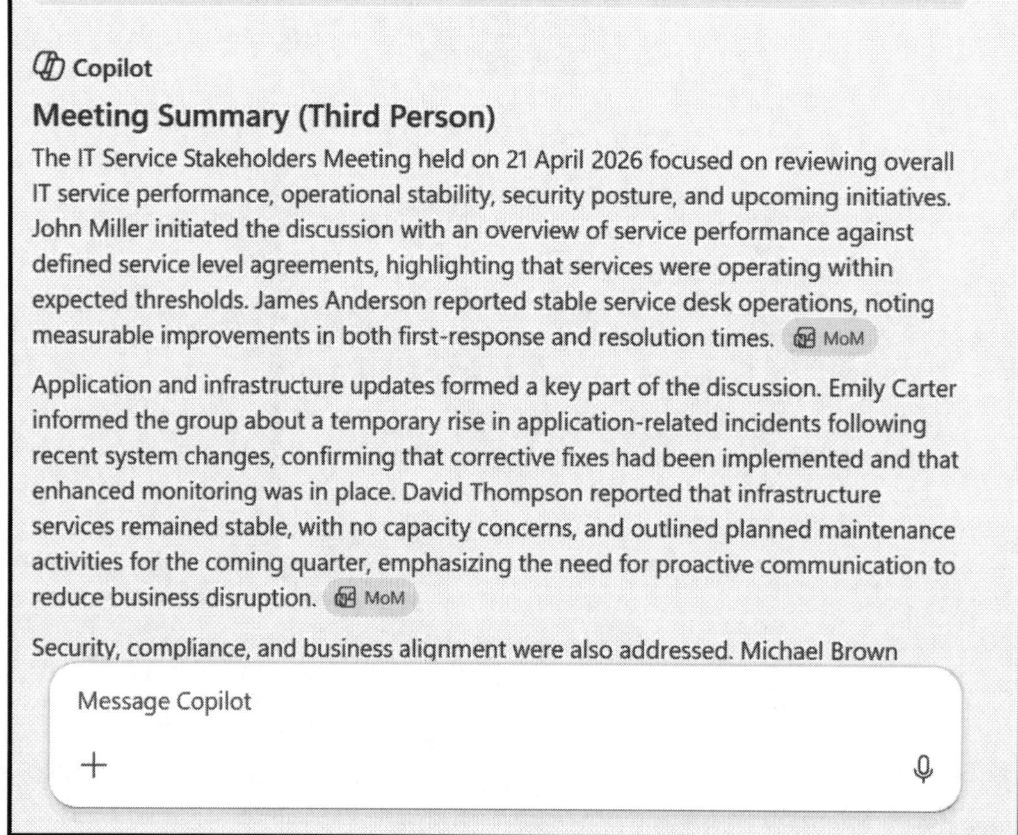

Figure 4-20. *Summary created by Copilot*

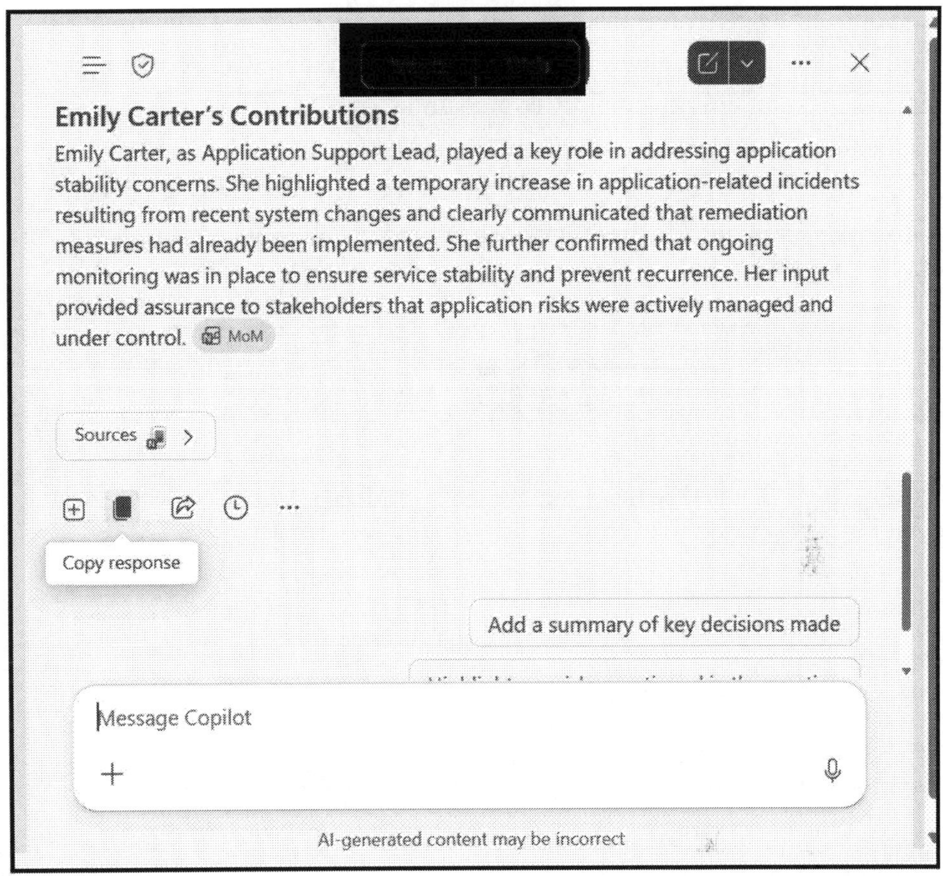

Figure 4-21. *Entire summary copy option*

Create a To-Do List

Previously, we demonstrated how Copilot can efficiently generate summaries from your notes, including action items and follow-up tasks. Another effective method for utilizing Copilot is to request the generation of a structured to-do list. This functionality is particularly beneficial when managing extensive notes and determining priority tasks may seem challenging or overwhelming.

In this scenario, I am working with meeting notes involving John, Emily, David, and Sarah. Each participant is assigned specific tasks, as referenced within the notes. To streamline these responsibilities, we will navigate to the Copilot pane, enter a prompt requesting extraction of to-do lists organized by individual meeting participants, and submit this request as shown in Figure 4-22.

Copilot promptly generates distinct to-do lists for each attendee, complete with citations that allow you to easily verify the source of each item within your notes. The resulting task lists can be conveniently copied and shared via email or integrated into other applications to assist team members in tracking and completing their assignments as shown in Figure 4-23. Further, you can convert these into a OneNote checklist format, create a task table suitable for sharing in Teams or Outlook, or generate a follow-up reminder text based on these to-dos as shown in Figure 4-24.

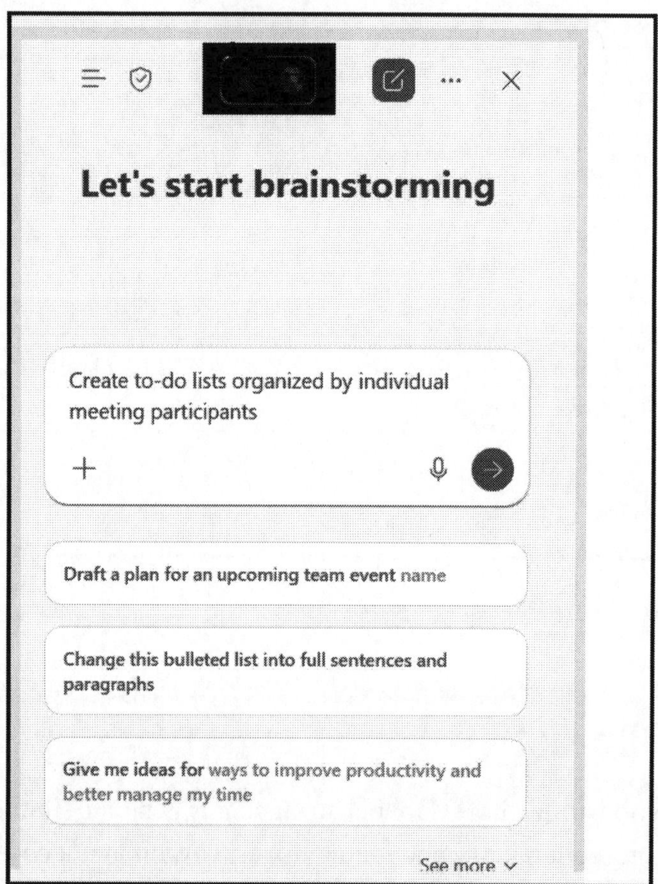

Figure 4-22. *Prompt to create a to-do list*

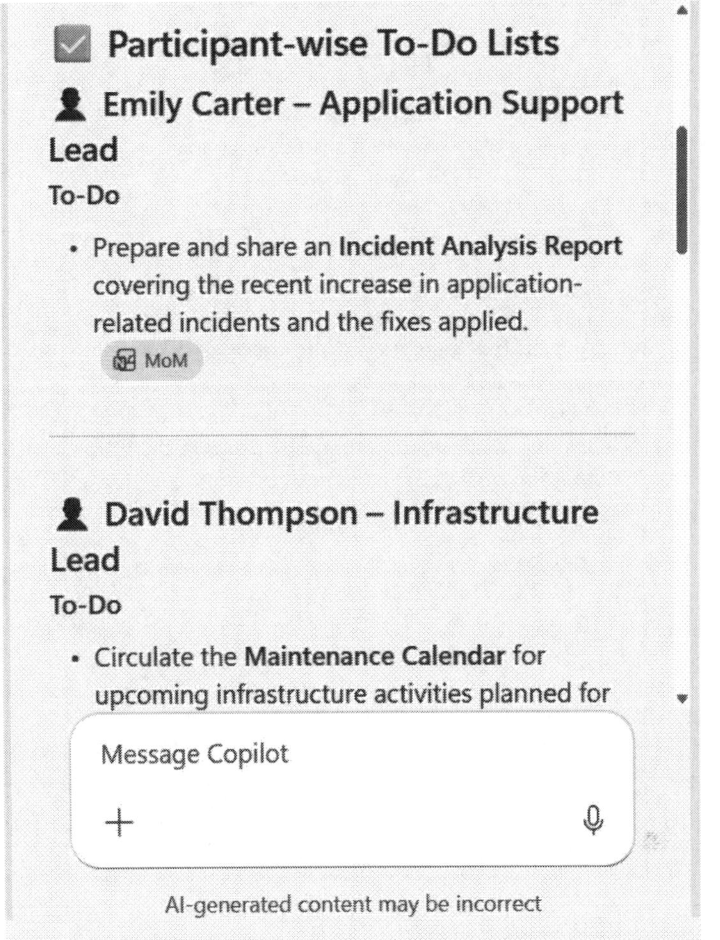

Figure 4-23. *Generated to-do list*

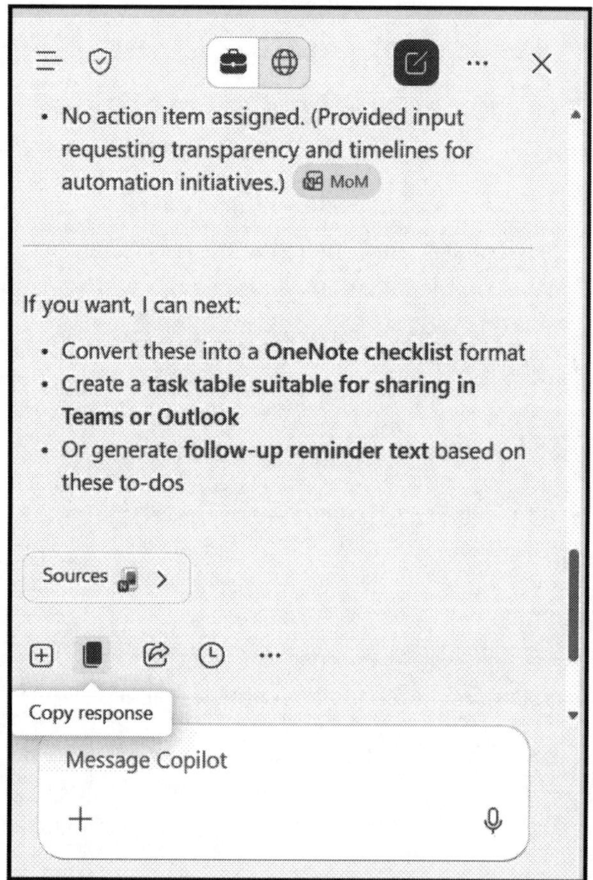

Figure 4-24. *More options to process to-do list*

Generate a Project Plan

Here is an example of how Copilot in OneNote can facilitate the efficient organization of meeting notes into a structured, actionable plan. In this scenario, we have compiled notes from a meeting focused on an IT Project: Enterprise IT Service Management (ITSM) Transformation project, encompassing various aspects such as budgets, timelines, design concepts, legal considerations, marketing, and more. When tasked with developing a comprehensive project plan to outline and prioritize the necessary development tasks, Copilot offers a streamlined solution as shown in Figure 4-25.

Rather than manually parsing extensive information, copying, pasting, and arranging details, users can utilize Copilot by entering a prompt—such as "extract the main tasks from these notes and organize them into an actionable project plan" as shown in Figure 4-26. Within moments, Copilot generates an organized plan, which can then be copied and transferred to applications like Word for further editing and refinement as shown in Figure 4-27.

This approach significantly enhances efficiency compared to manually constructing the project plan while reviewing the notes. Additionally, users can return to OneNote to request further analyses, generate milestone goals, or assign tasks using prompts like "Convert this into a RACI matrix," "Create a management-ready one-page roadmap," or "Reformat it into a PowerPoint/project plan–friendly structure."

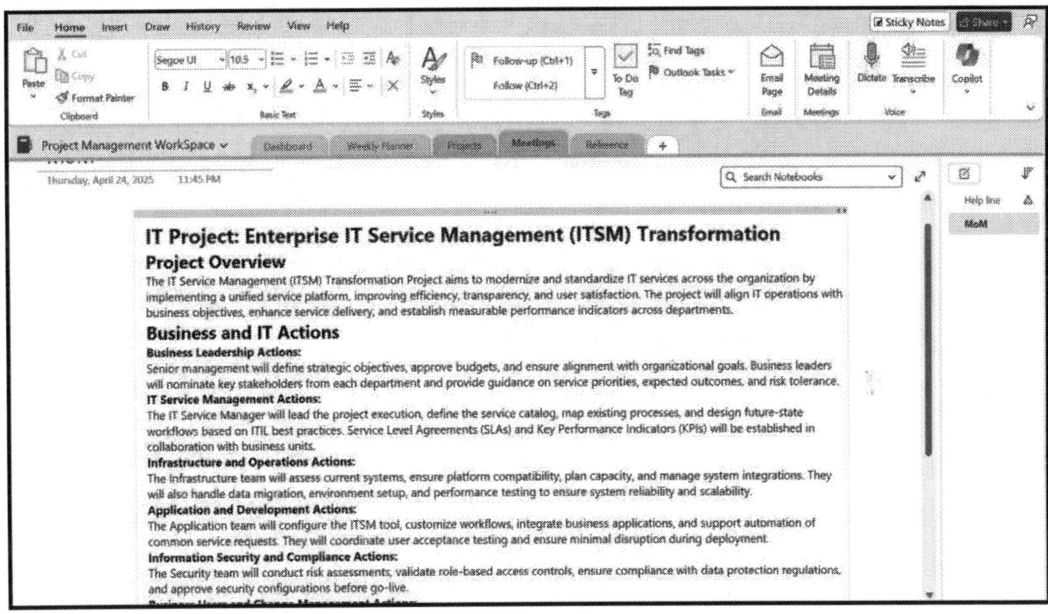

***Figure 4-25.** ITSM project plan*

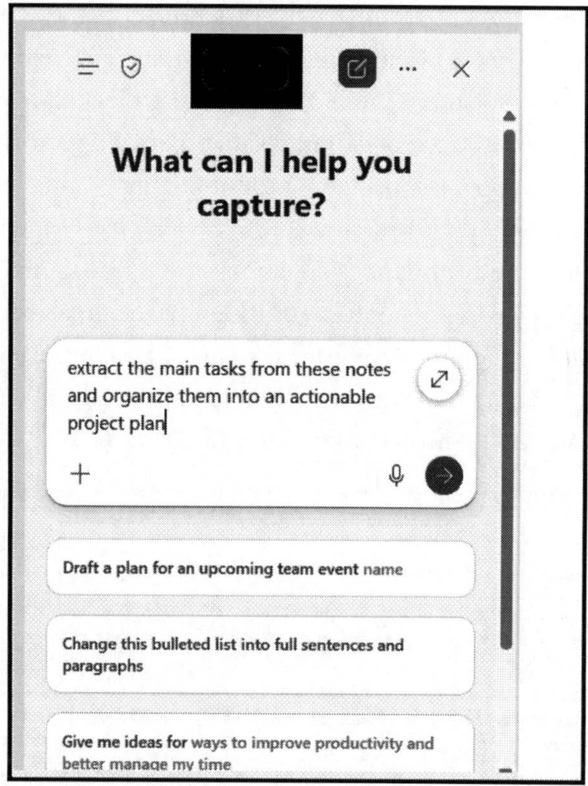

Figure 4-26. *Prompt to generate actionable items*

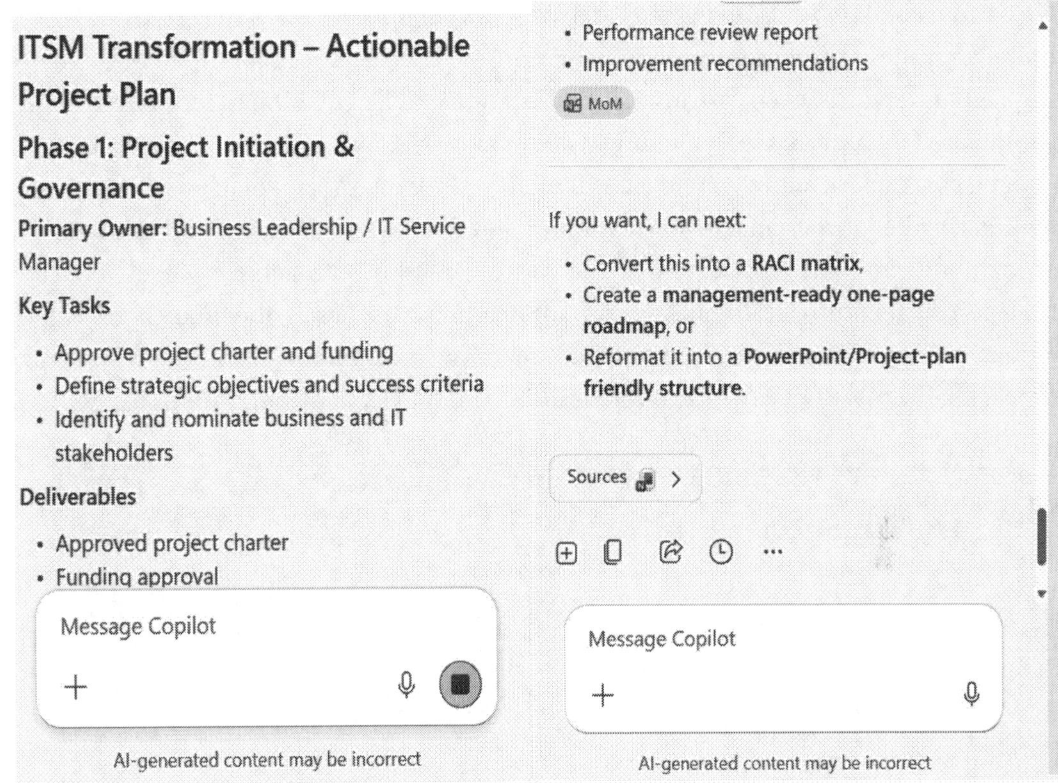

***Figure 4-27.** Automated plan generated by Copilot*

Research Your Notes with Copilot

OneNote is a highly effective application for organizing essential information, events, and tasks. However, managing and retrieving specific details can become challenging when dealing with extensive collections of notes. While OneNote offers a search feature to locate words or phrases, Copilot significantly streamlines the process of finding targeted information across numerous pages. Copilot in OneNote can answer questions using the content of your current notebook page, and it can also use other Microsoft 365 files you have access to as well as information from the internet.

Within OneNote, however, Copilot proves invaluable for efficiently locating information. For example, if you need to recall specific suggestions Emily made regarding marketing and social media plans, you can use Copilot's conversational search in the relevant section, such as Quick Notes. By querying, "*What are the buzzwords that*

Emily said we should be using in the marketing campaign?", as shown in Figure 4-28. Copilot identifies and cites relevant information, such as Emily's recommendation to use campaign buzzwords, even providing direct citations and navigation to the source note.

Similarly, if preparing for a meeting with Sarah and seeking her input on crucial project tasks, Copilot allows you to ask, "Which parts of the project plan has Sarah identified as the most crucial to address immediately?" as shown in Figure 4-29. If no pertinent information is found, ensure the entire section is searchable by deselecting any text. Upon correction, Copilot may report, for instance, that Sarah, the finance manager, emphasized the importance of obtaining itemized costs for approval and exploring bulk purchasing for cost savings, again offering direct references to the relevant notes.

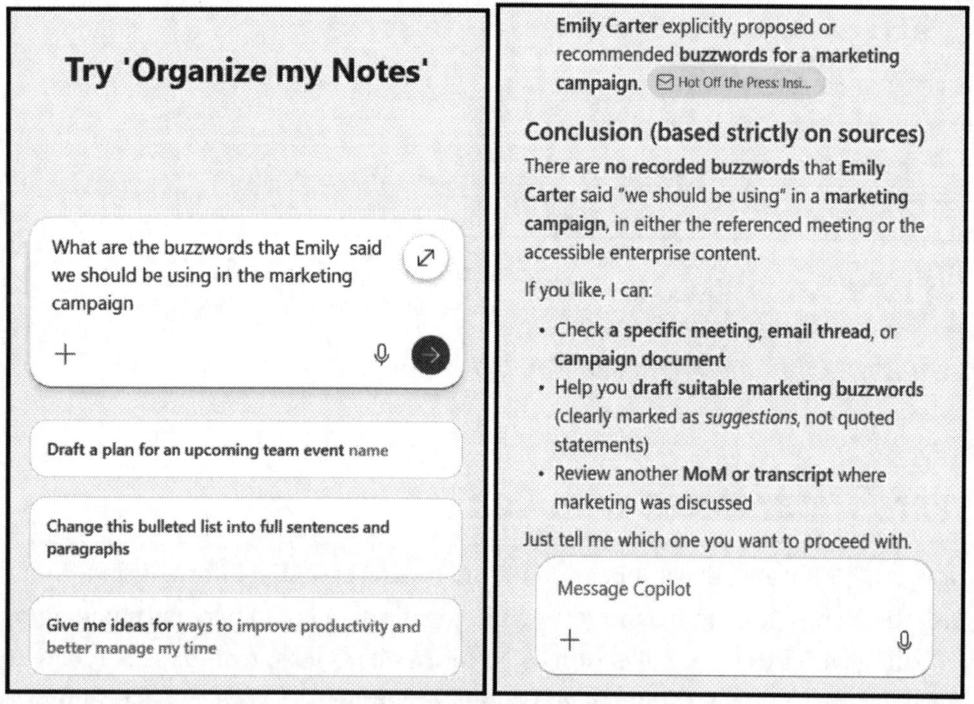

Figure 4-28. *Prompt for Emily's buzzword and no word found*

Unlike the traditional search field, which would require scanning multiple instances individually, Copilot rapidly locates and summarizes the pertinent content. Additional queries might include "Which parts of the project plan does John have reservations about?",

"Which tasks should Sarah be working on?", or "Which vendors are being considered for fixture installations?" Copilot enhances productivity by enabling users to quickly identify and act upon key information without extensive manual review.

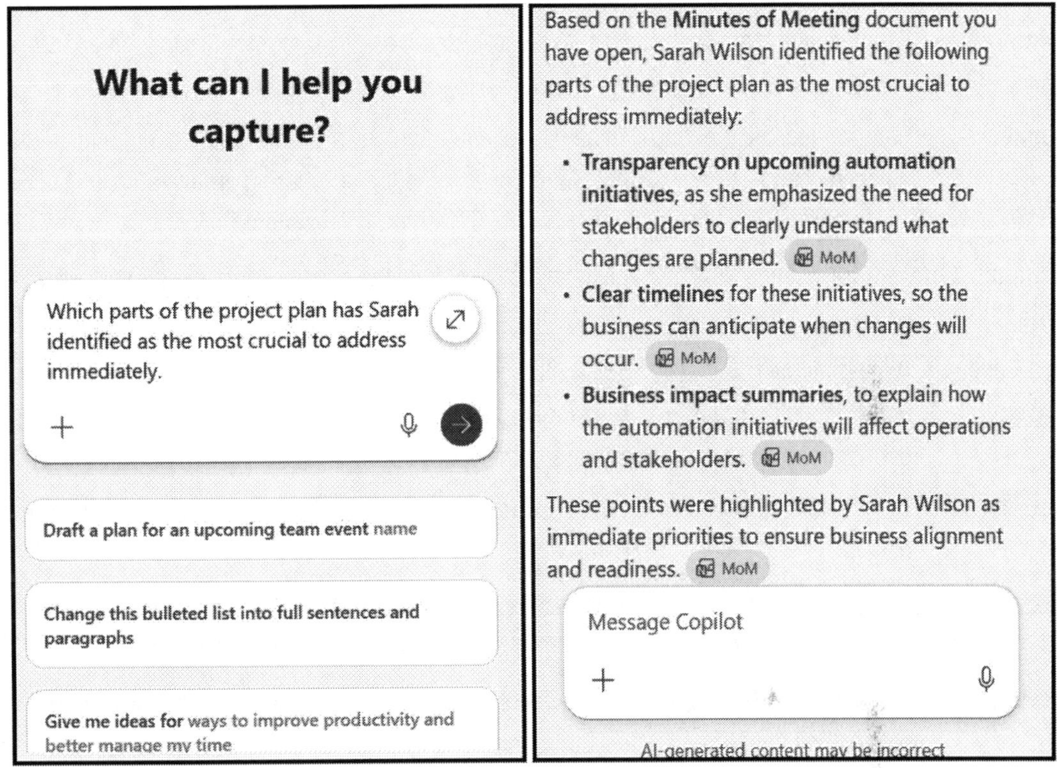

Figure 4-29. *Sarah's critical points were discovered through Copilot*

When to Use OneNote, Microsoft Loop, and SharePoint Online

Along with multimedia and AI capabilities as shown in this chapter for content management, Microsoft offers several workplace tools, each with unique roles for collaboration and content management. OneNote is suitable for flexible note-taking and capturing ideas. Microsoft Loop enables real-time, dynamic teamwork with instant updates. SharePoint acts as an enterprise platform for secure document management and compliance. Choosing the right tool improves productivity, streamlines workflows, and supports effective information control as shown in Table 4-1.

Table 4-1. Comparison between OneNote, Loop, and SharePoint

Scenario/ Purpose	OneNote	Microsoft Loop	SharePoint
Primary Use	Personal and team note-taking	Real-time collaborative workspaces	Document management and intranet
Best For	Capturing ideas, meeting notes, research	Dynamic collaboration and co-creation	Storing, managing, and sharing organizational content
Content Type	Free-form notes (text, images, drawings, audio)	Live components (tables, lists, tasks)	Structured documents, files, and pages
Use Case Example	Writing meeting notes, study material, brainstorming	Team planning, task tracking, project collaboration	Department document repository, policies, records
Structure	Notebook → sections → pages	Workspaces → pages → components	Sites → libraries → folders/ files
Ideal Users	Students, individuals, small teams	Agile teams, project groups	Organizations, departments, enterprise teams
When to Use	When you need flexible note-taking and idea capture	When teams need live collaboration and evolving content	When you need structured, secure, and compliant document storage

Microsoft Copilot integrates AI with productivity tools to speed up decisions, increase creativity, and simplify workflows. By automating tasks and improving collaboration, it serves as a powerful assistant for the modern digital workplace.

This chapter outlined how Microsoft OneNote enables rich content creation by embedding multimedia like YouTube and Vimeo videos, supporting in-app video recording, and integrating files, images, links, Excel sheets, and Visio diagrams for centralized resource management. It also introduced Copilot, an AI assistant that streamlines note management by summarizing meetings, generating action items, creating tailored to-do lists, and turning unstructured notes into project plans. Finally, we explored how we can use different Microsoft services such as Microsoft OneNote, Loop, and SharePoint Online for content management.

In the next chapter, we will discuss features that help manage OneNote more effectively, such as adding or removing tags, searching within OneNote, applying styles from other content to your text, and formatting notes with bullets and tables.

CHAPTER 5

Managing and Searching OneNote

In the previous chapter, we discovered different features which help in collaborating and sharing OneNote such as embedding videos into OneNote, inserting documents in OneNote, sharing notebooks with teams and organizations, OneNote + Microsoft Teams integration, OneNote for shared projects. In this chapter, we will explore functionalities which will assist in managing OneNote such as adding remove tags, searching in OneNote, applying the look of other content to the text, and formatting notes with bullets and tables.

Add Remove Tags

Tags can be applied to notes to facilitate locating all content associated with the same topic as shown in Figure 5-1, which displays a list of tags. This functionality extends beyond individual pages, sections, or notebooks, allowing cross-referencing across multiple open notebooks. Figure 5-2 illustrates examples of a tag, using which one can tag content. Tags can be created and deleted by the end user. By searching for tags, users can quickly find all items sharing a specific tag.

C. Waghmare, *Mastering Microsoft OneNote*, https://doi.org/10.1007/979-8-8688-2866-9_5

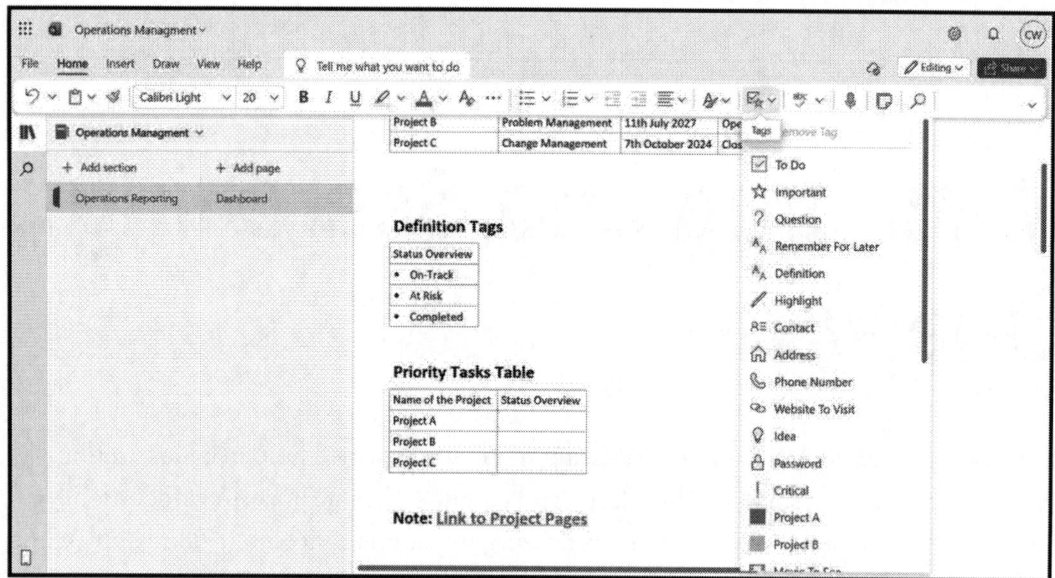

Figure 5-1. *Tagging feature in Microsoft OneNote*

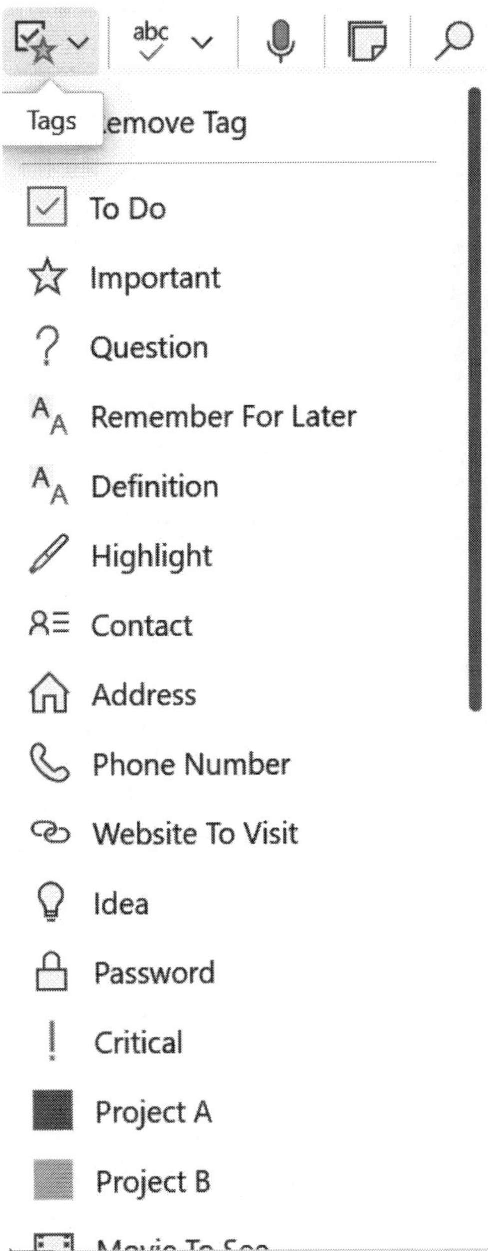

Figure 5-2. *Manage the list of tags*

One can add a tag to a page as shown in Figure 5-3, one can tag a text as shown in Figure 5-4, or one can tag a table as shown in Figure 5-5. One can remove tag as shown in Figure 5-6.

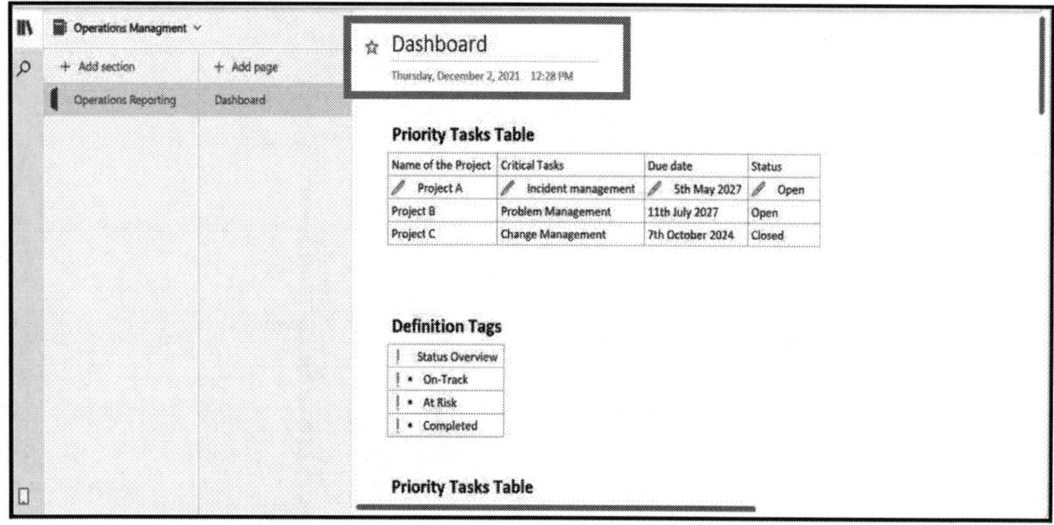

Figure 5-3. *Tagging a page*

Priority Tasks Table

Name of the Project	Critical Tasks	Due date	Status
Project A	Incident management	5th May 2027	Open
Project B	Problem Management	11th July 2027	Open
Project C	Change Management	7th October 2024	Closed

Figure 5-4. *Tagging a text inside a table*

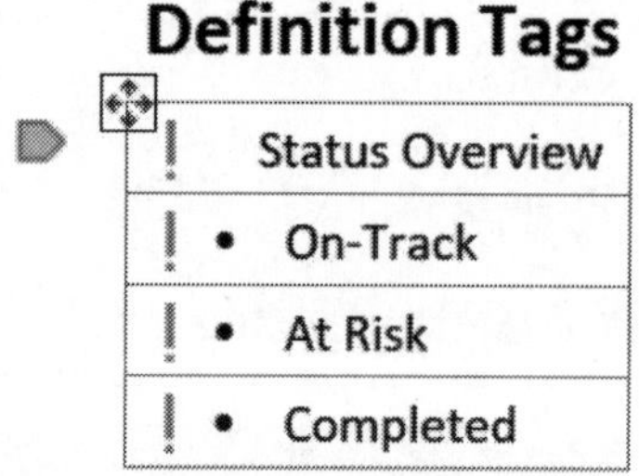

Definition Tags

Status Overview
• On-Track
• At Risk
• Completed

Figure 5-5. *Tagging a table*

Should you wish to delete custom tags, return to the Tags menu, and choose "Remove." Deleting a tag from the list does not remove its assignments within containers. Utilizing tags effectively enables efficient retrieval of notes in the future.

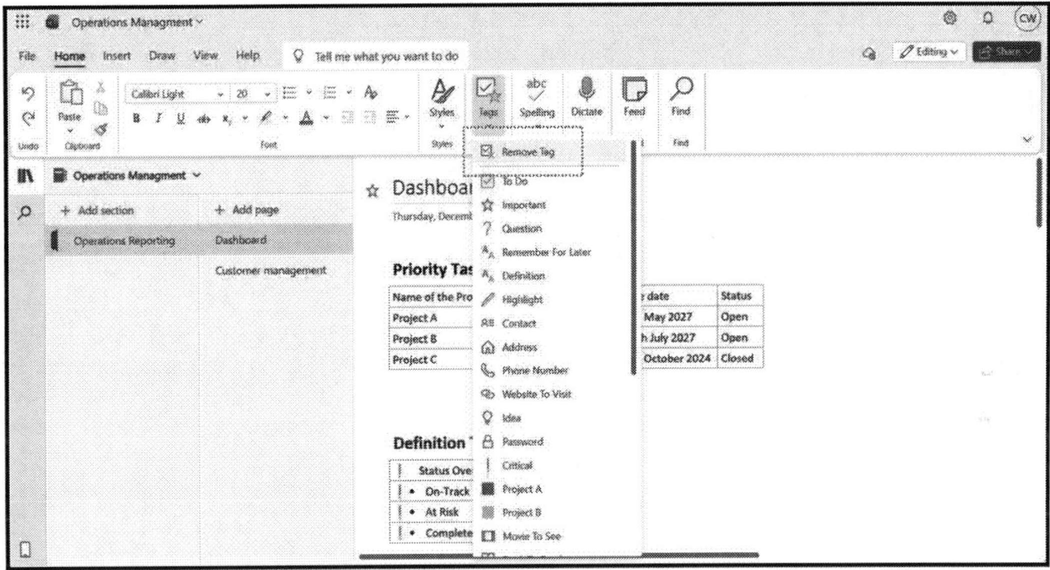

Figure 5-6. *Remove tags*

Search for Microsoft Notes

OneNote offers comprehensive search capabilities that enable users to locate notes efficiently. The platform allows searching by keyword within a page, section, entire notebook, or across all open notebooks, as well as locating tagged notes. To initiate a search, select the magnifying glass icon on the navigation rail, which opens the search pane as shown in Figure 5-7. Search results can be filtered between sections and pages as shown in Figure 5-8. Enter your desired keyword or phrase to search the content you need.

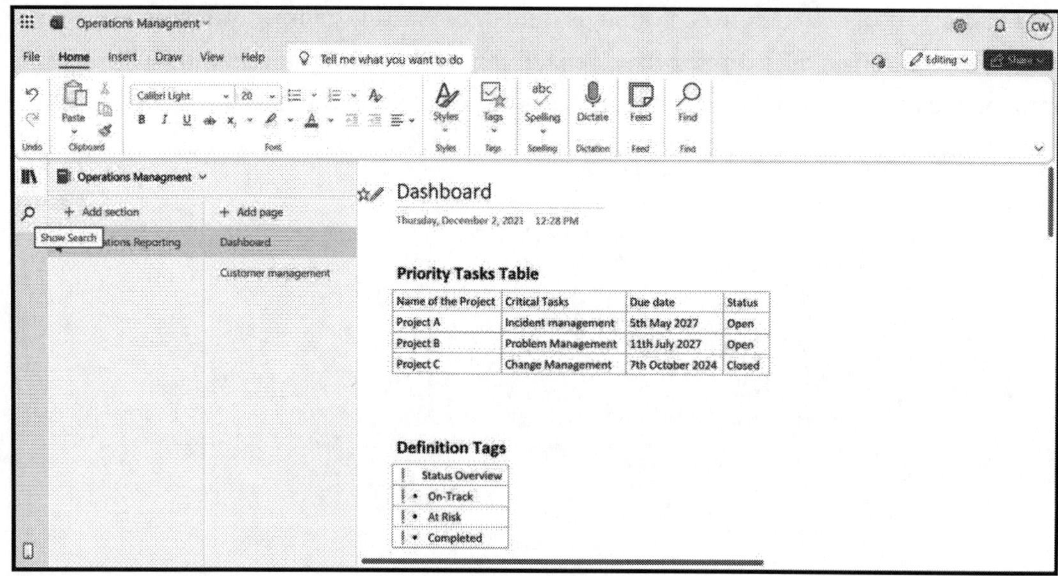

Figure 5-7. *Access search functionality*

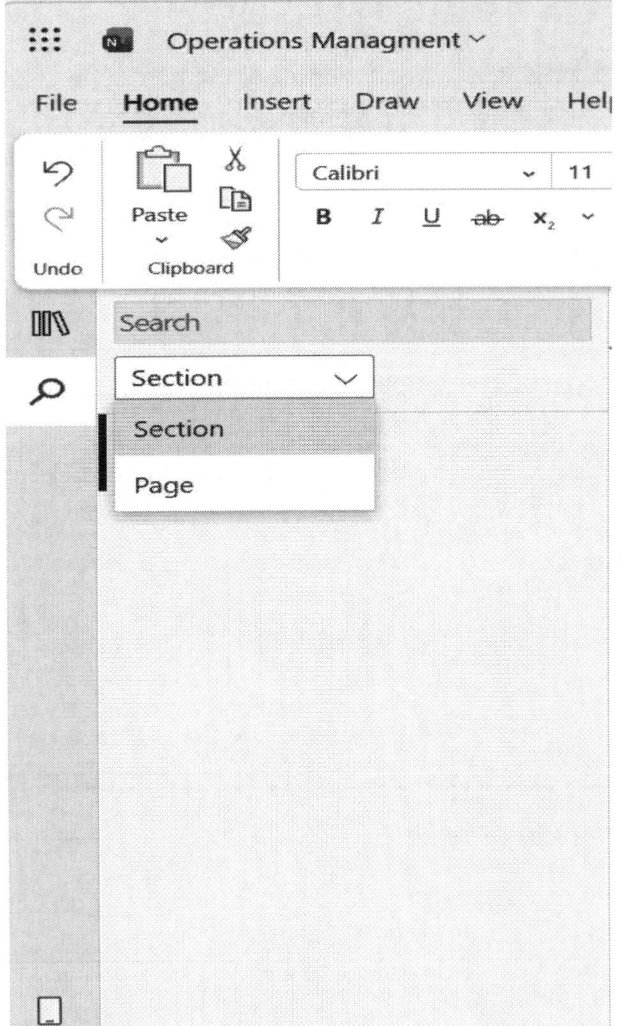

Figure 5-8. *Limiting search results between section and page*

For example, entering "Incident" displays search results categorized into pages and sections. OneNote will indicate pages with "Incident," highlighting matching criteria. Once the keyword “incident” is entered and the scope of search is section as shown in Figure 5-9, the keyword match will get highlighted, and all pages corresponding to the section where there is a match will be displayed in the search result as shown in Figure 5-10. In the figure, the keyword match is seen in two pages: Dashboard and Incident Management.

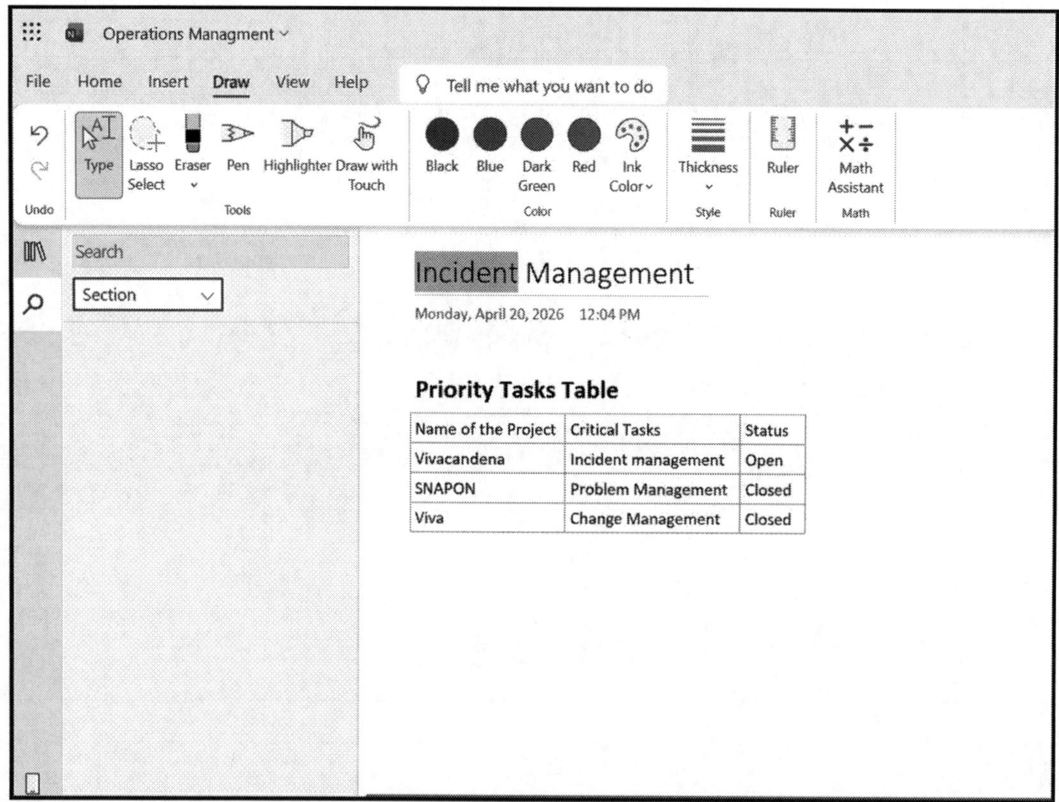

Figure 5-9. *Defining scope search*

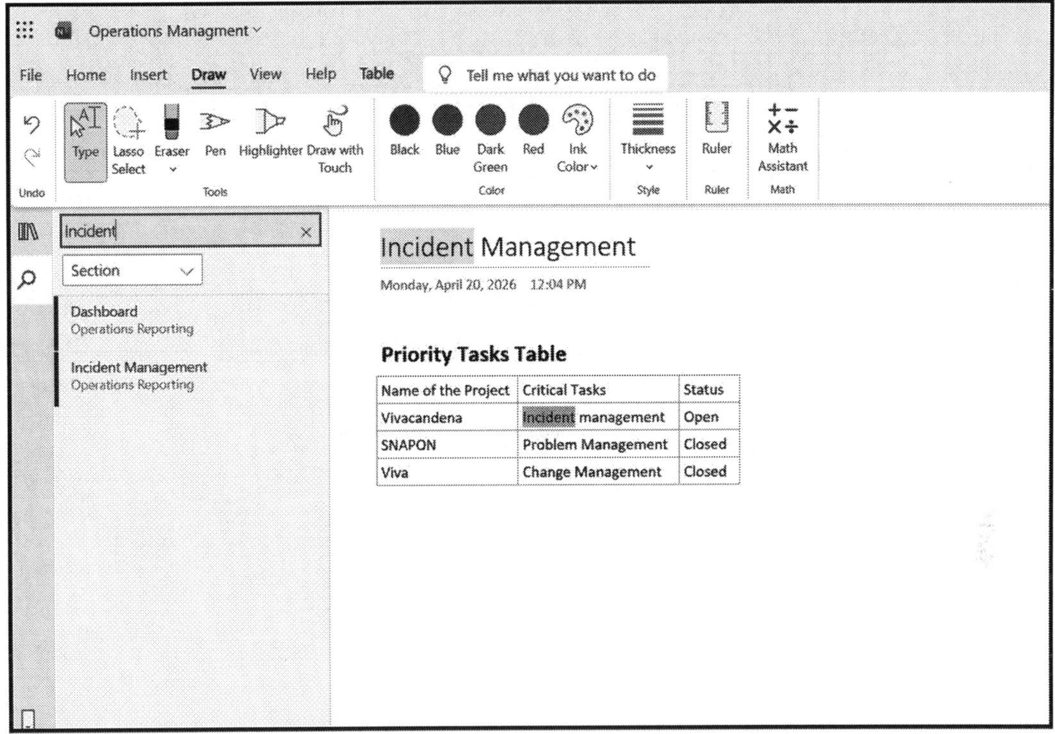

***Figure 5-10.** Search result*

One can define the scope of search to a specific page only, in this case "Incident Management," as shown in Figure 5-11, and the search result will display matches from that page only as shown in Figure 5-12. To exit search results, simply click the magnifying glass once again to hide the search pane as shown in Figure 5-13. Additionally, keyboard shortcuts enhance navigation: Ctrl+E initiates a search across all open notebooks, while Ctrl+F focuses the search on the current page. These features collectively facilitate rapid and precise note retrieval within OneNote.

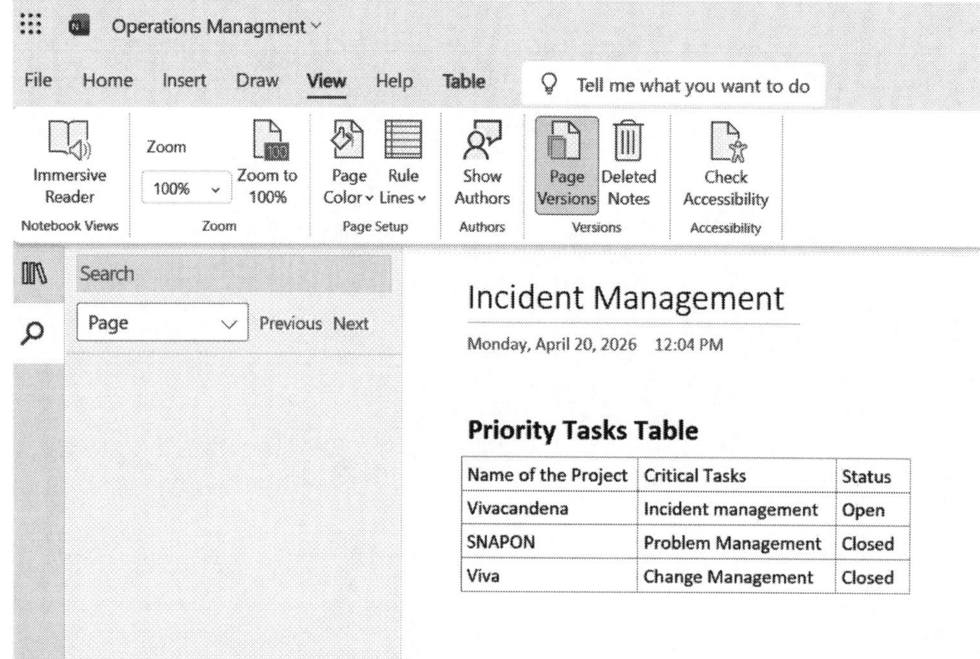

Figure 5-11. *Scope of search limited to a specific page*

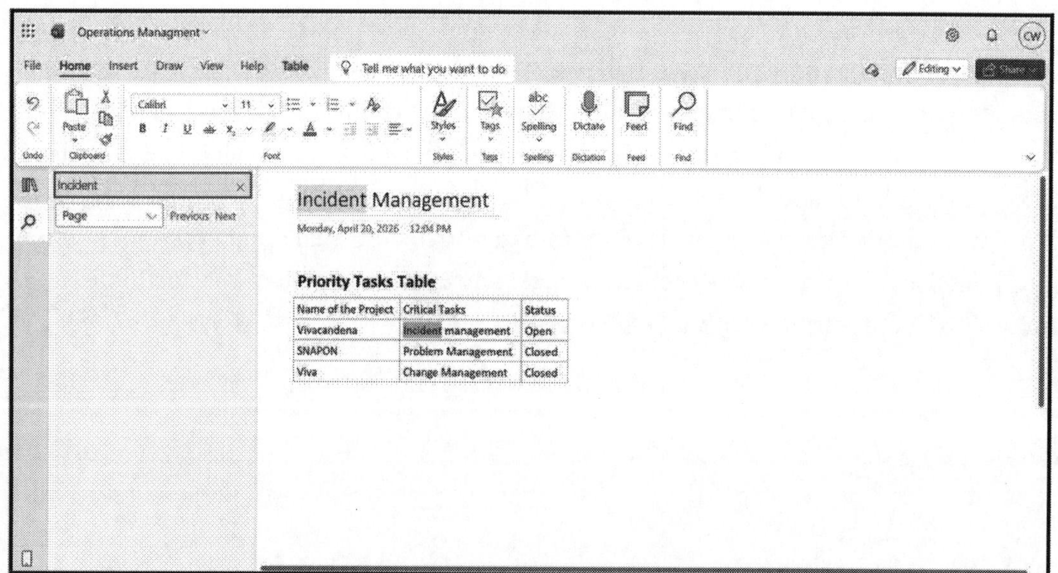

Figure 5-12. *Search result from a specific page chosen*

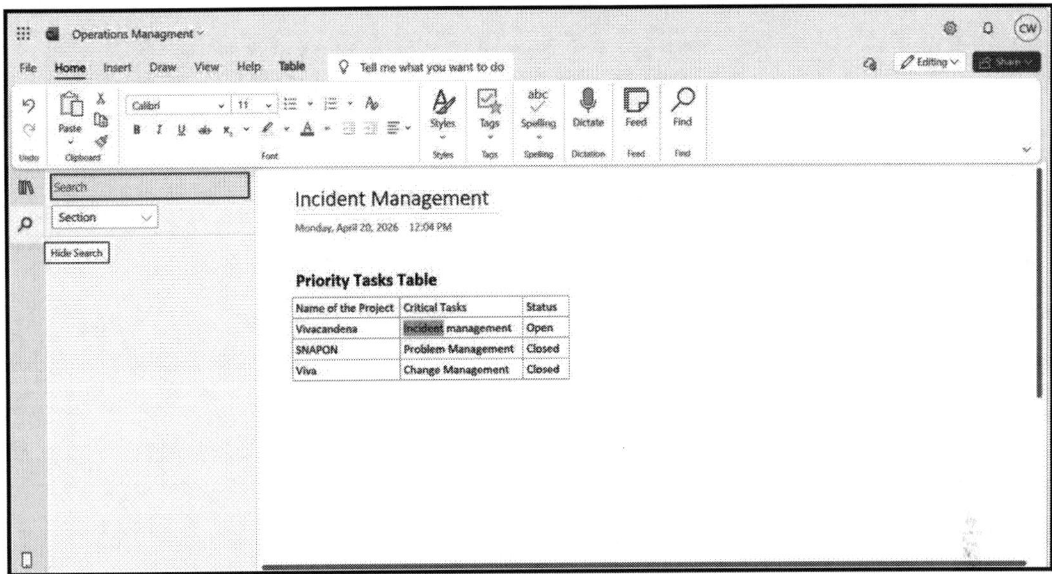

Figure 5-13. *Hide Search*

Each note container in a notebook includes metadata such as the creation date, time, and author information. To identify the author of a note, from the View menu click Show Authors, and to find versions of a page, click Page Versions as shown in Figures 5-14 and 5-14-1.

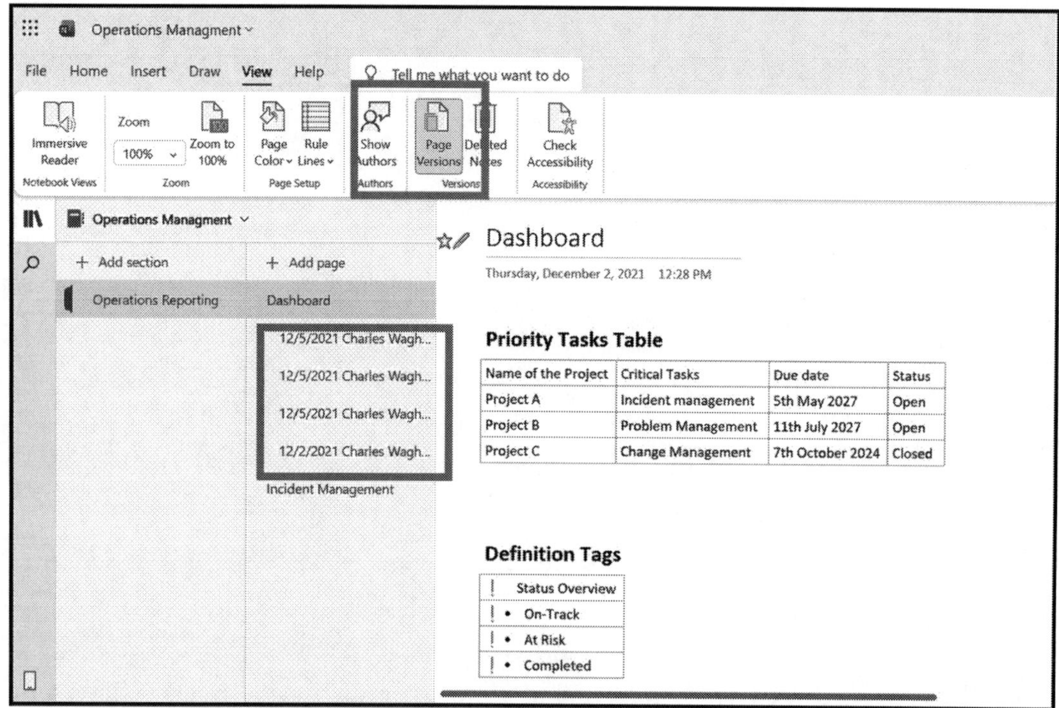

***Figure 5-14.** Access OneNote metadata*

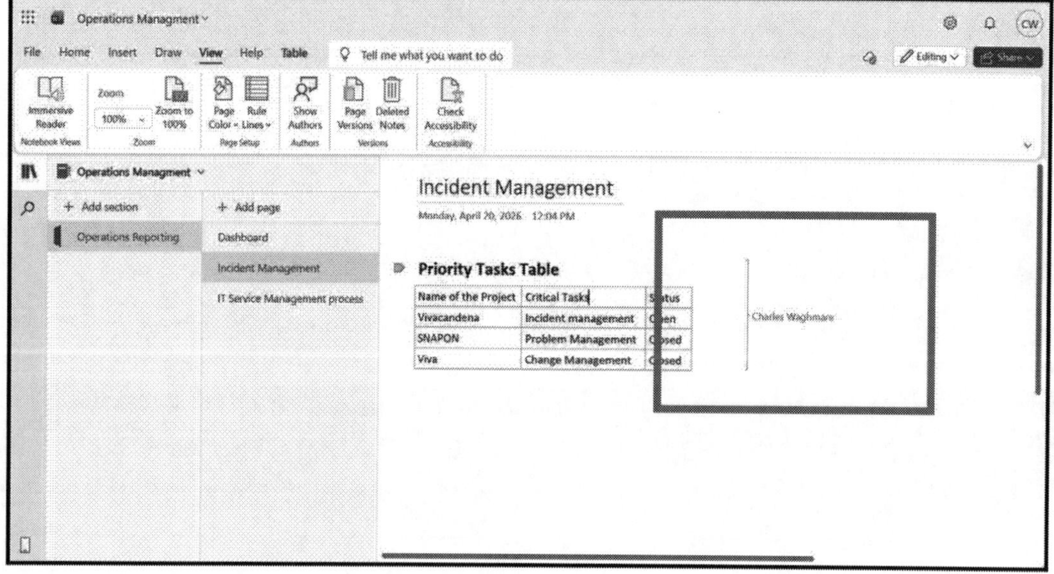

***Figure 5-14-1.** Displayed author name*

Once version history is accessed, we can restore or delete previous versions as shown in Figure 5-15.

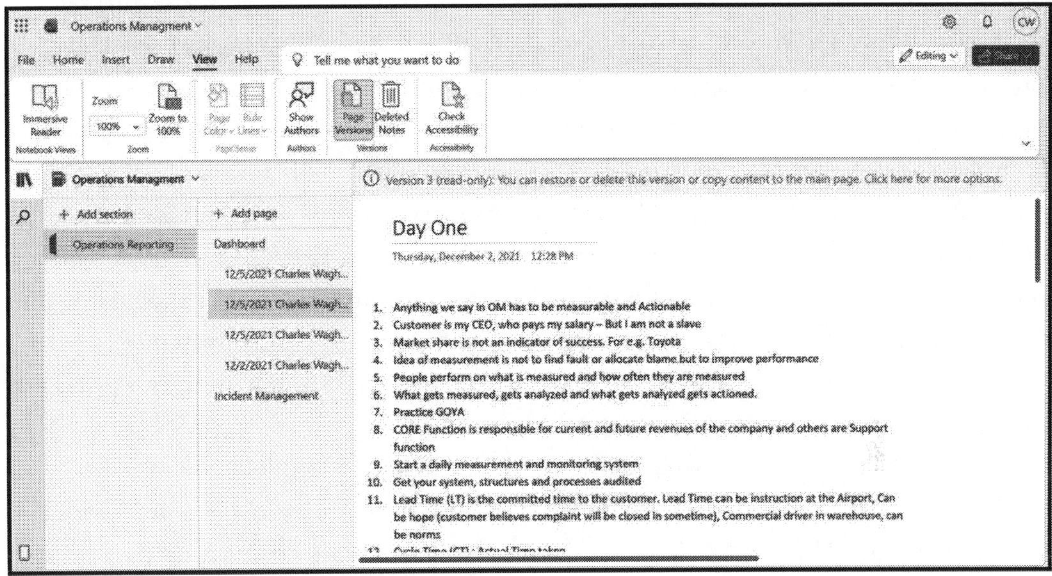

Figure 5-15. *Access version history*

Search Capability with OCR-Based Search, Audio Transcript Search, and Handwritten Notes

Microsoft OneNote offers advanced search features thanks to its optical character recognition (OCR) technology. This lets users find information not just from typed text, but also from images and embedded files, turning OneNote into a powerful knowledge store. When you add an image, scanned document, or screenshot to a page, OneNote uses OCR to extract any readable text automatically, so even content that isn't typed becomes searchable. This is especially helpful in workplaces where people save whiteboard photos, printed reports, or meeting notes as images. Searching across different content types saves time and boosts productivity by removing the need to rewrite or reorganize info. You can search within pages, sections, or entire notebooks, whether they're local or synced with OneDrive. While OCR accuracy depends on image quality and formatting, this feature makes OneNote a versatile tool for handling both organized and unstructured visual data.

OneNote allows users to search within audio recordings, making it a powerful tool for capturing information. You can record meetings, lectures, or discussions right in a OneNote page, with the app linking these recordings to any notes you take during the session. Although OneNote may not provide complete transcripts like dedicated transcription tools, it lets you index recordings by time when you type notes as you listen. This syncing of written notes and audio means you can easily jump to specific parts of the recording by clicking on your notes. Some versions, especially those integrated with Microsoft 365, offer speech recognition that turns spoken words into searchable text. This is helpful if you miss something important during a live discussion—you can later search keywords and quickly find the related audio segments. Together, note linking and partial transcription make it easier to retrieve information, especially from meetings or training sessions. However, how well this works depends on how detailed your notes are during the recording and the quality of the captured audio.

OneNote excels at handling handwritten notes, thanks to its advanced ink recognition technology. Users can search their handwritten notes just like they would with typed entries. This is especially handy for people who enjoy using a stylus or touchscreen—such as on tablets or digital pens. When you write by hand, OneNote's recognition engine converts your handwriting into searchable text without changing how your original script looks. This means you get the authentic feel of handwriting along with powerful digital search tools. Students and professionals alike can quickly jot down ideas, diagrams, or meeting notes, then effortlessly find what they need later simply by typing keywords into the search bar. This makes reviewing large volumes of notes much easier. The system supports multiple languages and adapts to different handwriting styles, becoming more accurate as you use it. However, neat handwriting is important because messy writing may lead to less precise searches. Ultimately, this feature brings together traditional note-taking and modern digital convenience in a seamless way.

As Microsoft OneNote notebooks become larger and more complex, performance issues may arise that impact both usability and efficiency. High volumes of content, such as multimedia files and substantial note collections, can lead to slower processing, synchronization difficulties, and diminished responsiveness—particularly within collaborative or cloud-based settings. Some challenges are shown below:

- **Slow Loading Times**: Notebooks containing extensive sections, numerous pages, and multimedia elements may experience prolonged opening and synchronization durations, potentially impacting user productivity.

- **Search Performance Degradation**: The efficiency of searching within large notebooks may decrease, particularly when optical character recognition (OCR), handwritten notes, and embedded files are involved.
- **Sync Delays and Conflicts**: Frequent modifications in voluminous notebooks can result in synchronization challenges across devices, including version conflicts and delayed updates.
- **Navigation Challenges**: Managing and retrieving information in notebooks with complex structures and substantial content volumes can become increasingly difficult.
- **Application Lag and Freezing**: Notebooks comprising images, attachments, and lengthy pages may contribute to reduced application responsiveness, lag, or occasional crashes.

In summary, OneNote's integrated search capabilities, spanning OCR, audio, and handwritten content, greatly improve information retrieval and knowledge management. Although there are some minor limitations regarding accuracy and performance with more complex or extensive data, these advanced features collectively establish OneNote as a versatile and effective solution for capturing, organizing, and accessing a wide range of information formats.

Apply the Look of Other Contents to Text

Typed notes in a notebook page offer the same text formatting tools you'd find in other programs like Microsoft Word, PowerPoint, WordPad, or Notepad. To copy font formatting from one section of text to another, first highlight the formatted text. Once selected for an example "Incident management" as shown in Figure 5-16, go to the Home ribbon or menu which pops after selection, and click on Format Painter. When you move your mouse across the page, you'll see a paintbrush icon appear—this means the Format Painter has captured all the characteristics of your selected text, such as bold, italics, underline, font size, color, and style as shown in Figure 5-17. Imagine it like dipping a brush into paint: you pick up the exact finish and shade, ready to apply elsewhere.

Next, find the section where you want to paste this formatting. The destination text in our case “Incident Management” doesn’t need to be preselected; simply position your cursor next to it as shown in Figure 5-18, then left-click and drag to highlight the target text. When you release the mouse, all the formatting from your original selection will apply instantly, just like painting over an area for a fresh look as shown in Figure 5-19. Format Painter updates text quickly and consistently, reducing the number of clicks you need, and maintains precise details like font color and size.

You can use this feature across other Microsoft Office apps, including Excel, PowerPoint, and Word—it’s always found in the clipboard area of the Home ribbon.

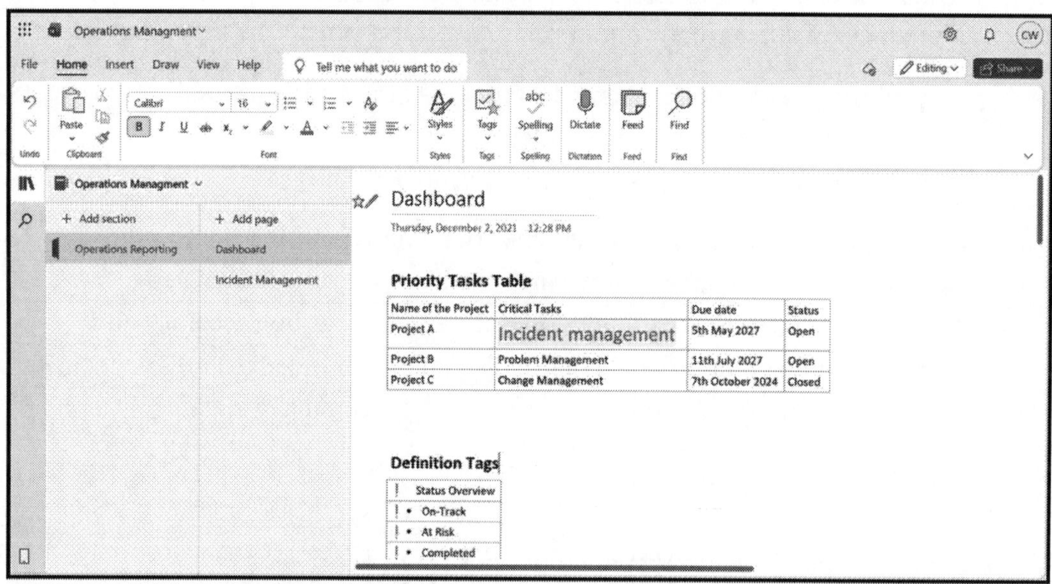

Figure 5-16. *Selection of text*

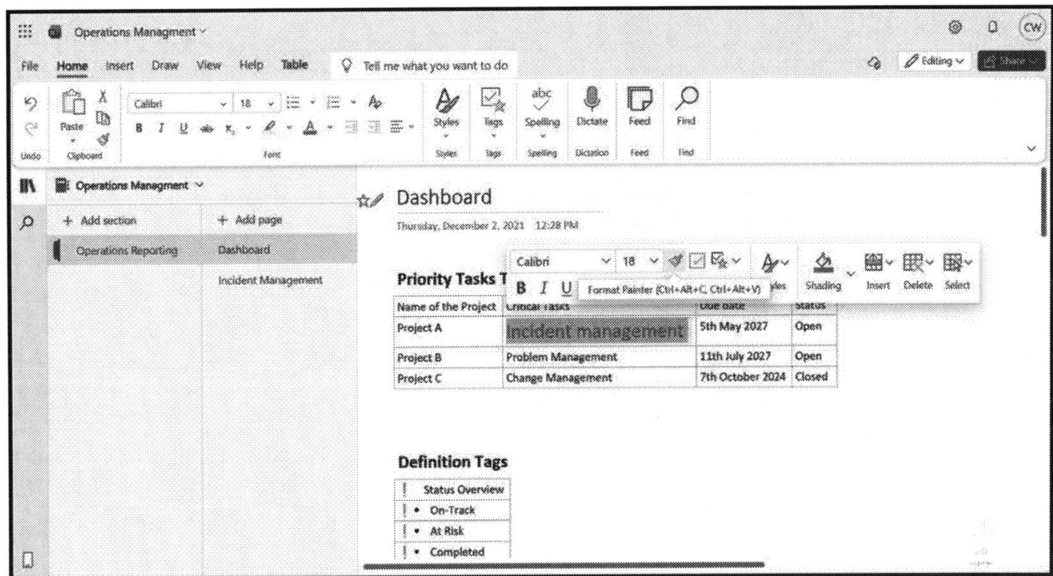

Figure 5-17. *Apply paint brush to selected text*

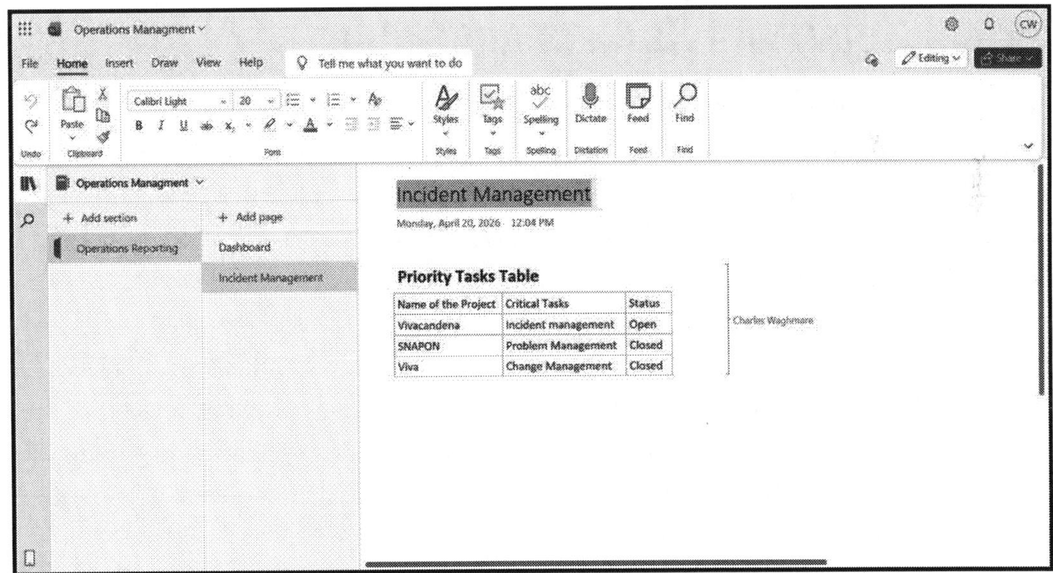

Figure 5-18. *Pre-select desired text*

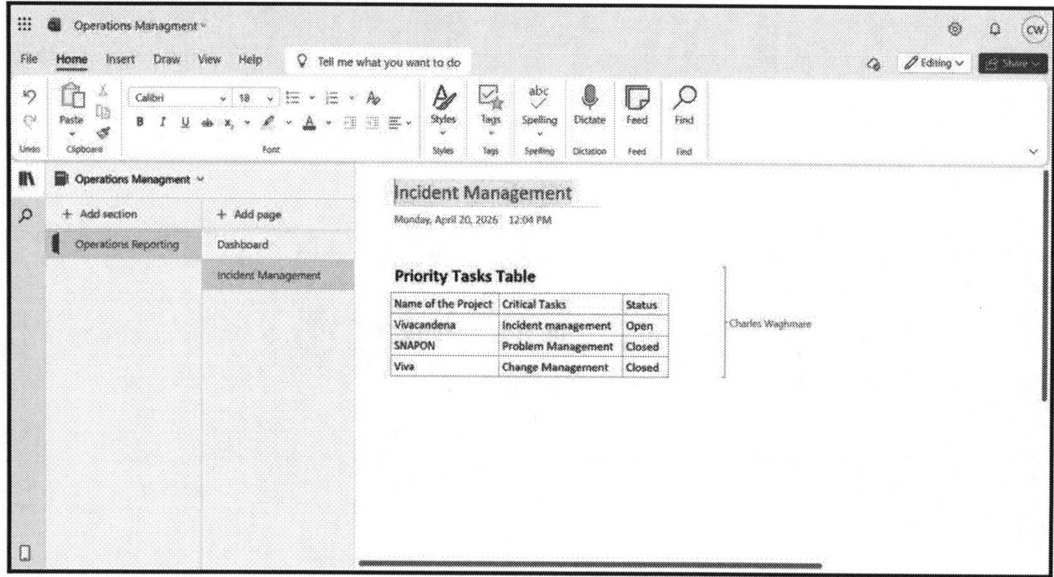

Figure 5-19. Formatting changed

Format Notes with Bullets and Tables

You can organize information on a notebook page using bullet lists as shown in Figure 5-20. If you already have typed text, start by selecting it as shown in Figure 5-21. You can access bullet options from the Home ribbon; simply select either the default bullet or pick another style from the gallery as shown in Figure 5-22. If you want a different look, click "Bullets" symbol again and use the downward arrow to see other styles—like hollow circle bullet as shown in Figure 5-23—which will change the list's appearance as shown in Figure 5-23-1. Also, from the mini toolbar that pops up, choose "Bullets" to apply the default bullet style to each item as shown in Figure 5-25. To remove bullets, select the list of bullet pointers and choose "Bullets" as shown in Figure 5-25. As you add more items, pressing Enter will keep the bullet formatting going. If you press Enter on a blank new line as shown in Figure 5-26, the bullets will stop as shown in Figure 5-26-1.

Numbered lists work similarly. Select your items, then choose "Numbering" either from the mini toolbar or Home ribbon. The drop-down arrow lets you pick different number styles as shown in Figure 5-27. To remove numbering, select the list and use "Clear All Formatting" from the Home ribbon. Note this resets all formatting—including font styles and sizes—to plain text. One can insert table into page using Table option under insert menu as shown in Figure 5-28. By selecting 4x4 configuration of table containing 4 rows and 4 columns, a table a inserted into Page as shown in Figure 5-29. Under Home, there is clear formatting feature which helps to clear existing formatting. Select text as shown in Figure 5-30 and after applying "Clear formatting" formatting is gone as shown in Figure 5-31.

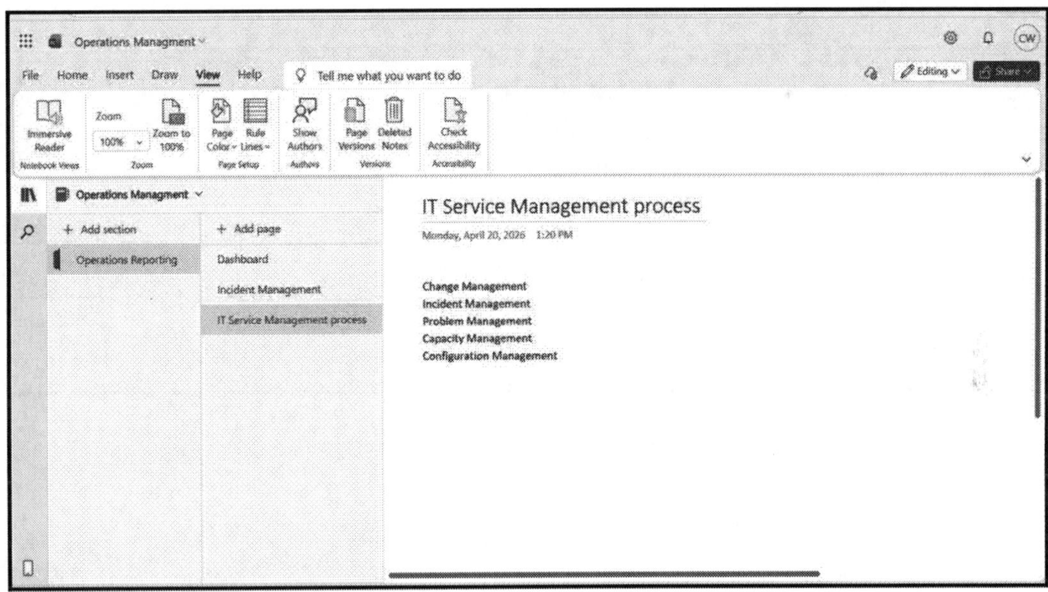

Figure 5-20. *Unbulleted text*

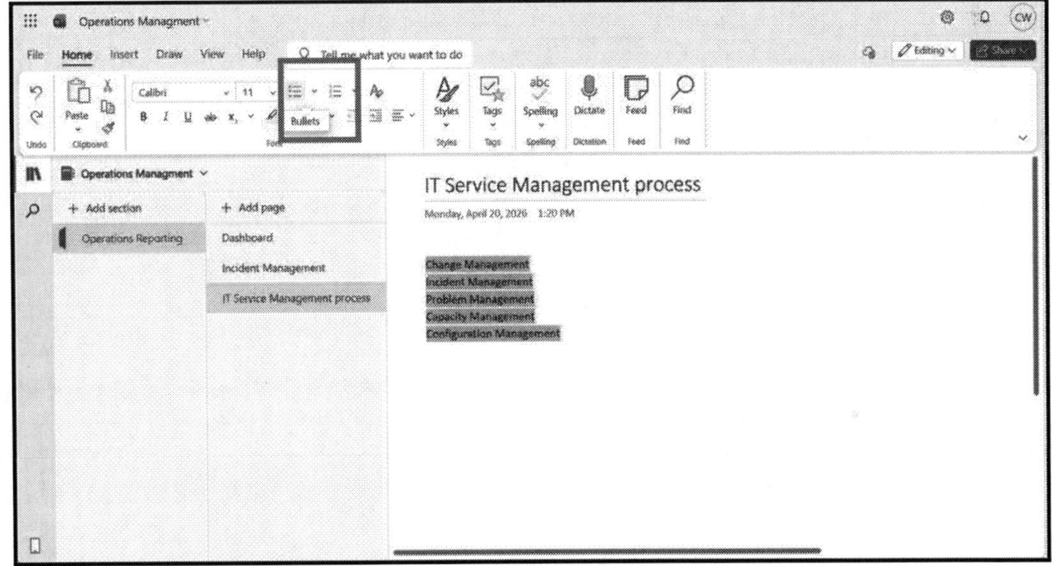

Figure 5-21. *Apply bullets to selected text*

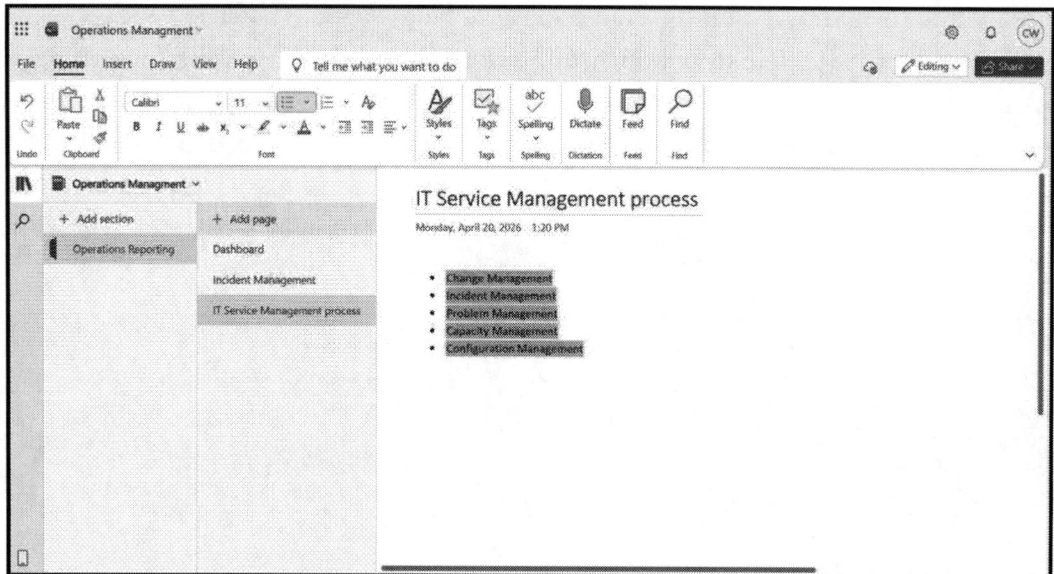

Figure 5-22. *Select bulleted text*

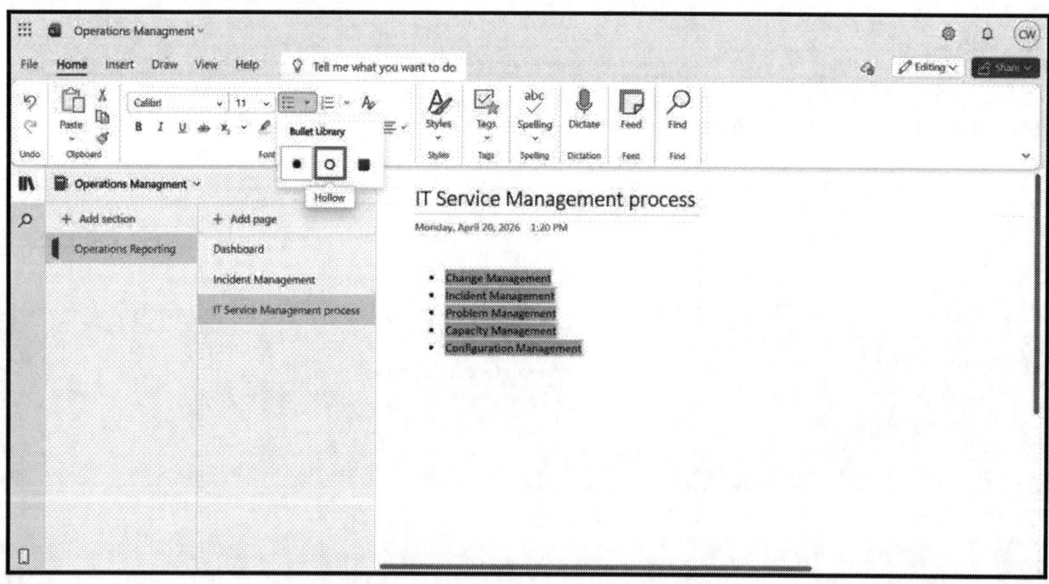

Figure 5-23. *Change bullet type*

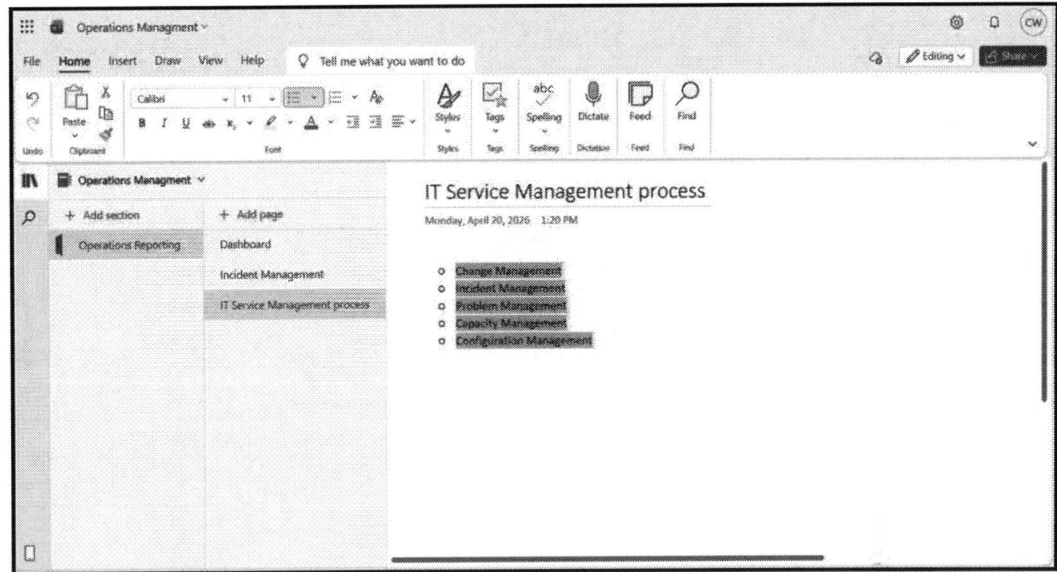

Figure 5-23-1. *Apply new bullet type*

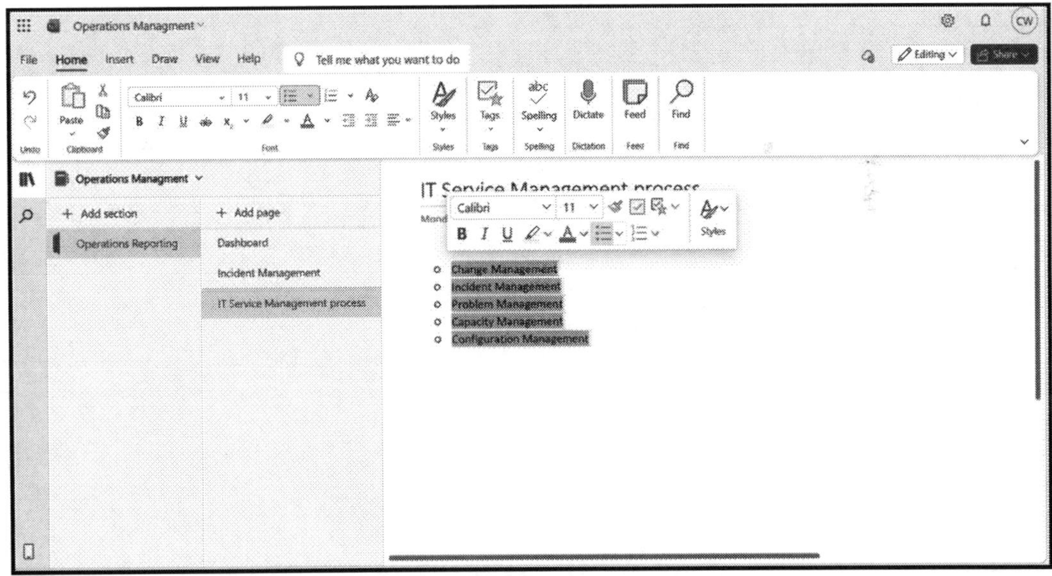

Figure 5-24. *Apply bullet from the mini window*

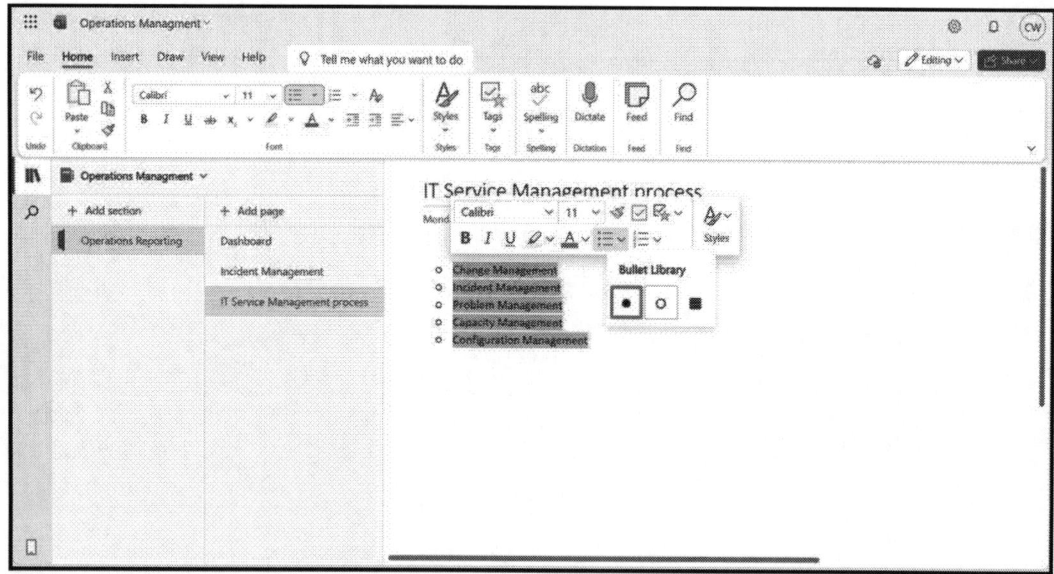

***Figure 5-25.** Change bullet type from the mini window*

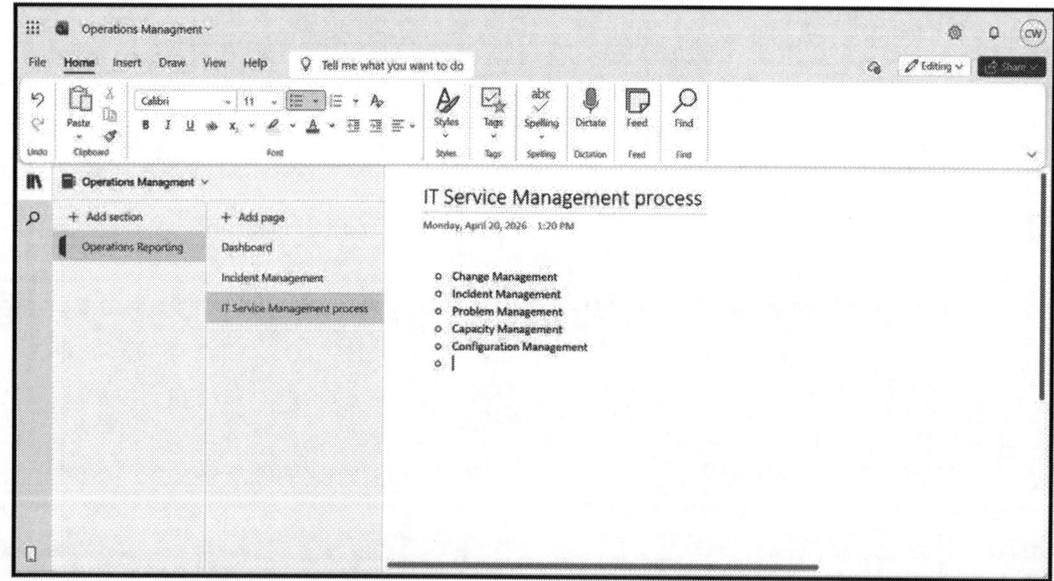

***Figure 5-26.** Enter a blank bullet line to remove bullets*

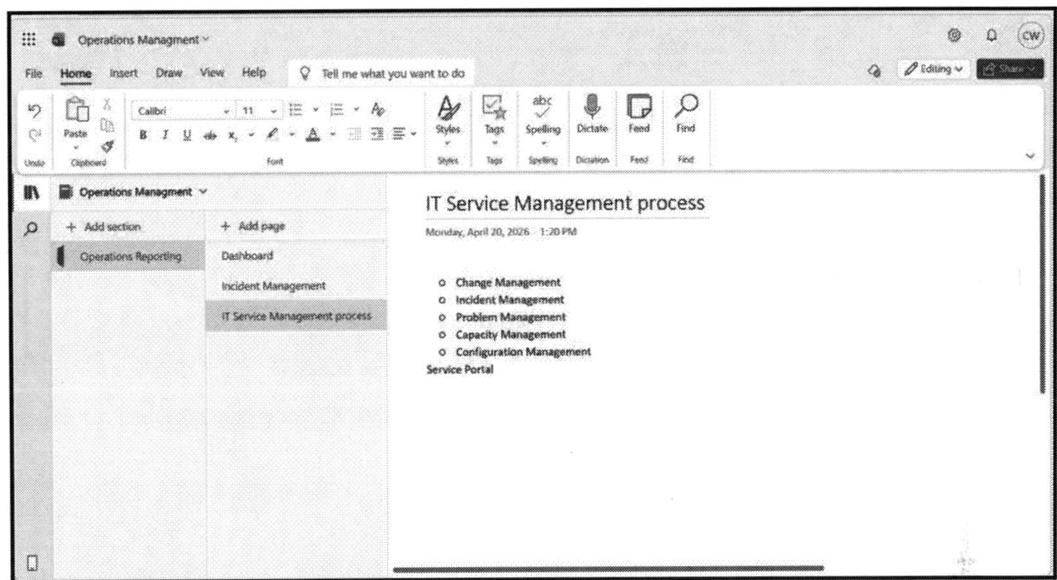

Figure 5-26-1. *Bullets disappear*

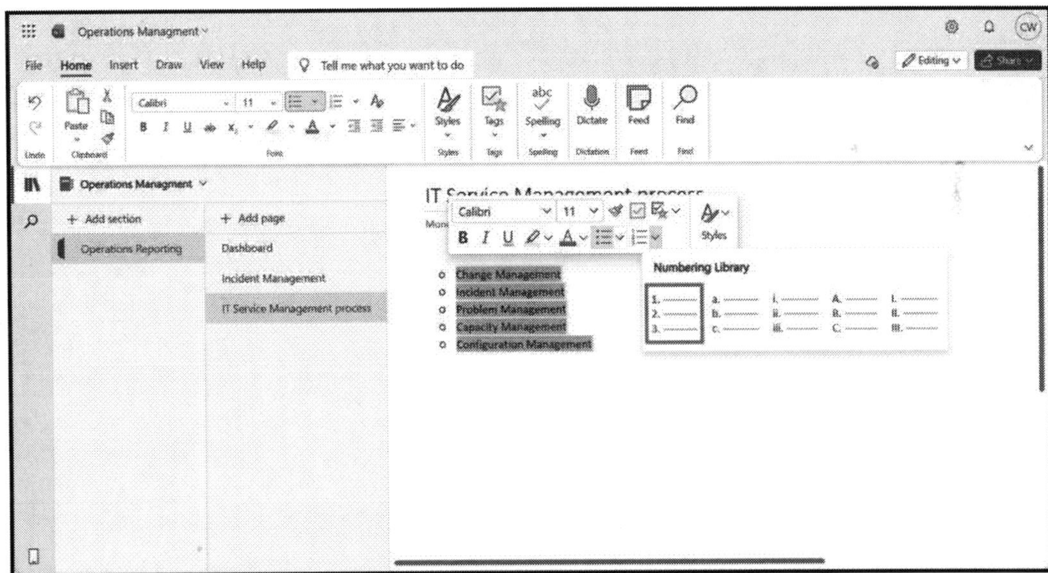

Figure 5-27. *Alternate way of bulleting using numbers*

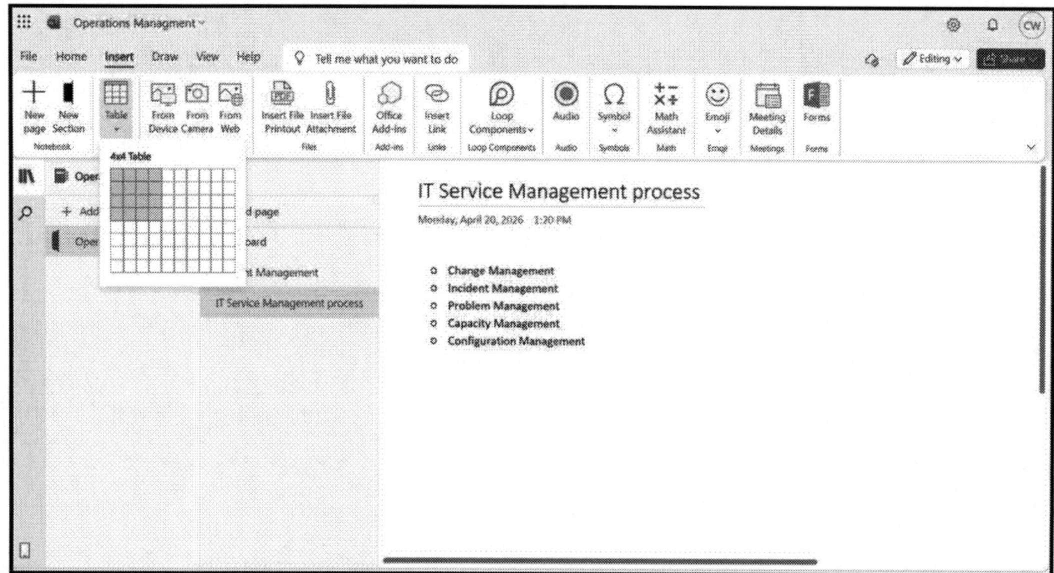

Figure 5-28. Insert a 4x4 table

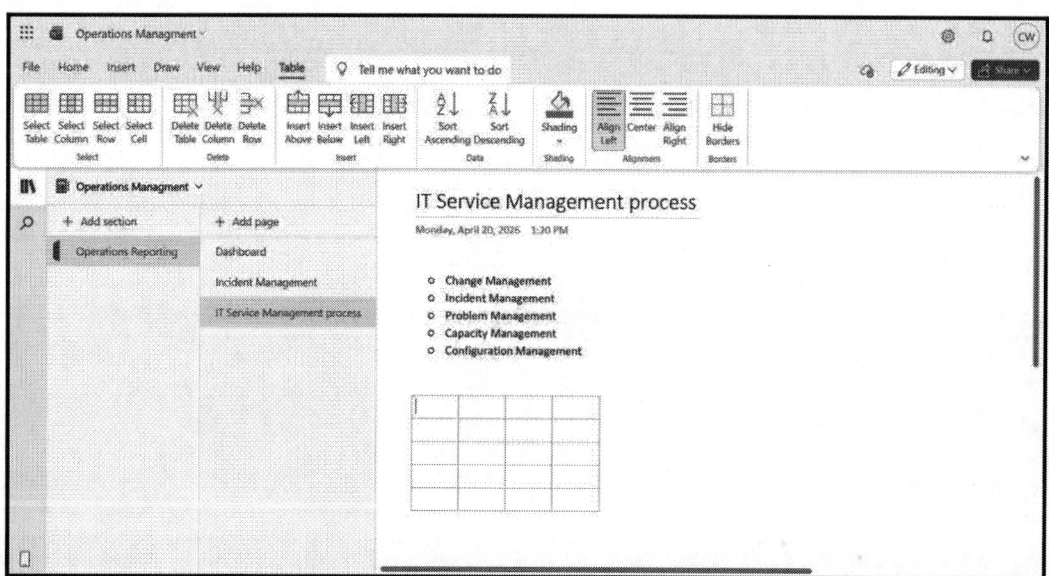

Figure 5-29. Table inserted

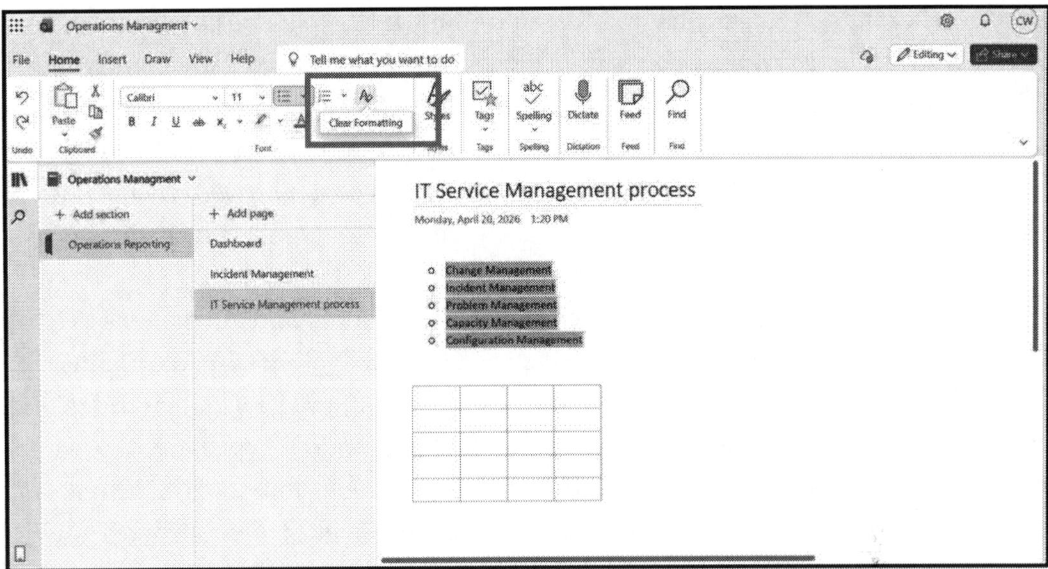

__Figure 5-30.__ Select text to apply Clear Formatting

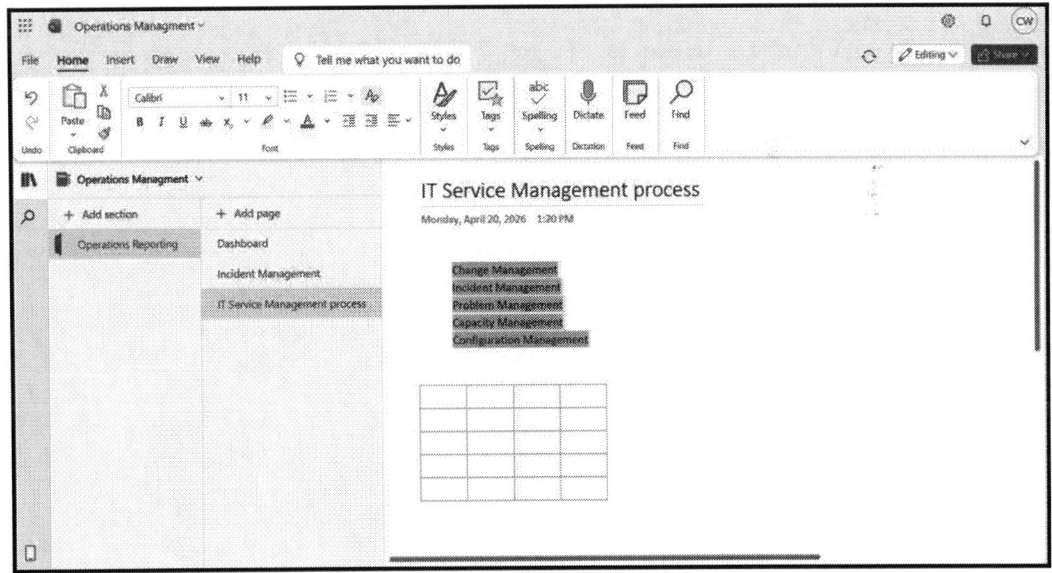

__Figure 5-31.__ Clear Formatting applied

This chapter reviewed ways to manage and search content in Microsoft OneNote, highlighting tools for organization, retrieval, and formatting. It explained tagging for categorizing information, searching by tags and keywords, refining the scope of search, and using shortcuts. Metadata features like author info and version history were discussed for tracking changes. Formatting tools—including Format Painter, lists, and tables—were covered to improve note readability. Overall, strategic use of tags, search, metadata, and formatting makes OneNote an efficient platform for organized and accessible digital notes. Besides, we have also seen search capability with OCR-based search, audio transcript search, and handwritten notes along with challenges of searching OneNote with large sizes.

The next chapter covers advanced techniques, automation, and integrations to boost Microsoft OneNote's appearance and productivity. It shows how users can combine visual enhancements with automation and cross-app workflows for a better note-taking experience. The chapter explains converting handwritten notes to typed text for clearer presentation, which is helpful for stylus users in meetings or lectures. It also introduces keyboard shortcuts for faster task execution and editing. Finally, it demonstrates how integrating OneNote with Power Automate enables workflows for reminders, tasks, and content updates, streamlining repetitive actions.

CHAPTER 6

OneNote Power Tips, Automation, and Integrations

The previous chapter explored techniques for managing and searching content in Microsoft OneNote, focusing on tools for organization, retrieval, and formatting. It described how tagging can be used to categorize information, methods for searching by tags and keywords, ways to narrow search results, and the use of shortcuts. It also addressed metadata features such as author details and version history for tracking changes. Additionally, formatting options—including Format Painter, lists, and tables—were discussed to enhance the readability of notes. By applying these strategies for tags, search, metadata, and formatting, OneNote becomes an effective platform for keeping digital notes organized and accessible.

In this chapter, we will learn about adding Outlook meeting details to a notebook, taking notes in an MS Teams meeting, and automatically generating MS Teams meeting notes and explore the top ten power shortcuts for automations.

Adding Outlook Meeting Details to a Notebook

If you need to take notes during a meeting, adding Outlook meeting details to your notebook is easy with Outlook and OneNote. When viewing your Outlook meeting, focus on the ribbon at the top of the screen. The steps may differ depending on your version—whether you're using the web app, Classic Outlook (the desktop app), or New Outlook. Here, we'll use New Outlook as an example but be aware that features and locations may vary by application.

C. Waghmare, *Mastering Microsoft OneNote*, https://doi.org/10.1007/979-8-8688-2866-9_6

Open your event—the meeting you're about to attend. On the ribbon, click the ellipsis (More Options), then select "Send to OneNote" as shown in Figure 6-1. If it's your first time using this function, you'll need to log in with your Microsoft 365 account so Outlook can connect to OneNote and display your notebooks for sending meeting details. Logging in is required when integrating these apps.

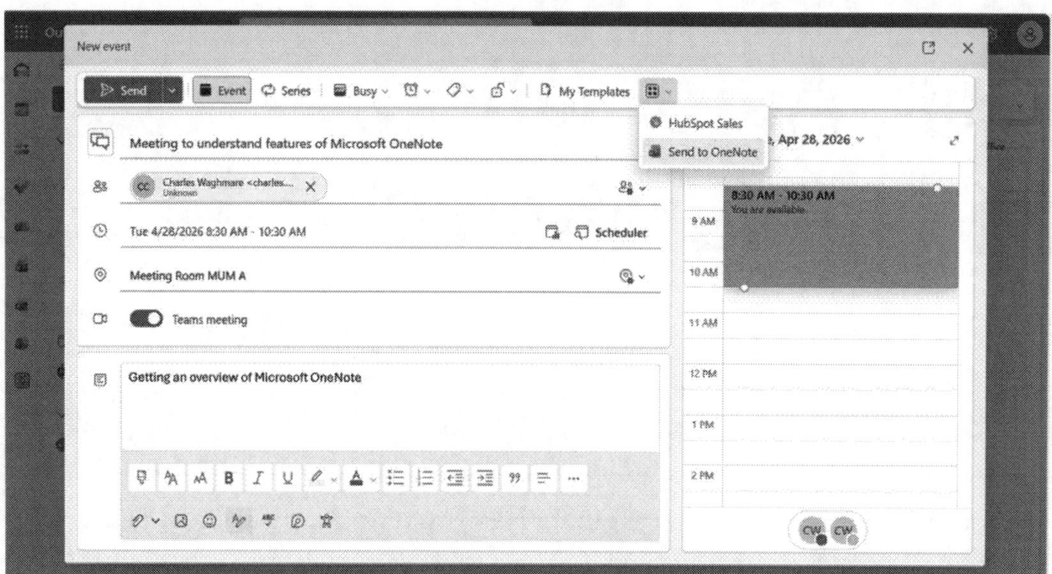

***Figure 6-1.** Use "Send to OneNote" feature in MS Teams*

Once you apply "Send to OneNote," on the right side of the meeting invitation, a Onenote Tree structure will appear and choose a location from this list as shown in Figure 6-2.

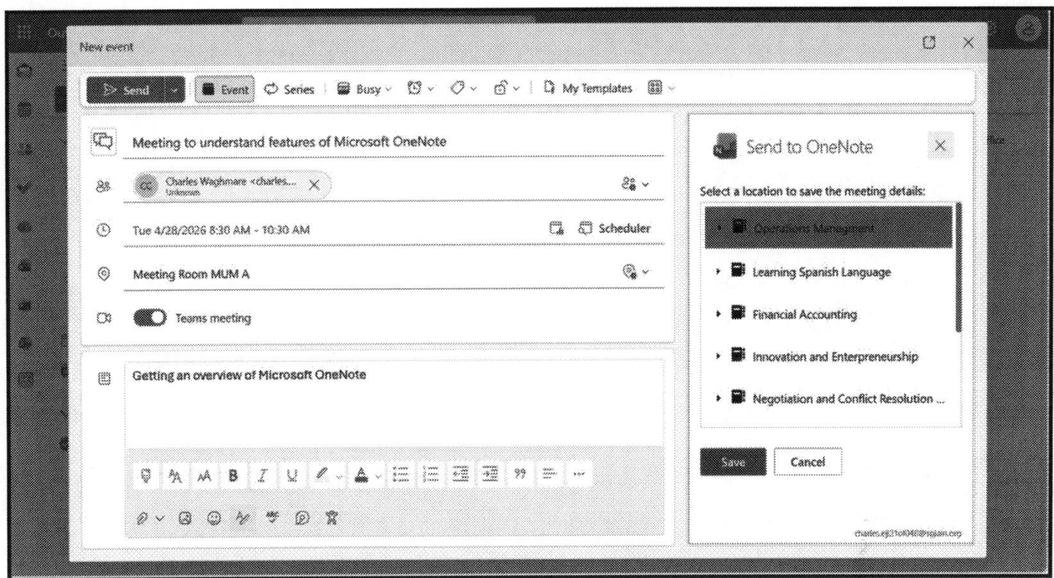

Figure 6-2. *Choose the desired location for copying meeting details*

Once the destination is selected as "Operations Management," information is saved and you are now asked to open OneNote as shown in Figure 6-3.

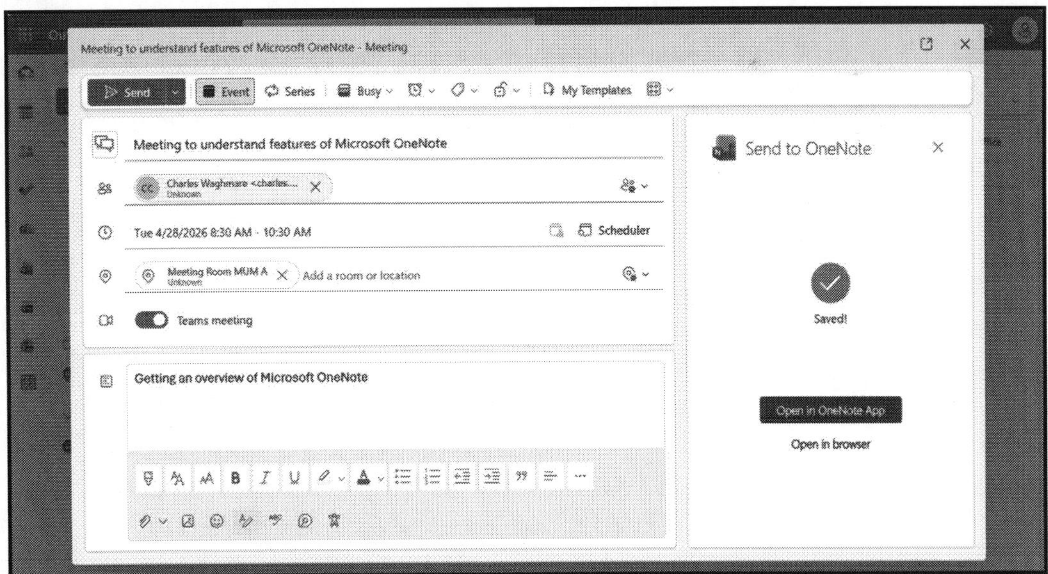

Figure 6-3. *Send to OneNote is successful*

Once you open OneNote as shown in Figure 6-4, you will see a page with a title. This title comes from the meeting name in Outlook, and the page will contain a table listing meeting details such as the subject, a link to return to the Outlook item, who created the invitation, and required attendees—marked with tags for tracking attendance. Additional information includes date, time, location (in this case, a Teams meeting), agenda, and how to join as shown in Figure 6-4-1.

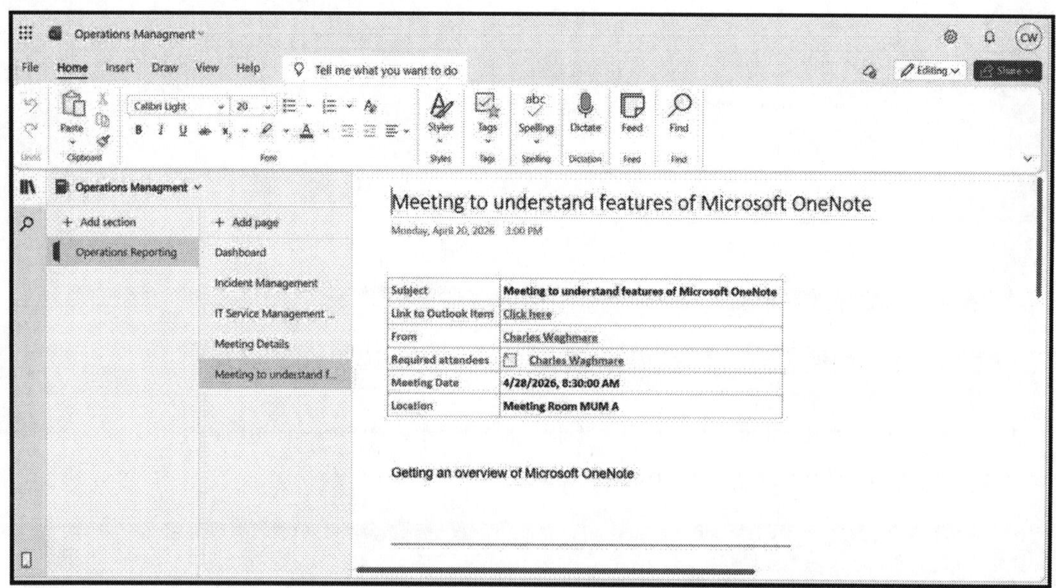

Figure 6-4. *Meeting invitation copied successfully into OneNote*

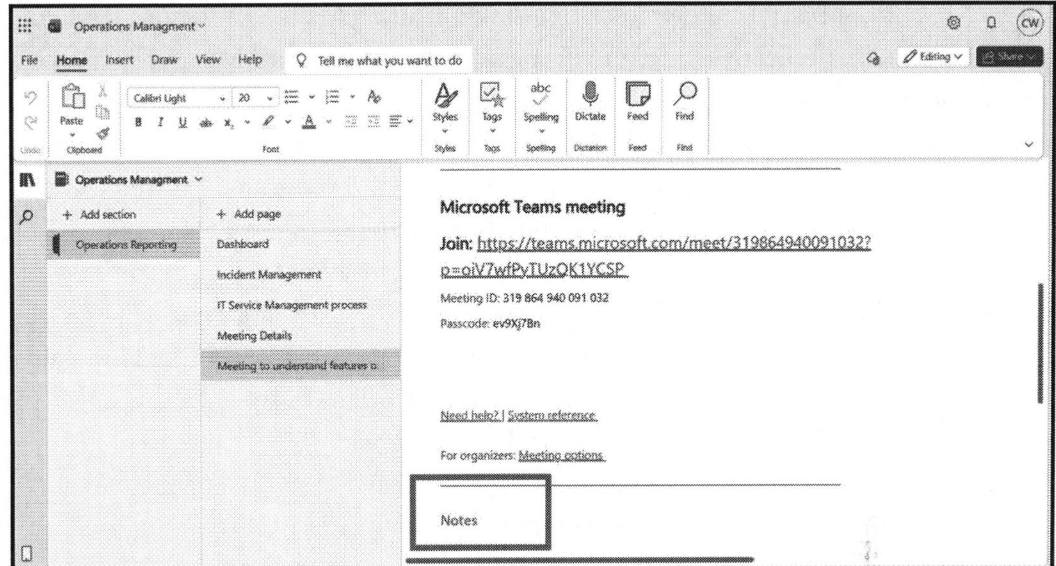

Figure 6-4-1. *Meeting details accessed via OneNote*

This method gets you started quickly, since all essential info is automatically placed on your page—you don't have to manually type or copy and paste. At the bottom, there's a notes section for recording discussions, action items, follow-ups, and takeaways. That's how you add Outlook meeting details to OneNote to kick off your note-taking efficiently.

Taking Notes in an MS Teams Meeting

Microsoft OneNote serves as an essential note-taking solution during meetings conducted via Microsoft Teams, facilitating the efficient capture, organization, and preservation of meeting information in a structured format. When a Teams meeting is scheduled, OneNote can be directly integrated with the meeting context, enabling participants to prepare targeted notes for discussions, agendas, and actionable items. Users have the capability to access OneNote alongside Teams during live sessions, recording key points in real time to ensure accurate documentation of decisions, explanations, and references. Meeting notes may be systematically arranged using headings, bullet points, tables, and checklists, reflecting the logical sequence of the meeting and supporting subsequent review. This integration ensures that notes remain linked to the relevant Teams channel, chat, or project, thereby assisting participants in maintaining continuity across recurring meetings and collaborative initiatives.

OneNote also supports collaborative note-taking during Microsoft Teams meetings, making it particularly effective for group discussions and shared projects. When a OneNote notebook is stored in OneDrive or SharePoint and linked to a Teams channel, multiple participants can simultaneously contribute to the same set of notes. This co-authoring capability ensures that ideas from different contributors are captured without duplication or loss of context. During meetings, team members can add comments, highlight key decisions, tag action items, and insert links to shared files or recordings discussed in Teams. Because changes sync automatically, all participants see updates in near real time, reducing the need for follow-up clarification emails. This collaborative approach transforms meeting notes from a personal record into a shared knowledge asset that reflects collective understanding and accountability.

OneNote streamlines post-meeting follow-up and knowledge management in Teams. Notes from meetings can be turned into actionable tasks linked to Outlook, Planner, or To Do. Users can quickly search notebooks for past discussions using keywords or tags. Meeting content from Teams—like recordings or documents—can be directly embedded in OneNote, providing a central reference. This approach builds a searchable meeting history, aiding project continuity and onboarding. Integrating OneNote with Teams connects meetings, notes, and actions within Microsoft 365 for an efficient workflow.

Effective note-taking extends beyond the meeting itself; it begins with a collaborative agenda involving all participants and remains valuable during and after the meeting as a centralized reference for notes, decisions, and actionable items. In Microsoft Teams, when scheduling a new meeting titled "Events Planning," attendees can be added and details such as date and time specified. A notable feature is the option to include an agenda, which generates a Loop component—an interactive file providing consistency and expectations for meeting documentation as shown in Figure 6-5.

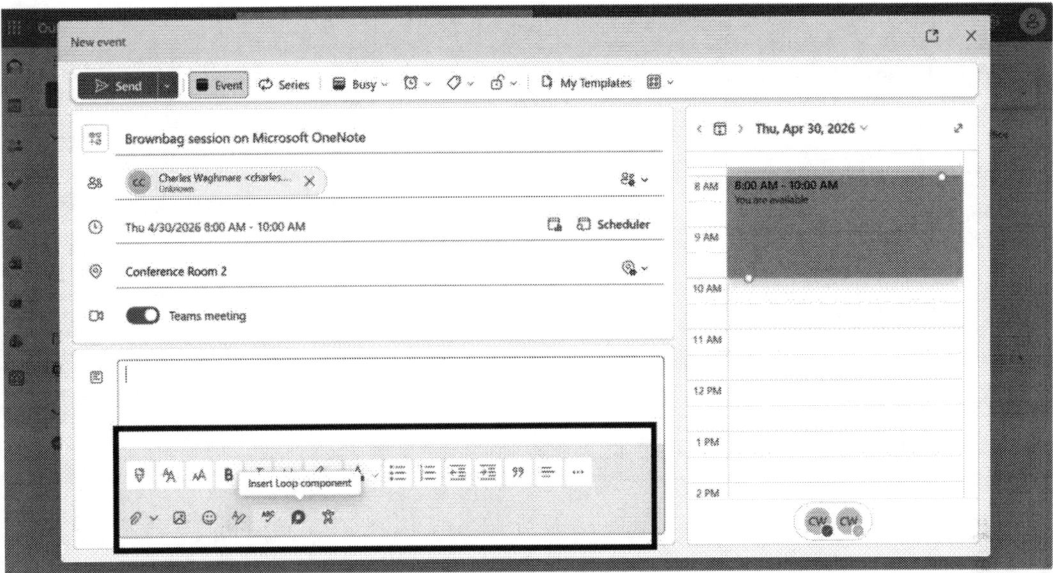

Figure 6-5. *Loop component inside MS Teams*

Microsoft Loop, identifiable by its distinct icon as seen in Figure 6-5, offers workspaces with pages and subpages, containing portable components usable across applications like Word and Outlook as shown in Figure 6-6. Updates made to these components are synchronized, supporting real-time collaboration. The Loop component encompasses areas for agendas, meeting notes, and follow-up tasks, enabling structured preparation and participation once you click on Agenda as shown in Figures 6-7 and 6-8.

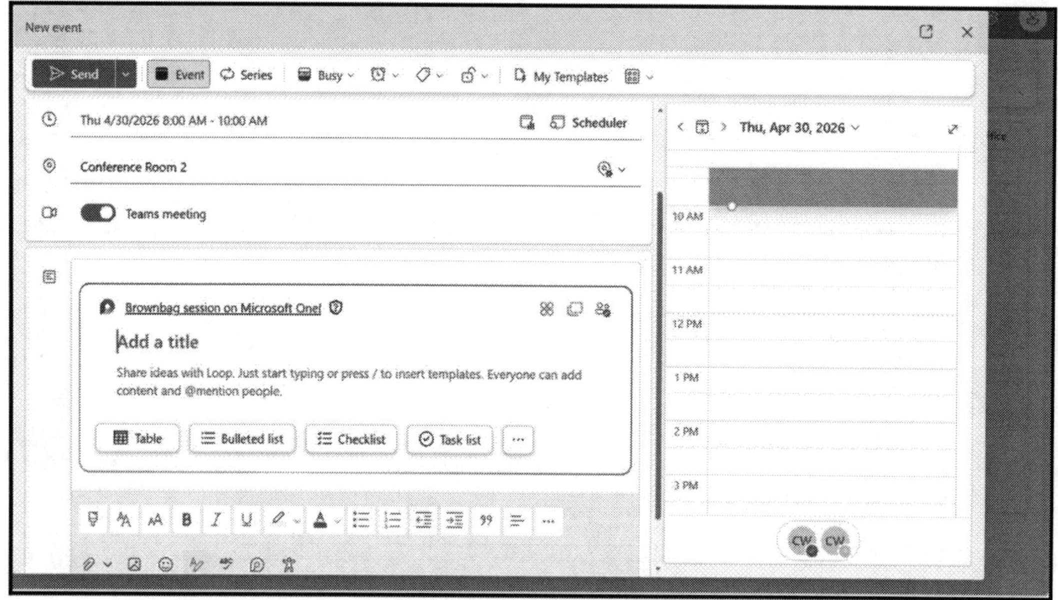

***Figure 6-6.** Interactive features of Microsoft Loop*

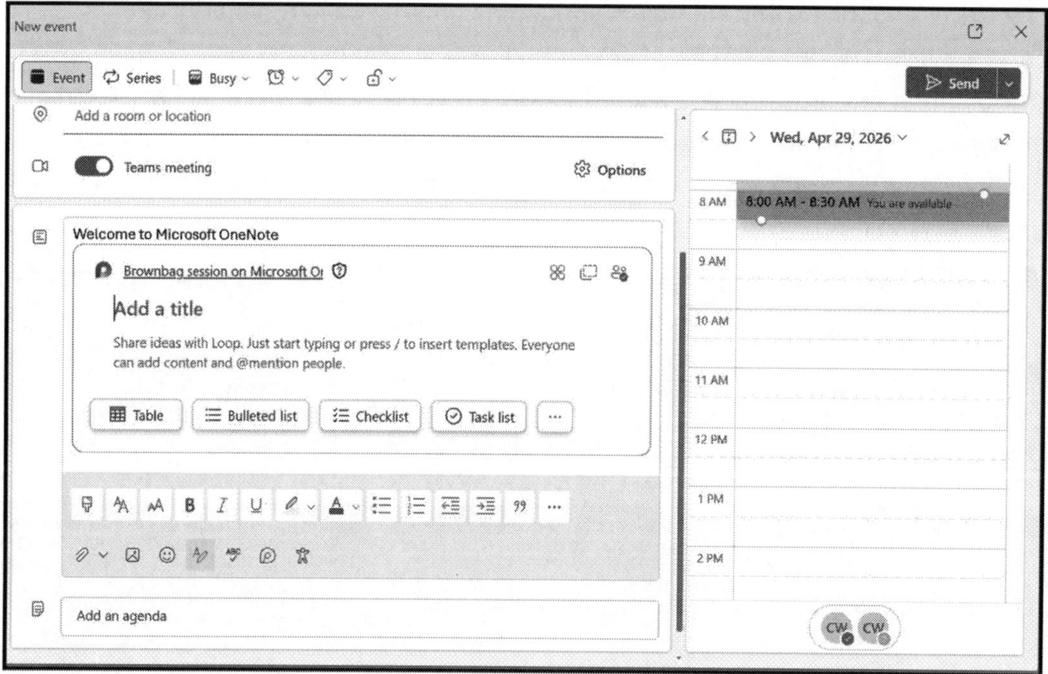

***Figure 6-7.** Add agenda*

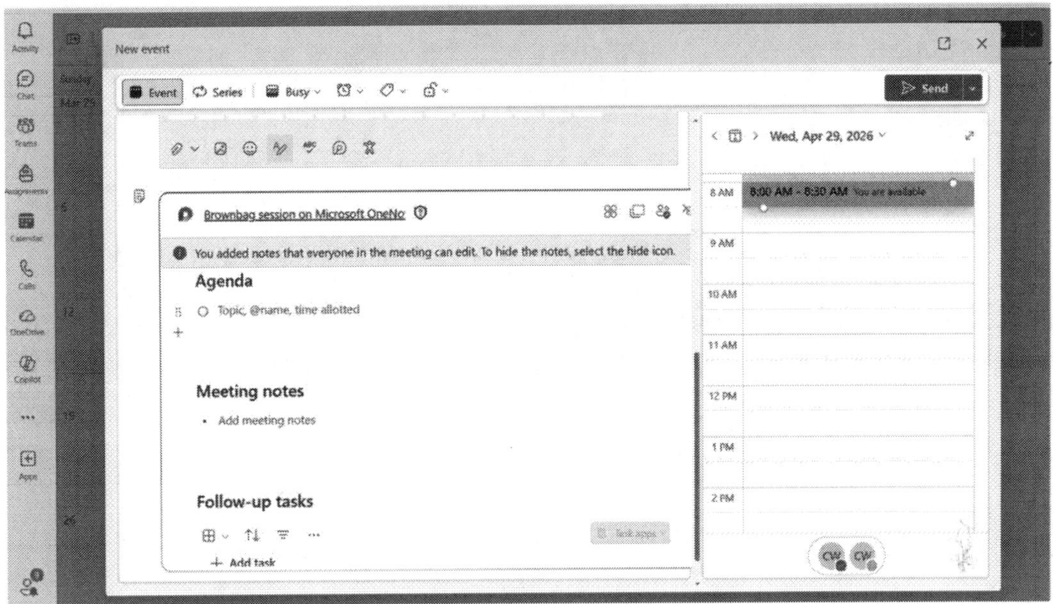

Figure 6-8. *Structured agenda gets created*

The Microsoft Loop opens in the form of notes during Microsoft Teams meetings to capture notes as shown in Figure 6-7. Headings such as Agenda, Meeting notes, and Follow-up tasks can be created into Loop while creating a meeting invitation so that they appear as shown in Figure 6-9.

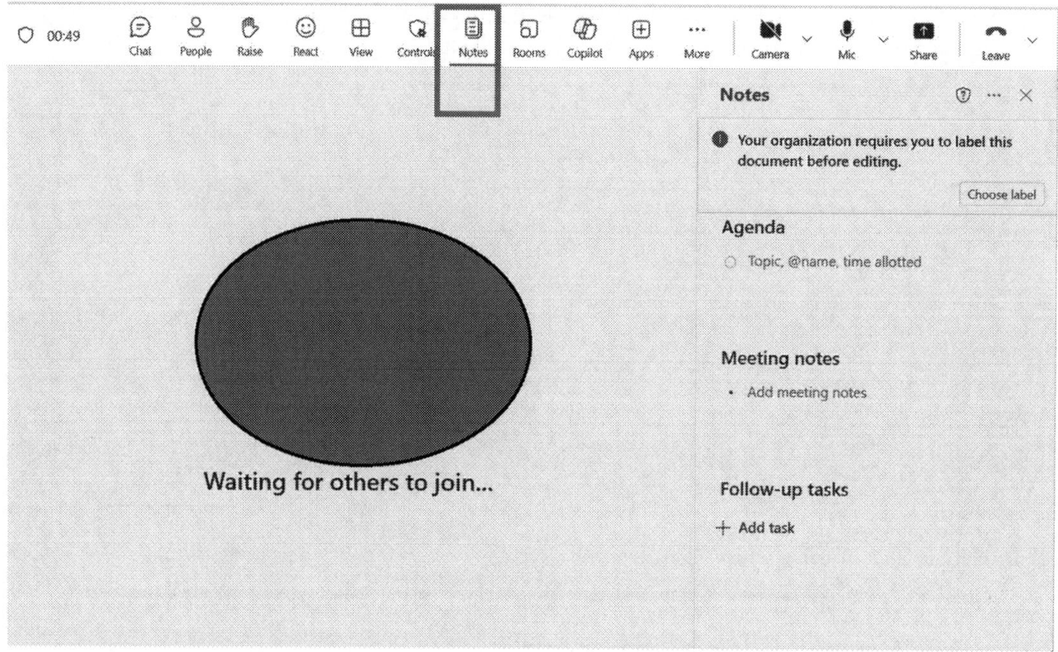

Figure 6-9. *Take meeting notes using Loop*

Automatically Generate Teams Meeting Notes

If you participated in a Teams meeting and needed to review content afterward, you would typically search multiple locations for shared files, meeting notes, or recordings. Now, all of this content is conveniently located within the Recap tab of each meeting as shown in Figure 6-10. Every Teams user has access to the Recap tab, where they can find meeting materials.

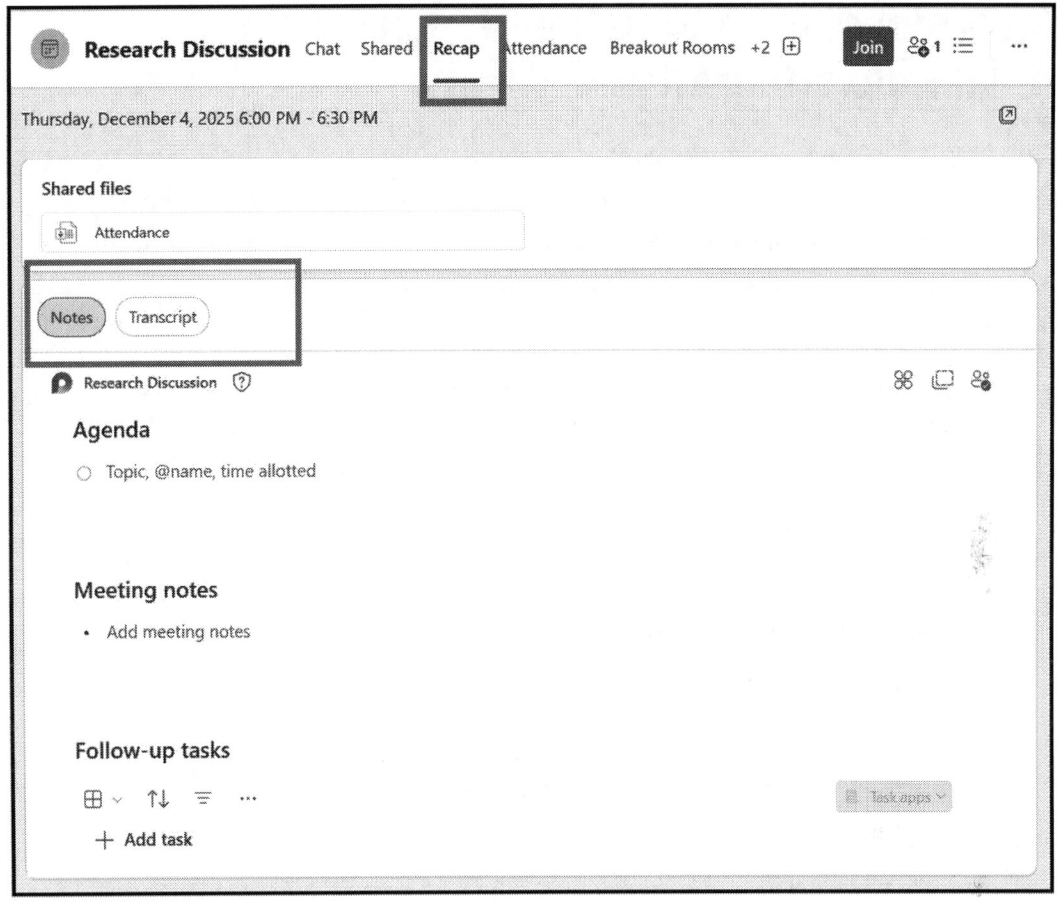

Figure 6-10. *Recap button*

Once you click Recap, recordings, transcripts, and manual notes become available to all users as highlighted in Figure 6-10. Where Teams premium adds value is through Intelligent Recap, which uses AI to offer suggested notes and tasks based on meeting discussions. Regardless of your license, when accessing this information, you'll use the Recap tab; we're simply distinguishing between standard and premium features so you can understand what AI-powered content comes with the premium license.

Intelligent Recap compiles content from meeting data including recordings, transcripts, attendance reports, and participant names. To capture Intelligent Recap details, you must record the meeting, which also enables transcription. As topics, decisions, and tasks are discussed, AI generates recommended notes and tasks within the Recap section.

Understanding Automation Dependencies in OneNote Integrations

While Microsoft OneNote offers seamless integration with Teams, Outlook, and Loop, it is important to note that most "automation" scenarios are **driven by dependencies rather than being fully autonomous.** These functionalities require support from various Microsoft 365 services, specific configurations, and user engagement.

Key dependencies include

- **OneDrive or SharePoint**: Essential for storing notebooks, enabling sharing, and facilitating real-time collaboration
- **Microsoft Teams Meeting Recording**: Required for accessing transcripts and Recap features
- **Transcription Services**: Must be activated in order to produce searchable meeting content
- **Microsoft Loop Components**: Rely on cloud-based platforms for real-time synchronization
- **Power Automate**: Necessary for comprehensive workflow automation, such as setting triggers and sending notifications

If these dependencies are not correctly configured, several advanced features outlined in this chapter may not operate as intended. Certain capabilities mentioned in this chapter may appear as general features but are **license-dependent**, which can lead to confusion if not explicitly stated as in Table 6-1.

Table 6-1. License information

Feature	Availability	Clarification
Basic Teams Recap (recordings, notes, files)	Standard Microsoft 365	Available to most users
Intelligent Recap (AI summaries, tasks)	Teams Premium	Requires additional license
Transcription & recording	Admin-controlled	Must be enabled in tenant settings
Loop collaboration	Standard (cloud-based)	Requires online storage and access
Workflow automation	Power Automate	Requires configuration and connectors

It is essential to note that integration does not necessarily result in complete automation within Microsoft 365. Numerous AI-driven insights are contingent upon appropriate licensing, and advanced features require correct configuration and seamless interoperability among services. Awareness of these aspects allows users to establish realistic expectations and facilitates the development of efficient, scalable, and integrated workflows.

To conclude, clarifying dependencies and licensing distinctions enhances the practical integrity of this chapter. By explicitly detailing system requirements, configuration parameters, and limitations related to premium features, users are provided with a comprehensive understanding of actual capabilities. Such transparency facilitates informed decision-making, minimizes misunderstandings, and contributes to the creation of reliable, efficient, and scalable solutions within Microsoft 365 environments.

System Boundaries: OneNote vs. Teams vs. Loop vs. Power Automate

A thorough understanding of the functional distinctions among OneNote, Teams, Loop, and Power Automate is crucial for optimizing Microsoft 365 utilization. Each application fulfills a specific role—whether it pertains to knowledge management, communication, or workflow automation. Articulating the capabilities and limitations of each tool minimizes confusion, promotes appropriate usage, and contributes to streamlined, integrated business processes.

OneNote: Capabilities vs. Boundaries

What OneNote DOES	What OneNote DOES NOT DO
Stores and organizes notes in notebooks, sections, and pages	Does NOT host meetings or communication (no chat/video)
Supports rich content (text, images, audio, handwriting, tables)	Does NOT generate AI meeting summaries
Provides tagging, search, and OCR text extraction from images	Does NOT automate workflows independently
Allows real-time co-authoring (via OneDrive/ SharePoint)	Does NOT execute tasks or workflows (only tracks them)
Integrates with Outlook (Send to OneNote)	Does NOT replace task management tools (Planner/To Do)
Maintains version history and content tracking	Does NOT act as a live collaboration workspace like Loop

Microsoft Teams: Capabilities vs. Boundaries

What Teams DOES	What Teams DOES NOT DO
Enables meetings, chats, and team collaboration	Does NOT provide deep structured note organization (like OneNote)
Stores meeting recordings, transcripts, and shared files	Does NOT act as a long-term knowledge repository
Provides Recap features (recordings, notes, transcripts)	Does NOT automate workflows beyond built-in features
Supports integration with OneNote and Loop	AI recap requires premium license (not standard)

(continued)

What Teams DOES	What Teams DOES NOT DO
Enables real-time communication and collaboration	Does NOT manage structured knowledge across projects
Central hub for teamwork and coordination	Does NOT replace automation tools (Power Automate)

Microsoft Loop: Capabilities vs. Boundaries

What Loop DOES	What Loop DOES NOT DO
Provides real-time, editable components (tables, lists, tasks)	Does NOT store long-term structured knowledge like OneNote
Syncs content across Teams, Outlook, and Word instantly	Does NOT support deep hierarchy (limited structure)
Enables collaborative agendas, notes, and task lists	Does NOT execute workflows or automation
Supports co-authoring with live updates	Does NOT replace formal task tools (Planner/To Do)
Works as a fluid, portable content layer	Does NOT act as a document management system
Enhances meeting preparation and collaboration	Does NOT replace Teams communication features

Power Automate: Capabilities vs. Boundaries

What Power Automate DOES	What Power Automate DOES NOT DO
Automates workflows across apps (M365 & external)	Does NOT store content (relies on other apps)
Connects OneNote, Teams, Outlook, SharePoint, etc.	Does NOT create meeting notes or summaries on its own
Triggers actions (alerts, approvals, task creation)	Does NOT replace Teams, OneNote, or Loop functionality

(continued)

What Power Automate DOES	What Power Automate DOES NOT DO
Enables business process automation (flows)	Requires setup, connectors, and permissions
Supports scheduled and event-based automation	Does NOT provide user interface for note-taking or meetings
Integrates multiple systems into workflows	Does NOT function without underlying services

These distinctions demonstrate that each Microsoft 365 tool serves a unique, complementary role. OneNote facilitates knowledge management, Teams streamlines communication, Loop enhances real-time collaboration, and Power Automate orchestrates workflows. A clear understanding of these roles supports realistic expectations, reduces reliance on any single tool, and empowers users to develop effective, integrated digital productivity solutions.

Top Ten Power Shortcuts

Take a Screenshot of Any Area on Your Screen

Screen clipping, or capturing a screenshot, is a common functionality that can be accessed through various methods. The print screen key on the keyboard and the Snipping Tool within the Windows operating system are both frequently used. Additionally, OneNote provides a built-in feature for taking screen clippings of any content displayed on your monitor.

To utilize this feature, navigate to the Insert ribbon in OneNote and select Screen Clipping from the Images group as shown in Figure 6-11. The tool tip will display the keyboard shortcut, Windows+Shift+S, which activates the same function. Upon clicking Screen Clipping, OneNote will minimize, revealing the window previously open. The faded effect on the background indicates that you may use the cursor to click and drag, thereby defining the area to capture. Once the area is selected, release the mouse button to insert the screen clipping directly onto the active OneNote page as shown in Figure 6-12.

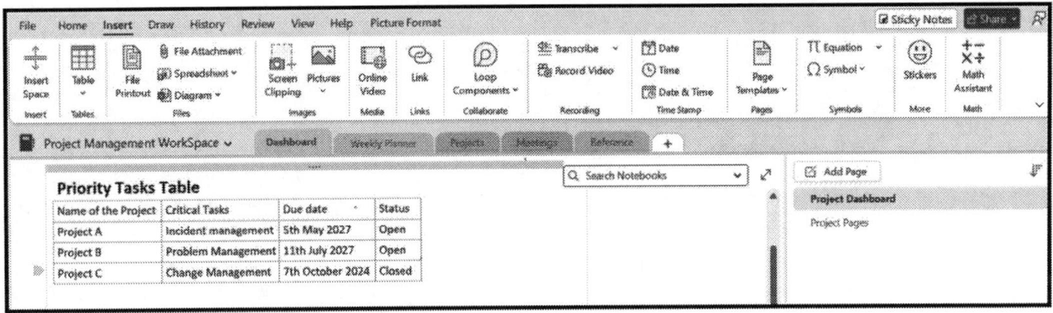

Figure 6-11. *Screen Clipping feature*

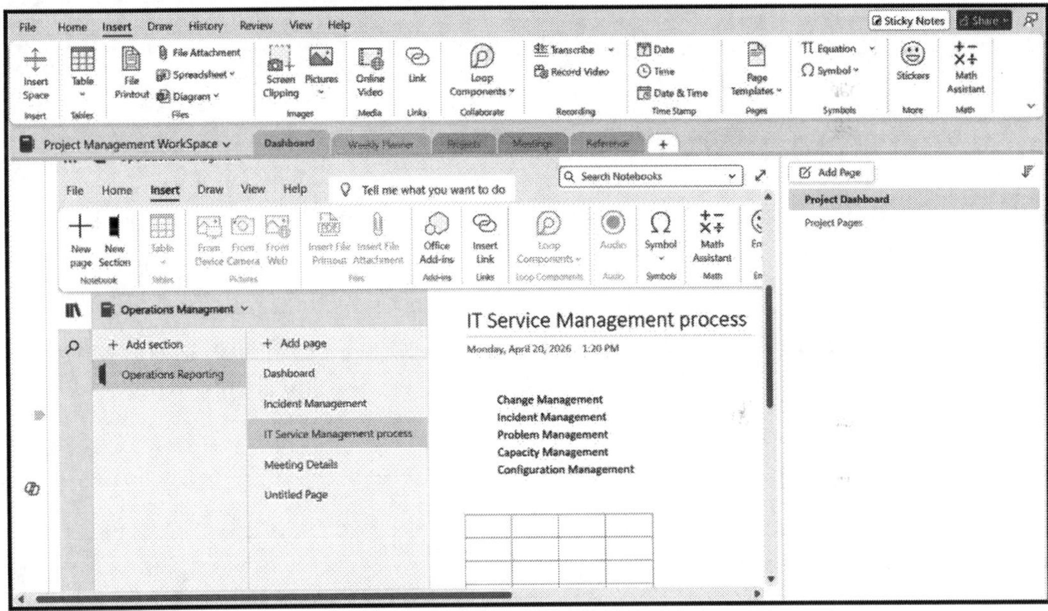

Figure 6-12. *Successfully copied into active page*

A date and timestamp is automatically added beneath the screen clipping, providing a useful reference for tracking changes to websites, instructions, or training materials over time as shown in Figure 6-13. This feature is invaluable for documentation and maintaining an accurate record of content as it appeared at the moment of capture.

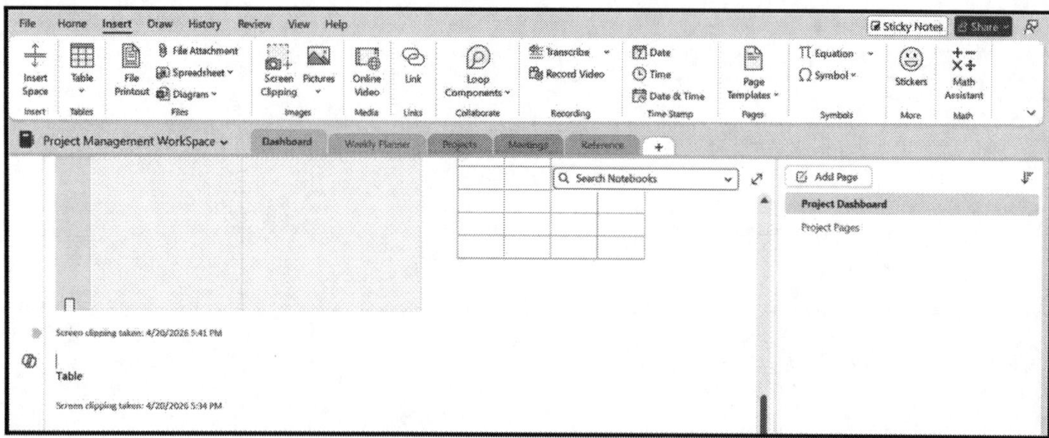

Figure 6-13. *Timestamp of the screen clipping*

Copy Text from a Picture

Extracting text from an image or screenshot isn't always straightforward, as you can't simply select the text like regular content. However, OneNote offers a handy tool for this purpose. For example, it's just a static image, so the text can't be highlighted directly. If you right-click on the picture as shown in Figure 6-14, you'll see an option to extract text from the image. Selecting this prompts OneNote to recognize any visible text.

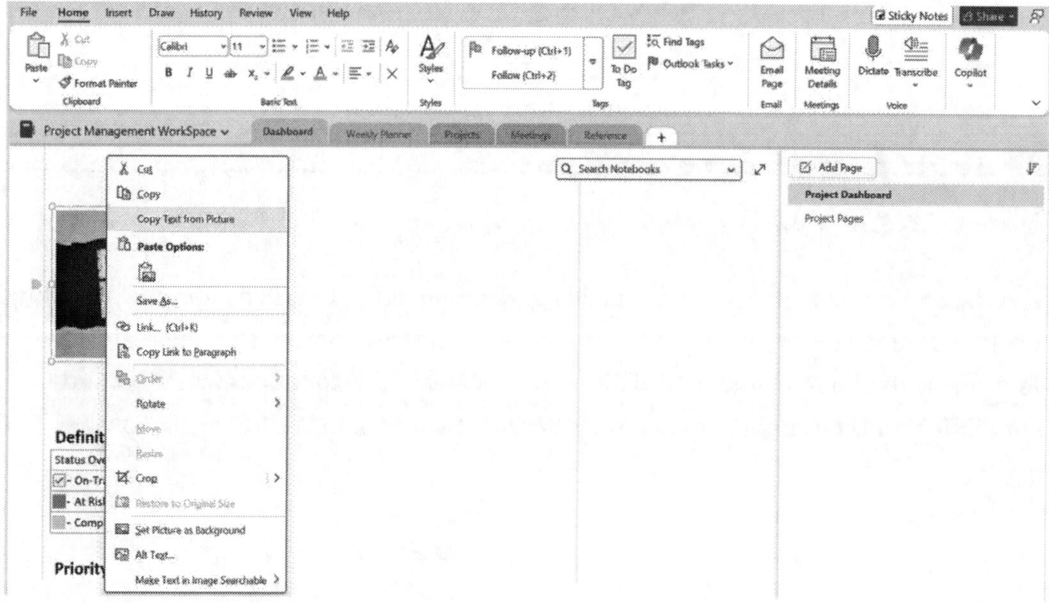

Figure 6-14. *Extract text from image*

Once the text is acknowledged, you can copy it by choosing "Copy All Text and Close." The text is then saved to your clipboard and can be pasted anywhere, such as in emails, Word documents, PowerPoint presentations, or even elsewhere within OneNote itself. Just press Enter a few times and use CTRL to paste—the extracted text will appear, ready to reuse as shown in Figure 6-15.

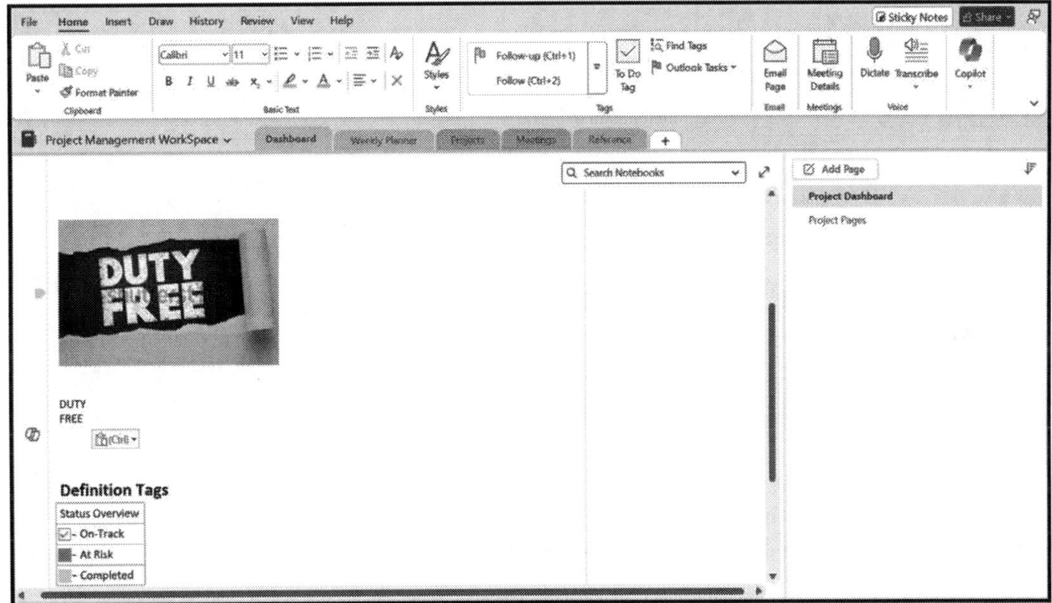

***Figure 6-15.** Copied text from the image*

If this feature isn't working for you, check your settings. Go to File ➤ Options ➤ Advanced, and scroll to the section labeled "Text recognition in pictures." Ensure that "Disable text recognition in pictures" isn't checked. Uncheck it if necessary and click OK to enable the function as shown in Figure 6-16.

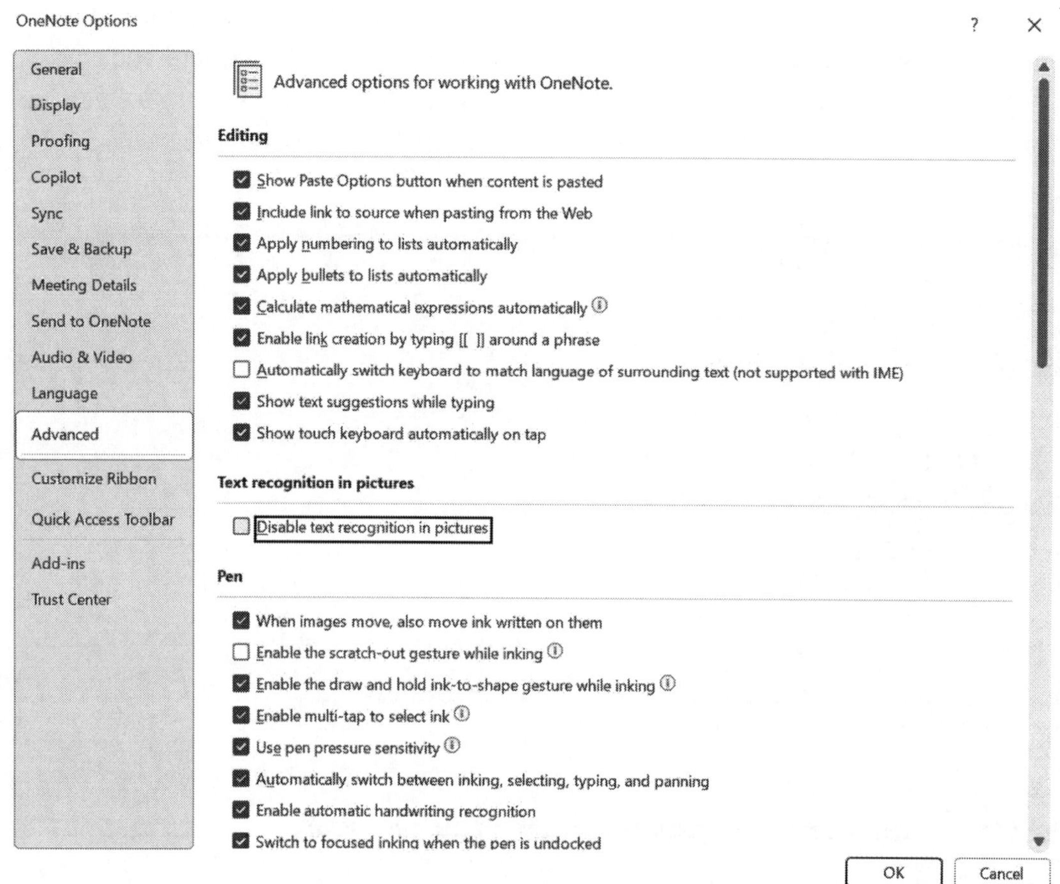

***Figure 6-16.** Keep disabled text recognition in pictures disabled*

Quickly Create a Table in OneNote

If you've ever added tables in Microsoft Word or PowerPoint, you can do the same in a notebook. Simply go to the Insert ribbon—just as you would in other Office apps—and find the Tables group. Click Table, and you have several options: hover over cells to build your table, use Insert Table for a dialog box, or even create a new Excel spreadsheet. This process we have already seen in Chapter 5 under the "Format Notes with Bullets and Tables" section.

Instead of always using the Insert ribbon, there's a handy keyboard shortcut. Begin by typing your first table heading, for instance, "SLA", as shown in Figure 6-17. Press Tab to move to the next cell as shown in Figure 6-18, and type the next heading as "Time". Keep pressing Tab as you add headings. Once finished, press Enter; this drops you to the next row for entering data as shown in Figure 6-19.

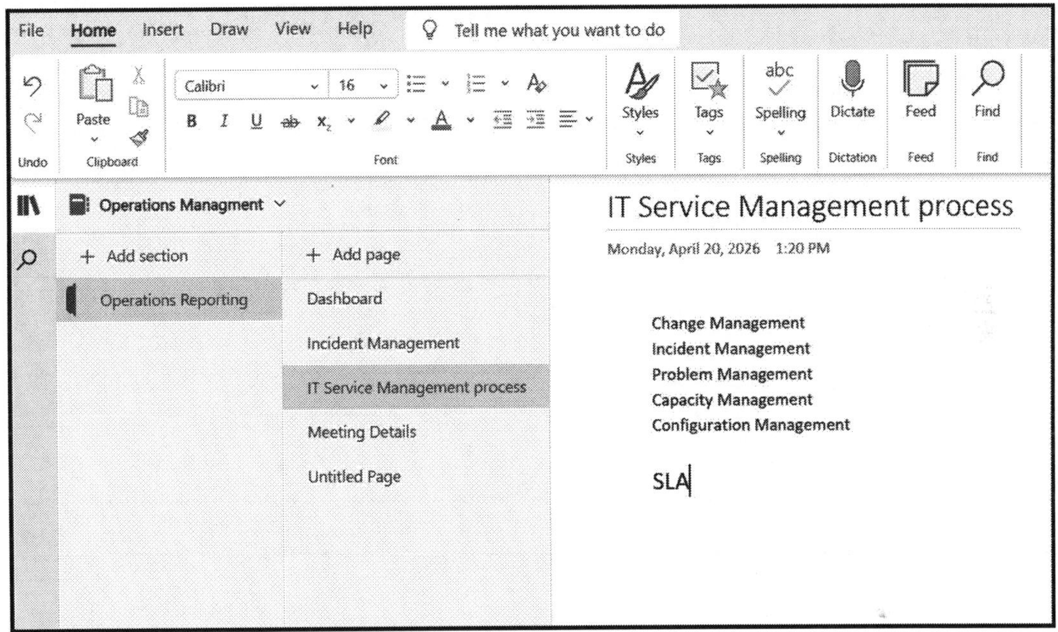

Figure 6-17. *Text SLA is typed*

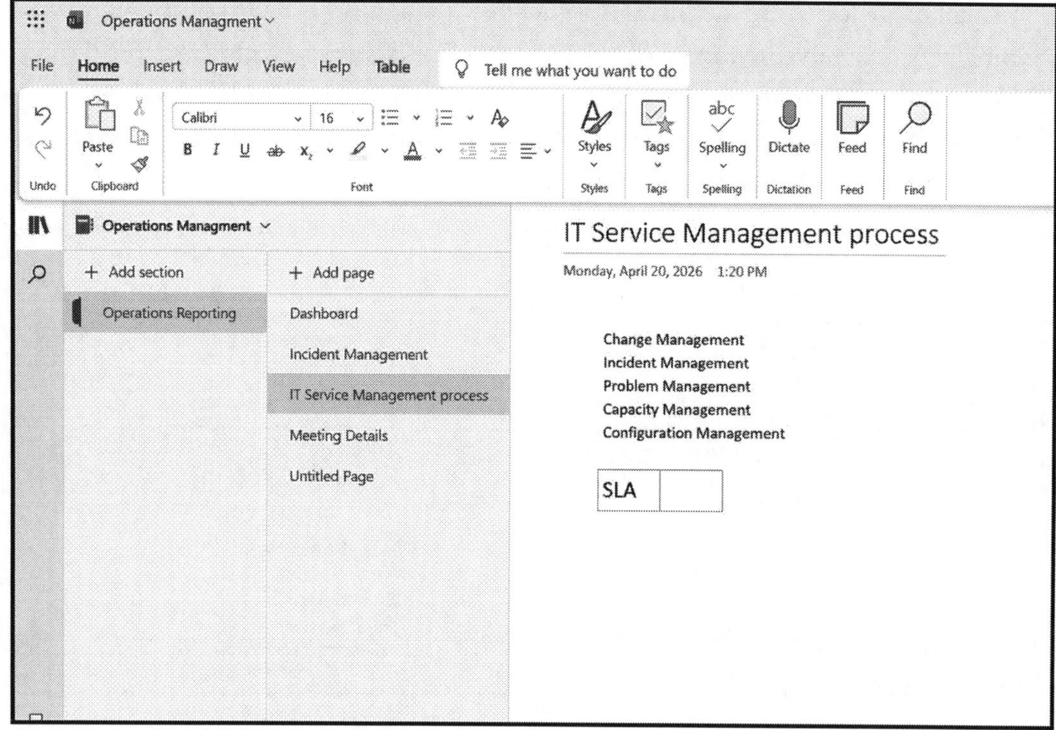

***Figure 6-18.** New column gets created*

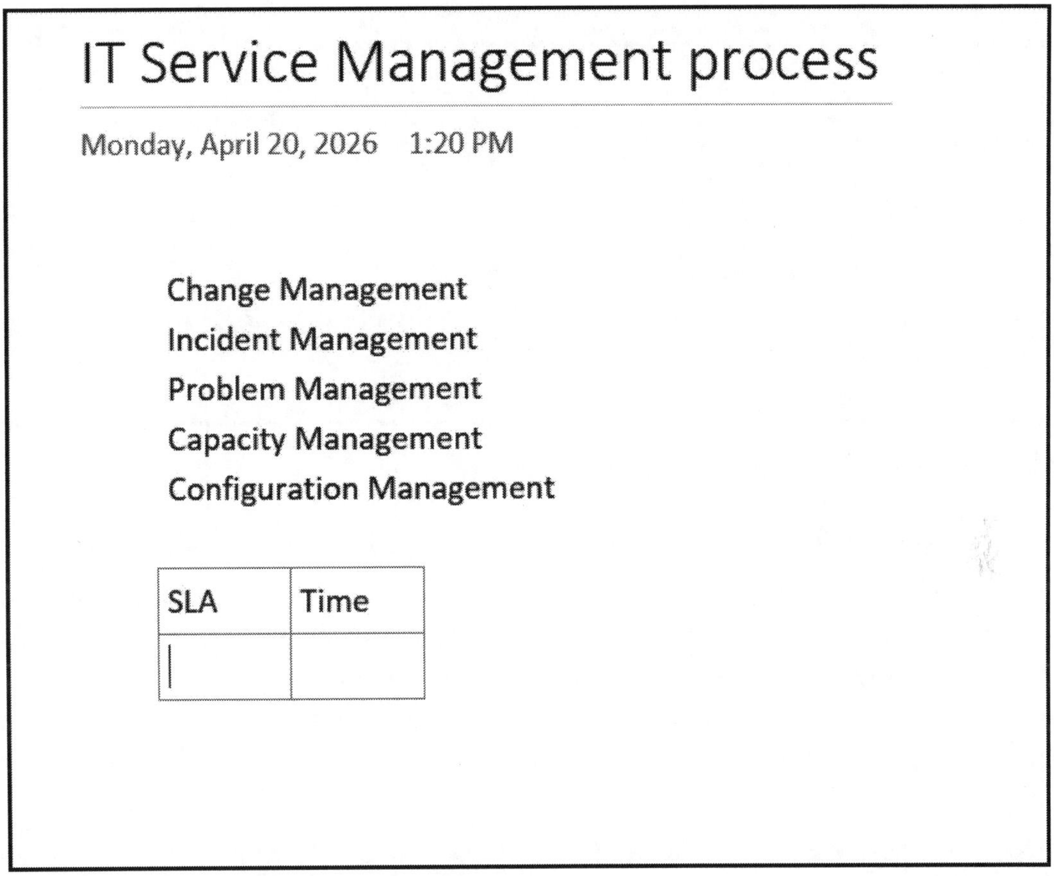

Figure 6-19. *New row gets created*

While your cursor is inside a table cell, you'll see a new, contextual Table ribbon appear at the top. This ribbon vanishes if you click off the table but returns when you're back in a cell. On this Table ribbon, you can select columns and rows, delete parts of the table, insert columns or rows where needed, and apply formatting.

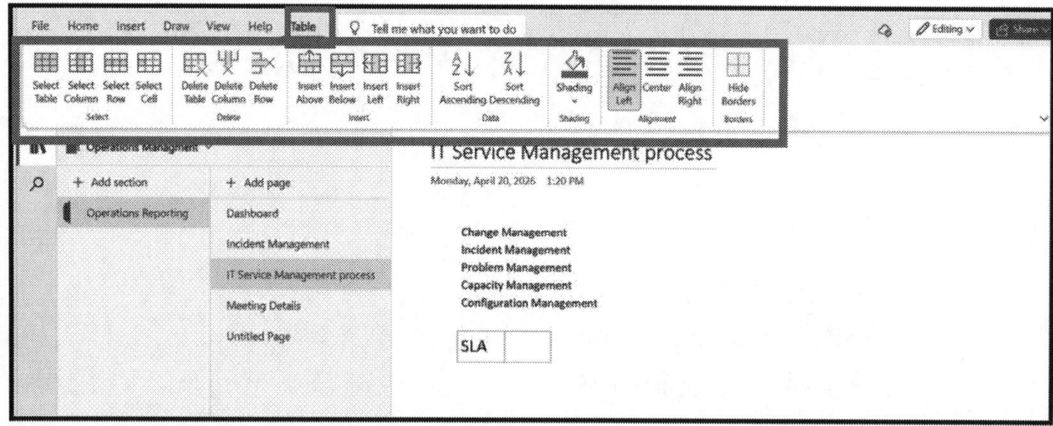

Figure 6-20. *Table menu to format table*

To style your table, select a row by clicking and dragging, then choose Shading from the format area and pick a color. If borders aren't necessary, such as when arranging pictures—you can hide them for a cleaner layout, then bring them back later if desired. You also have the option to center your headings rather than align them left. With the Tab key shortcut and the Table contextual ribbon, creating and customizing tables is quick and straightforward as highlighted in Figure 6-20.

Change the Default Font Type, Size, and Color

If you frequently modify the font, size, or color each time you take notes in OneNote, consider configuring the default settings to streamline your workflow. By default, OneNote uses Calibri 11 in black font. To customize these preferences, navigate to the File tab and select Options from the backstage menu as shown in Figure 6-21. This will open the OneNote Options dialog box. In the General section, locate the Default Font area, where you can specify the preferred font, size, and color.

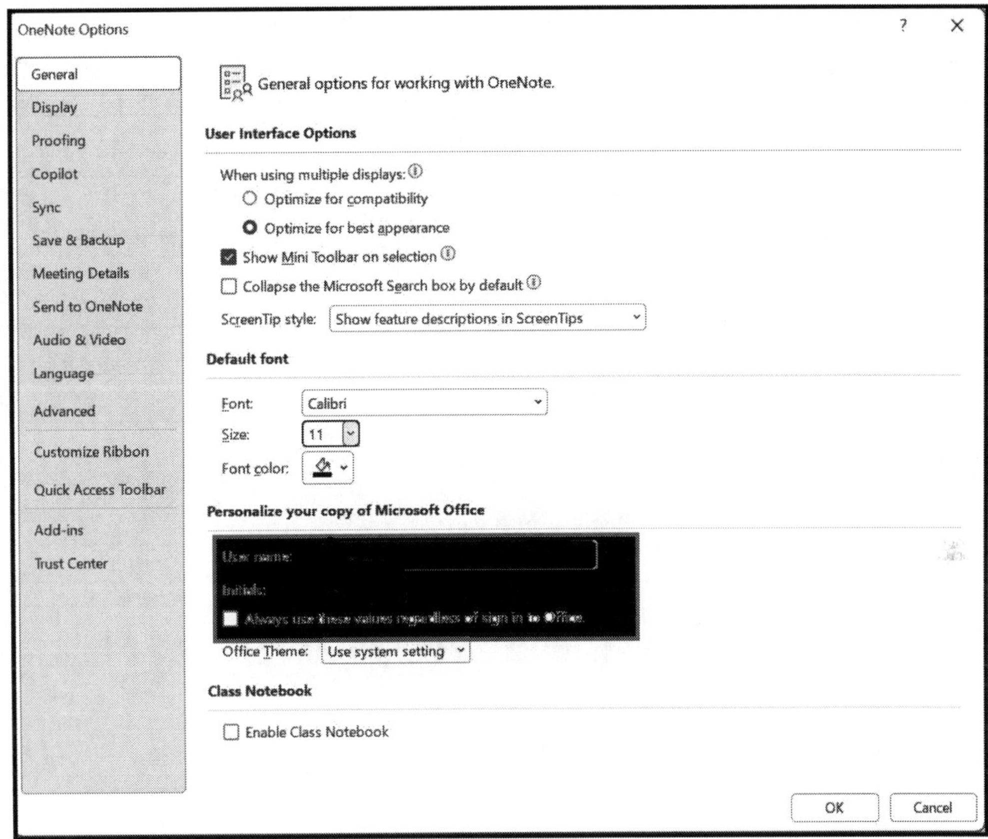

Figure 6-21. *Access default font settings*

To change the font, use the dropdown menu to browse available options, or type the initial letter of the desired font for quicker access. For example, entering "S" will allow you to efficiently locate "Segoe UI" as shown in Figure 6-22. Next, update the font size as needed—such as changing it to 12 as shown in Figure 6-23—and select your preferred color from the palette, such as standard dark blue as shown in Figure 6-24. After making your selections, click OK. The ribbon will now display your updated default font preferences.

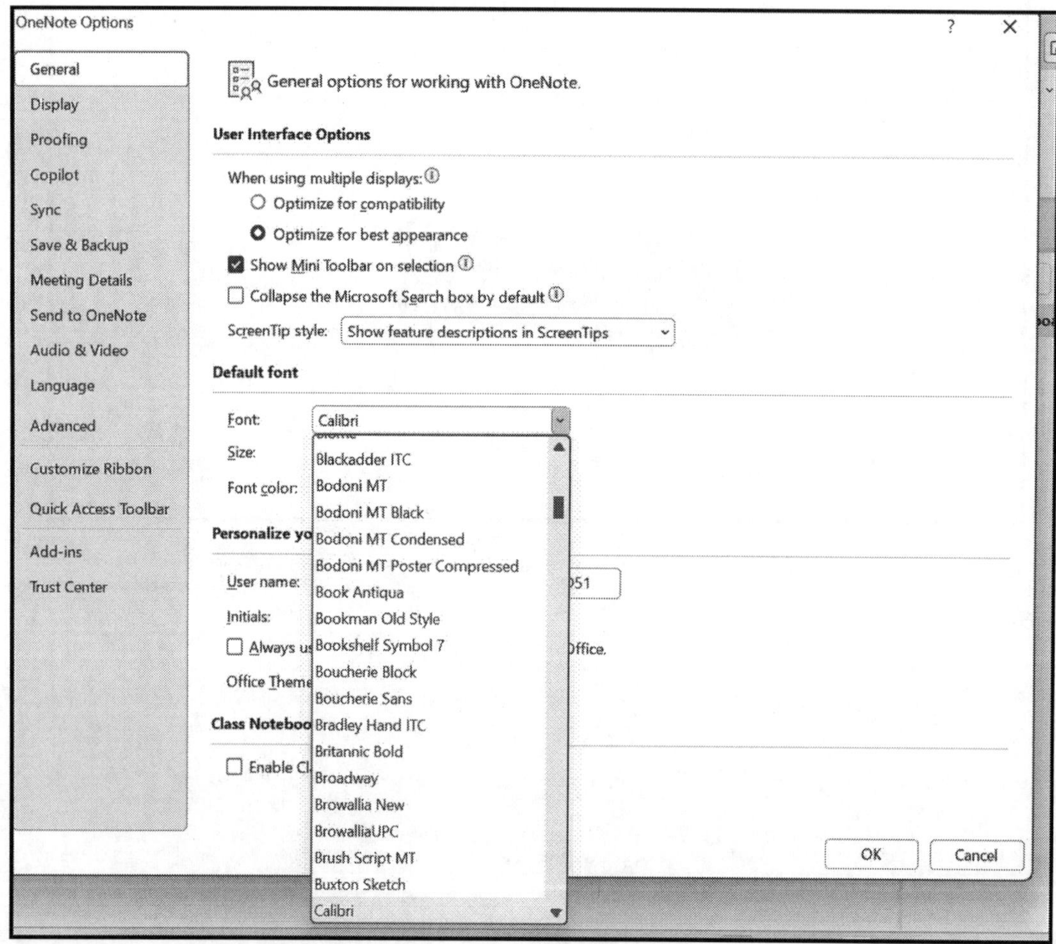

Figure 6-22. *Available fonts*

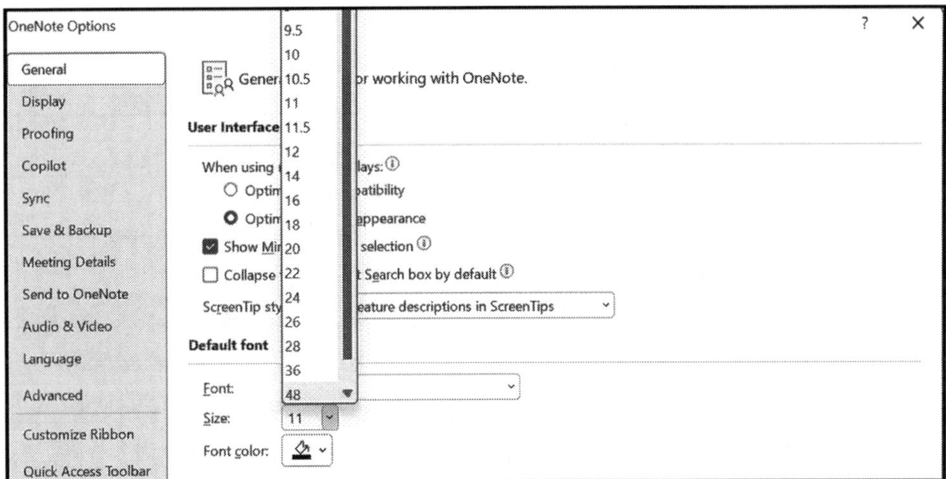

Figure 6-23. Available font preferences

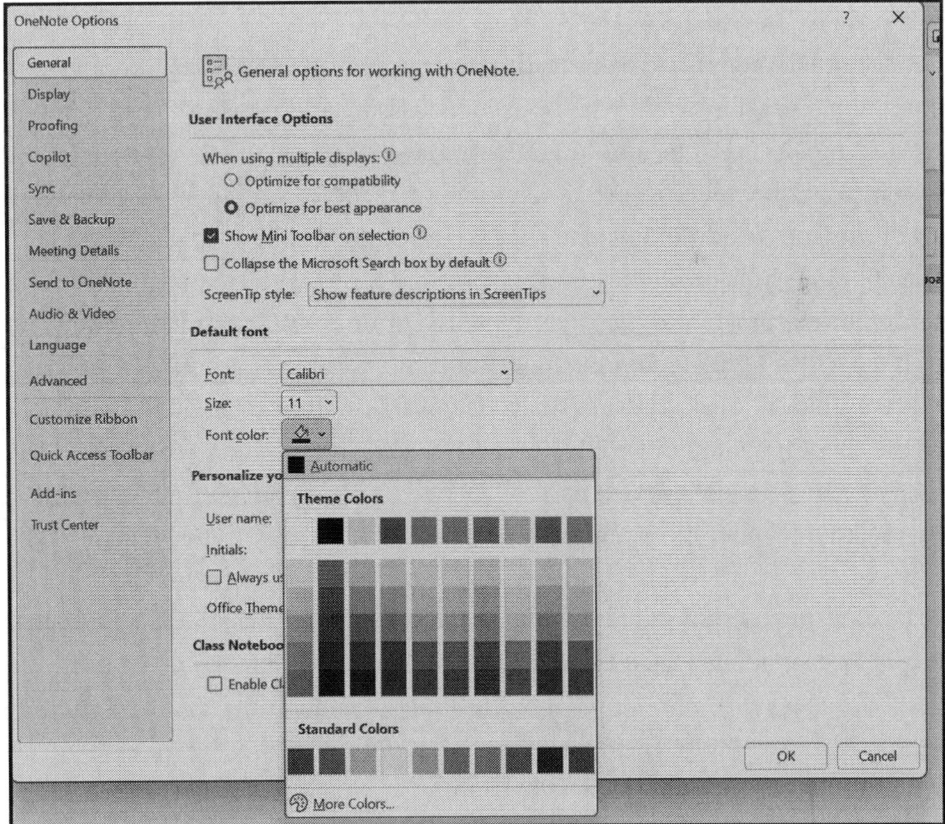

Figure 6-24. Available font colors

When you begin typing a new note, you will see these changes in effect. It is important to note that when navigating to different notebook sections, the original default settings may briefly appear, but once you click on a page and start typing, your custom settings will be applied. These default preferences remain consistent across all sections and will also carry over to newly created or accessed notebooks. This ensures your notes maintain a uniform appearance throughout your work. With this, the chapter ends.

This chapter explored advanced tips, automation tools, and Microsoft OneNote integrations that improve meeting records, boost productivity, and keep visuals consistent. It detailed how Outlook meeting details can be imported straight into OneNote, so agendas, attendee lists, dates, and Teams links are automatically included—cutting down on manual work and creating an organized space for meeting notes. The chapter also covered using OneNote during Microsoft Teams meetings, allowing real-time note-taking and collaboration, so several people can contribute at once and everyone stays on the same page.

Further this chapter provided an in-depth examination of Microsoft Loop and Teams Recap functionalities, illustrating methods for accessing and reusing agendas, meeting notes, recordings, transcripts, and AI-generated summaries. It detailed Intelligent Recap features, emphasizing how suggested notes and tasks are automatically produced from meeting discussions. Additionally, the chapter introduced advanced user shortcuts such as screen clipping with automatic timestamps, extracting text from images, efficiently creating and formatting tables through keyboard commands, and implementing advanced table formatting techniques. Customization options for default font type, size, and color were also addressed to maintain visual consistency throughout notebooks. Overall, the chapter demonstrated that OneNote, when integrated with Teams, Outlook, Loop, and automation tools, serves as a robust and unified workspace that optimizes meetings, fosters collaboration, and increases productivity within the Microsoft 365 environment.

The next chapter demonstrates how Microsoft OneNote can serve as a practical, flexible tool for managing projects and tasks in personal, academic, and professional settings. Building on earlier productivity techniques, it shows how OneNote simplifies structured planning without the complexities of traditional project management software. The chapter covers applying the Getting Things Done (GTD) methodology; organizing tasks and ideas with notebooks, sections, pages, and tags; and creating dashboards and weekly planners for clear priority and progress tracking. Integration with Outlook Tasks is discussed for reminders and deadlines, along with visual task tracking using Kanban boards in OneNote. It also introduces project templates and multi-project notebook designs for consistency and scalability. By the end, readers will see OneNote as an effective, adaptable project management tool for structured productivity and collaboration.

CHAPTER 7

Use Microsoft OneNote for Project Management

The previous chapter covers advanced methods to make Microsoft OneNote more productive and visually appealing. It explains handwriting to text for clarity, keyboard shortcuts for efficiency, and Power Automate integration for workflow automation like note creation and task syncing. Examples show how OneNote connects with Excel, Word, Outlook, Planner, and To Do for reporting and task management. Collaboration tools like Whiteboard and Loop support real-time sharing, while advanced copy-paste and linking techniques help organize notebooks. Overall, readers gain expert strategies to enhance OneNote's appearance, functionality, and collaboration features.

This chapter presents Microsoft OneNote as a practical project and task management tool, offering structured planning and oversight without the complexity of traditional systems. It introduces using the Getting Things Done (GTD) methodology in OneNote, showing readers how to capture, prioritize, and organize tasks efficiently. The chapter highlights creating dashboards and planners for clear task tracking, leveraging integration with Outlook for actionable reminders, and building Kanban-style boards within OneNote for visual task progress. Professional templates help standardize project documentation, and guidance is provided on managing multiple projects through effective notebook organization. By the end, readers understand how OneNote serves as a flexible solution for managing tasks and coordinating projects across various professional settings.

Introduction

Effectively managing projects and tasks has grown increasingly complex within contemporary professional environments. Both individuals and teams must oversee multiple initiatives, foster cross-departmental collaboration, adhere to deadlines, and

C. Waghmare, *Mastering Microsoft OneNote*, https://doi.org/10.1007/979-8-8688-2866-9_7

sustain comprehensive documentation while minimizing cognitive strain. Microsoft OneNote offers a flexible, lightweight, and adaptable platform for project and task management, empowering users to plan, execute, and monitor work without the constraints of traditional project management software.

Distinct from conventional tools that separate planning and documentation, OneNote integrates ideation, planning, and execution into a unified workspace. Its notebook-based structure enables users to capture concepts, define goals, record meeting results, track tasks, and store supporting materials in context. This functionality is particularly advantageous for projects that develop organically, require continuous collaboration, or involve diverse information sources.

This chapter examines how the Getting Things Done (GTD) methodology can be applied within OneNote. Readers will gain insight into capturing tasks, organizing actionable items, and maintaining clarity using pages, sections, and tags. The discussion extends to the creation of dashboards and weekly planners, offering centralized and visual overviews of priorities, deadlines, and progress, thereby transforming fragmented notes into structured action plans.

Integration is crucial for bridging planning with execution. OneNote's synergy with Outlook Tasks connects notes to reminders, due dates, and accountability measures. The chapter further guides readers in implementing Kanban-style boards within OneNote, illustrating visual task tracking through tables and tags. This method allows both teams and individuals to intuitively manage workflows without the need for supplemental tools.

Microsoft OneNote also provides professional project templates designed to standardize planning, documentation, and reporting across various initiatives. Additionally, strategies are presented for designing multi-project notebooks to efficiently organize concurrent projects while ensuring clarity, consistency, and scalability. By the conclusion of this chapter, readers will appreciate OneNote's role as a practical companion for project managements supporting structured productivity, collaborative execution, and flexible planning across personal, academic, and organizational settings.

Using OneNote for GTD (Getting Things Done)

As shown in Figure 7-1, the Getting Things Done (GTD) methodology, introduced by David Allen, emphasizes capturing everything that demands attention, clarifying what each item means, organizing outcomes into trusted systems, reflecting regularly, and engaging with confidence. Microsoft OneNote aligns naturally with GTD principles due to its flexible structure, intuitive organization, and seamless integration with Microsoft 365 services. Rather than forcing users into rigid task hierarchies, OneNote enables contextual thinking, making it an effective platform for applying GTD in dynamic professional environments.

At its core, OneNote acts as a trusted external brain where commitments, ideas, reference material, and actionable tasks coexist in a single ecosystem. Its ability to capture unstructured input—typed notes, handwritten ideas, audio recordings, emails, and web content—makes it ideal for the GTD "capture" phase. When implemented correctly, OneNote allows users to transition smoothly from idea capture to actionable execution while maintaining clarity and mental focus.

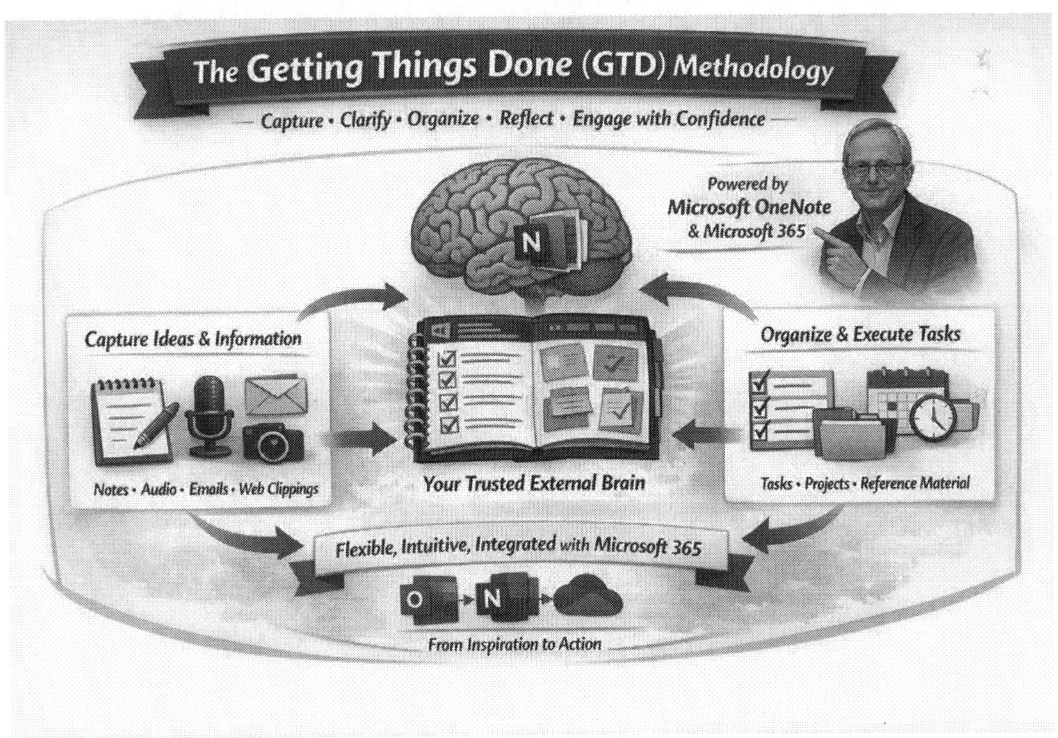

Figure 7-1. *GTD using Microsoft OneNote*

Capturing, Clarifying, and Organizing Work in OneNote

Figure 7-2 shows a synopsis of this section. OneNote's primary advantage in implementing GTD is its ability to facilitate the rapid and seamless capture of inputs. Users may designate an inbox section within a notebook to log all incoming tasks, ideas, meeting notes, and spontaneous thoughts without initial assessment. This approach aligns with the GTD methodology, which advocates immediate capture to reduce cognitive overload. Additionally, OneNote's cross-device synchronization enables consistent access and consolidation of inputs recorded on mobile devices, tablets, or desktops.

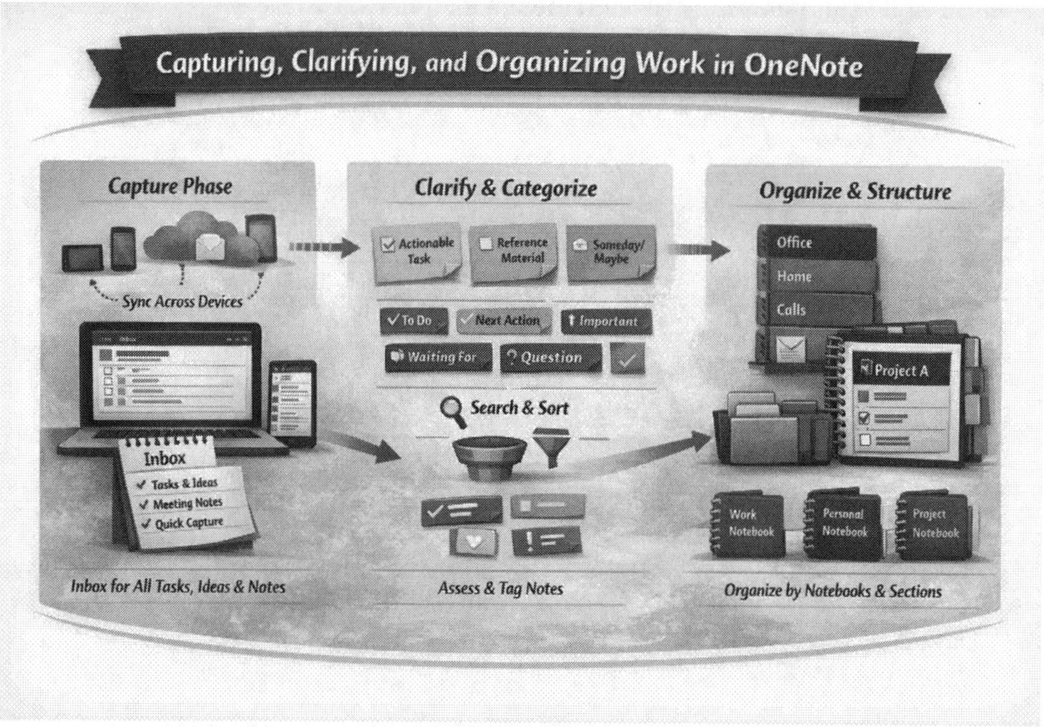

Figure 7-2. *Capturing, clarifying, and organizing work in OneNote*

After the initial capture phase, clarification is the subsequent step. Each note or item is systematically assessed to determine whether it constitutes an actionable task, reference material, or deferred content. OneNote's organizational structure, including pages and subpages, enables users to distinguish actionable items from supporting information while maintaining contextual connections. Tags such as To Do, Important, and Question, along with custom GTD tags like Next Action, Waiting For, or Someday, facilitate both visual and functional categorization of tasks. Leveraging these tags in conjunction with OneNote's robust search and summary capabilities ensures efficient retrieval of actions without the need to navigate through large volumes of notebook content.

OneNote enables efficient organization through a structured hierarchy comprising notebooks, sections, and pages. Projects can be allocated dedicated sections, while individual tasks may be categorized within context-specific pages such as office, home, or calls. This approach ensures that tasks are systematically grouped according to their purpose, facilitating engagement with the appropriate actions at the optimal time, a key principle of GTD.

Planning, Reviewing, and Maintaining Clarity

To keep your GTD system effective as shown in Figure 7-3, it's important to review it regularly—and OneNote helps by offering flexible weekly review pages and dashboards. You can set up a weekly review page where unfinished tasks, upcoming responsibilities, and project progress are all gathered in one spot. With internal links, you can quickly navigate from your review summary to detailed project notes, making your reflection sessions smoother and more efficient.

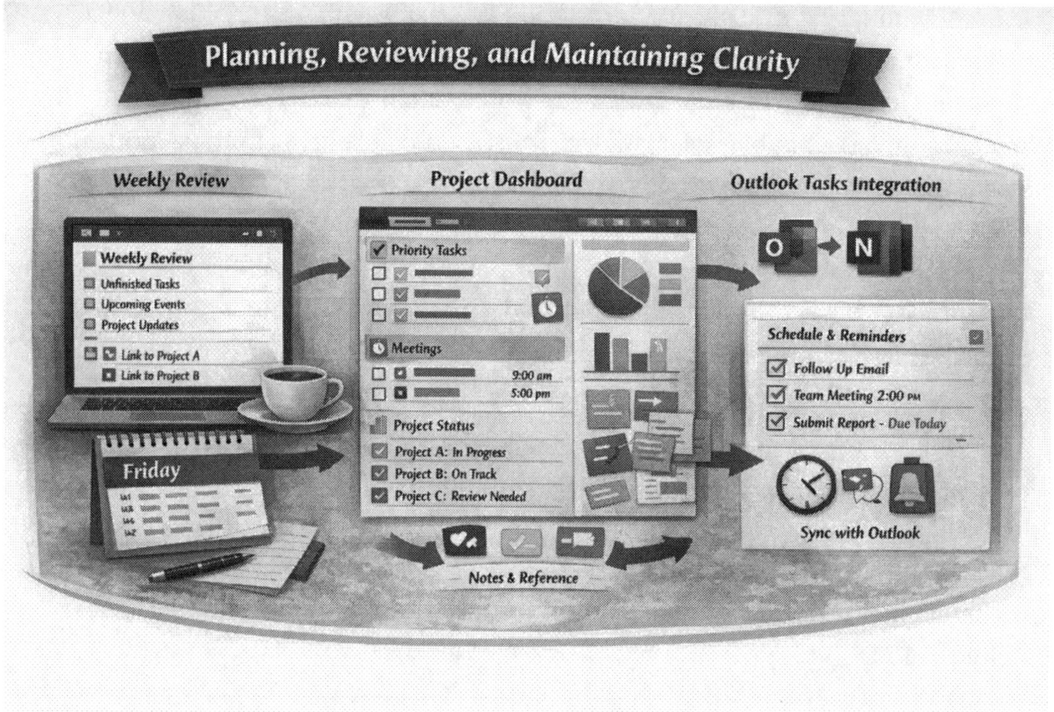

Figure 7-3. *Planning, reviewing, and maintaining clarity*

Dashboards can use tables, tags, icons, and links to create a real-time summary of what's important. Rather than splitting tasks from their context like dedicated task managers do, OneNote lets users view their tasks together with related notes, meeting details, and reference materials. This complete picture helps people make well-informed decisions, rooted in the relevant information.

OneNote integrates efficiently with Outlook Tasks, facilitating the conversion of action items identified during GTD clarification into scheduled tasks with reminders. This integration maintains OneNote as the dedicated space for planning and ideation, while Outlook oversees task execution and timing, achieving a clear separation of functions within the GTD framework. Collectively, these tools enable sustained productivity without redundant efforts.

Executing Actions and Scaling GTD Across Projects

Effective implementation of GTD depends on maintaining confidence in the system's completeness and reliability as shown in Figure 7-4. OneNote supports this assurance by enabling users to incorporate checklists, assign categories, and link tasks to relevant materials. In the context of complex projects, sections may include meeting minutes, task inventories, risk registers, and reference documents, all conveniently located within a unified project workspace.

As responsibilities grow, OneNote scales effortlessly. Users managing multiple projects can design a master projects notebook, with standardized templates for each initiative. Tags and search filters allow users to focus on high-priority tasks across all projects, while page links maintain navigation efficiency. This scalability makes OneNote especially effective for professionals managing parallel commitments across roles or teams.

By combining structure with flexibility, OneNote enables GTD implementation without forcing users into rigid workflows. Instead, it adapts naturally to individual thinking styles while maintaining methodological discipline.

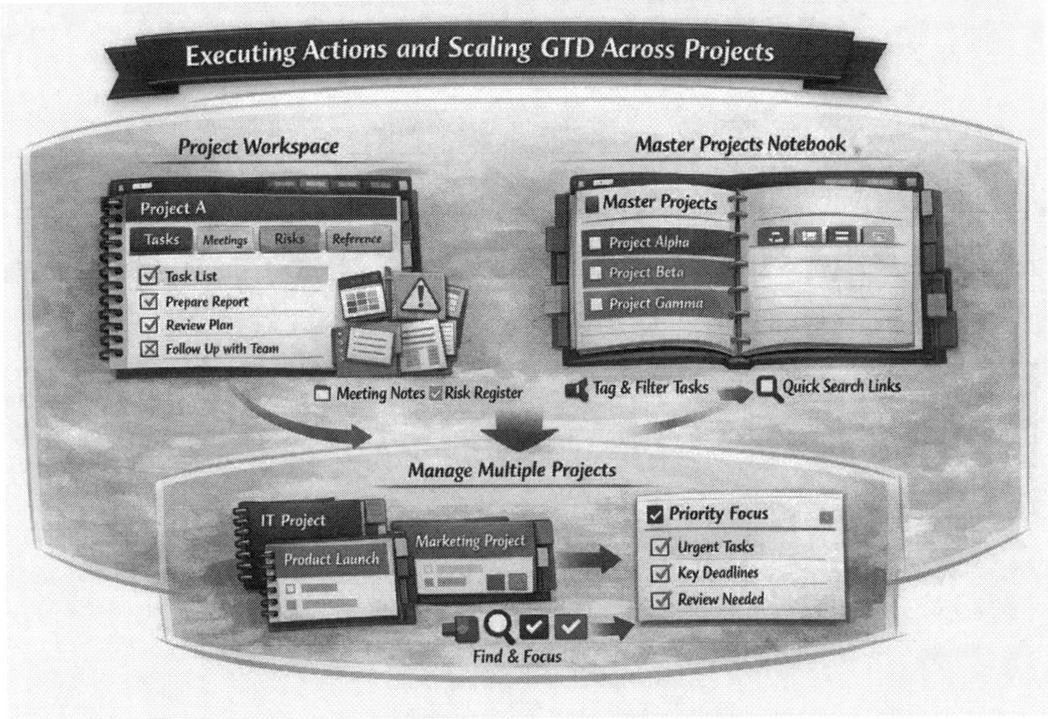

Figure 7-4. *Executing actions and scaling GTD across projects*

An Example: Implementing GTD in OneNote for a Project Manager

The project manager establishes a notebook entitled "GTD Workspace," incorporating sections such as inbox, next actions, projects, waiting for, and reference. During meetings, all notes and action items are systematically recorded in the inbox. At the close of each day, the manager reviews the inbox, clarifies tasks, and appropriately reallocates them to relevant sections.

Each project is assigned a dedicated page under the projects section, which includes objectives, task lists, meeting notes, and stakeholder information. Actionable items are designated as next actions and, when necessary, their deadlines are coordinated with Outlook Tasks. On Fridays, the manager conducts a weekly review to evaluate outstanding tasks, update project statuses, and establish priorities for the upcoming week. Through this setup, OneNote becomes both a strategic planning environment and an operational command center—fully aligned with GTD principles as shown in Figure 7-5.

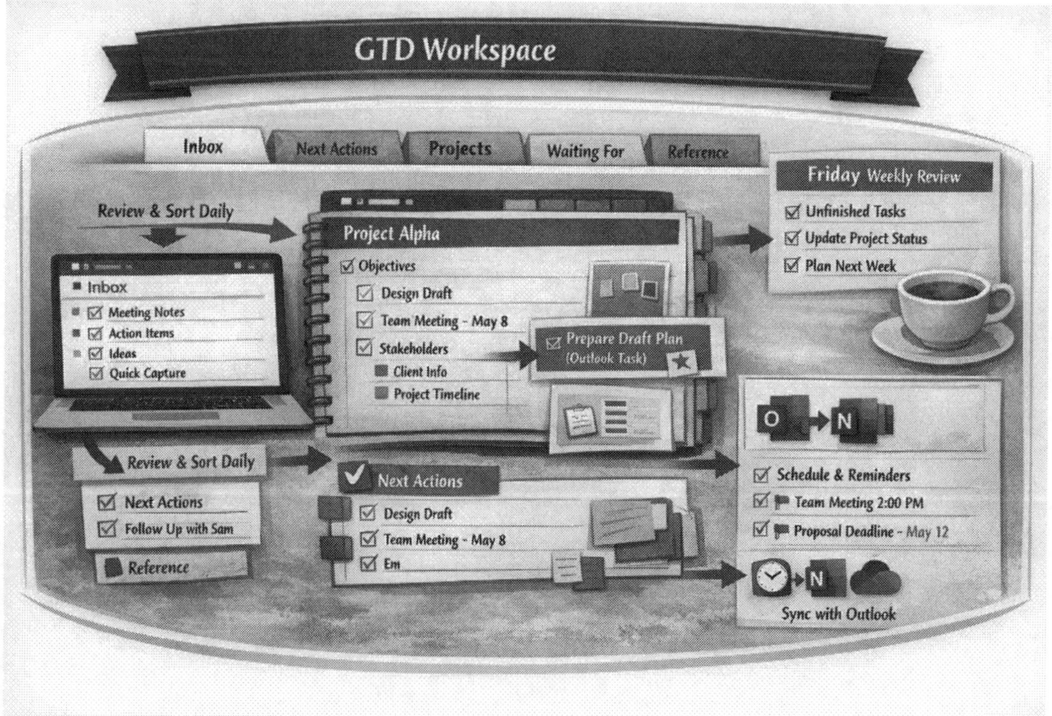

Figure 7-5. *Implementing GTD in OneNote for a project manager*

Creating Dashboards and Weekly Planners

In contemporary professional and academic settings, individuals are often tasked with managing substantial volumes of information while concurrently monitoring priorities, deadlines, and ongoing responsibilities. Absent a structured planning approach, tasks may become dispersed among emails, documents, and meeting notes, resulting in diminished focus and increased decision fatigue. Microsoft OneNote addresses these challenges by enabling users to create tailored dashboards and weekly planners, thereby fostering organization, transparency, and clarity in both daily operations and long-term objectives. Distinct from conventional task management systems, OneNote integrates planning activities with relevant contextual data, making it an optimal platform for comprehensive productivity management.

At its core, OneNote dashboards serve as centralized control panels offering comprehensive overviews of tasks, projects, schedules, and reference materials. Through the integration of tables, tags, icons, internal links, and visual indicators, users are able to construct dashboards tailored to their specific workflows and responsibilities. Weekly planners developed within OneNote facilitate the translation of overarching objectives into actionable steps, enabling effective time allocation while preserving adaptability. Rather than imposing rigid schedules, these planners function as flexible frameworks that can be adjusted in response to shifting priorities. By consolidating all planning resources within OneNote, users maintain seamless connections between planning activities and the associated notes, discussions, and decisions that inform their work.

Dashboards and weekly planners within OneNote facilitate a continuous review approach, which is vital for maintaining productivity over time. A dedicated weekly review page allows users to consolidate incomplete tasks, impending deadlines, and project updates in one central location, supporting reflection on progress and proactive adjustment of plans. Internal linking streamlines navigation from overview pages to detailed project records, minimizing reliance on multiple tools or applications. This integrated methodology reduces cognitive burden and assures individuals that critical items are consistently addressed. By unifying planning and execution, OneNote provides a reliable, comprehensive workspace for effective management.

An important benefit of utilizing OneNote for dashboards and planners lies in its capacity to accommodate diverse roles and responsibilities. Whether it is employed by an individual contributor managing daily tasks, a project manager coordinating several initiatives, or an executive monitoring strategic objectives, OneNote adjusts seamlessly to varying levels of complexity. Weekly planners may be tailored for personal productivity, team collaboration, or project scheduling, while dashboards can be configured to emphasize key metrics, progress milestones, or urgent actions. This versatility allows users to move beyond standard templates, enabling them to develop planning systems that align with their distinct cognitive styles and professional requirements.

Additionally, OneNote boosts planning efficiency by integrating seamlessly with Microsoft 365 tools like Outlook, Planner, and To Do. You can connect action items from your weekly planners directly to scheduled tasks with reminders, which helps align your planning with actual execution. Outlook handles time-specific duties, while OneNote serves as a hub for reflection, prioritization, and strategic decision-making. By maintaining this division between tools, users gain clarity and avoid unnecessary duplication, leading to more confident and consistent workflows.

Ultimately, using dashboards and weekly planners turns OneNote into a central productivity hub. They offer visibility, context, and flexibility, encouraging a shift from simply reacting to tasks toward thoughtful planning. This chapter covers the core strategies for building effective dashboards and planners in OneNote, giving readers the tools to stay focused, track their progress consistently, and manage work with confidence and precision.

Steps to Create Project Dashboards and Weekly Planners in Microsoft OneNote

Creating dashboards and weekly planners in Microsoft OneNote transforms the application into a centralized planning and execution workspace. The following steps guide you through designing effective, reusable, and scalable dashboards and planners aligned with real-world productivity and project management needs.

Step 1: Set Up the Planning Notebook Structure

Begin by creating a dedicated notebook for planning and project oversight, such as "Project Management WorkSpace" or "Weekly Planning Hub." Within the notebook, create key sections: Dashboard, Weekly Planner, Projects, Meetings, and Reference as shown in Figure 7-6.

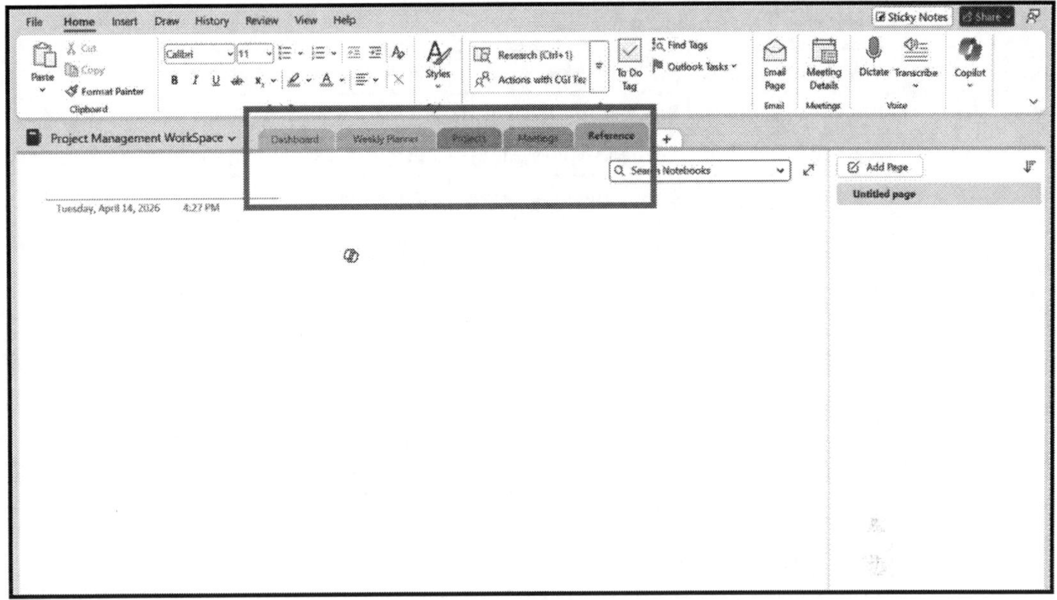

***Figure 7-6.** Creating dedicated notebooks*

This structure ensures clear separation between overview, planning, and detailed execution while keeping all content interconnected.

Step 2: Create a Project Dashboard Page

In the Dashboard section, create a new page titled "Project Dashboard." This page serves as a high-level control center. Add the following elements as shown in Figure 7-7:

- **Priority Tasks Table**: A simple table listing critical tasks, due dates, and status
- **Project Status Overview**: Bullet points or tables showing each project (e.g., On Track, At Risk, Completed)
- **Links to Project Pages**: Use OneNote page links to connect directly to detailed project notes
- **Visual Indicators**: Icons, emojis, or color formatting for quick recognition

Priority Tasks Table

Name of the Project	Critical Tasks	Due date	Status
Project A	Incident management	5th May 2027	Open
Project B	Problem Management	11th July 2027	Open
Project C	Change Management	7th October 2024	Closed

Definition Tags

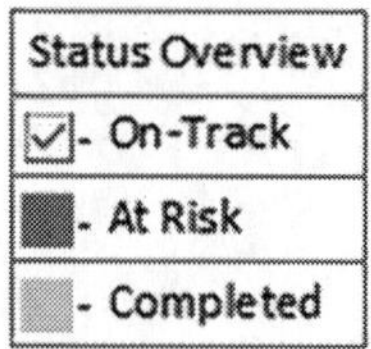

Status Overview
☑- On-Track
- At Risk
- Completed

Priority Tasks Table

Name of the Project	Status Overview
Project A	☑
Project B	
Project C	

Note: Link to Project Pages

Figure 7-7. *Creation of project dashboard page*

The dashboard should remain concise and scannable, focusing on visibility rather than detail.

Step 3: Design the Weekly Planner Page

Create a page in the Weekly Planner section titled "Weekly Planner – [Week Date]." Structure the page with clear subheadings, such as Weekly Goals, Top 5 Priorities, Daily Planning (Monday–Friday), Meetings & Deliverables, and Notes & Follow-Ups. Use checklists, tables, and tags (To Do, Important, Follow Up) to track progress as shown in Figure 7-8. Consider duplicating this page weekly to maintain consistency.

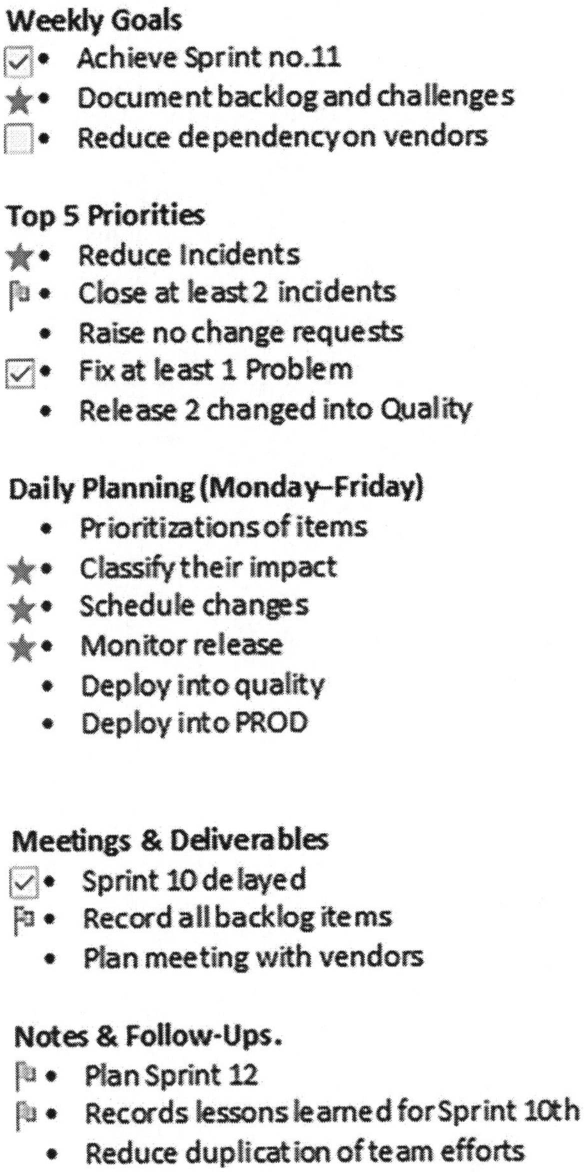

Weekly Goals

- Achieve Sprint no.11
- Document backlog and challenges
- Reduce dependencyon vendors

Top 5 Priorities

- Reduce Incidents
- Close at least 2 incidents
- Raise no change requests
- Fix at least 1 Problem
- Release 2 changed into Quality

Daily Planning (Monday–Friday)

- Prioritizations of items
- Classify their impact
- Schedule changes
- Monitor release
- Deploy into quality
- Deploy into PROD

Meetings & Deliverables

- Sprint 10 delayed
- Record all backlog items
- Plan meeting with vendors

Notes & Follow-Ups.

- Plan Sprint 12
- Records lessons learned for Sprint 10th
- Reduce duplication of team efforts

Figure 7-8. *Design of weekly planner*

Step 4: Link Weekly Planner to Projects and Dashboard

Strengthen navigation by linking as shown in Figures 7-9 and 7-10:

- Tasks in the weekly planner to their respective project pages.
- Dashboard items to relevant planner or project pages.
- Use Copy Link to Page in OneNote to create seamless cross-references. This reduces search time and ensures planning remains connected to execution context.

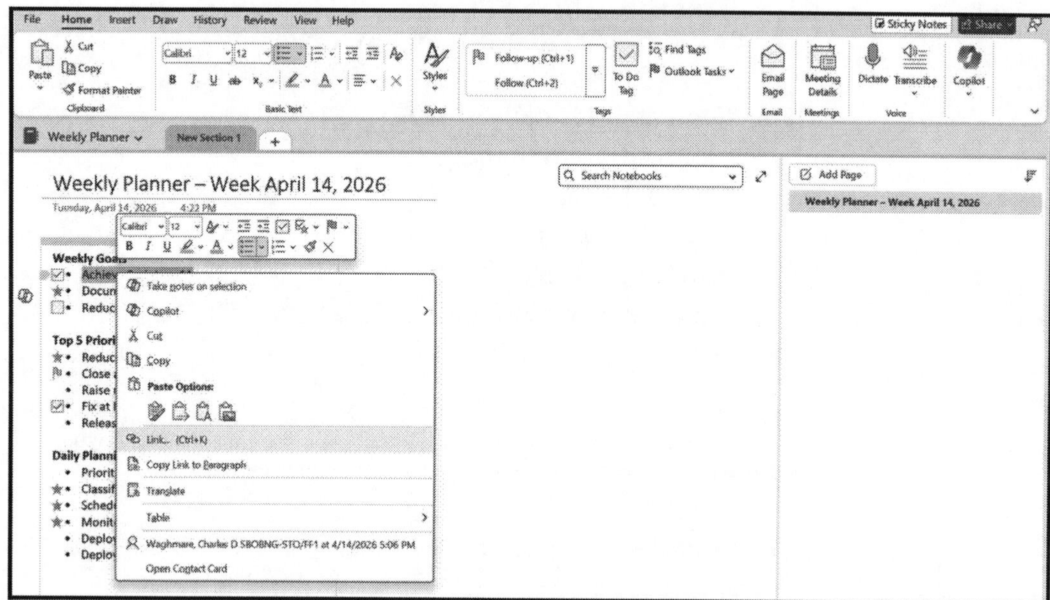

Figure 7-9. Right-click on the task to access Link option

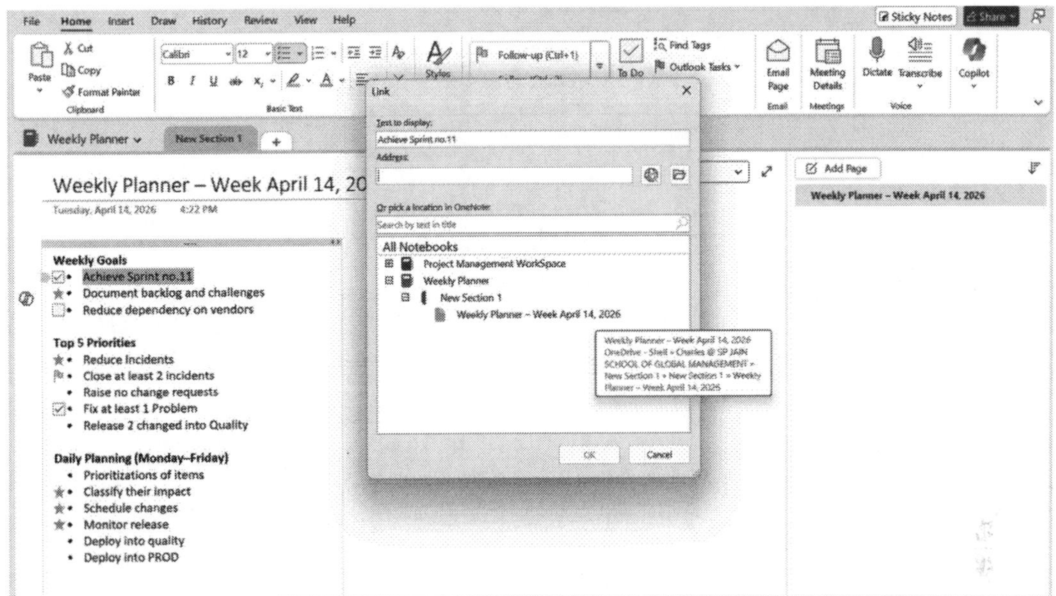

***Figure 7-10.** Link weekly task to pages*

Step 5: Use Tags, Search, and Summary for Visibility

Apply tags such as To Do, Important, Question, and Next Action. As shown in Figure 7-11, use OneNote's Find Tags feature to generate task summaries across dashboards, planners, and project pages. This makes it easy to review open actions during weekly or daily planning sessions.

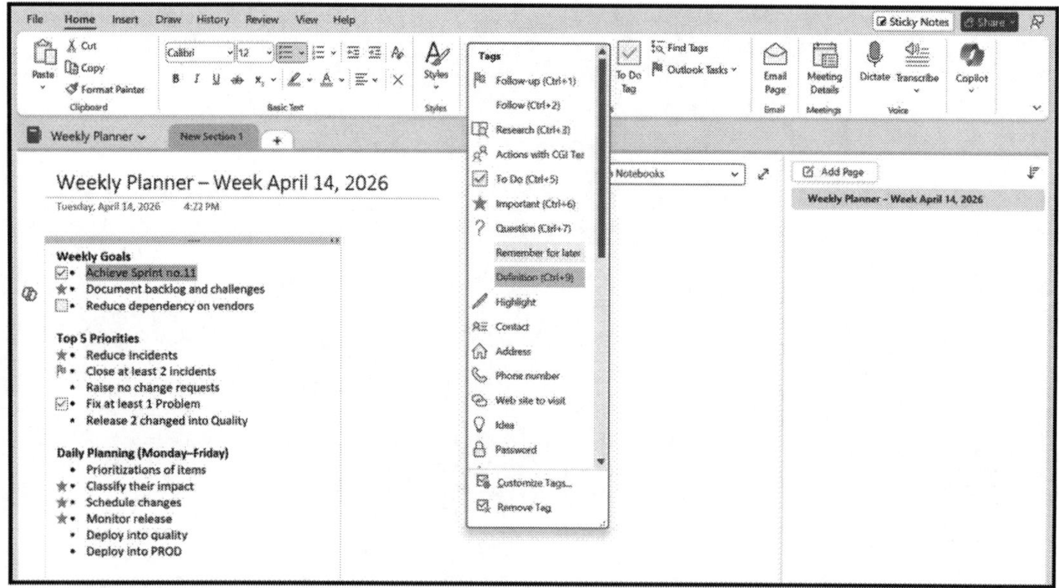

Figure 7-11. *Figure to explore and assign tags*

Step 6: Integrate OneNote with Outlook Tasks (Optional)

For time-bound actions, as shown in Figure 7-12, right-click checklist items and create Outlook Tasks. Assign due dates and reminders in Outlook. This allows OneNote to remain the planning and thinking hub, while Outlook manages execution timing and notifications.

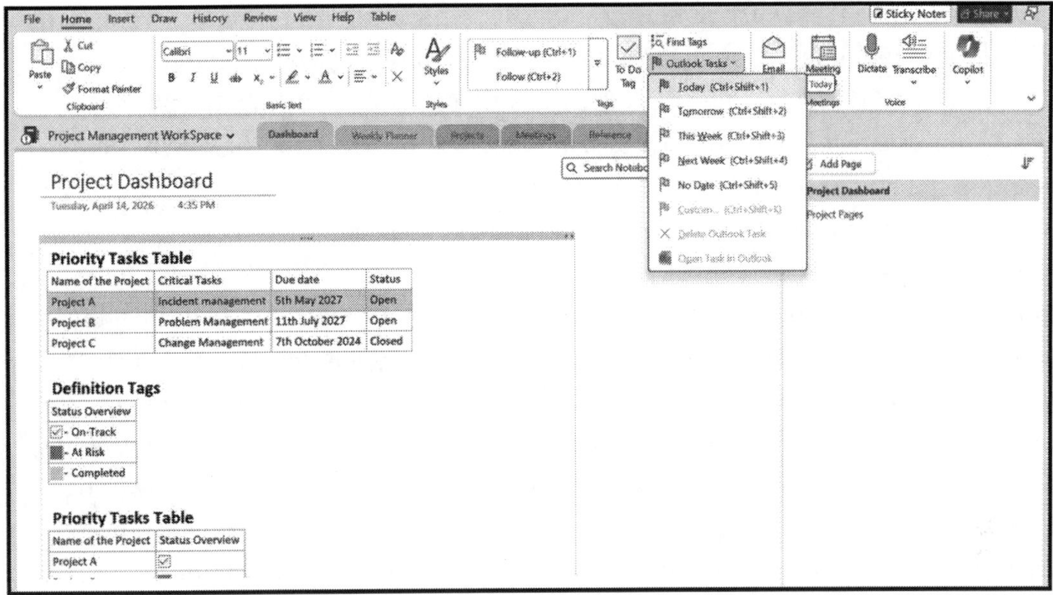

Figure 7-12. *Assign Outlook Tasks*

Step 7: Review and Maintain Weekly

At the end of each week, update task status, archive completed weekly planners, refresh dashboard priorities, and prepare the next week's planner by copying the template. Regular reviews maintain clarity, trust in the system, and alignment with goals. By following these steps, Microsoft OneNote becomes a dynamic planning system that combines dashboards, weekly planners, project tracking, and contextual documentation. This approach supports consistent productivity, clear prioritization, and informed decision-making—without the complexity of traditional project-management tools.

OneNote + Outlook Tasks Integration

The integration between Microsoft OneNote and Outlook Tasks bridges the gap between thoughtful planning and disciplined execution, allowing users to convert ideas and notes into time-bound actions without disrupting their workflow. While OneNote serves as a flexible space for capturing thoughts, meeting discussions, project details, and strategic considerations, Outlook Tasks provides the structure required to manage deadlines, reminders, and follow-ups. When these tools are used together, they form a cohesive productivity system in which planning and scheduling reinforce one another rather than compete for attention. Action items identified during meetings or planning sessions in OneNote can be transformed directly into Outlook Tasks, ensuring that important commitments are not lost within extensive notes or overlooked during busy schedules. As shown in Figure 7-12, a task is added to an item once the item is selected, and from the displayed menu the Outlook Tasks option can be selected.

This integration preserves clarity by maintaining a clear distinction between thinking and doing. OneNote remains the environment for reflection, prioritization, and contextual understanding, where tasks are recorded alongside supporting information such as objectives, reference materials, and stakeholder notes. Once an action requires a deadline or reminder, Outlook takes responsibility for execution by managing alerts, due dates, and time-sensitive tracking. This separation minimizes cognitive overload, as users no longer need to remember when to act—Outlook provides timely prompts—while OneNote continues to serve as the source of truth for why the task exists.

From a project management perspective, the OneNote–Outlook connection enhances accountability and follow-through. Tasks linked from OneNote retain meaningful context, enabling users to revisit the originating notes when clarification is needed. During weekly reviews, planners can confirm that scheduled tasks in Outlook accurately reflect project priorities captured in OneNote. This review loop fosters confidence in the system's completeness and reliability, which is essential for sustained productivity. Importantly, integration avoids duplication; updates occur without the need to re-enter information across platforms.

The combined use of OneNote and Outlook Tasks is particularly valuable in complex, multi-project environments. Professionals managing concurrent responsibilities can plan comprehensively in OneNote while relying on Outlook to orchestrate daily execution. Meetings generate tasks, tasks carry deadlines, and deadlines prompt action—yet all remain traceable to their original strategic context. As a result, users operate with greater focus, improved follow-through, and reduced stress.

Ultimately, OneNote and Outlook Tasks together enable a disciplined yet flexible productivity framework. By aligning thoughtful planning with structured execution, this integration ensures that ideas evolve into outcomes, commitments are honored, and productivity remains sustainable over time.

Kanban Boards in OneNote

Kanban boards are valued for visualizing tasks, preventing overload, and making progress visible across distinct workflow stages. When integrated with Microsoft OneNote, they go beyond simple task movement by merging visual organization with robust documentation. Unlike standalone Kanban platforms, OneNote lets users track tasks next to meeting notes, project goals, reference items, and decisions, turning Kanban into a full-featured project management tool that enhances both clarity and continuity. Thanks to OneNote's flexible pages, free-form layouts, and tagging features, users can customize Kanban boards to suit changing project needs, instead of sticking to strict guidelines.

Designing a Kanban Board Structure in OneNote

To create a Kanban board in OneNote, start by outlining workflow stages that track progress from beginning to completion. Typical stages like *to do, in progress, waiting,* and *completed* can be set up using tables, page sections, or aligned content containers, and replicated in OneNote with tags (see Figure 7-11). Each column gives a clear visual update on the status of tasks. You can display tasks as checklist items, brief descriptions, or linked pages according to their complexity. Smaller tasks may stay as checklist entries, while larger projects might use links to dedicated pages with schedules, stakeholders, and supporting materials.

OneNote's tagging system augments Kanban boards by introducing additional layers of information without compromising the visual structure. Tags such as *Important, Question, Follow Up,* or *Next Action* assist users in prioritizing tasks both visually and operationally. Leveraging OneNote's search and tag summary capabilities, individuals can efficiently filter tasks across multiple Kanban boards and projects. Visual elements like color coding, icons, and emojis further aid in workload assessment and rapid identification of bottlenecks. The flexible formatting options available in OneNote allow Kanban boards to be customized according to individual preferences or organizational requirements.

Using Kanban Boards for Execution and Review

Kanban boards in OneNote work best when they're used as dynamic tools instead of static charts. As you work on tasks, you manually move them between columns, which heightens your awareness of your workflow and prompts careful decision-making. This hands-on process—physically shifting a task from *In Progress* to Done—helps reinforce a sense of accomplishment and accountability. In contrast to automated tools that update tasks silently, OneNote's manual method encourages users to pause and consider whether a task is truly finished or needs more attention.

Regular reviews are vital for keeping a Kanban system effective. By checking the board daily or weekly, users can spot where tasks are piling up, adjust workloads, and keep things moving smoothly. OneNote makes it easy to integrate Kanban boards with checklists, dashboards, and meeting notes, so reviews happen alongside other planning activities. If a task requires a deadline or a reminder, it can be linked to Outlook Tasks—keeping scheduling separate while letting OneNote handle planning and tracking. This setup fits well with productivity systems like GTD, because it supports clear decision-making through visualization without automating the process away.

Scaling Kanban Boards Across Projects and Teams

OneNote's key strength is its ability to scale. Individuals can use personal Kanban boards for daily tasks, while project managers set up boards for whole teams or initiatives. Using standardized Kanban templates helps maintain consistency across projects, yet each project still has room for customization. For example, a master projects notebook could have separate Kanban pages for every project, all linked to a main dashboard that shows the most urgent tasks from each board. Thanks to tags and search features, urgent actions are easy to find no matter where they are in the notebook.

When collaborating, shared notebooks let multiple people update Kanban boards at once. This enables teams to track progress together, discuss items during meetings, and connect decisions directly to specific tasks. With OneNote's version history, changes are always recorded, encouraging accountability and transparency. Notably, OneNote's Kanban boards give structure without imposing strict rules—teams can adapt columns, change stages, or create new views as their projects develop.

In summary as shown in Figure 7-13, Kanban boards in Microsoft OneNote offer a powerful balance between visualization, flexibility, and context. By embedding task flow within a rich documentation environment, OneNote enables users to see not only *what* needs to be done, but *why* it matters and *how* it connects to broader objectives. This combination makes OneNote-based Kanban boards an effective solution for individuals and teams seeking practical, scalable, and adaptable workflow management.

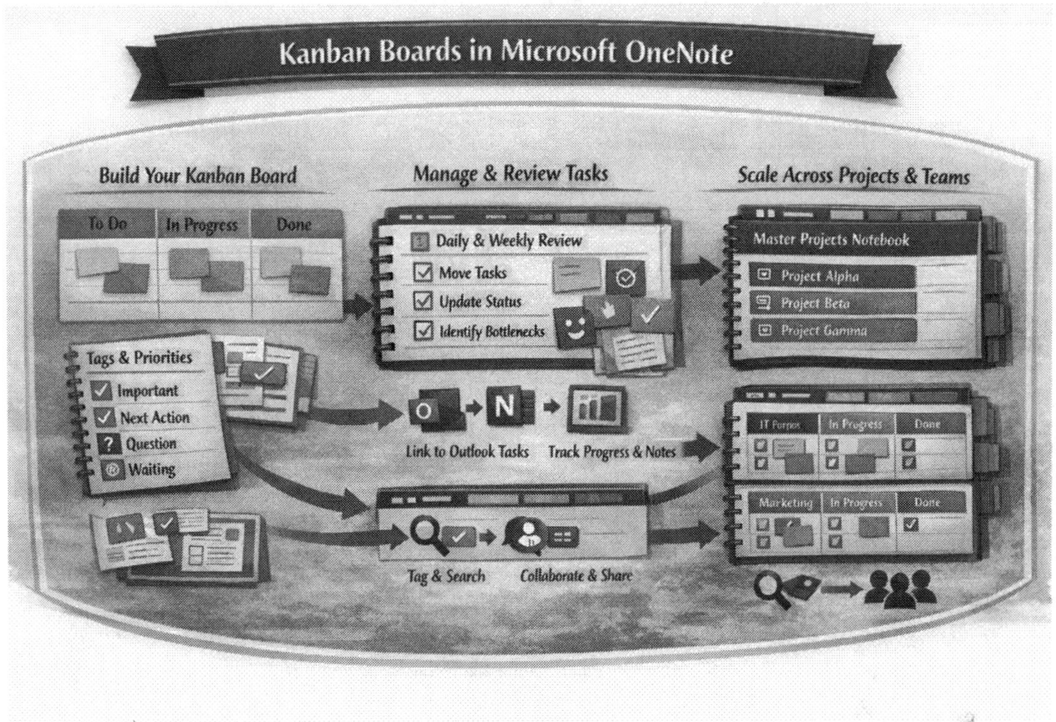

Figure 7-13. *Overview of Kanban in OneNote*

At the end of this chapter, we will have a glimpse of professional templates for project and multi-project notebook design in Microsoft OneNote.

Professional Templates for Projects

Professional project templates play a vital role in establishing consistency, clarity, and efficiency across project planning and execution. In Microsoft OneNote, templates provide a structured starting point that eliminates repetitive setup while ensuring that essential project elements are systematically addressed. Well-designed project templates typically include sections for project objectives, scope definition, task breakdowns, timelines, risk tracking, stakeholder information, and meeting notes. By standardizing these components, OneNote templates help users focus on decision-making and progress rather than formatting or organizational concerns.

OneNote's flexibility allows templates to be customized according to professional roles and project complexity. For instance, an IT project template may emphasize incident logs, change records, and technical documentation, whereas a business or academic project template may prioritize milestones, deliverables, and review notes. Once created, templates can be reused across projects, ensuring uniform documentation practices and reducing the likelihood of overlooking critical information. Additionally, templates facilitate collaboration by providing shared expectations and familiar layouts for team members.

As shown in Figure 7-14, by combining structured layouts with OneNote's tagging, linking, and multimedia capabilities, professional templates transform project documentation into actionable workspaces. They promote clarity, reduce setup time, and support disciplined project execution while remaining adaptable to changing requirements.

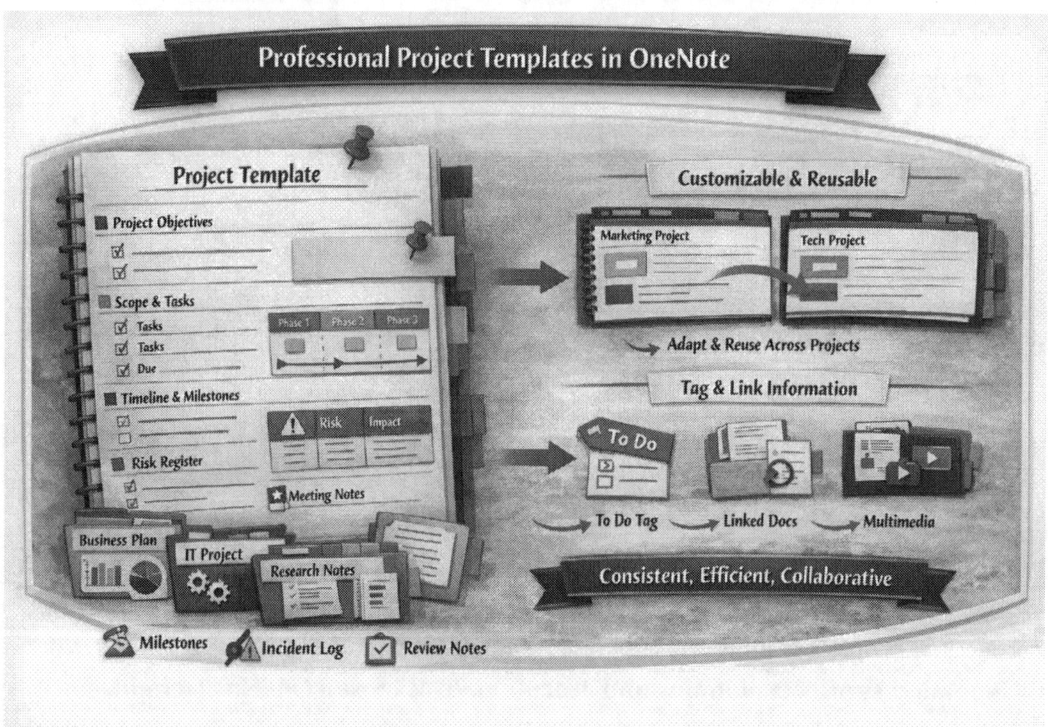

Figure 7-14. *Professional customized project templates in OneNote*

Multi-project Notebook Design

Effectively managing multiple projects at once necessitates an organizational framework that ensures visibility, scalability, and ease of navigation. Microsoft OneNote facilitates this objective through well-considered multi-project notebook structures, empowering users to monitor concurrent initiatives within a unified environment. A comprehensive multi-project notebook generally consists of a master dashboard or overview section, dedicated sections for each project, shared reference resources, and designated review pages. This arrangement enables clear separation among projects while maintaining centralized oversight and strategic insight.

Each project section contains dedicated pages for planning, execution, meetings, and documentation, thereby ensuring that information relevant to each project is systematically organized and readily accessible. The adoption of consistent naming conventions, standardized layouts, and color-coded divisions streamlines navigation and reduces cognitive demand. Internal hyperlinks facilitate efficient cross-referencing between projects without content duplication, while tags and search filters expedite the identification of high-priority tasks throughout the notebook.

A thoughtfully structured multi-project notebook as shown in Figure 7-15 provides both strategic oversight and operational clarity. It allows professionals to transition seamlessly between initiatives without sacrificing context, supporting informed decision-making. As responsibilities grow, OneNote adapts to increasing complexity, serving as a dependable platform for effective project management, sustained focus, and productivity across varied portfolios.

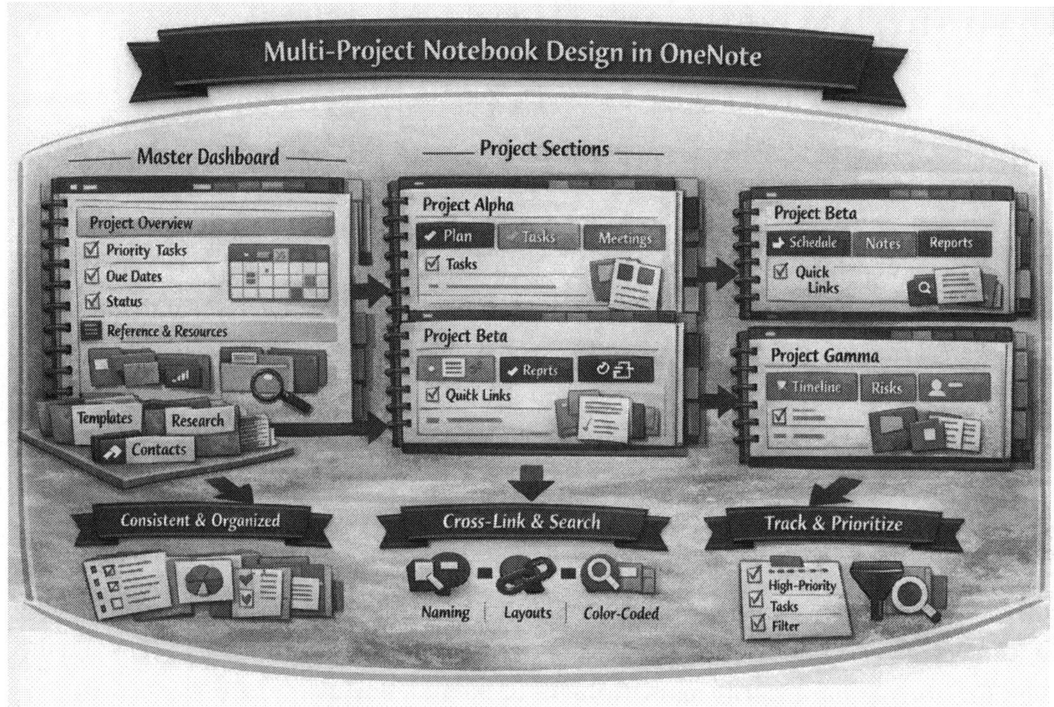

Figure 7-15. *Multi-project notebook design in OneNote*

Limitation of OneNote As a Project Management Tool

Microsoft OneNote is a flexible digital note-taking tool that supports organization and collaboration, but it is not a comprehensive project management solution. Many teams use OneNote for project tasks because of its simplicity and integration with Microsoft 365; however, as projects grow in complexity, OneNote's limitations—such as lack of task tracking, resource management, automation, and real-time dashboards—become evident. Unlike dedicated tools like Microsoft Project or Planner, OneNote primarily serves as an information repository and may create inefficiencies and governance issues when used as a primary project management platform, especially for complex projects. Below are some limitations:

- **Lack of Task Management Features**: OneNote does not offer native capabilities for task assignment, deadline tracking, or monitoring progress, unlike specialized project management tools.
- **No Gantt Charts or Timelines**: The platform is unable to provide visual project planning resources, such as timelines or dependency mapping.
- **Limited Reporting Capabilities**: Dashboards and automated reporting functions for project status and performance are absent.
- **Absence of Workflow Automation**: OneNote does not facilitate automated workflows, approval processes, or notifications within its native environment.
- **Weak Resource Management**: The system does not efficiently support team workload management, resource allocation, or utilization.
- **Scalability Issues**: Organizing large-scale projects is challenging due to unstructured content and navigation limitations.
- **Limited Integration for PM Functions**: Although OneNote integrates with Microsoft 365, it does not feature deep connectivity with project-
specific tools necessary for comprehensive management.

OneNote excels as a note-taking and collaboration platform, but it does not provide all the features required for comprehensive project management. Because it lacks structured planning, tracking, and reporting capabilities, OneNote cannot efficiently handle complex projects on its own. To achieve better efficiency and control, it's best to use OneNote alongside specialized project management tools.

This chapter outlines how Microsoft OneNote can serve as a robust platform for managing projects and tasks. It shows how to turn OneNote into a structured productivity system supporting planning, execution, and review for both individuals and teams, leveraging the notebook's flexibility with proven project management methods. The chapter demonstrates using the Getting Things Done (GTD) method within OneNote for capturing and organizing tasks and explains how dashboards and planners help track priorities and progress.

Integration with Outlook Tasks allows action items from OneNote to be scheduled and tracked, creating an efficient workflow between planning and execution. Kanban boards in OneNote offer visual task tracking and support collaboration. Also, this chapter concludes with tips on scalability through templates and multi-project notebook design for consistent, clear, and efficient navigation. Readers gain practical tools to streamline project management and use OneNote as a central productivity hub. Also, in the end we have seen some limitations of OneNote from a project management perspective.

As OneNote becomes a key platform for managing information, security, compliance, and data protection are increasingly vital. The next chapter explains how OneNote and Microsoft 365 protect user data, highlighting features like password-protected sections, secure storage via OneDrive and SharePoint, and enterprise governance controls. The chapter also covers privacy practices, access management, retention, auditing, and compliance considerations for regulated industries, positioning OneNote as a secure choice for professionals.

CHAPTER 8

Security, Compliance, and Industry Regulations with OneNote

The previous chapter illustrates how Microsoft OneNote serves as a versatile platform for project management, extending its functionality beyond standard note-taking. It examines the application of methodologies such as Getting Things Done (GTD) to systematically capture tasks, organize priorities, and sustain focus across diverse initiatives. The discussion includes techniques for constructing dashboards and weekly planners, offering enhanced visibility into key priorities, timelines, and deliverables. Readers are guided through the integration of OneNote with Outlook Tasks, enabling seamless transition of action items from notes into formal task management systems. Additionally, the chapter addresses the implementation of Kanban boards within OneNote for visual oversight of work stages and workflow progression. The inclusion of professional project templates and recommendations for designing multi-project notebooks demonstrates how OneNote can effectively support both individual contributors and teams managing concurrent projects.

In this chapter on security, compliance, and backup strategies, the focus shifts to protecting and governing the content created within OneNote. It introduces security features such as password-protected sections. The chapter explains enterprise governance concepts, including permissions, audit considerations, and data ownership. It also addresses data privacy requirements and the use of OneNote in regulated industries, reinforcing its suitability for professional and enterprise environments.

C. Waghmare, *Mastering Microsoft OneNote*, https://doi.org/10.1007/979-8-8688-2866-9_8

Introduction

This chapter presents a pivotal aspect of Microsoft OneNote that encompasses not only productivity but also trust, governance, and information security. As OneNote increasingly becomes a primary repository for business decisions, project data, academic records, and personal information, safeguarding the integrity and confidentiality of this data is paramount. The chapter establishes OneNote's role within contemporary digital workplaces, where information is dynamically generated, shared, and synchronized across multiple devices and teams. It emphasizes that maintaining robust security measures is an indispensable requirement when OneNote is utilized for professional or organizational purposes.

Integrated with the Microsoft 365 ecosystem, OneNote offers comprehensive protection for content. The discussion includes password-protected sections to secure sensitive notes, as well as the access, sharing, and ownership controls enabled through OneDrive and SharePoint security models. Moving beyond fundamental safeguards, the chapter introduces enterprise governance principles such as permission management, notebook lifecycle administration, and audit protocols. By contextualizing these controls specifically for OneNote, readers gain insight into how individual notebooks relate to wider organizational security policies while supporting seamless workflow integration.

The chapter underscores the importance of resilience, compliance, and regulatory awareness—issues that have become increasingly significant across various sectors. Strategies are outlined for backing up notebooks, restoring content, and exporting data to mitigate risks of loss or corruption. Additionally, the text addresses data privacy obligations, especially for professionals who manage confidential, personal, or regulated information. In conclusion, the chapter explores OneNote's application within regulated industries, demonstrating compliance alignment in healthcare, finance, education, and government settings. Collectively, these themes equip readers to leverage OneNote as a secure, compliant, and enterprise-grade knowledge management platform.

Password-Protected Sections

As Microsoft OneNote increasingly serves as a central repository for knowledge across individuals, teams, and enterprises, safeguarding sensitive data within notebooks becomes paramount. OneNote is routinely utilized to record meeting discussions, strategic initiatives, credentials, personal reflections, academic records, and regulated business information. Unrestricted access to notebook contents may present significant privacy and security concerns, particularly when notebooks are shared or synchronized across multiple devices and users. Password-protected sections offer a solution by enabling granular security controls within a single notebook environment. Instead of segregating sensitive notes in separate applications or files, OneNote allows users to maintain an integrated workspace while selectively limiting access where necessary. This chapter examines password-protected sections as a fundamental security capability promoting responsible information stewardship, regulatory compliance, and trust in contemporary digital note-taking.

How Password-Protected Sections Operate in Microsoft OneNote

Password-protected sections in Microsoft OneNote function by encrypting an entire section and requiring authentication to access its contents. Users establish a password through OneNote's security settings, rendering all pages within that section inaccessible until the correct credentials are provided. Upon locking, content remains concealed, excluded from search results, and unavailable for modification or duplication. Additionally, OneNote automatically secures protected sections following periods of inactivity, thereby reducing exposure risk if devices are left unattended. Encryption is performed locally; Microsoft does not store passwords, nor can they be recovered once lost. Despite these safeguards, notebooks continue to synchronize across devices via OneDrive or SharePoint, ensuring users enjoy cloud accessibility alongside stringent control over sensitive information. The feature is designed for simplicity and reliability, promoting security without necessitating technical proficiency or ancillary encryption tools.

The Importance of Password-Protected Sections

The imperative for password-protected sections is shaped by the evolving role of OneNote in both professional and personal spheres. As OneNote becomes central to confidential information management, risks of inadvertent disclosure increase. Shared workspaces, collaborative notebooks, and multi-device synchronization can unwittingly expose private data absent proper protection. Password-protected sections facilitate open collaboration while preserving discretion over select content—supporting privacy, ethical conduct, and organizational compliance. In corporate contexts, this mitigates risks of data leakage, insider threats, and unauthorized access. In educational settings, it safeguards student records and evaluations. For individuals, it protects journals, financial records, and health-related information. Rather than hindering collaboration, password protection enables confident participation by delineating boundaries around sensitive material and reinforcing mutual trust among stakeholders.

Scope and Limitations of Password-Protected Sections

Password-protected sections secure all forms of content within them, including typed entries, handwritten notes, images, audio files, attached documents, scanned materials, and hyperlinks. When locked, section contents are excluded from indexing, search, and tag summaries, preventing inadvertent disclosure. This comprehensive security makes the feature ideal for high-value information. However, notable constraints accompany these protections. Forgotten passwords render the content irretrievable, highlighting the necessity for diligent password management. Locked sections temporarily suspend background operations such as OCR processing and synchronization until unlocked. Further, protected material cannot be copied or linked externally while secured. These limitations are intentional, underscoring the seriousness associated with password protection. Users must exercise responsibility and awareness to balance convenience against robust security.

Integration Within Microsoft 365

Password-protected sections contribute to a layered security approach within the Microsoft 365 ecosystem. While OneDrive and SharePoint manage external access permissions, retention, and compliance, OneNote's section-level passwords afford internal content confidentiality. This integration enables secure collaboration across platforms—including Microsoft Teams channels, Class Notebooks, and enterprise libraries. Protected sections remain secure irrespective of access location, whether on desktop, mobile, or the web, though optimal password management occurs via the desktop application. In organizational environments, this layered model ensures broad notebook accessibility while maintaining privacy for critical information, making OneNote suitable for hybrid work, cross-functional collaboration, and distributed teams where openness and discretion must coexist.

Recommended Users for Password-Protected Sections

Password-protected sections are essential for users storing sensitive information in OneNote, most notably professionals in roles with elevated responsibilities. Executives employ them for strategic documents, board deliberations, and performance reviews. IT personnel safeguard credentials, infrastructure details, and investigative documentation. Educators and administrators protect student assessments, behavioral reports, and private correspondence. Consultants and freelancers differentiate client-confidential information from general project notes. Individuals use password protection for personal journals, financial planning, legal materials, and medical records. In regulated sectors such as finance, healthcare, education, and government, password-protected sections fulfill privacy and compliance mandates. Ultimately, any OneNote user prioritizing controlled access, accountability, and trust will regard password-protected sections as a vital aspect of conscientious digital note management.

Steps to Apply Password Protection in Microsoft OneNote

Launch the OneNote desktop application and open the notebook that contains the section you want to protect. Password protection is best managed from the desktop version.

Step 1: As shown in Figure 8-1, navigate to the Review tab that contains sensitive information.

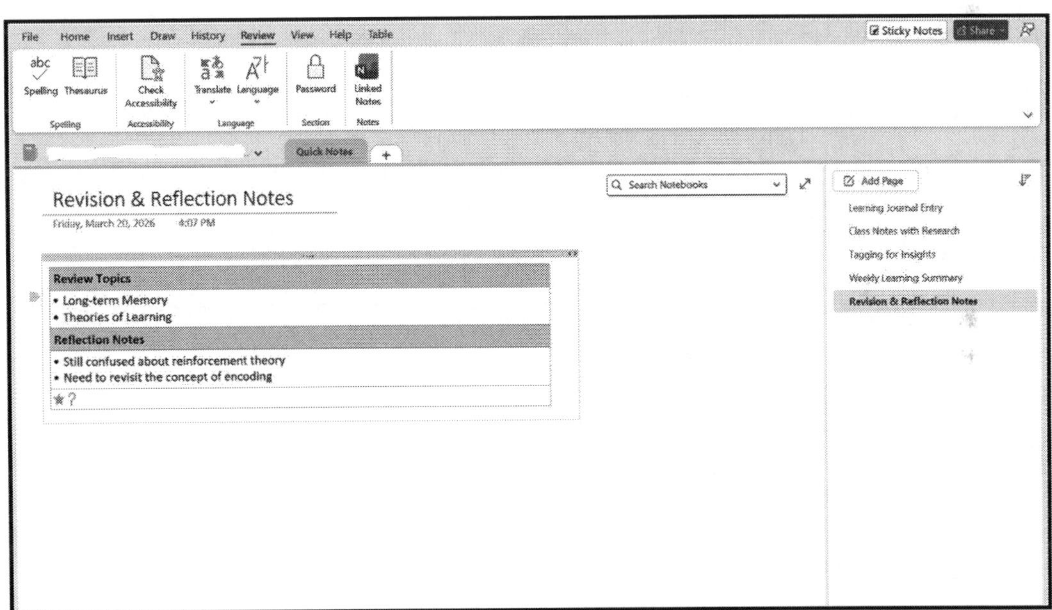

Figure 8-1. Navigate to the Review tab

Step 2: As shown in Figure 8-2, click on the Password option and the "Password Protection" menu will appear.

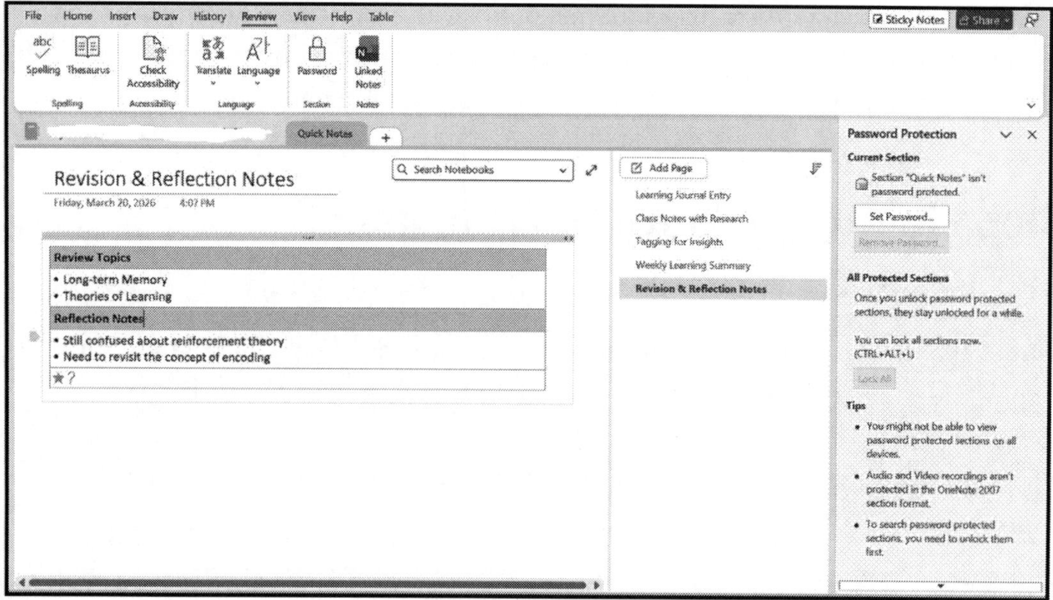

Figure 8-2. *Access the Set Password tab*

Step 3: As shown in Figure 8-3, a password creation window pops up once the Set Password tab is clicked; however, before password creation, chose delete backups or keep existing backups because they will not be password protected.

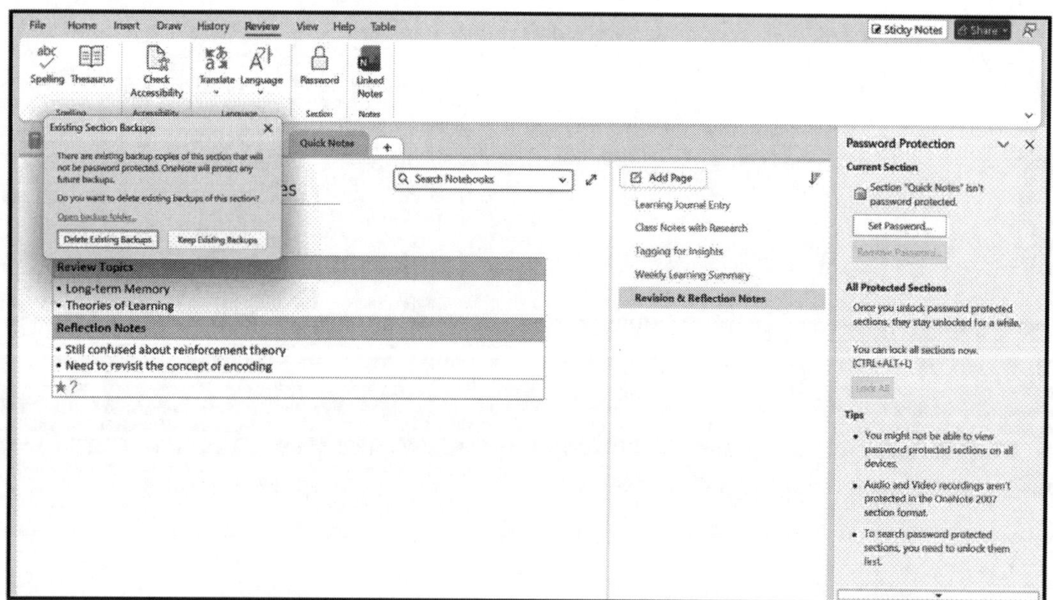

Figure 8-3. *Set password*

Step 4: As shown in Figure 8-4, now the password can be changed or removed.

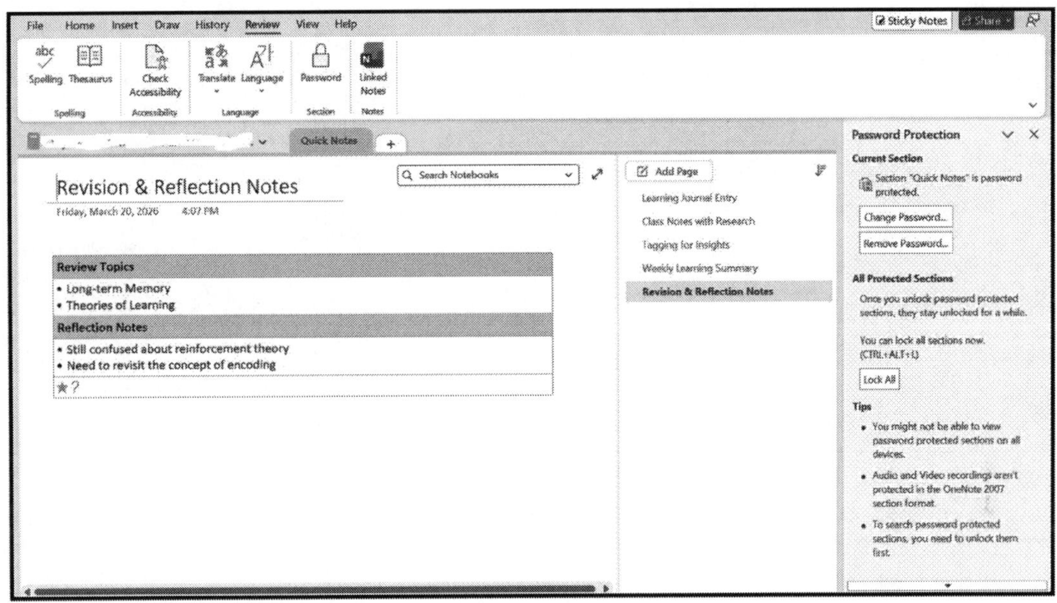

Figure 8-4. *Change or remove password*

Step 5: As shown in Figure 8-5, to remove password, the existing password needs to be entered, and while changing the password, the old and new passwords need to be entered as shown in Figure 8-6.

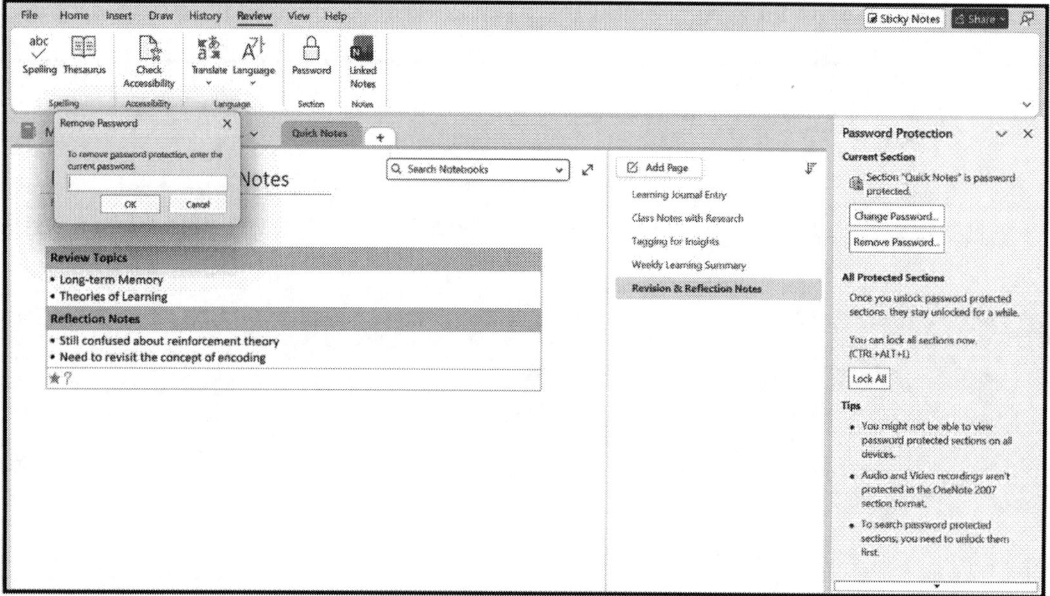

Figure 8-5. *Remove password*

Step 6: Enter the existing password to change the password.

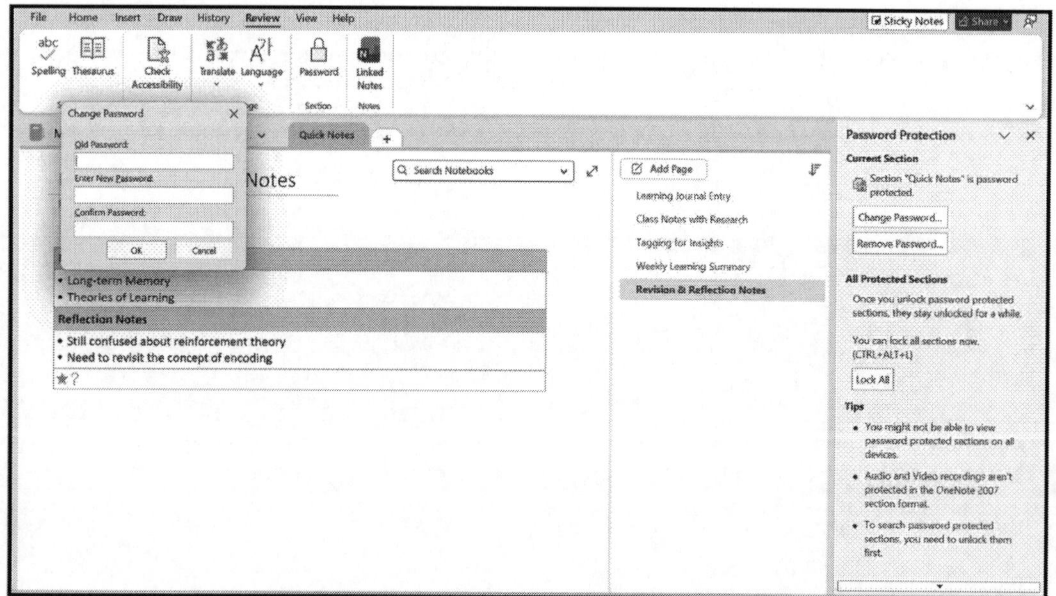

Figure 8-6. *Change password*

With this we conclude this section on password protection where we have learned how important it is to apply the password protection feature when the content is confidential and thereby safeguard its value. The steps described on how to apply password protection features are pretty straightforward which makes OneNote easy to handle when it comes to handling critical content.

Enterprise Governance with Microsoft OneNote

Enterprise governance utilizing Microsoft OneNote offers a systematic framework for managing information in dynamic environments where collaboration, efficiency, and knowledge sharing are paramount. As organizations increasingly leverage OneNote to document operational insights, project records, strategic initiatives, and institutional knowledge, effective governance becomes critical to maintain consistency, security, and long-term value. Establishing a comprehensive governance vision ensures that OneNote is aligned with organizational goals, elevating it to a reliable knowledge management platform rather than a casual note-taking tool. This vision clarifies appropriate content usage within OneNote, its role in supporting business processes, and its integration within the broader Microsoft 365 suite.

Defining clear roles, ownership, and accountability is essential for establishing responsibility over notebook integrity, content accuracy, and access control. Designated ownership mitigates risks associated with orphaned notebooks, outdated information, and improper sharing, thereby ensuring operational continuity as teams evolve. Additionally, robust governance encompasses access, classification, and boundary controls to effectively balance collaboration and confidentiality. By specifying access permissions and delineating information boundaries, organizations can safeguard sensitive data while facilitating productive cross-departmental collaboration.

Furthermore, lifecycle governance ensures the longevity and relevance of information by mandating regular review, retention, archival, or disposal of content in adherence to business and compliance standards. This approach preserves the reliability and trustworthiness of information stored in OneNote. Lastly, governance operations operationalize policies through well-defined standards, templates, regular audits, and ongoing training. Collectively, these governance pillars empower Microsoft OneNote to scale efficiently across the enterprise, promoting seamless collaboration while upholding rigorous standards of control, accountability, and regulatory compliance.

In the upcoming section, we will take an intensive look at Microsoft OneNote governance vision, access classification, boundary controls, roles, ownership, accountability, lifecycle governance, and governance operations.

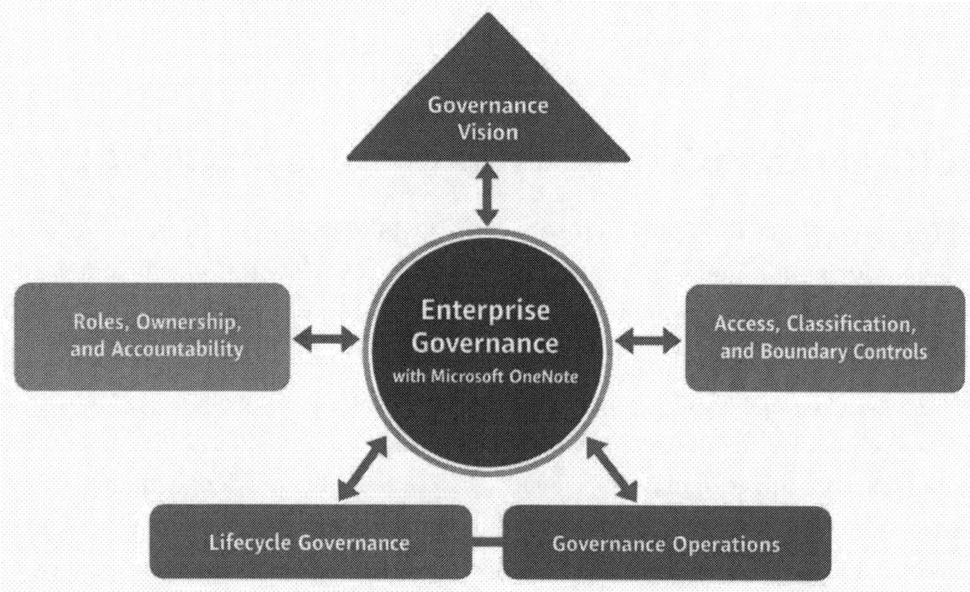

Figure 8-7. *Enterprise governance with Microsoft OneNote*

Governance Vision: Establishing OneNote As a Controlled Knowledge System

Enterprise governance with Microsoft OneNote commences when an organization transitions from perceiving it as a personal notebook to recognizing it as a governed knowledge system that impacts decision-making, operational activities, and risk management. In practice, OneNote frequently serves as the "shadow repository," capturing meeting outcomes, project rationales, client information, technical solutions, and policy interpretations faster than these details reach formal systems. Governance therefore requires a vision that is pragmatic: maintaining OneNote's agility and adaptability while ensuring content remains reliable, accessible, and defensible. This vision typically begins by defining what constitutes "official" content within OneNote. Some entries are ephemeral—such as brainstorming notes or initial concepts—while others become records: approved procedures, audit evidence, or finalized handover documentation. Governance delineates the boundary between draft and authoritative knowledge, establishing processes for draft material to transition into standardized assets. This distinction influences naming conventions, storage locations, and the controls that apply. A governed OneNote environment also implements a shared information architecture. Absent a unified structure, teams develop notebooks according to individual preferences, resulting in inconsistent section naming, redundant templates, and fragmented knowledge. Governance-driven architecture introduces reusable patterns: notebooks organized by function or program, sections aligned to processes, and pages structured around repeatable artifacts like meeting minutes, status reports, decision logs, and incident reviews. Such standardization enhances flexibility and reduces cognitive burden, enabling cross-team collaboration by providing familiar patterns. Furthermore, governance clarifies purpose: is OneNote primarily a workspace, an institutional memory, a lightweight knowledge base, or a connector to formal systems such as SharePoint and ticketing tools? Many organizations adopt a hybrid approach: OneNote is used for rapid knowledge capture and refinement, with promotion to formal repositories when lifecycle controls, enterprise search, or compliance retention are required. When this vision is effectively communicated, OneNote evolves into a strategic enterprise asset governed proactively rather than reactively.

Roles, Ownership, and Accountability: Transforming Notebooks into Managed Assets

A governance model becomes effective only when roles and ownership are explicitly defined. In unmanaged settings, notebooks are created as needed, stored wherever convenient, and often abandoned following personnel changes, resulting in orphaned knowledge and access issues. Governance establishes a clear chain of ownership: a business owner responsible for the value and accuracy of the notebook, a technical owner tasked with storage and access configurations, and content stewards managing specific sections such as procedures, templates, and compliance documentation. This allocation of responsibilities mitigates the common failure of treating access control as a one-time setup. Ownership fosters ongoing accountability through regular reviews, de-duplication, and content maintenance. For instance, a "service operations notebook" may designate an operations lead as business owner, a SharePoint site owner as technical owner, and section stewards for incident reviews, known errors, and change notes. Governance also defines contributor roles—editors, reviewers, and readers—where editors can update content, reviewers verify accuracy and compliance, and readers access information without modification. Role clarity supports quality assurance while facilitating efficient knowledge capture. Typically, broad contributions are allowed in "working" sections, whereas "reference" sections are reserved for reviewers and stewards, creating a pipeline from draft to approved material. Notebooks benefit from page-level conventions documenting authorship, date, and status. While OneNote's metadata is limited compared to traditional document management systems, governance compensates with standardized page headers such as "owner, last reviewed, next review, classification, and source links." This enhances content auditability and reduces institutional risk associated with critical notes. Governance also ensures continuity; when employees depart or assume new roles, notebooks remain accessible to relevant functions, not restricted to individuals. Governance-critical notebooks should be stored in organizational locations (e.g., SharePoint team sites), with ownership assigned to groups or roles, supporting both technical and governance objectives. Behavioral expectations are also defined: specifying appropriate content for OneNote, prohibiting storage of sensitive information when regulated, and mandating transfer of certain records to formal systems (contracts, legal documents). Defining roles and accountability stabilizes OneNote usage over time and ensures resilience during organizational transitions.

Access, Classification, and Boundary Controls: Regulating Collaboration Without Impeding Productivity

Access governance is fundamental in enterprise environments given OneNote's collaborative nature. The primary goal is not to limit sharing indiscriminately but to enforce appropriate boundaries for different types of information. Governance starts with classification—a labeling scheme distinguishing public internal knowledge from confidential business data and regulated information. Classification can take the form of naming conventions ("FIN-Confidential," "HR-Restricted"), page header tags, or section labels indicating handling requirements. Once established, classification is mapped to access controls. General collaboration notebooks may permit broad team access, while restricted notebooks require group-based permissions to minimize maintenance and prevent unauthorized access. Boundary controls extend to external sharing policies, determining whether and under which conditions notebooks may be shared outside the organization. Given that OneNote often resides on OneDrive or SharePoint, governance relies on these platforms for monitoring, restricting, and aligning sharing practices with policy. Section passwords within OneNote provide additional compartmentalization for sensitive areas, but governance recommends using them sparingly, as they present operational risks if mishandled. Instead, passwords should facilitate temporary restrictions—with long-term access managed through group permissions and secure storage. Governance addresses "permission sprawl"—the proliferation of edit rights that undermines content integrity—by dividing "collaboration sections" from "policy/reference sections" and instituting review checkpoints. This preserves the stability and reliability of reference materials without hindering workflow. Device and session risks are also considered; accidental exposure from unlocked screens or personal devices poses significant threats. Governance mandates practices such as auto-locks, device compliance standards, and session management guidance. It also details protocols for accessing notebooks on shared workstations or during travel. Ultimately, access governance instills confidence: teams collaborate knowing information boundaries are intentional, permissions are structured, and sensitive data is handled appropriately.

Lifecycle Governance: Managing Retention, Review Cadence, and Records in OneNote

Lifecycle management is often overlooked in OneNote governance, yet it is essential to determining the validity, usability, and legal relevance of captured notes. Without defined lifecycle rules, OneNote can become cluttered with outdated decisions and incomplete drafts, diminishing trust as users struggle to distinguish current guidance from obsolete information. Governance introduces lifecycle stages—draft, active, approved reference, archived, and disposed—each with corresponding handling protocols. Draft and active content is editable; approved reference material is stable and version controlled; archived content is retained for learning or audits but not used for daily operations; disposed content is deleted per retention policy. These stages are implemented via page tags, section naming, and routine housekeeping; robust lifecycle management does not necessitate complex tooling. A scheduled review cadence is crucial. Organizations often employ a "90-180-365" pattern: quarterly reviews for critical operational content, semi-annual reviews for departmental standards, and annual reviews for enduring policies. Cadence is adapted to risk: for instance, incident response playbooks require more frequent evaluation than brainstorming templates. Governance identifies triggers for immediate review, including process changes, technology upgrades, security incidents, or organizational restructuring. Retention is both a compliance and operational concern. Notes qualifying as records—formal approvals, audit evidence, and regulated documentation—must be clearly located, preserved, and readily available for audits. Frequently, OneNote serves as a working space rather than the final record system; accordingly, governance defines workflows for promoting content to controlled repositories (e.g., SharePoint libraries with retention labels), retaining links in OneNote for context. Governance also counters notebook proliferation—multiple notebooks for the same program, lacking a canonical source—by maintaining a registry listing official notebooks, owners, purposes, and storage locations. This registry, often housed in OneNote, provides an internal map of institutional knowledge. Content hygiene practices are also incorporated: archiving inactive sections, segmenting oversized notebooks to enhance performance, and standardizing backup/export procedures for critical content. With established lifecycle rules, OneNote remains trustworthy, with content that is current, historical items properly identified, and records preserved deliberately.

Governance Operations: Controls, Audits, Training, and Culture to Sustain Enterprise OneNote Usage

Governance is most successful when integrated into routine operations, rather than existing solely as documentation. For OneNote, core governance operations include periodic audits, standardized onboarding, template oversight, and continuous improvement initiatives. Practical audits need not be punitive; they might consist of quarterly assessments evaluating notebook ownership, permission alignment, reference section reviews, proper storage of sensitive notebooks, and elimination of duplicative notebooks. Governance dashboards track notebooks by business unit, last review date, and risk classification. Governance operations also maintain a dynamic template library, ensuring consistency and eliminating the need for users to create new structures. Mature OneNote environments utilize standardized templates for meeting minutes (with explicit decisions and actions), project status reports (detailing scope, milestones, blockers, and risks), incident logs (documenting timeline, impact, root cause, and corrective actions), and handover checklists. Template stewardship ensures continued relevance and prevents fragmentation arising from competing formats. Training is equally crucial; governance-related training educates users on responsible OneNote use: when to store content, when to link to record repositories, and how to label and classify information, manage shared notebooks, and safeguard sensitive data. Etiquette is also addressed: clear documentation, rationale recording, consistent tagging, and avoidance of ambiguous shorthand. Cultivating a governance-oriented culture is vital. When governance is perceived as enhancing trust and efficiency, adoption increases; leaders reinforce this by referencing governed notebooks in meetings, accepting OneNote pages as official artifacts, and recognizing teams for maintaining clean, updated knowledge. Governance operations prepare OneNote for expansion, supporting mergers, reorganizations, and cross-team projects through unified knowledge management. An established governance framework transforms OneNote into a scalable collaboration platform where content is portable, permissions are manageable, and knowledge remains coherent amid organizational change. Ultimately, enterprise governance with OneNote is dedicated to ensuring information reliability, security, and reusability. When operationalized through templates, regular reviews, audits, and targeted training, OneNote becomes a robust platform that balances speed with control and collaboration with accountability.

In summary, implementing enterprise governance with Microsoft OneNote fundamentally enhances how organizations manage and safeguard their knowledge assets. By establishing a clear governance framework for OneNote usage, organizations align collaboration efforts with strategic objectives, minimizing operational silos. Clearly defined roles, ownership, and accountability help maintain content quality and sustainability, effectively reducing risks and ambiguity over time. Access controls, classification protocols, and boundary guidelines facilitate open information sharing while ensuring that sensitive data is properly protected and managed.

Lifecycle governance further guarantees that the information within OneNote remains current, accurate, and compliant, thereby preventing outdated or duplicate materials from compromising decision-making processes. The ongoing reinforcement of these governance principles through systematic execution, training initiatives, and continuous improvement establishes a strong foundation of trust in OneNote as an enterprise-grade platform.

Effective governance does not constrain user innovation or productivity; instead, it empowers users by providing clarity, structure, and assurance. When executed successfully, governance transforms Microsoft OneNote into more than a simple note-taking tool—it becomes a secure, scalable, and dependable knowledge management platform that drives organizational collaboration, accountability, and long-term success.

Data Privacy Inside Microsoft OneNote

In today's digitally connected workplaces, data privacy has moved from being an IT concern to a shared organizational responsibility. Microsoft OneNote is increasingly used to capture and store a wide range of information—ranging from meeting discussions and project documentation to personal reflections and regulated business data. Because OneNote notebooks are often synchronized across devices and shared among teams, privacy considerations become critical. Users may unknowingly store confidential, personal, or sensitive information in OneNote, assuming it will remain private by default. However, without adequate privacy awareness and controls, such content may be exposed through sharing, synchronization, or improper access configuration. Understanding how Microsoft OneNote handles data privacy is therefore essential for professionals, educators, and organizations seeking to use the platform responsibly and securely.

Notebook Location, Ownership, and Privacy Implications

A primary factor influencing data privacy in OneNote is the location and ownership of notebooks. Notebooks stored within personal OneDrive accounts provide privacy at an individual level but may lack organizational oversight, audit capabilities, and retention controls. Conversely, notebooks housed on SharePoint sites are governed by enterprise policies, including access management, audit trails, and compliance functionality. This distinction holds significant implications for privacy. Personal notebooks priorities individual confidentiality, whereas SharePoint-hosted notebooks emphasize controlled sharing and institutional accountability. Organizations must establish clear guidelines regarding the storage of various data types and educate users on the consequences of keeping professional or regulated information in personal repositories. Comprehensive governance surrounding notebook storage is therefore an essential component of data privacy.

Access Management and Responsible Sharing Practices

OneNote enables detailed privacy controls through permission settings and access management inherited from OneDrive and SharePoint. Users can assign view-only or editing rights to collaborators, thereby ensuring sensitive data is not modified or disseminated unnecessarily. However, privacy risks frequently arise not from deliberate actions, but from inadvertent oversharing. Broadly distributed notebooks or invitations extended to external users without due diligence may result in unintended exposure of private content. Implementing access discipline, such as group-based permissions over individual sharing, mitigates privacy risks and streamlines ongoing access management. This underscores the importance of responsible sharing in maintaining data privacy within OneNote.

Protecting Sensitive Content with Password-Protected Sections

At the content level, OneNote offers password-protected sections as an internal mechanism for safeguarding privacy. This feature allows the encryption of specific notebook sections, protecting sensitive pages even when the overall notebook is shared. Password-protected sections are particularly effective for segregating personal, confidential, or restricted business information within collaborative notebooks. When these sections are locked, they are excluded from search results and previews, minimizing indirect data exposure. However, password protection places additional responsibility on users, as lost passwords cannot be recovered. This emphasizes that privacy controls are most effective when combined with informed user practices.

Device Synchronization, Mobility, and Privacy Risks

Data privacy in OneNote is also closely linked to synchronization, device usage, and offline access. Notebooks may be accessed across laptops, mobile devices, and browsers, enhancing convenience but expanding the potential privacy risk. Synchronized notebooks on unsecured or shared devices may unintentionally expose information. OneNote addresses this through automatic locking of protected sections and reliance on device-level security measures such as operating system authentication and screen locks. Nonetheless, organizations should reinforce these technical safeguards with explicit guidance on secure device use, especially in hybrid and remote working environments where personal and professional spheres intersect.

Data Lifecycle, Retention, and Residual Privacy Management

Another important consideration is the data lifecycle and residual information. Notes created within OneNote may persist beyond their initial purpose, potentially retaining outdated or sensitive details. Deleted pages are often recoverable for a period, and shared notebooks might contain historical data no longer suitable for continued access. Effective privacy management requires routine reviews, data cleanup processes, and adherence to retention policies. In regulated sectors, organizations may be obligated to restrict the retention duration of personal or sensitive information. Integrating OneNote with Microsoft 365's broader retention and compliance frameworks helps ensure privacy throughout the information lifecycle.

Enhancing Privacy Through Strategic OneNote Utilization

Data privacy within Microsoft OneNote is shaped by both technical measures and sound governance, user awareness, and responsible utilization. While Microsoft offers robust encryption, identity management, and section-level protection, their effectiveness relies on conscientious application by users. Choices regarding notebook storage, sharing permissions, password management, and device security directly influence privacy outcomes. Individual users benefit from understanding these mechanisms for safer personal knowledge management, while organizations achieve compliance and trust by aligning OneNote practices with enterprise privacy policies.

In conclusion, when data privacy is regarded as an integrated process rather than a mere configuration, OneNote stands as a dependable platform for capturing and sharing information. By combining its inherent privacy features with clear governance and well-informed user behavior, Microsoft OneNote supports collaboration and productivity without sacrificing confidentiality or ethical standards in data handling.

Microsoft OneNote in Regulated Industries

Regulated industries like healthcare, banking, insurance, energy, and government must follow strict rules around confidentiality, auditability, retention, and information sharing. In these sectors, data—such as patient details or legal records—must comply with both internal and external regulations. Microsoft OneNote is popular for its efficient note-capturing features, but its flexibility can lead to compliance issues if not managed properly, such as oversharing, improper storage, or mixing sensitive content.

To use OneNote securely in regulated environments, it should be treated as a monitored workspace, aligned with governance practices including classification, access control, retention policies, and audit protocols. Best practices include using SharePoint for regulated data storage, establishing role-based access, standardizing templates, and maintaining regular content reviews.

This section, as shown in Figure 8-7, outlines how organizations can leverage OneNote as a compliant and secure knowledge platform through "Governance-First Notebook Architecture for Regulated Work," "Access Control, Least Privilege, and Secure Collaboration Boundaries," "Evidence-Ready Documentation: Turning Notes into Defensible Records," "Lifecycle Governance: Retention, Review, and Controlled Archiving," and "Compliance-Aligned Usage Patterns in Industry Scenarios."

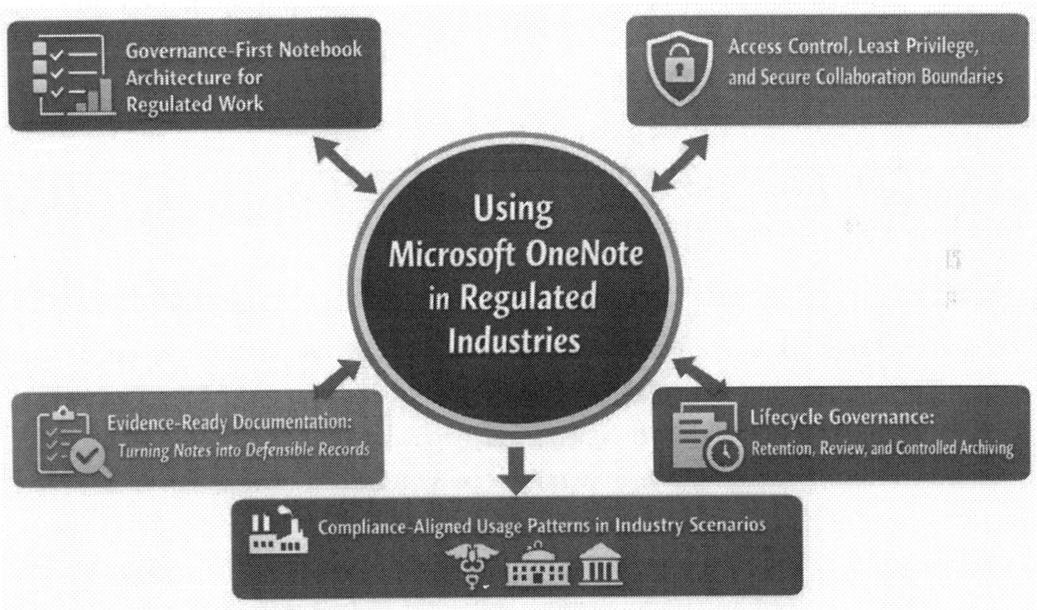

Figure 8-8. *OneNote in regulated industries*

Governance-First Notebook Architecture for Regulated Work

As shown in Figure 8-8, In regulated industries, notebook design is not just a productivity choice—it is a compliance safeguard. Start by defining the notebook purpose and scope in governance terms: each notebook should represent a business function, program, or controlled process (e.g., "Quality Management," "Clinical Trial Operations," "Financial Controls," or "Safety and Incident Management"). Within each notebook, structure sections to reflect regulated workflows, such as "Policies," "SOPs," "Training Evidence," "Audits," "Risk Register," and "Corrective Actions." This structure makes it easier to locate authoritative content and distinguish working drafts from approved reference information. A best practice is to clearly separate "Working Notes" from "Controlled Reference." Working areas can remain flexible, while controlled reference sections should follow stricter editing rules and review cycles. Add lightweight metadata at the top of key pages—owner, last reviewed date, version status, classification level, and links to authoritative repositories—so that pages are audit-friendly without turning OneNote into a rigid system.

Access Control, Least Privilege, and Secure Collaboration Boundaries

Regulated environments require controlled sharing that prevents overexposure while still enabling teamwork. Use role-based permissions rather than ad hoc individual sharing wherever possible, and ensure notebook ownership is assigned to teams or functions instead of a single individual. For sensitive notebooks, limit editing rights to authorized contributors and use view-only access for broader audiences. Where collaborative input is needed, implement a "contribute here" model: dedicate sections for submissions (draft notes, field inputs, inspection observations) while keeping official sections (approved procedures, audit artifacts, final decisions) restricted to stewards or reviewers. If certain content is highly sensitive—such as investigation details, legal discussions, or restricted personal data—use internal boundaries such as password-protected sections carefully, with clear operational rules for password custody. The goal is to maintain a defensible access posture: the right people can access the right content for the right reason, and sensitive information does not leak through convenience sharing.

Evidence-Ready Documentation: Turning Notes into Defensible Records

Audits and investigations often fail not because work wasn't done, but because evidence is incomplete, unclear, or inconsistent. OneNote can strengthen audit readiness by standardizing how evidence is captured. Use templates that force clarity: meeting minutes templates should separate "decisions," "actions," "risks," and "approvals"; incident templates should capture timeline, impact, root cause, corrective actions, and verification steps; quality templates should document control checks, exceptions, and sign-offs. Encourage consistent language—avoid vague phrases like "fixed" or "handled," and instead record what was done, when, by whom, and with what result. Where applicable, link to source artifacts stored in controlled repositories (policies in SharePoint libraries, tickets in ITSM tools, approvals in email or workflow systems). This creates traceability: OneNote provides context and narrative, while authoritative records remain in systems designed for retention and governance.

Lifecycle Governance: Retention, Review, and Controlled Archiving

In regulated industries, data that is accurate today can become a liability tomorrow if retained unnecessarily or left outdated. OneNote should follow lifecycle governance rules that define how long content stays active, when it must be reviewed, and when it must be archived or disposed. Establish review cadences based on risk: safety procedures, financial controls, or clinical protocols should be reviewed more frequently than general team notes. Use clear page markers such as "Draft," "In Review," "Approved," and "Archived," and align these markers to organizational retention policy. When a project closes, archive the notebook or sections to prevent uncontrolled edits, and create a summary page that links to final deliverables stored in official repositories. This approach prevents notebook sprawl and protects teams from relying on outdated guidance. Lifecycle governance also improves performance and usability by reducing clutter, ensuring OneNote remains a reliable system for current operations rather than a dumping ground of historical content.

Compliance-Aligned Usage Patterns in Industry Scenarios

Different regulated sectors can use OneNote safely when usage patterns reflect sector risks. In healthcare or life sciences, OneNote can support non-clinical collaboration such as process documentation, training notes, quality improvement logs, and meeting records—while avoiding unnecessary storage of sensitive patient data unless policy explicitly permits it. In banking and insurance, OneNote is effective for control narratives, policy interpretation notes, audit preparation checklists, and incident coordination—while access controls and retention become paramount. In energy, manufacturing, and safety-critical operations, OneNote can consolidate incident learnings, maintenance checklists, and safety meeting outcomes, helping organizations demonstrate continuous improvement. Public sector teams can use OneNote for controlled program documentation, stakeholder meeting records, and operational planning while maintaining strict sharing and archiving practices. Across all these scenarios, the principle is consistent: OneNote becomes compliant when it is used intentionally—with defined boundaries, documented ownership, disciplined templates, and lifecycle rules that prevent uncontrolled exposure and unmanaged retention.

In conclusion, Microsoft OneNote can be effective in regulated industries when managed as a governed workspace, not just for informal notes. Its strengths—quick capture, flexible organization, and collaborative editing—are valuable for compliance-driven documentation. However, without proper governance, risks may arise, such as oversharing or unclear ownership. To meet regulatory standards, organizations should implement intentional notebook structures, role-based access, evidence-ready templates, and clear collaboration boundaries.

Lifecycle governance ensures notebooks remain compliant through regular reviews, archiving, and retention practices. Sector-specific adaptations allow OneNote's use across healthcare, finance, government, and safety-critical fields. By combining these practices, OneNote becomes a secure platform that enables efficient collaboration, controlled knowledge sharing, and evidence preservation for regulated organizations.

This chapter underscores that security, compliance, and data protection are essential for digital note-taking platforms like Microsoft OneNote. OneNote serves as more than just a productivity tool; with proper management, it supports secure, compliant information handling for sensitive business and personal data.

Key features—including password-protected sections, clear access controls, and governance—help organizations safeguard content and prevent data risks, especially in hybrid or remote environments. OneNote's tools meet regulatory needs, making it relevant for industries requiring strict documentation and ongoing accountability.

Effective security relies not only on technology but also on user awareness and sound processes. By following the principles discussed, organizations can use OneNote confidently, maintaining both productivity and robust data protection.

The upcoming chapter explains how OneNote helps business teams in sales, marketing, consulting, HR, and operations. It covers standardized meeting notes for clarity, structured client call documentation for accountability, and streamlined project handovers to prevent information loss. The chapter also introduces enterprise knowledge libraries—shared notebooks that preserve expertise and guidance. By highlighting real-world examples, it demonstrates how OneNote boosts productivity, communication, and teamwork across an organization.

CHAPTER 9

Improve Productivity Using OneNote

The previous chapter provides an in-depth examination of securing, governing, and protecting notebooks within professional settings. The section details how implementing password-protected areas enhances confidentiality for sensitive content, while OneDrive and SharePoint offer robust solutions for secure storage through advanced permissions management, access control mechanisms, and comprehensive version histories. Further, the chapter discusses organizational governance, encompassing regulatory compliance, data retention policies, and audit requirements. It supplies actionable recommendations regarding backup procedures, restoration processes, and notebook export capabilities to mitigate the risk of data loss. The discussion concludes by addressing considerations for data privacy and examining the deployment of OneNote within highly regulated industries such as finance, healthcare, and legal, emphasizing best practices for responsible information stewardship.

This chapter transitions to the subjects of collaboration and productivity, illustrating how OneNote serves as a valuable resource for business teams. It outlines practical scenarios across various domains, including sales, marketing, consulting, human resources (HR), and operations. This chapter introduces methodologies for maintaining structured meeting records, documenting client communications, overseeing project documentation, and facilitating effective handovers. Additionally, it highlights strategies for constructing enterprise knowledge repositories that support shared learning, promote consistency, and preserve institutional knowledge over time.

C. Waghmare, *Mastering Microsoft OneNote*, https://doi.org/10.1007/979-8-8688-2866-9_9

Improve Productivity Sales, Marketing, Consultants, HR, and Operations Using Microsoft OneNote

As shown in Figure 9-1, Microsoft OneNote serves as a pivotal tool in enhancing team productivity by effectively addressing a core challenge prevalent in modern organizations: the fragmentation of information across various tools, individuals, and workflows. Teams frequently invest considerable amounts of time searching through emails, chat logs, documents, and personal notes to reconstruct previous discussions, decisions, or assignments. OneNote resolves this inefficiency by consolidating disparate information into a unified, continuously updated workspace where ideas, discussions, decisions, and action items are easily accessible. By functioning as a central knowledge repository, OneNote empowers teams to operate with greater speed, strategic collaboration, and sustained context throughout projects and roles.

Figure 9-1. *OneNote helping improve productivity*

Fundamentally, OneNote supports productivity by aligning with natural working styles, eschewing rigid documentation protocols. Team members can promptly capture insights during meetings, client interactions, brainstorming sessions, and fieldwork without being constrained by formatting requirements. This immediacy in documentation mitigates productivity loss tied to delayed recordkeeping. Storing real-time information collectively enhances the quality of shared knowledge and clarifies subsequent actions. Over time, such practices foster a dependable organizational memory, reducing reliance on individual recollection and ensuring critical insights remain within reach.

For **sales professionals**, productivity hinges on managing multiple client relationships while upholding context and consistency. OneNote enables the creation of comprehensive, continuously maintained client profiles that include account details, meeting records, stakeholder analyses, objections, pricing discussions, and follow-ups—all within a single platform. By serving as a narrative chronicle of the customer journey, OneNote allows sales teams to respond promptly and knowledgeably to client needs, thereby accelerating sales cycles and bolstering customer trust.

The platform further enhances sales productivity by offering structured yet adaptable note-taking capabilities. Sales professionals can accurately document customer statements, objections, and delineate next steps during calls and negotiations. Sharing these notes across the team provides managers and colleagues with clear visibility into deal progress, minimizing the need for additional status meetings. This transparency streamlines communication and ensures alignment among sales, presales, finance, and leadership. Additionally, OneNote supports sales enablement by curating best-practice scripts, objection responses, and successful proposal templates, promoting efficient reuse of proven strategies.

Marketing teams, operating at a fast pace to execute campaigns and maintain brand cohesion across multiple channels, benefit significantly from OneNote's centralized approach. The tool functions as a campaign management hub, integrating strategy, implementation, and assessment. Key elements such as campaign objectives, audience insights, creative drafts, feedback loops, and performance metrics are consolidated, facilitating seamless collaboration among copywriters, designers, reviewers, and stakeholders.

Utilizing OneNote as a content pipeline streamlines content production by tracking ideas from inception to publication, preserving essential context around messaging and target audiences. Feedback is more actionable when decisions and discussions remain linked to specific content entries. As libraries expand, OneNote allows for the reuse of previously validated messaging, editorial guidelines, and campaign blueprints, ensuring efficiency and brand consistency across teams and timeframes.

Consulting teams, whose efficacy depends on the quality and continuity of information, leverage OneNote as an engagement intelligence hub. Consultants can methodically document client interactions, insights, decisions, and deliverables, mirroring final project outputs. This systematic approach shortens the transition from meeting notes to actionable reports and presentations, enhancing both accuracy and relevance.

As consulting engagements progress and assumptions shift, OneNote offers a clear chronological record of decision-making. This transparency safeguards against scope confusion and aligns both consultants and clients. Furthermore, building reusable knowledge assets—such as methodologies, workshop outlines, and best-practice templates—in OneNote accelerates future projects and supports the rapid onboarding and development of junior consultants.

Human resources departments experience measurable productivity improvements by adopting OneNote for documentation, knowledge sharing, and communication. Centralized onboarding materials guide new employees efficiently, reducing repetitive queries for HR staff. Structured policy repositories and FAQs improve accessibility and ensure consistent interpretation of procedures, while organized documentation of interviews and employee relations cases fosters transparency, compliance, and holistic institutional learning.

Operations teams see gains in standardization and process reliability through OneNote's capacity to host and update standard operating procedures, thereby ensuring all personnel access current information. Documented handover notes and incident logs enhance shift continuity and minimize the risk of errors due to information gaps. Over time, OneNote evolves into an operational knowledge archive that advances organizational resilience and supports continuous improvement.

Across all business functions, OneNote fosters productivity by instilling consistency in documentation and information-sharing practices. Standardized templates reduce cognitive load and streamline administrative processes, allowing teams to concentrate on critical thinking and execution rather than formatting.

A notable advantage of OneNote is its seamless integration with Microsoft 365 applications. Teams can link communications in Microsoft Teams directly to OneNote pages, preserve Outlook meeting notes, and access SharePoint files without redundancy.

This interoperability positions OneNote as the connective narrative layer of work, strengthening the ties between conversations, tasks, and documentation.

Finally, as organizations grow and evolve, OneNote preserves institutional memory in an accessible format, mitigating knowledge loss due to staff turnover. By capturing both data and contextual rationale, OneNote ensures new team members can quickly assimilate past decisions and methodologies. This continuity underpins organizational scalability and long-term productivity.

In summary, Microsoft OneNote elevates team productivity not through rigid processes but by striking an optimal balance between structure and adaptability. It nurtures effective collaboration and knowledge management across sales, marketing, consulting, HR, and operations, ultimately transforming each project, campaign, and process into a foundation for ongoing success.

Meeting Notes Framework in Microsoft OneNote

Meetings represent a critical yet often inadequately documented asset within contemporary organizations. Key decisions pertaining to projects, clients, budgets, and personnel are frequently made orally and subsequently dispersed through emails, chat threads, or fragmented personal notes. The primary productivity challenge lies not in the volume of meetings but in the lack of an effective system to transform spoken conversations into actionable, shared knowledge. Microsoft OneNote addresses this issue by serving as a structured environment where meetings become occasions for documentation, accountability, and learning.

A robust meeting notes framework transcends simple transcription, aiming to preserve intent, rationale, and direction to facilitate continued progress after the meeting concludes. The framework includes preparation, decisions and insights, review and follow-up, line and share, archive and learn, action items, and capture discussion as shown in Figure 9-2. OneNote equips teams to capture exchanges in real time, organize them systematically, and link discussions directly to subsequent decisions and actions. Unlike static documents or rigid templates, OneNote accommodates the dynamic nature of meetings, making it suitable for both formal and informal discussions.

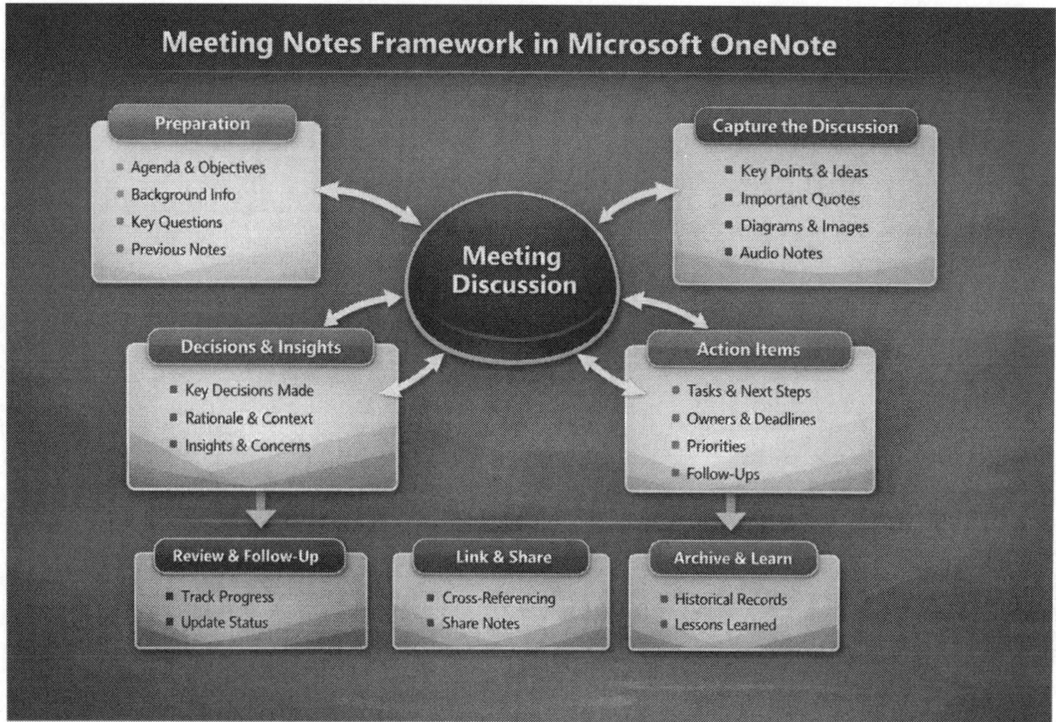

Figure 9-2. *Meeting notes framework*

OneNote's flexibility is a significant advantage in meeting documentation, as it allows departure from linear constraints typical of traditional minutes. Meetings frequently shift between topics and ideas in a manner that chronological lists cannot accurately reflect. Through its adaptable canvas, OneNote enables independent yet interconnected topics, capturing both outcomes and the cognitive processes behind them.

As shown in Figure 9-2, **preparation** is integral to effective meeting notes frameworks. OneNote integrates pre-meeting materials such as agendas, background information, references, key questions, and objectives within a single page, fostering a unified understanding among participants before discussion begins. This approach transforms meetings into purpose-driven sessions, enhancing dialogue quality and minimizing inefficiency.

Throughout meetings, OneNote facilitates unobtrusive note-taking via typing, handwriting, audio, and visual annotations, enabling comprehensive capture without sacrificing engagement. This capability is particularly beneficial in complex meetings featuring diverse perspectives and clarifications, ensuring that rich dialogue is preserved rather than oversimplified.

A well-constructed OneNote framework emphasizes decisions as central outputs. As shown in Figure 9-2, **decisions**, often under-documented, are visually distinguished within notes, maintaining clarity regarding their rationale and context. This decision-centric strategy mitigates confusion over past choices and promotes alignment and trust among team members.

Also, as shown in Figure 9-2, **action** clarity is another essential aspect of high-quality documentation. Tasks are often lost due to ambiguous definition rather than neglect. OneNote supports precise task documentation adjacent to relevant discussions, preserving original intent and reducing misinterpretation. Accountability is supported transparently in OneNote without fostering a surveillance culture. Responsibilities are recorded neutrally, reinforcing collective ownership. Progress can be tracked effectively, diminishing dependency on additional meetings or reminder communications.

Recurring meetings, such as **weekly reviews or project updates**, benefit markedly from OneNote's structured frameworks as shown in Figure 9-2. Continuous sections for regular meetings allow for accumulation of historical notes, facilitating pattern recognition, progress tracking, and priority management across time. This perspective elevates recurring meetings from routine to strategic assets.

Linking past and present meetings is a further strength of OneNote, preventing unnecessary revisitation of resolved issues as shown in Figure 9-2. References to prior discussions and outcomes streamline organizational momentum and enhance morale. OneNote's versatility accommodates various meeting types—from strategic to operational and exploration—without enforcing uniformity. Its adaptability ensures that documentation reflects specific objectives, whether preserving high-level reasoning, recording execution status, or accommodating creative ideation.

In virtual and hybrid meeting contexts, OneNote serves as a shared reference, mitigating fragmentation and loss of context. Participants unable to attend live can reconstruct discussions, improving inclusivity and alignment across distributed teams. Capturing emotional and relational context within meeting notes is crucial. While maintaining professionalism, documenting concerns and dependencies informs future execution and stakeholder engagement. OneNote's structure allows these nuances to coexist alongside formal outcomes.

Repetition and reinforcement through regular review of meeting notes fosters knowledge retention and builds collective memory, enhancing decision-making and execution within teams. Integration with calendars and collaboration platforms ensures seamless association of notes with events, simplifying retrieval and reducing barriers to thorough documentation.

Adaptability is a hallmark of OneNote frameworks; teams can refine note-taking practices continuously, sustaining relevance and usability over time. From a leadership standpoint, systematic meeting notes provide visibility into team progress, issue identification, and overall health without necessitating attendance at every session. This reduces meeting overload and encourages autonomy.

Meeting notes also support **coaching and reflective learning** as shown in Figure 9-2. Reviewing past meetings allows individuals to understand decision-making processes and improve communication skills. For new team members, historical notes are a valuable resource. OneNote minimizes documentation redundancy in project environments, permitting direct extraction of context-rich summaries for reports and updates. In compliance-driven settings, OneNote enables maintenance of auditable records of deliberations and approvals without excessive formality, supporting defensible documentation.

The visual integration capabilities of OneNote enhance clarity through diagrams, sketches, and visuals, which are especially pertinent in technical or design meetings. Consistent use of meeting notes frameworks in OneNote drives cultural change, fostering focus, thoughtful discussion, and improved follow-through. This transformation restores meetings as productive tools for organizational advancement. Reducing cognitive stress is another notable benefit; reliable documentation allows participants to engage fully without the burden of memorizing details, thereby promoting creativity and collaboration.

As organizations scale, OneNote increases informational efficiency per meeting. Structured, accessible, and connected notes reduce the need for excess meetings and enable asynchronous information flow. Over time, accumulated meeting notes create a knowledge archive, revealing decision patterns and cultural values that serve as strategic assets. Ultimately, Microsoft OneNote redefines meeting productivity, converting transient conversations into enduring knowledge and visible commitments. Leveraging

OneNote as an organizational thinking and memory platform ensures meetings facilitate meaningful action and continuous progress.

Microsoft OneNote for Client Call

Client calls play a critical role in safeguarding revenue, strengthening client relationships, identifying risks early, and establishing clear expectations for subsequent interactions. However, in many organizations, the essential details from these conversations are often lost immediately after the call concludes—scattered across individual memory, fragmented chat messages, rushed notes, and selective email follow-ups that capture only a partial record of what transpired. This loss can result in considerable productivity setbacks: repeated queries, unfulfilled commitments, misaligned priorities, and redundant efforts to regain context that should have been preserved initially. Implementing a robust client call documentation system within Microsoft OneNote addresses these challenges by transforming every call into a structured, searchable, and shareable record that preserves intent, clarity, and continuity.

OneNote excels as a platform for client call documentation because it seamlessly combines organizational structure with adaptability. Rarely do client discussions adhere strictly to predefined scripts; instead, they often traverse topics such as needs, constraints, stakeholders, timelines, and unforeseen issues. The flexible page layout in OneNote facilitates capturing the organic flow of conversation while maintaining order. Users can preserve the integrity of the call narrative while segmenting content into logical blocks including objectives, discussion threads, action items, and follow-up tasks. This approach ensures that notes are both faithful to the actual dialogue and easily accessible for future reference, supporting operational efficiency rather than creating administrative overhead.

A dependable OneNote-based documentation process centers around the principle of maintaining a "single source of truth" for each client interaction. Rather than allowing individual team members to keep disparate notes in personal files or drafts, all documentation resides in a shared notebook organized consistently by client and engagement. This strategy serves not merely as an archive but as a vehicle for operational clarity. When notes are consolidated in a predictable, shared location, any authorized team member can access them, continue the conversation intelligently, respond accurately to client inquiries, and deliver a consistent client experience. Such continuity is particularly beneficial when teams are geographically distributed, roles change, or multiple functions engage with the same client account. Call details, key discussion topics, commitments and decisions, client quotes and insights, reference materials, and summary and next steps form the basis of the client meeting template as shown in Figure 9-3, and we will go through each of these aspects.

Figure 9-3. *Client meeting OneNote template*

Client Call Details

To establish this system in OneNote, begin by developing a notebook framework aligned with your organization's client engagement model. A practical approach is to create separate notebooks per client or account group, subdivided into sections reflecting the client lifecycle: discovery and onboarding, recurring meetings, escalation management, commercial negotiations, delivery coordination, and relationship management. Each client call is documented on an individual page. It is important to adopt a systematic page titling convention—such as "YYYY-MM-DD | Call Type | Client Name | Topic"—

which ensures efficient retrieval of records even months later. This practice effectively mitigates one of the most common documentation pitfalls: possessing information that cannot be readily accessed.

Once the notebook structure is established, the next step involves designing a call page template that converts conversational content into actionable documentation. The optimal template offers a balance between thoroughness and practicality; overly elaborate pages discourage consistent use, while minimal documentation fails to retain critical details. A standard OneNote call page typically opens with a concise "Call Header" section outlining key metadata: date, time, attendees, client organization, primary participants, and meeting purpose. This overview provides immediate context and helps prevent confusion when similar topics are discussed across various stakeholders.

Subsequently, the call objective should be articulated in a dedicated paragraph. Rather than generic descriptions such as "weekly sync" or "project update," the objective should specify the desired outcomes for that particular meeting. Clearly stated objectives serve as a reference point for evaluating whether the meeting achieved its goals and identifying areas requiring further attention. Over time, this habit enhances meeting discipline, as articulating objectives before discussion fosters clarity and focus.

Finally, OneNote's value is maximized when call discussions are organized into thematic sections rather than recorded as chronological transcripts. As conversations naturally revisit and interweave multiple topics, OneNote's flexible interface allows for distinct blocks devoted to themes like "current situation," "client priorities," "constraints," "risks," "open questions," and "requested deliverables." Thematic documentation aligns with the way individuals search for information retrospectively, enabling quick navigation to specific areas of interest—be it risk management, pricing, project scope, or stakeholder expectations—without the need to review the entire transcript.

Key Discussion Topics

Among the thematic sections, capturing the client's precise words—especially when they express priorities, worries, or criteria—is invaluable. During client calls, key phrases reveal what truly matters: their fears, values, definitions of success, or potential obstacles. When these are preserved in OneNote, future communication becomes anchored and aligned, protecting against the common pitfall of translating client intent into internal jargon that distorts meaning. Using the client's wording minimizes misinterpretation and strengthens follow-up responses by mirroring their perspective.

A robust documentation process also includes a distinct "Commitments and Agreements" area. Relationships falter most when commitments aren't clear or are recalled differently. OneNote enables teams to record commitments distinctly within call notes, emphasizing specificity about what will be delivered, by whom, when, and which dependencies apply. Clear commitments make writing follow-up emails and handing off tasks internally much more efficient, reducing the risk of forgotten promises. In many organizations, consistently documented commitments drive the greatest productivity gains by preventing rework and escalation.

Commitments and Decisions

Additionally, maintaining a "Decisions and Rationale" section is crucial for client calls. Internal meetings often prioritize decision tracking, but client interactions involve negotiation, compromise, and mutual understanding. Simply recording decisions isn't sufficient; the rationale, considered alternatives, and accepted assumptions must also be captured. When reasoning is documented, it's easier to address future questions about specific choices or scope boundaries with clarity, avoiding repeated debates or conflicting explanations.

OneNote offers tools for mapping stakeholders and gathering relationship intelligence, a commonly overlooked aspect. Subtle insights emerge about approval dynamics, influence, and stakeholder perspectives during client conversations. Storing operationally relevant details such as who shapes decisions, who is risk-averse, who prioritizes cost, or who advocates internally enhances team engagement. The purpose is factual clarity, not personal opinions. Thoughtful documentation of stakeholder intelligence streamlines communication and reduces wasted effort.

Client calls often generate unresolved questions. Without structured processes, these questions can be lost, resurface later, or become inconvenient bottlenecks. A dedicated "Open Questions" section in OneNote distinguishes pending items from decisions and commitments. This separation is beneficial both psychologically and operationally, ensuring the team doesn't mistakenly treat unresolved issues as settled. Explicit tracking of questions sharpens follow-up efforts and enables subsequent calls to start with answers instead of confusion, turning OneNote into a bridge that connects conversations and fosters progress.

Client Quotes and Insights

An effective OneNote page concludes with a concise “Call Summary”—a brief narrative of key outcomes and next steps written right after the discussion. Busy leaders rely on this summary, and teammates can grasp the call’s essence in under a minute. Summarizing forces note-takers to clarify intent, resolve ambiguities, and emphasize priorities. Over time, these summaries create an accessible archive that tracks the evolution of client interactions.

Linking client call pages to related artifacts amplifies OneNote’s utility. Many discussions rely on documents like proposals, statements of work, presentations, plans, security questionnaires, or design drafts. By attaching or referencing these resources in OneNote, the documentation seamlessly connects conversations to deliverables, saving time spent hunting for the latest versions and improving responsiveness.

Sustainable client call documentation relies on a blend of real-time capture and post-call refinement. Key themes, commitments, and questions should be jotted down with minimal friction during the call, followed immediately by a brief review to clarify unclear points, ensure commitments are specific, add missing context, and craft a clean summary. This two-step approach acknowledges that perfect notes rarely happen in real time, but disciplined revision transforms fragments into useful records without requiring extensive rewrites.

Recurring client calls benefit from structured documentation in OneNote. For ongoing meetings, organize a dedicated section where each session gets its own page and maintain a “running log” summarizing milestones, recurring issues, and long-term commitments. Individual pages provide detail, while the log offers continuity, helping new participants quickly get up to speed.

OneNote also standardizes post-call communication. After a call, teams typically email summaries of decisions and next steps. With well-structured notes, crafting these emails is faster and less error-prone. Consistent follow-up builds trust with clients, demonstrating professionalism and organization, which accelerates approvals and smooths future interactions.

Another productivity boost comes from recording implicit signals during client calls—urgency, confidence, risk tolerance, and internal constraints. Documenting these insights helps teams prioritize realistically, plan around approval cycles, and avoid overpromising. Ignoring these cues leads to missed expectations and strained relationships, but OneNote makes capturing them routine.

For teams managing multiple accounts, OneNote turns scattered notes into a comparative knowledge base. Patterns emerge—common objections, repeat requests, timeline delays. Systematic documentation shapes better playbooks, sharper planning, and stronger messaging. Even simple searches across notebooks reveal recurring client concerns and how successful teams respond, transforming OneNote from a personal tool to a collective intelligence resource.

Sensitive information, including pricing, contract positions, and security issues, is common in client calls. OneNote supports safe handling through notebook permissions and thoughtful organization, separating general from sensitive content using restricted sections or separate notebooks. Designed permission controls foster collaboration while maintaining confidentiality.

Reference Material

Quality documentation ties directly to effective handovers. As accounts change hands, consultants rotate, and leadership seeks briefings, thorough notes in OneNote make transitions seamless. New owners can review call summaries, commitments, and stakeholder dynamics, engaging confidently without reconstructing history, impressing clients with continuity.

Escalation or difficult calls demand clear, factual documentation more than ever. OneNote provides a framework to record events, client experiences, impacts, agreed resolutions, and timelines. Focused on verifiable actions and outcomes, this protects both relationships and organizations by tracking resolution steps and follow-through.

Technical discussions benefit from OneNote's blend of text and visuals. Diagrams, annotated screenshots, and sketches stored alongside narratives clarify concepts, reducing misunderstandings and simplifying downstream work.

OneNote allows for layered documentation—a summary and action list upfront cater to those seeking quick insights, while detailed thematic blocks offer depth for others. Executives can scan the highlights, contributors can delve deeper, and new members can familiarize themselves with the entire relationship's progression.

Summary and Next Steps

Preparation for future calls is enhanced by a "Next Call Preparation" section listing key topics, questions, and objectives. This transforms documentation into a living bridge between meetings, eliminating last-minute scrambles and making preparation a natural extension of note-taking.

Consistency across teams is fostered by shared templates in OneNote. Templates should guide narrative flow—from headers and objectives to discussion themes, decisions, commitments, risks, and open questions, concluding with a summary and preparation cues. Uniform pages simplify scanning and auditing, speeding operations and reducing confusion.

Though some worry that thorough documentation slows teams, a well-designed structure does the opposite. Time spent clarifying commitments and decisions is reclaimed many times over via fewer follow-up clarifications, reduced repetition, and aligned delivery. Habitual use lowers mental strain, spreading calm and efficiency as knowledge is reliably stored and accessed.

Documenting client calls in OneNote improves engagement quality as well. Knowing commitments and rationale will be recorded, teams ask clearer questions, make explicit assumptions, and summarize decisions to ensure alignment—enhancing the call experience and reducing misunderstandings.

At its highest level, OneNote documentation builds a strategic narrative from individual notes. Reviewing summaries reveals shifting priorities, increasing risks, changing stakeholder dynamics, and evolving relationships, supporting proactive rather than reactive client management.

Immediate benefits drive adoption, with OneNote serving as a valuable reference for follow-ups, planning, and preparation. Shared notes multiply collaborative advantages. Keeping the system straightforward, consistent, and outcome-focused sustains its usefulness.

Ultimately, documenting client calls in OneNote is a mark of respect for time, clarity, and trust—for both clients and teams. It ensures concerns are addressed, reduces repeated work, and demonstrates professionalism and continuity, especially with multiple points of contact. Microsoft OneNote combines swift capture, flexible structure, easy sharing, and lasting searchability in a single workspace.

Thoughtfully implemented, OneNote transforms calls into enduring assets. Each page records what mattered, what was agreed, next steps, and the reasoning behind choices. Over months and years, these pages tell the story of the client relationship, laying the foundation for consistent delivery and growth. That's the true productivity impact: OneNote turns conversation into continuity and continuity into results.

Project Documentation and Handovers Using Microsoft OneNote

Project documentation is most valuable when it captures not only what was delivered, but how the work evolved over time and why specific choices were made. In many organizations, documentation is produced at the end of a project as a compliance activity, which leads to outdated, incomplete, or unused records. Microsoft OneNote enables a different approach by supporting documentation as a continuous, living knowledge system that grows alongside the project. Teams can record goals, assumptions, evolving scope, and contextual notes as part of daily work rather than as a separate task. Because OneNote pages are easy to edit, reorganize, and expand, documentation remains aligned with reality instead of freezing an early version of understanding. This living nature ensures that when the project reaches its later stages, the documentation already reflects the true journey of delivery, making it far more reliable for future reference and handover. As shown in Figure 9-4, we will go through each phase of documentation from structured project knowledge to decisions and design evolution, reliable handover process, and sustainable knowledge.

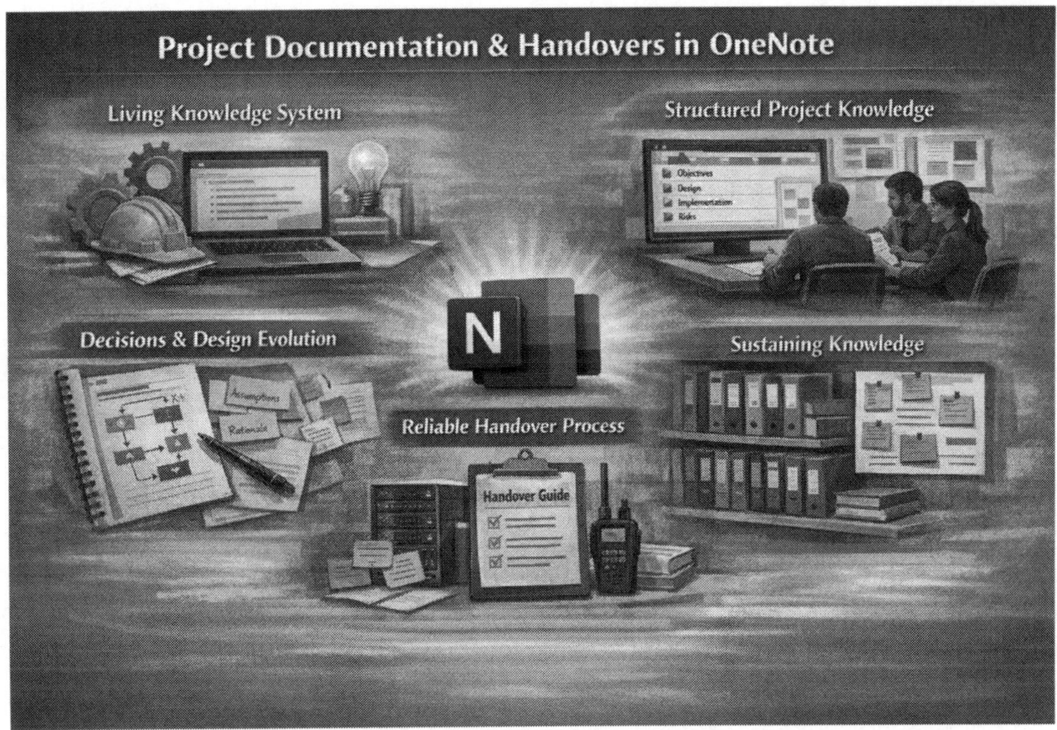

Figure 9-4. *Project documentation and handovers using Microsoft OneNote*

Structuring Project Knowledge

The effectiveness of project documentation depends heavily on how information is structured. OneNote excels in this area by allowing teams to organize content in notebooks, sections, and pages that mirror the project lifecycle. Rather than grouping information by role or tool, strong project notebooks are structured around enduring concepts such as objectives, design decisions, implementation details, risks, validation, and operations. This structure makes the documentation intuitive even for someone who was not involved in the original work. When information is grouped logically and linked clearly, readers do not need to rely on tribal knowledge to navigate the material. This clarity reduces onboarding time for new contributors and prevents confusion during audits, reviews, or future enhancements. Over time, a well-structured OneNote project notebook becomes a dependable reference point rather than a collection of disconnected notes.

Decisions and Design Evolution

One of the most common weaknesses in project handovers is the loss of rationale behind key decisions. Teams may understand what was built, but not why it was built that way. Microsoft OneNote supports decision awareness by making it easy to document assumptions, alternatives considered, constraints faced, and trade-offs accepted at each stage of the project. Because these decision notes can live alongside design sketches, technical explanations, and meeting outcomes, the reasoning remains visible and understandable in context. This is particularly important when future teams modify or extend the solution. Without access to past rationale, they risk undoing critical design safeguards or repeating earlier mistakes. By preserving the evolution of thinking rather than just final outcomes, OneNote ensures continuity of understanding and supports more confident decision-making long after the original team has moved on.

Reliable Project Handovers

A successful project handover is not simply the transfer of files; it is the transfer of operational confidence. The receiving team must understand how the solution works, how it should be monitored, how changes are deployed, and how issues should be handled. OneNote supports this by allowing teams to curate a focused handover section within the project notebook that draws together essential knowledge from across the project. This section can highlight system behavior, environmental details, operational risks, validation steps, and known limitations in a format that is readable and practical. Because OneNote allows explanatory text, visual references, and links to authoritative artifacts to coexist, the handover information is both comprehensive and approachable. When teams use OneNote in this way, handovers become smoother, questions decrease, and dependency on outgoing team members is significantly reduced.

Sustaining Knowledge

The long-term value of project documentation depends on whether it continues to be used and updated after handover. OneNote encourages sustainability because it integrates naturally into everyday workflows and does not require specialized tools to maintain. When ownership of the notebook is clearly assigned, teams can update documentation as systems evolve, lessons are learned, or processes improve. This ongoing maintenance transforms project documentation from a historical artifact into an operational knowledge base. Over time, these notebooks accumulate into a rich organizational memory that supports resilience, scalability, and learning. By using Microsoft OneNote for project documentation and handovers, organizations ensure that knowledge survives beyond individual projects and contributors, enabling smoother transitions, reduced risk, and more effective long-term operations.

Building Enterprise Knowledge Libraries Using Microsoft OneNote

In large organizations, knowledge is created continuously through projects, decisions, problem-solving, and day-to-day operations, yet much of this knowledge remains fragmented or transient. Emails are deleted, chats disappear, documents become outdated, and critical understanding often resides with individuals rather than the organization itself. Building enterprise knowledge libraries using Microsoft OneNote addresses this challenge by providing a shared, flexible environment where institutional knowledge can be captured, refined, and accessed over time. OneNote supports a narrative form of documentation that preserves context, rationale, and learning, rather than storing information as isolated files. When used purposefully across teams, OneNote transforms knowledge management from an administrative obligation into an integral part of how the organization learns, operates, and evolves.

Enterprise knowledge libraries using OneNote can be built using scalable and trustworthy knowledge architecture and organizational learning through embedded knowledge practices as explained in Figure 9-5, and we will look into the details of these.

Figure 9-5. *Creation of knowledge libraries using OneNote*

Designing a Scalable and Trustworthy Knowledge Architecture

The efficacy of an enterprise knowledge library is determined by the intuitiveness of its information structure and the reliability with which it mirrors actual business conditions. Microsoft OneNote enables organizations to develop scalable knowledge frameworks by systematically organizing content into notebooks, sections, and pages that correspond to enduring business concepts such as policies, processes, domain expertise, project histories, and best practices. Unlike traditional document repositories, OneNote facilitates the creation of comprehensive pages that integrate explanations, examples, references, and timely updates within a unified space. This narrative arrangement empowers employees to appreciate both procedural steps and the underlying intent, supporting informed decision-making. As organizational knowledge evolves, incremental page revisions ensure guidance remains aligned with current practice. Such adaptability fosters confidence in the knowledge library, assuring users that information is up-to-date, accurate, and grounded in authentic experience rather than static policy statements.

A thoughtfully structured OneNote knowledge library also minimizes cognitive load for users by reflecting natural search behaviors. High-level overview pages provide initial orientation, while subordinate pages deliver detailed guidance, contextually linked to supplementary material. This hierarchical approach supports both quick reference and extensive learning, eliminating unnecessary duplication. Gradually, documented patterns highlight recurring challenges, preferred solutions, and established norms within the organization. Leaders and subject-matter experts can leverage these insights to refine standards and promote greater consistency across teams. By enabling direct practitioner contributions, the library ensures decentralized yet coherent knowledge creation, lessening reliance on a dedicated documentation function. Governance is maintained through defined notebook ownership and review protocols, preserving quality and alignment as the repository expands.

Sustaining Organizational Learning Through Embedded Knowledge Practices

An enterprise knowledge library is effective only when integrated into daily workflows, rather than being a separate resource accessed infrequently. Microsoft OneNote facilitates this integration by simplifying both the contribution and retrieval processes. Employees are able to document insights immediately following issue resolution, project completion, or process enhancement, thereby capturing learning at its inception. This timely documentation mitigates knowledge loss and ensures lessons learned remain contextually relevant. When teams consistently consult the OneNote library during onboarding, planning, and execution, the use of organizational knowledge becomes routine. This regularity enhances the library's value and promotes ongoing improvement, as employees directly experience benefits such as expedited problem-solving and minimized redundant efforts.

Over time, the enterprise knowledge library develops into a robust repository of organizational intelligence. As personnel transition between roles or depart, their expertise is preserved through shared knowledge resources. New employees benefit from reduced adjustment periods, as the library offers insights on standard practices, decision-making rationale, and favored methodologies. This continuity fosters organizational resilience and decreases operational risk during transitions. Furthermore, leadership can leverage the library to assess adaptive strategies, gain perspective on cultural strengths, and identify systemic challenges. By maintaining knowledge as an evolving resource supported by Microsoft OneNote, organizations progress beyond mere information storage, cultivating a culture where learning, transparency, and collective understanding drive sustained performance and adaptability.

With these we have come to the end of this chapter. We have seen that Microsoft OneNote boosts team productivity by providing a collaborative workspace for documentation and knowledge sharing. The chapter outlined how OneNote is used in various functions—such as sales, marketing, consulting, HR, and operations—to organize daily tasks, structure meeting notes, and document client calls. It highlighted OneNote's role in ensuring smooth project handovers, preserving both deliverables and decision rationale, and maintaining enterprise knowledge libraries to support learning and continuity.

The next chapter covers how Microsoft OneNote boosts personal productivity by supporting habit tracking, learning journals, home and finance management, digital bullet journaling, and knowledge archiving. By uniting these functions in one workspace, OneNote helps users stay organized and balance both professional and personal life.

CHAPTER 10

OneNote for Personal Productivity and Life Management

Upon completion of the previous chapter, we gained insights into the strategic application of Microsoft OneNote to enhance team productivity within professional settings. We have experienced how organizations—across functions such as sales, marketing, consulting, human resources, and operations—can centralize information, facilitate effective collaboration, and maintain organizational clarity through well-structured notebooks. It covered best practices for creating robust meeting notes frameworks, documenting client interactions, managing project documentation and handovers, and developing enterprise knowledge libraries. Overall, Chapter 9 established OneNote as a key resource for fostering collective efficiency, accountability, and operational continuity.

Moving to this chapter, the emphasis transitions from group collaboration to individual effectiveness. This chapter examines the integration of OneNote into daily routines to optimize the management of personal goals, schedules, and information. Topics include habit tracking, the use of learning journals, home management solutions, and finance tracking templates—all illustrating how OneNote can consolidate multiple functionalities within a single adaptable digital platform. Additionally, the chapter introduces concepts such as digital bullet journaling and personal knowledge archiving, empowering readers to systematically organize their thoughts, ideas, and experiences. By the chapter's end, readers will possess a comprehensive understanding of leveraging OneNote not only as a note-taking tool but also as an all-encompassing life management solution that promotes personal development, focus, and productivity. The overview of the chapter is shown in Figure 10-1.

C. Waghmare, *Mastering Microsoft OneNote*, https://doi.org/10.1007/979-8-8688-2866-9_10

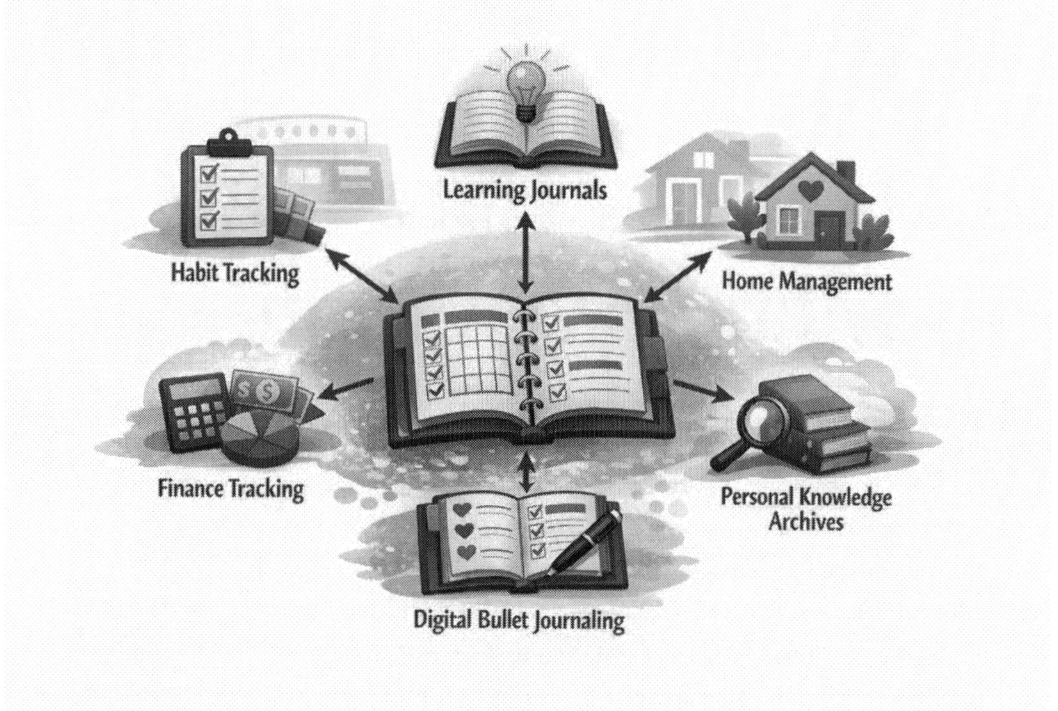

Figure 10-1. *Personal productivity and life management*

OneNote for Habit Tracking

Habit tracking serves as an effective strategy for fostering consistency, self-discipline, and sustained personal development. Whether aiming to enhance health, acquire new skills, or uphold a balanced lifestyle, systematically monitoring habits enables measurable progress and greater visibility. Microsoft OneNote provides a versatile and intuitive digital platform, allowing users to construct habit-tracking systems tailored to individual requirements. Unlike conventional habit-tracking applications, OneNote delivers comprehensive freedom for customizing layouts, formats, and tracking methodologies.

The initial step in leveraging OneNote for habit tracking involves establishing a dedicated tracker page. This can be situated within a personal notebook or sections such as "Personal Productivity" or "Life Management." Utilizing clear titles like "Daily Habit Tracker" or "Monthly Habits" aids in maintaining organizational clarity as shown in Figure 10-2. This central hub facilitates consistent tracking across all chosen habits, and duplicating the page for each month or week supports systematic recordkeeping over time.

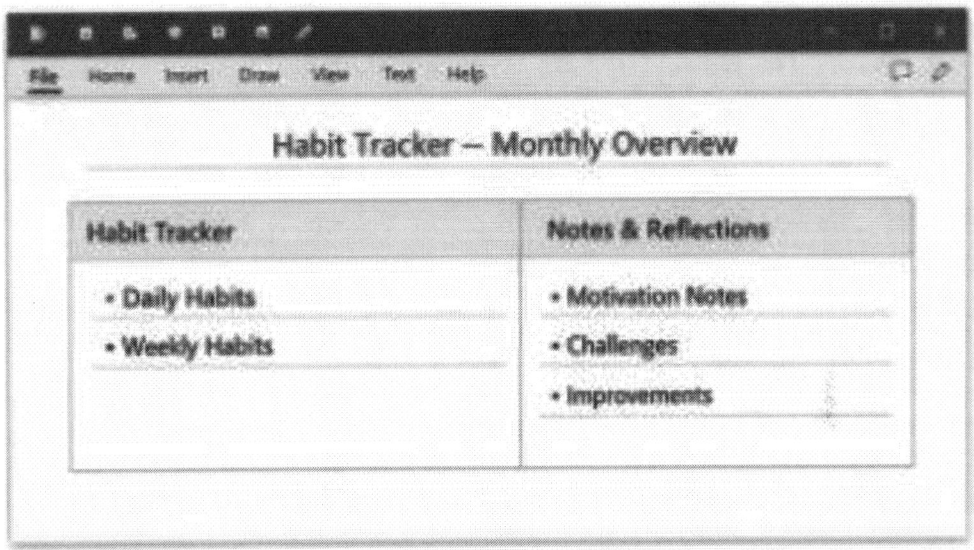

Figure 10-2. *Monthly habit tracker overview*

Following page creation, it is recommended to construct a habit-tracking table. OneNote's robust table features make it suitable for structured recording. The leftmost column should list targeted habits—such as exercise, reading, early rising, meditation, or sufficient water intake—while the top row comprises days of the week or specific dates as shown in Figure 10-3. This grid layout offers transparent visualization of obligations and achievements, and its simplicity helps reduce overwhelm, thereby supporting sustained engagement.

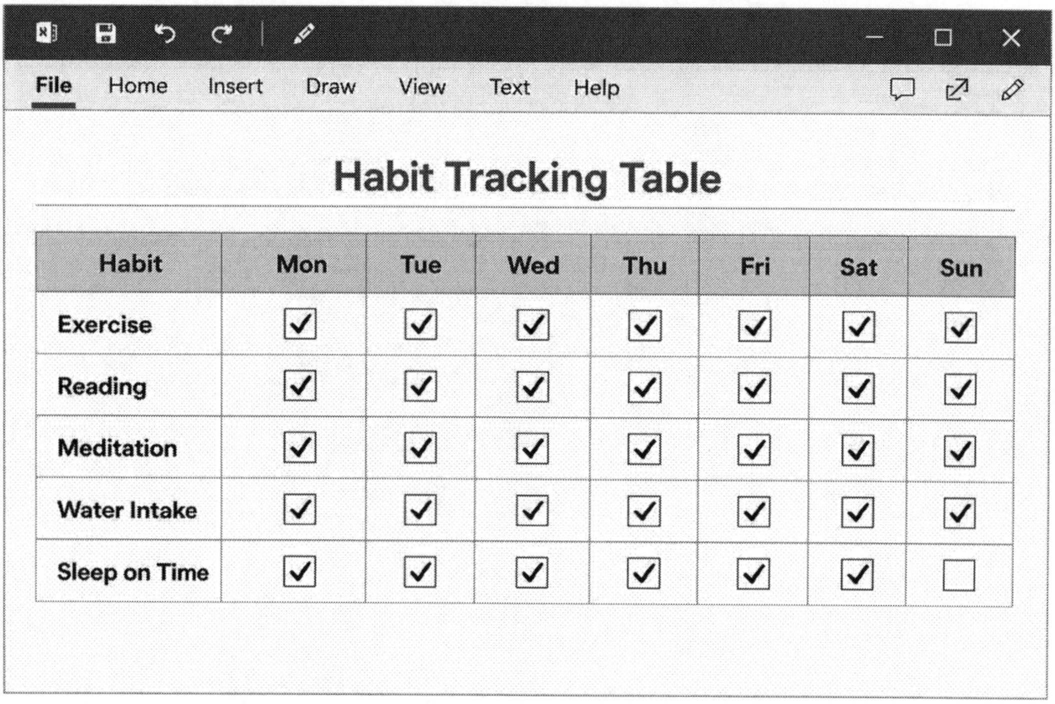

File Home Insert Draw View Text Help

Habit Tracking Table

Habit	Mon	Tue	Wed	Thu	Fri	Sat	Sun
Exercise	☑	☑	☑	☑	☑	☑	☑
Reading	☑	☑	☑	☑	☑	☑	☑
Meditation	☑	☑	☑	☑	☑	☑	☑
Water Intake	☑	☑	☑	☑	☑	☑	☑
Sleep on Time	☑	☑	☑	☑	☑	☑	☐

Figure 10-3. *Habit-tracking table*

With the table established, monitoring daily progress with checkboxes becomes integral to reinforcing desirable behaviors. OneNote's built-in checkbox tags can be easily placed within table cells to indicate completion as shown in Figure 10-4. Marking these boxes provides immediate visual feedback, which strengthens accountability and motivation. Over time, accumulating checkmarks encourages ongoing adherence and continuity, making this a distinct advantage of using OneNote for habit management.

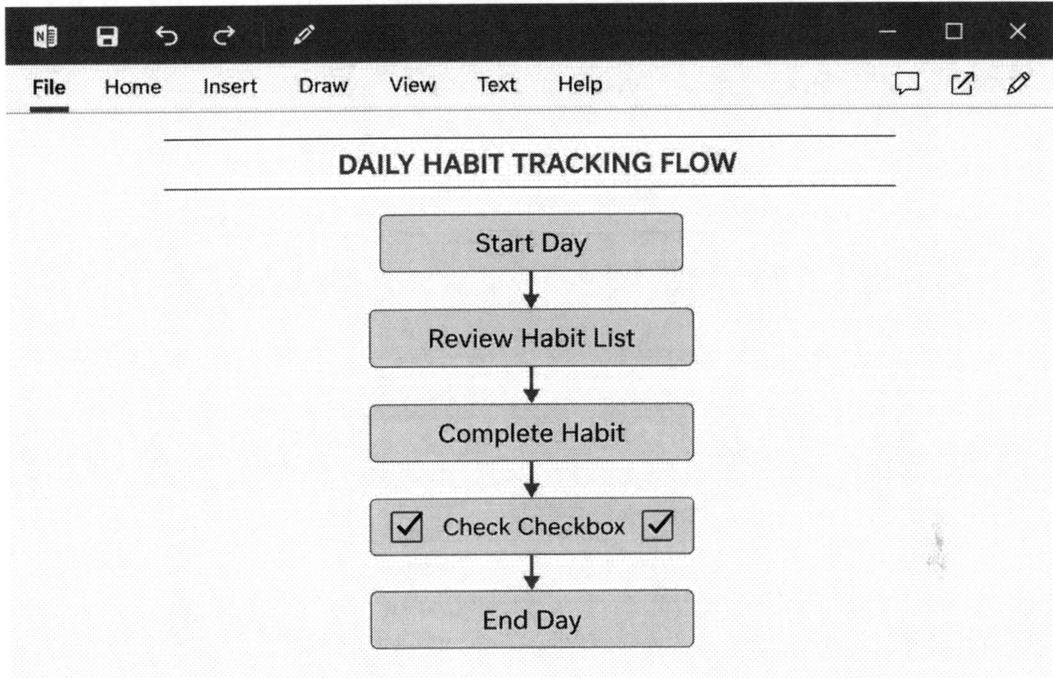

Figure 10-4. *Daily habit-tracking flow*

To further enrich self-engagement and awareness, users are encouraged to incorporate notes, reflections, and reminders alongside their trackers. Designating a space below the table for concise reflections on daily experiences, challenges encountered, or factors contributing to outcomes adds depth to the process. Leveraging OneNote's tagging options—such as "Important," "To Do," or customized categories—helps highlight vital insights as shown in Figure 10-5. Additionally, users may include motivational quotes, set personal objectives, or add habit-specific reminders, thereby transforming tracking into a comprehensive self-improvement practice.

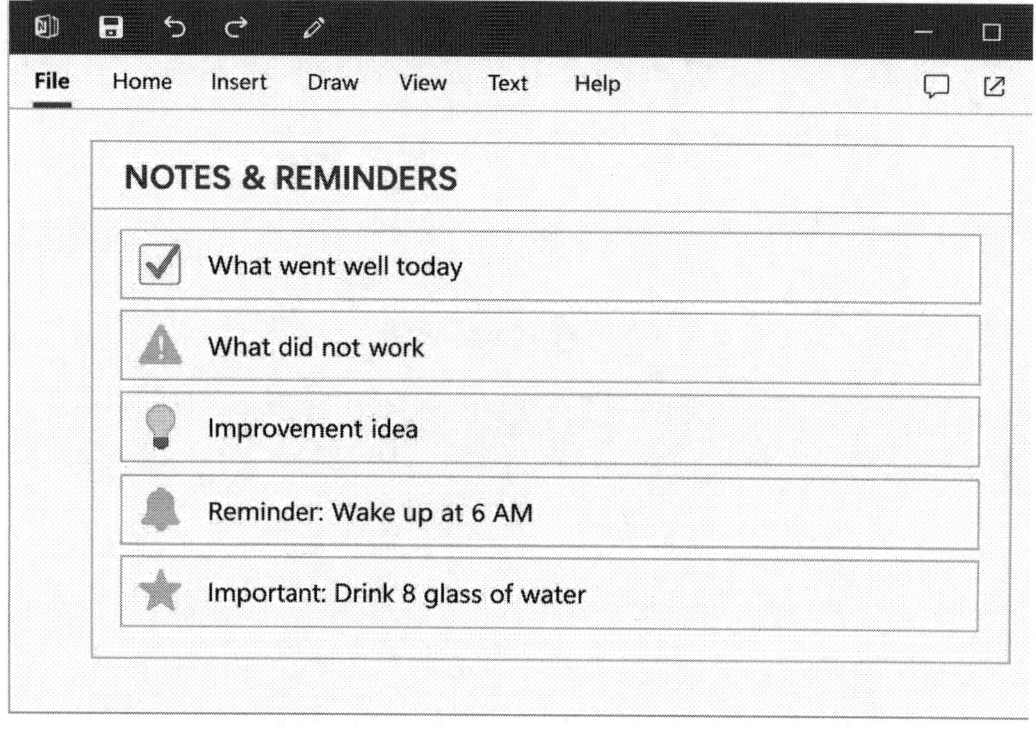

Figure 10-5. *Notes and reminders*

A crucial element of successful habit monitoring is routine review and progress evaluation. At weekly or monthly intervals, reviewing recorded data allows for identification of consistent patterns as shown in Figure 10-6. Habits that present challenges may necessitate modifications, while those regularly achieved can be reinforced. OneNote supports the creation of summary sections, basic charts, and evaluative notes to facilitate this review. Such analyses foster enhanced accountability and provide an objective understanding of one's behavioral trends.

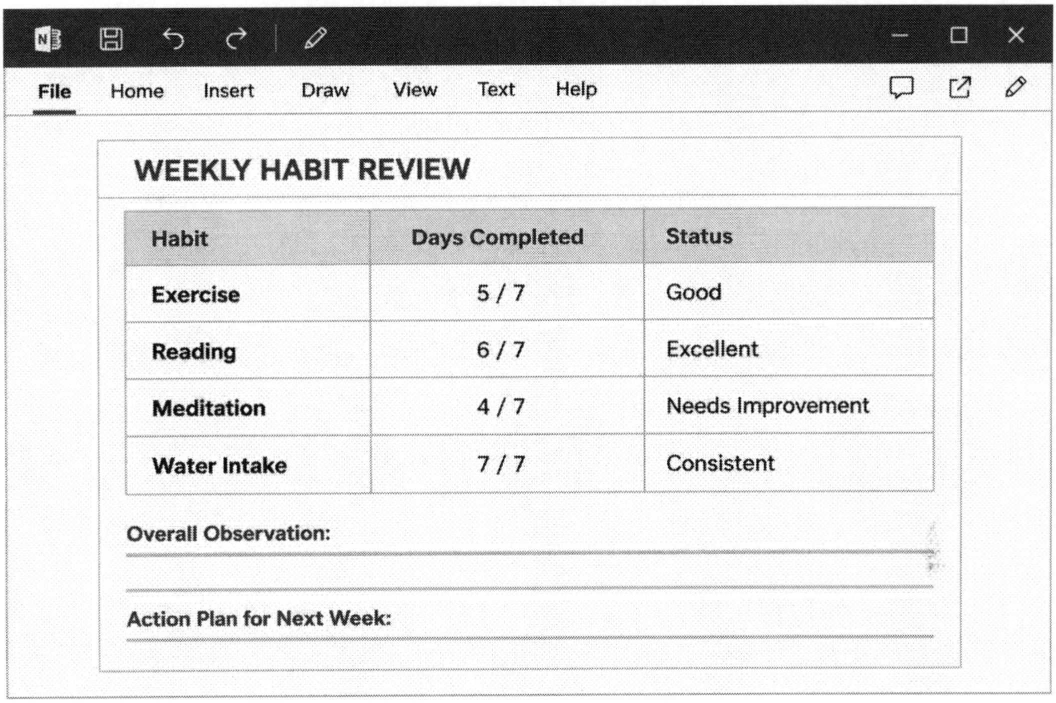

File Home Insert Draw View Text Help

WEEKLY HABIT REVIEW

Habit	Days Completed	Status
Exercise	5 / 7	Good
Reading	6 / 7	Excellent
Meditation	4 / 7	Needs Improvement
Water Intake	7 / 7	Consistent

Overall Observation:

Action Plan for Next Week:

Figure 10-6. *Weekly review dashboard*

Moreover, OneNote's cross-device functionality greatly benefits tracking. Synchronization across desktop, mobile, and tablet devices ensures habits can be updated promptly, regardless of location. This accessibility minimizes missed entries and maintains alignment with ongoing goals.

In summary as shown in Figure 10-7, utilizing Microsoft OneNote as a tool for habit tracking transforms it into a valuable instrument for personal productivity and holistic life management. Through structured organization, dynamic tables, actionable checkboxes, reflective journaling, and regular reviews, users can establish a robust and sustainable system for long-term behavioral growth. The flexibility, user-friendliness, and organizational capacity of OneNote make it exceptionally well suited for individuals pursuing consistent improvement and disciplined daily routines.

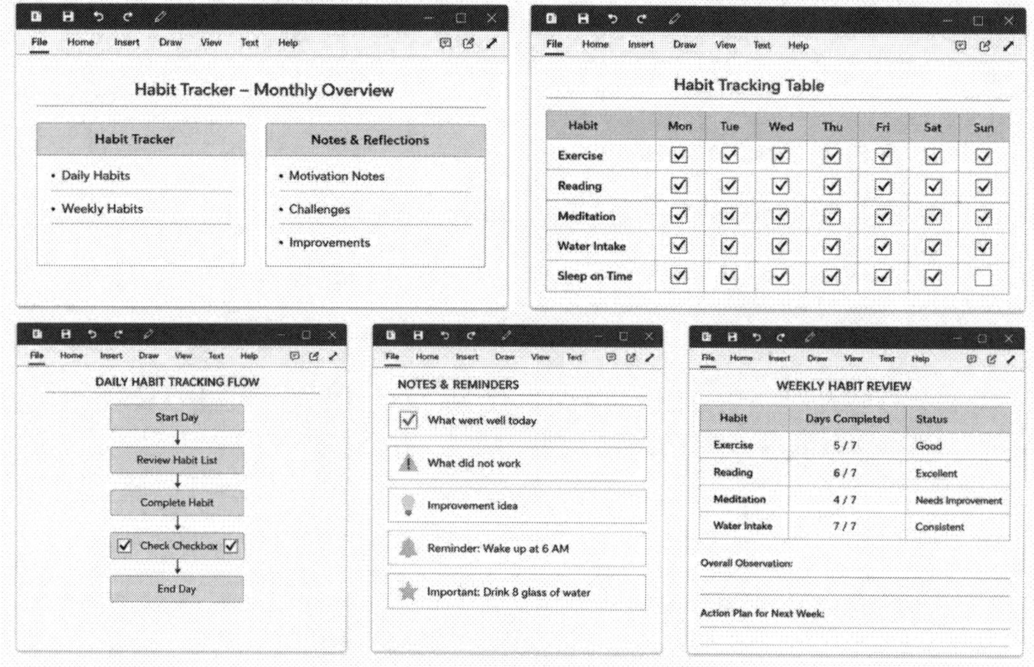

Figure 10-7. *Overview of habit tracking using OneNote*

Writing Learning Journals Using Microsoft OneNote

A learning journal is most effective when it is structured, reflective, and easy to update regularly. Microsoft OneNote is ideal for writing learning journals because it allows users to organize content into notebooks, sections, and pages. To begin, create a dedicated notebook or section titled Learning Journal. Each learning session should be recorded as a new page with a clear title, such as the topic or subject name. Using page titles, date entries, and tables, learners can structure their journal entries to include the learning date, topic, and objectives as shown in Figure 10-8. OneNote's free-form canvas allows content to be placed anywhere on the page, making personalized layouts easy and flexible.

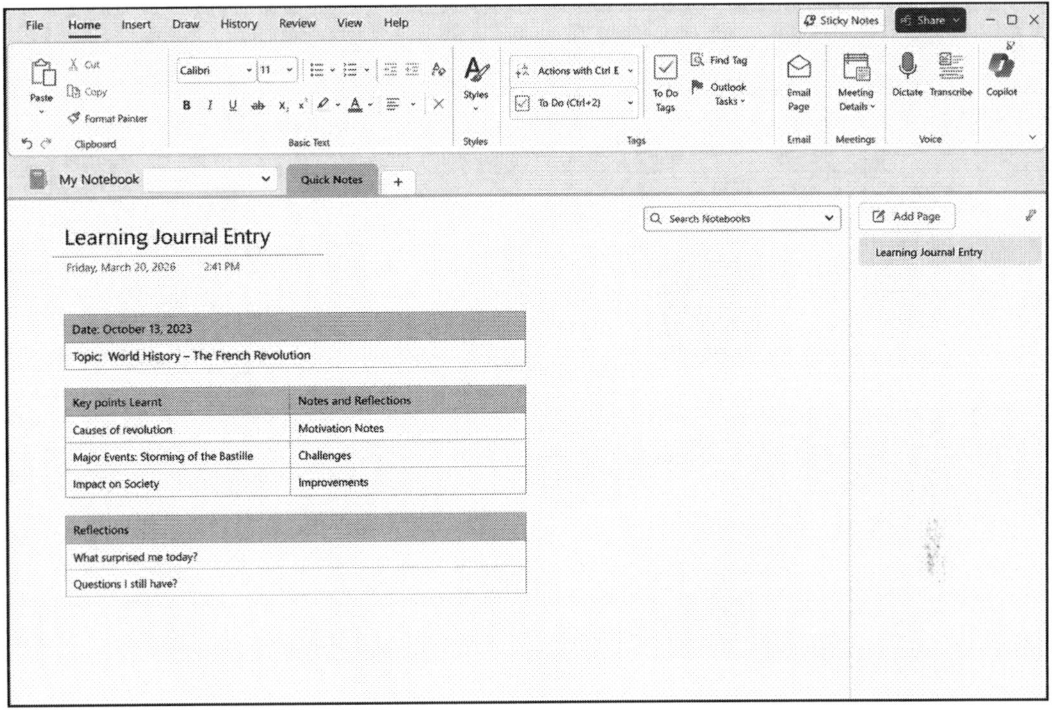

Figure 10-8. *Creating a learning journal*

An important feature of OneNote for learning journals is the ability to combine text with multimedia resources. While writing journal entries, learners can insert figures, PDFs, links, audio, or video references to support their understanding. Using the Insert tab, study materials such as lecture slides, research articles, and diagrams can be embedded directly into the journal page as shown in Figure 10-9. This helps learners connect theoretical knowledge with visual references. The integration of external resources within the same page reduces the need to switch between apps and strengthens contextual learning.

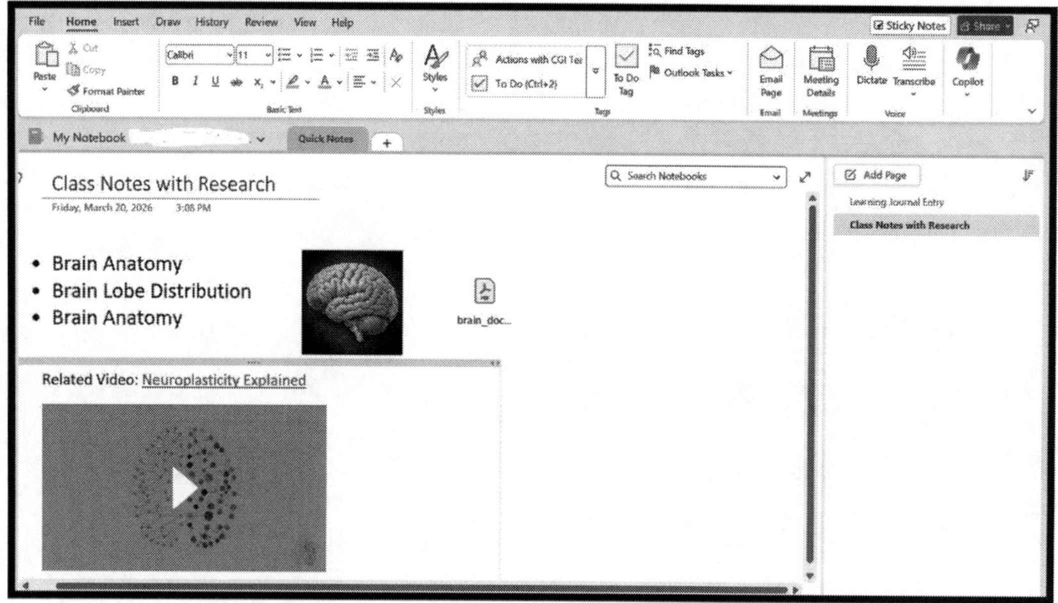

***Figure 10-9.** Multimedia features supporting learning journal*

Reflection is the core of a good learning journal, and OneNote supports this through its table, heading, and formatting tools. Users can create separate sections on the same page for key points learned, reflections, and questions. Tables are especially useful for dividing "What I Learned" and "What I Think" columns, encouraging critical thinking. Using bold text, bullet points, and headings, learners can clearly highlight important insights. This structured reflection helps transform passive note-taking into active learning.

OneNote's tags feature is one of the most powerful tools for maintaining a learning journal. Tags such as To Do, Important, Question, Idea, and custom tags can be applied to sentences or paragraphs. This makes it easy to identify doubts, follow-up tasks, or breakthrough ideas later. For example, a learner can tag unclear concepts with "Question" and revisit them before exams. The Find Tags feature allows users to quickly collect all tagged items across the notebook, making revision highly efficient as shown in Figure 10-10.

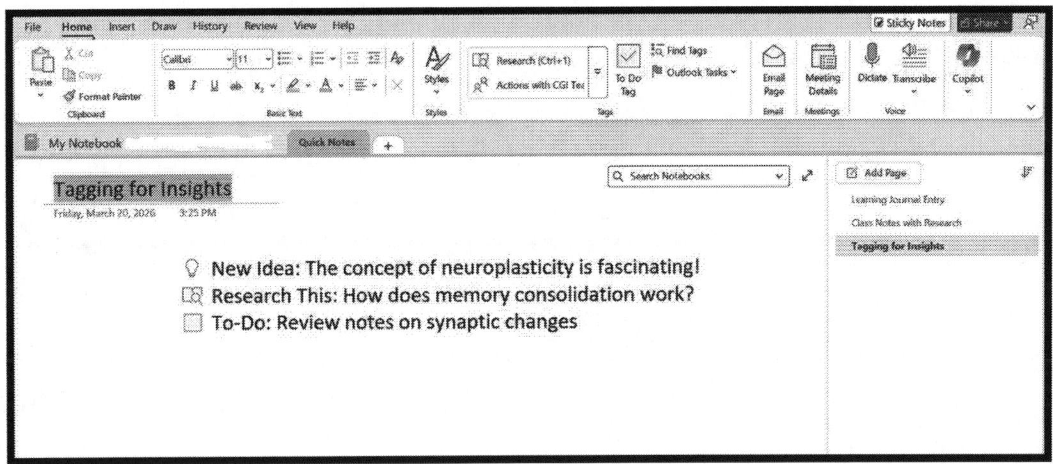

Figure 10-10. *OneNote tags*

Another valuable aspect of OneNote for learning journals is weekly or periodic summaries. Learners can create separate pages to summarize learning outcomes for the week or month. Using tables and checklist tags, they can record highlights, challenges, and learning goals as shown in Figure 10-11. This habit improves self-evaluation and helps track progress over time. OneNote's duplication feature allows users to copy the same summary template every week, maintaining consistency without extra effort.

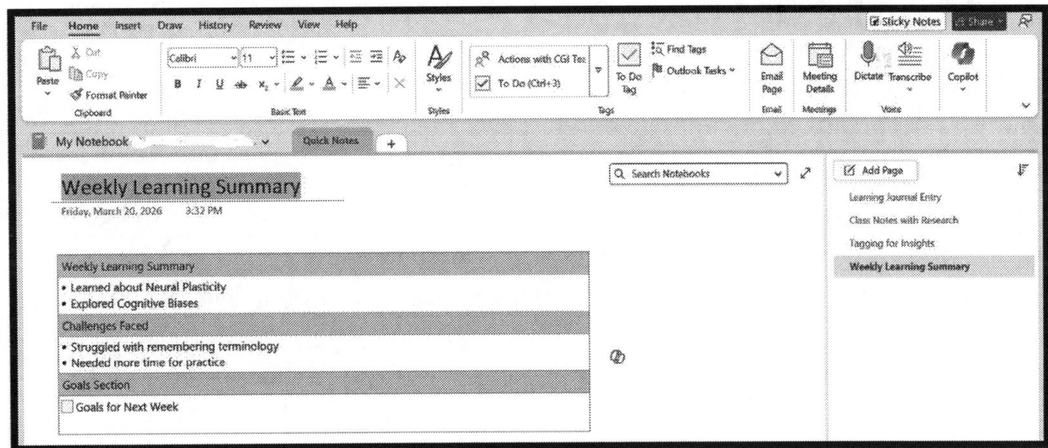

Figure 10-11. *Learning summary using OneNote*

Finally, OneNote supports long-term reflection and revision through its search, history, and synchronization features as shown in Figure 10-12. The powerful search tool allows learners to instantly locate keywords, even inside figures or handwritten notes. Page version history helps review how understanding has evolved over time. Since OneNote syncs across devices, learning journals can be updated anytime—during lectures, self-study, or revision. Together, these features make Microsoft OneNote an excellent digital platform for maintaining meaningful, organized, and reflective learning journals.

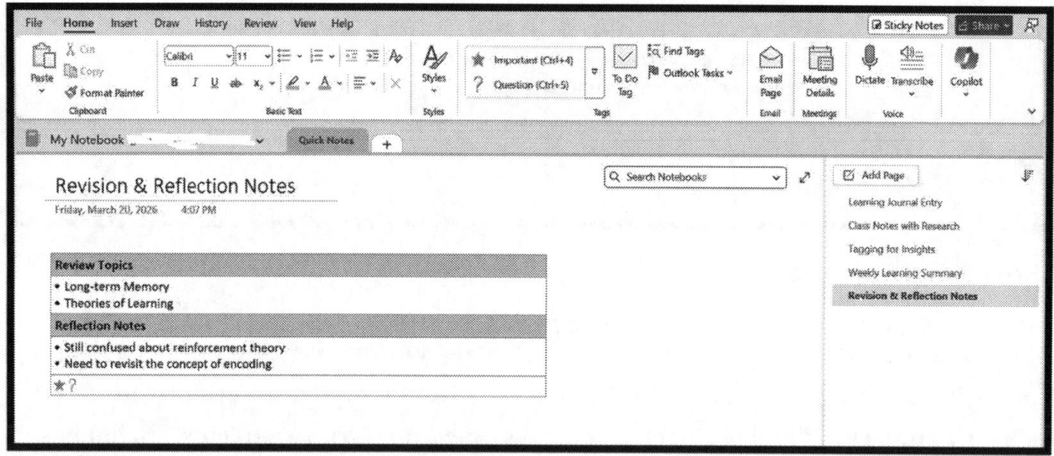

Figure 10-12. *Reflection of the journal*

Use of Microsoft OneNote for Home Management

Effective home management entails organizing a broad spectrum of responsibilities, including household operations, family schedules, documentation, meal planning, and ongoing projects. When managed informally, these tasks can quickly become unmanageable. Microsoft OneNote provides a robust digital solution, integrating all facets of home administration into a centralized, adaptable, and easily accessible platform. With careful configuration, OneNote serves as a comprehensive hub that fosters transparency, consistency, and streamlined coordination.

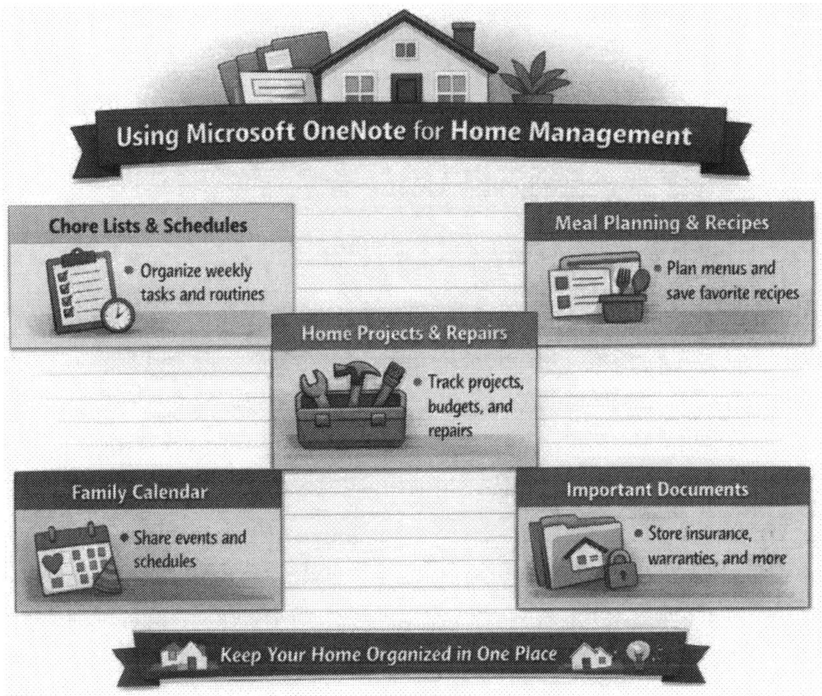

***Figure 10-13.** Use of OneNote in home management*

The initial step in leveraging Microsoft OneNote for domestic management is to establish a dedicated Home Management notebook. This notebook may be subdivided into sections such as chores and schedules, meal planning, family calendar, home projects and repairs, and important documents as shown in Figure 10-13. Each section encompasses pages devoted to specific functions or records, enabling logical categorization and effortless updates or retrievals. The notebook-section-page architecture supports systematic organization, as depicted in Figure 10-13 which illustrates interconnected home activities unified within one system.

OneNote's utility is particularly evident in maintaining chore lists and household schedules. By employing tables and checkboxes, users can construct daily, weekly, or monthly task lists. Responsibilities, such as cleaning, laundry, shopping, and maintenance, are clearly documented and assignable to various household members. The checkbox tool facilitates tracking task completion, fostering accountability and progress. Template duplication allows for weekly reuse, promoting efficiency and routine continuity.

In the realm of meal planning and recipe management, OneNote offers significant advantages. Users may designate pages for meal plans, menus, or special events, preserving recipes via text, figures, or web clippings and annotating ingredient notes or substitutions for future reference. Shopping lists can be linked directly to meal plans, enhancing workflow between planning and execution. As illustrated in the meal planning segment of Figure 10-13, this method alleviates decision fatigue and encourages organized, nutritious dining practices.

Microsoft OneNote also excels at documenting home projects and repairs. From renovations to appliance maintenance, all phases of a project can be recorded in dedicated pages, including timelines, budgets, contractor information, warranty details, and ongoing notes. Attachments such as receipts, invoices, and photographic evidence contribute to a thorough record, proving invaluable for long-term improvements and subsequent reference.

Family coordination and scheduling constitute another essential element. OneNote can host a shared calendar page to track key dates—school activities, healthcare appointments, birthdays, and travel. Real-time syncing across devices ensures all family members access current information, minimizing miscommunication and keeping household members aligned with collective obligations.

For important document management, OneNote is highly effective. Pages tailored for insurance policies, warranties, identification documents, medical history, and emergency contacts allow direct attachment of scanned files or PDFs. Clearly labeled sections facilitate immediate access in critical situations, a core function highlighted in Figure 10-13 as fundamental to home management.

Additionally, OneNote supports strategic household planning and review. Users may record notes on expenditures, maintenance cycles, or recurring concerns. Tags such as Important, To Do, or Question aid in prioritizing follow-up actions. The search capability enables swift information retrieval, even from handwritten entries and figures, making it particularly beneficial for dynamic households.

In summary, Microsoft OneNote elevates home management by transforming diverse responsibilities into a structured, efficient, and stress-reducing process. Consolidating schedules, tasks, meals, projects, documents, and coordination within a singular digital notebook empowers families to maintain organization and proactivity. As visualized in Figure 10-13, OneNote emerges as a central platform for harmonizing all aspects of home life, simplifying daily routines and enhancing effectiveness. With consistent application, it evolves beyond a mere note-taking tool into a dependable digital resource for sustaining a well-organized and balanced household.

Use of Microsoft OneNote for Personal Finance Tracking

Effective personal finance management demands clarity, discipline, and consistency. Tracking expenses, bills, savings targets, and debts can become challenging when information is dispersed across multiple applications or notebooks. Microsoft OneNote provides a versatile and unified platform for managing personal finances by consolidating all relevant financial data within a single digital environment. With proper utilization, OneNote serves as a comprehensive financial dashboard, facilitating budgeting, expense monitoring, savings planning, and ongoing assessment of financial health.

To leverage Microsoft OneNote for finance tracking, begin by establishing a Personal Finance notebook. Within this notebook, dedicated sections can be created to address key financial topics such as *budget planning, expense tracking, bills and payments, savings goals, debt management*, and *reports* (as illustrated in Figure 10-14). This notebook-section-page framework aligns with the typical approach to financial organization, thereby simplifying record maintenance and updates. Figure 10-14 outlines these principal components and demonstrates their integration within OneNote's centralized system.

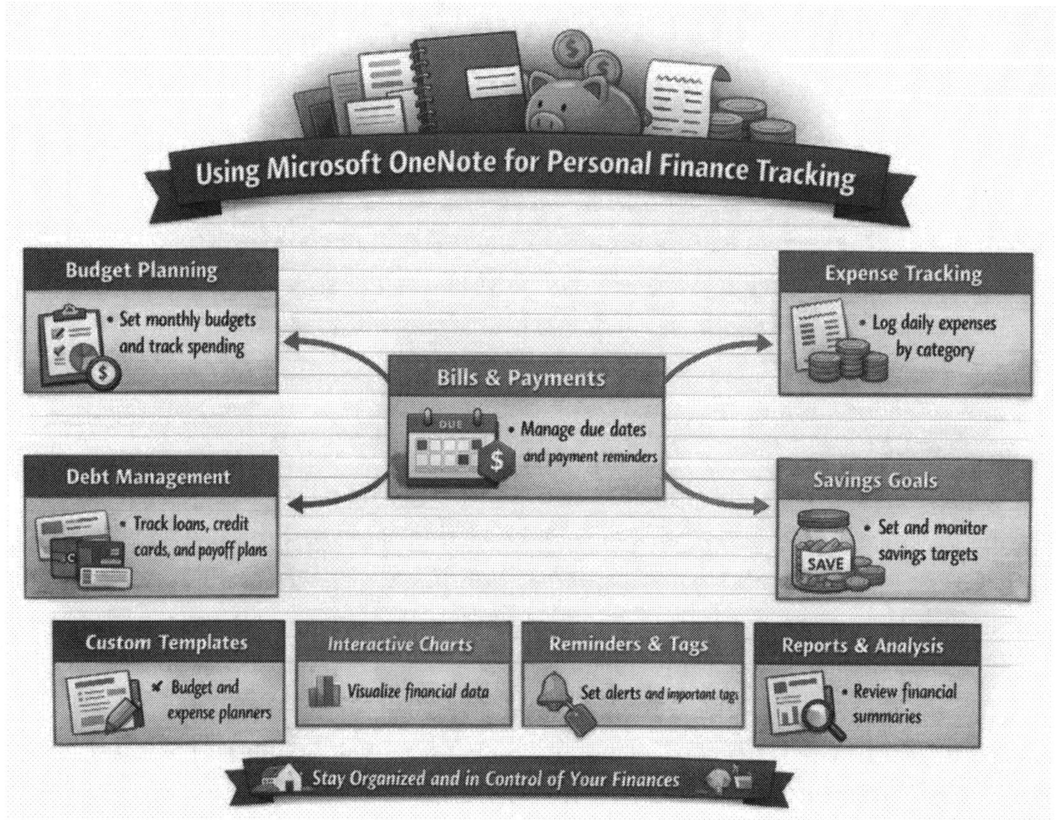

Figure 10-14. *Personal finance using OneNote*

OneNote offers significant value for budget planning. You can easily set up monthly or yearly budgets using tables to track income sources alongside planned expenses such as rent, groceries, transportation, utilities, and entertainment. Each expense category may feature columns for both allocated and actual spending. Since OneNote tables are simple to edit, duplicate, or revise, adapting your budget as circumstances change becomes straightforward. The ability to reuse these pages each month turns budgeting into a regular and manageable habit.

Expense tracking goes hand in hand with budget management. OneNote makes it convenient to log daily expenditures using basic tables or lists, organizing them under headings like food, travel, shopping, or subscriptions. Checkboxes and tags help you identify entries as verified, reimbursable, or out of the ordinary. Regular weekly or monthly reviews of these records offer insight into your spending habits, which is vital for building better financial discipline and avoiding unnecessary purchases.

Managing bills and payments becomes more effective with OneNote. You can dedicate pages to list recurring bills such as electricity, internet, rent, loan EMIs, and insurance premiums. Tables might include columns for due dates, amounts, payment methods, and payment status. Important bills can be flagged with OneNote's *Important* tag, and reminders like "Pay before the 10th" can be added as notes, reducing the risk of late fees and improving financial control.

Achieving long-term financial stability also relies on setting and tracking savings goals, for which OneNote provides helpful tools. Separate pages can be created for emergency funds, travel savings, education funds, or investment objectives—each detailing target amounts, current balances, and monthly contributions. You can also include motivational notes and progress updates. Frequently reviewing these pages helps reinforce savings habits and maintain focus.

Debt management is another area where Microsoft OneNote excels. You can monitor loans, credit cards, and other liabilities on dedicated pages, tracking information such as lender, outstanding balance, interest rate, EMI amount, and expected payoff date. Notes on repayment strategies or interest rate adjustments can be included as well. Centralizing all debt information enables informed decisions and supports timely debt repayment plans.

OneNote's versatility extends to custom templates and visual summaries. Finance templates for budgets, expenses, and savings can be created and reused each month. Charts, screenshots from bank statements, and summaries from other financial tools can be incorporated. Tags like *To Do*, *Important*, and *Question* support efficient follow-up. Over time, review pages can help summarize financial progress on a monthly or annual basis.

To sum up, Microsoft OneNote streamlines personal finance management by making it organized, transparent, and approachable. By bringing together budgets, expenses, bills, savings, and debts within one notebook, users gain full oversight of their finances. As shown in Figure 10-15, OneNote serves as a comprehensive finance center that encourages wise spending, punctual bill payment, continuous saving, and lasting financial confidence. With consistent use, OneNote evolves from a simple note-taking app into a trustworthy partner for personal finance management, and Figure 10-15 is an example of a template that can be used in OneNote to track personal finance.

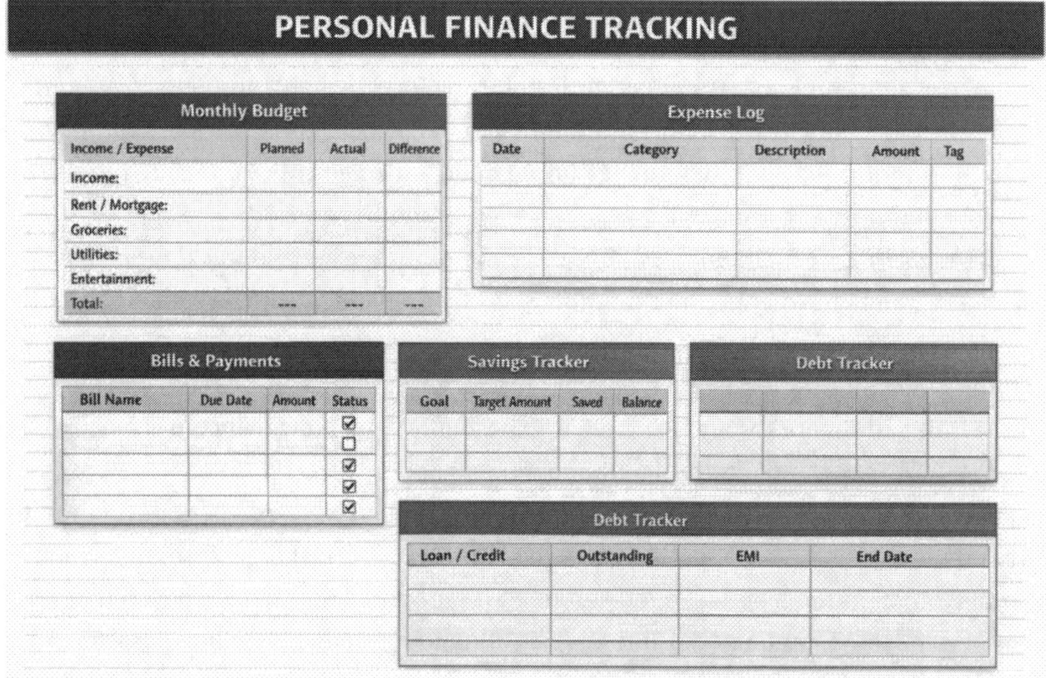

Figure 10-15. *Personal finance tracker in OneNote*

Using Microsoft OneNote for Digital Bullet Journaling

Digital bullet journaling integrates the straightforwardness of traditional bullet journals with the enhanced capabilities of digital platforms. Microsoft OneNote is particularly suited for this application due to its support for free-form layouts, advanced formatting options, tagging, figure insertion, and efficient navigation. When systematically implemented, OneNote can facilitate a digital bullet journaling system that is highly customizable for planning, tracking, reflection, and personal development.

To begin, establish a dedicated Digital Bullet Journal notebook in OneNote. Organize sections such as *daily logs, monthly overviews, collections, trackers,* and *reflections* as shown in Figure 10-16. This structure emulates the conventional bullet journal method while offering the adaptability of a digital environment. Daily or weekly entries should be created on separate pages, allowing important content to be easily duplicated or reorganized without manual transcription.

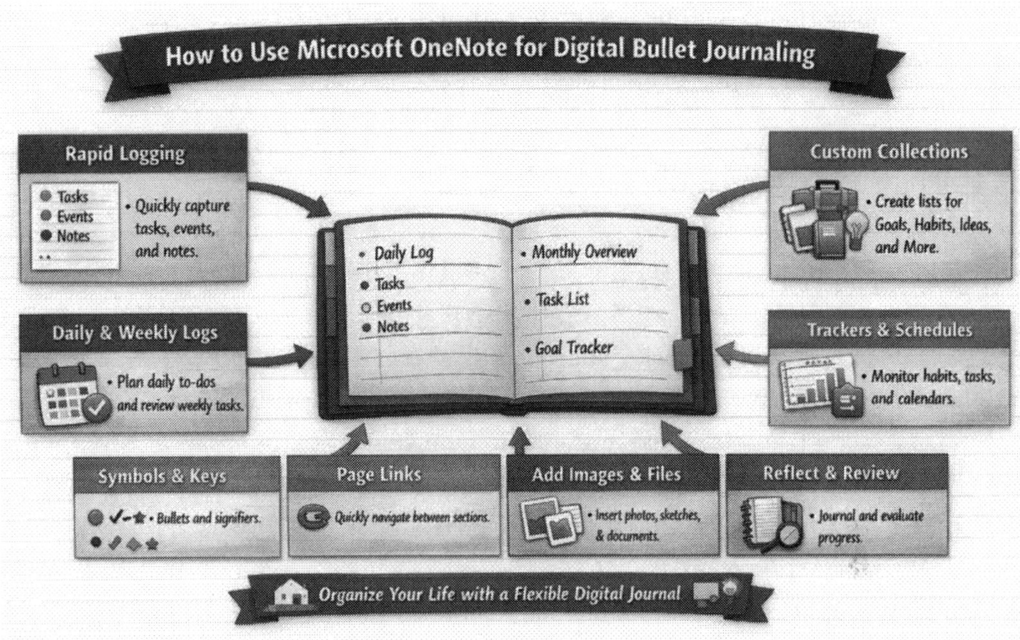

Figure 10-16. *Microsoft OneNote for digital bullet journaling*

Rapid logging constitutes the central function of digital bullet journaling. OneNote enables the swift recording of tasks, events, and notes using bullet points. Tasks may be tracked interactively through OneNote's *To Do* tag checkboxes. Events and notes are distinguishable via various bullet styles, symbols, or custom formatting. The automatic saving and syncing across devices ensures immediate entry recording whenever tasks or ideas arise.

Daily and weekly logs contribute to sustained focus and organization. Within OneNote, daily logs consist of task lists, appointments, and concise notes. Weekly logs provide summaries of completed tasks, outstanding items, and priorities for the subsequent week. Templates can be efficiently reused each week, streamlining processes and promoting uniformity. This unified approach supports both planning and reflective practices.

OneNote's digital bullet journaling excels in custom collections. Collections serve as thematic lists, including goals, habits, reading lists, project concepts, or wellness trackers. Each collection occupies a dedicated page within a section. The platform's versatility allows users to insert tables, checklists, figures, and quotes, enhancing both visual appeal and personalization.

Trackers and schedules represent further strengths of OneNote. Users can construct habit trackers, mood trackers, and goal trackers utilizing tables or checkboxes. Monthly tracking pages provide at-a-glance monitoring of progress. Unlike paper-based methods, digital tables can be modified or expanded as required, encouraging ongoing optimization of the bullet journaling process.

Symbol usage and custom keys play a significant role in the bullet journal methodology. Individuals may develop personal signifiers, such as stars for high-priority tasks, question marks for uncertainties, or lightbulbs for ideas. These symbols, combined with OneNote tags, create a robust visual organizational framework. The *Find Tags* feature facilitates the rapid aggregation of marked items, enhancing review efficiency.

A notable advantage of digital journaling in OneNote is the option to incorporate figures, files, and hyperlinks. Photographs, scanned documents, sketches, PDFs, and web links can all be embedded within journal pages. This functionality enriches entries and consolidates information from diverse sources in a single location. Internal page links further enable seamless navigation between logs and collections.

Periodic reflection and evaluation are integral components of the digital bullet journaling cycle. Pages for monthly or quarterly reviews can be established to assess progress, challenges, and insights gained. The search capability in OneNote allows for prompt retrieval and examination of past entries, fostering intentional reflection and continuous self-improvement. Over time, the digital bullet journal evolves into an exhaustive personal archive and management tool.

Use OneNote for Personal Knowledge Archives

A personal knowledge archive is an organized system for storing and managing information you want to keep over time—like ideas, research notes, learning materials, references, and insights. Microsoft OneNote is especially effective for creating such an archive, offering flexible note-taking, robust organization, powerful search, and multimedia support all in one app. With thoughtful use, OneNote becomes a lifelong repository of your knowledge—not just another note-taking tool as shown in Figure 10-17.

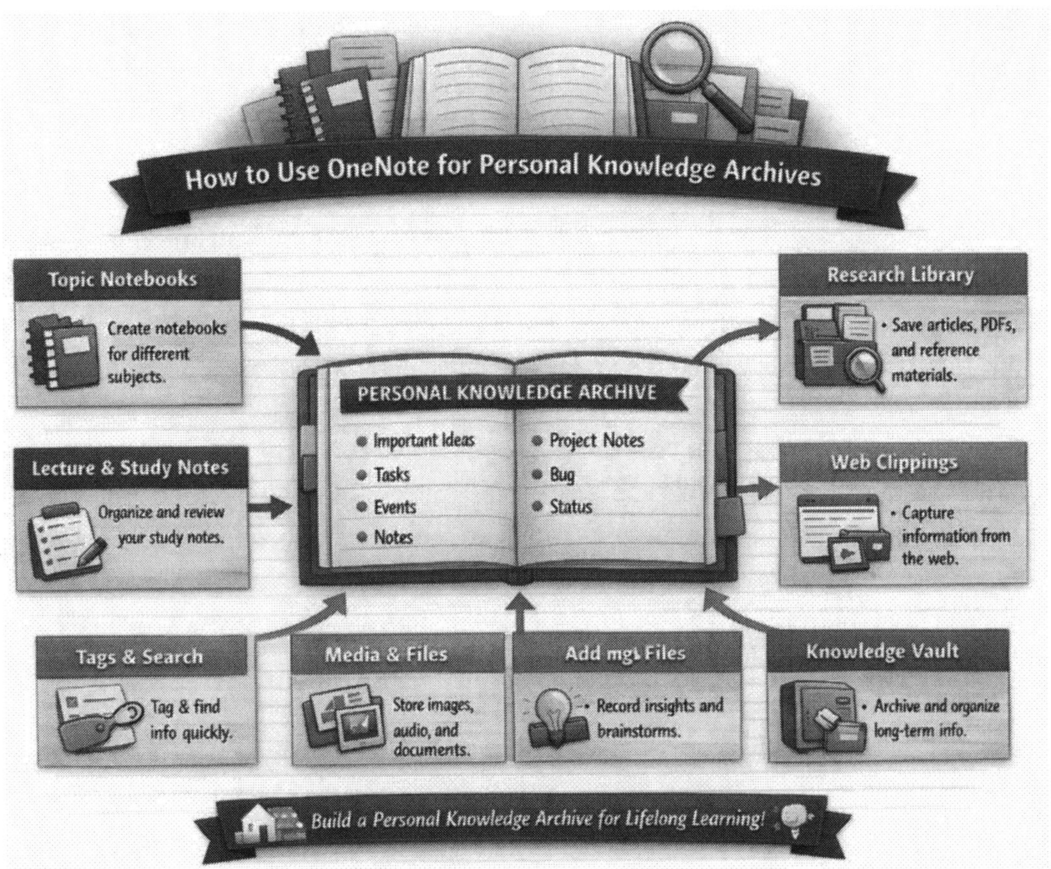

***Figure 10-17.** OneNote for personal knowledge archives*

To get started, **establish a clear notebook structure**. Make a notebook called *Personal Knowledge Archive* and add sections that reflect your main interests or areas, such as *subjects, research, projects, ideas,* and *reference materials.* Within each section, create pages for specific topics. This notebook-section-page setup mirrors the natural growth of knowledge and makes expansion easy without sacrificing clarity.

OneNote shines when used for **topic-based notebooks and subject notes**. For instance, if you're studying history, technology, or management, make individual sections for each field and dedicate pages to particular subjects. Capture key definitions, summaries, diagrams, and interpretations in your own words. This turns OneNote into a personalized resource built on your understanding rather than just copied content.

Another major advantage is OneNote's role as a **research library**. You can save articles, PDFs, lecture slides, and reference documents right in your pages. Clip web content with the browser tool or paste it manually, then add your thoughts or critiques beside the sources. Unlike scattered bookmarks, everything stays connected, making review and revision much more effective.

OneNote is also excellent for **collecting information from the web and different sources**. Easily embed web clippings, screenshots, figures, and links directly into your pages. This feature is valuable for academic work, professional growth, or personal hobbies. Over time, your curated resources become a dependable reference you can revisit anytime.

With large archives, **tags and search functions** are vital. Tag items as *Important, Question, Idea,* or *To Do* to highlight priorities and track insights. The search tool scans typed text, figures, and even handwritten notes, so nothing gets lost in the archive.

OneNote supports **storing media and files** alongside your notes: figures, audio, scanned documents, presentations, and video references can all be included. This enables you to keep knowledge in its most meaningful form, using visuals, recordings, or real-world examples to enrich your archive.

The platform encourages **idea development and reflection**, too. Create pages for insights, brainstorming, or conceptual links to connect previous knowledge with new discoveries. Over time, these pages record intellectual growth and evolving viewpoints, distinguishing a knowledge archive from simple storage.

Ultimately, a well-managed OneNote archive acts as a **long-term knowledge vault**. Its syncing across devices ensures your information remains accessible for years. Regular reviews and occasional reorganization keep your archive relevant. As shown in Figure 10-17, OneNote combines topic notebooks, research libraries, tagging, media, and search features into a unified personal knowledge system.

In short, Microsoft OneNote empowers you to build a structured, searchable, and enduring personal knowledge archive. By balancing organization, reflection, and digital flexibility, it fosters continuous learning and informed decision-making across your personal, academic, and professional life.

Coming to the closure, this chapter shows that Microsoft OneNote is more than just a digital notebook—it's a versatile platform for organizing daily life. OneNote integrates easily into productivity systems, helping users create structured routines and manage information efficiently.

The chapter began with habit tracking, demonstrating how tables, checklists, and tags in OneNote help maintain consistency and encourage self-reflection. Learning journals were featured next, showing how OneNote supports reflective learning through organized entries and multimedia tools, leading to better understanding and retention.

Home management was another focus, with OneNote centralizing family tasks, schedules, and important documents in one place for improved efficiency. The chapter also explained how OneNote templates aid in budgeting, expense monitoring, bill tracking, savings, and debt management, offering users clear insights for financial decisions. Digital bullet journaling was discussed as a dynamic method for planning and creative expression, with features like rapid logging and page linking surpassing paper alternatives. Lastly, OneNote's role as a knowledge archive highlights its value as a repository for research and ideas, supporting ongoing personal and professional growth.

In conclusion, the chapter emphasizes that intentional organization—not just increased output—is key to productivity. Consistently using OneNote equips users to track habits, manage tasks and finances, and store knowledge, making it an essential tool for staying organized and prepared for future goals.

Index

C. Waghmare, *Mastering Microsoft OneNote*, https://doi.org/10.1007/979-8-8688-2866-9

H

I, J

K, L

M, N

T, U, V, W, X,Y, Z

Zeitfracht Medien GmbH
Ferdinand-Jühlke-Straße 7
99095 Erfurt, Deutschland
produktsicherheit@kolibri360.de